AFRICAN LIBERATION MOVEMENTS

AFRICAN LIBERATION MOVEMENTS
Contemporary struggles against
white minority rule

RICHARD GIBSON

Published for the Institute of Race Relations, London

1972
OXFORD UNIVERSITY PRESS
New York and London

TO MY DEAREST SARAH

PREFACE

This survey of contemporary African liberation movements is the product of more than ten years' travel and research in Africa, the development and expansion of the notes of an Afro-American correspondent whose assignments carried him from Algeria to Zambia and who had the privilege of prolonged and friendly contacts with numerous liberation leaders, statesmen of many African countries and officials of the Organization of African Unity, as well as with men and women in the ranks of the movements who have borne patiently the heaviest burdens of the difficult struggles to extirpate the last vestiges of white-minority and colonial rule from the African continent. Without their assistance and encouragement, I could not have written this book; and I am particularly in the debt of several persons, whom I am not at liberty to name here, who displayed great personal courage and confidence in discussing frankly with me matters that others perhaps wished might be forever forgotten.

A 'brother' from Black America and a 'militant' after my own lights, I cannot therefore pretend to impartiality in this report of the battles for freedom of my own people; on the other hand, I am convinced that the truth, however harsh, can only hasten their successful conclusion. Hence, there has been no effort to gloss over the serious setbacks and deficiencies, especially factionalism, that have been major obstacles on a road I still believe will end in national liberation. To the extent of that belief, this is a committed book, written without shame or apology from the viewpoint of a black man.

Although my material is presented systematically, covering in turn each country and organization preceded by brief summaries of the background necessary for an understanding of the complexity of African realities, this is mainly a work of political history and analysis. Since today's battles are the consequence of earlier, if sometimes forgotten, struggles during the period of primary resistance to European encroachment and colonization, I have felt obliged to include a short account of them, as well as later African efforts to resist white aggrandizement within the framework of the colonial systems. Even at the risk of losing sight of the forest for the trees, I have considered it preferable to treat each country and every movement separately; as a consequence, there will be some repetition, but this is, I think, less onerous than omission, especially where time might prevent a hurried reader from examining closely sections of the book that might not seem of relevance to the study of a particular country or movement.

This book would probably have never been written if not for the encouragement of Mrs. Sheila Patterson, who thought it might have some value despite her reservations about some of the author's political opinions. A number of articles commissioned by Mrs. Patterson when she was editor of the *Newsletter* of the Institute of Race Relations have been incorporated in this work. Now entitled *Race Today*, that publication's succeeding editors, Peter Watson and later Alexander Kirby, encouraged me to continue. Simon Abbott, Deputy Director of the Institute, not only urged me to finish the book, but also edited the manuscript, with the assistance of Dale Gunthorp. I must acknowledge my great debt to Doreen Davis for typing a difficult manuscript and for the many helpful suggestions she made for improving the text.

I am of course indebted to many persons in Africa and I regret that I cannot acknowledge them all individually. I am especially grateful to the African friends who read various sections of the manuscript and attempted to correct my errors: Richard Hove of Zimbabwe, Tunguru Huaraka of South West Africa, Jorge Sangumba of Angola, and David Sibeko of South Africa. My thanks are also due to Mrs. Carole Piña of the International Labour Office in Geneva for thinking of me whenever she found any item in her own research on Africa that might be of relevance to my work.

Among the many authors to whom I am indebted, I must thank in particular my friend Gérard Chaliand, whose *Lutte armée en Afrique* (Paris, Maspero, 1967), as so much of his writing, has been in the vanguard of serious political works about contemporary liberation movements. John A. Marcum's *The Angolan Revolution* (Cambridge, Mass., The M.I.T. Press, 1969) provided me with a mine of pertinent information and a stunning example of a frank, but committed study of an African revolution. If other African liberation struggles are chronicled by scholars of such fairness and yet passionate concern, the future of African historiography will be brilliant.

Finally, I must express my gratitude to those loyal friends who insisted this book was needed and had to be written. They urged me on whenever I despaired of completing the task. I can only hope that the finished product resembles somewhat their original conception.

Richard Gibson

CONTENTS

Preface vii

Map of Africa xii

PART ONE: Introduction to the Concept of National Liberation in Africa 1

PART TWO: South Africa (Azania) 17
The Background 19
The Resistance 27
African National Congress (ANC) 38
Unity Movement (UMSA) 76
Pan Africanist Congress (PAC) 81

PART THREE: South West Africa (Namibia) 107
The Background 109
The Resistance 114
South West Africa National Union (SWANU) 120
South West African People's Organization
(SWAPO) 132

PART FOUR: Zimbabwe (Rhodesia) 143
The Background 145
The Resistance 151
Zimbabwe African People's Union (ZAPU) 158
Zimbabwe African National Union (ZANU) 174
Front for the Liberation of Zimbabwe
(FROLIZI) 183

PART FIVE: The Portuguese Colonies 185
I. Angola 197
The Background 199
The Resistance 202
Movimento Popular de Libertação de
Angola (MPLA) 211
Govêrno Revolucionário de Angola no
Exílio/Frente Nacional de Libertação de
Angola (GRAE/FNLA) 225

União Nacional para a Independência
Total de Angola (UNITA)   234

II. Guiné and the Cape Verde Islands   243
    The Background   245
    The Resistance   249
    Partido Africano da Independência da
    Guiné e Cabo Verde (PAIGC)   252
    Frente para a Libertação e Independência
    da Guiné Portuguesa (FLING)   ..   261

III. Mozambique   265
    The Background   267
    The Resistance   272
    Frente de Libertação de Moçambique
    (FRELIMO)   276
    Comité Revolucionário de Moçambique
    (COREMO)   287

IV. São Tomé e Príncipe   291
    Comité de Libertação de São Tomé e Prín-
    cipe (CLSTP)   296

PART SIX: The Horn of Africa and Some Islands   297
    I.   The French Territory of the Afars and Issas   299
        Front des Libération de la Côte des
        Somalis (FLCS)
        Mouvement de Libération de Djibouti
        (MLD)
    II. The Comoros..   307
        Mouvement de Libération Nationale des
        Comores (MOLINACO)   ..   ..
    III. The Canaries   315
        Mouvement pour l'Autodétermination et
        l'Indépendance de l'Archipel Canarien
        (MPAIAC)

PART SEVEN: A Conclusion and a Beginning   323

Tables   329

Selected Bibliography   333

Index   337

*I began my history at the very
outbreak of the war, in the belief
that it was going to be a great war. . . .*
                              THUCYDIDES

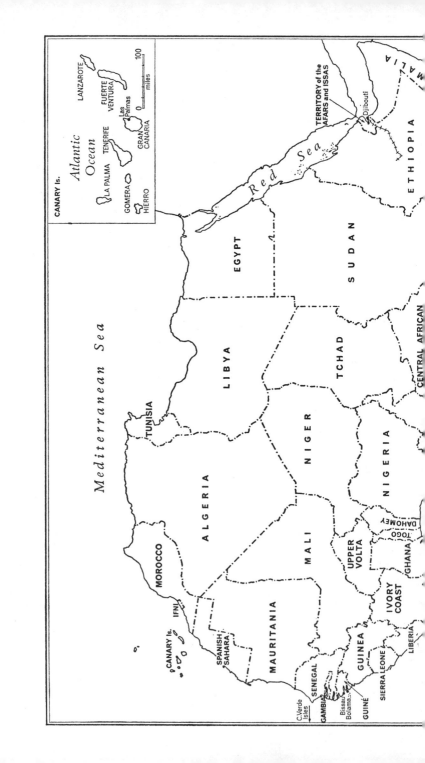

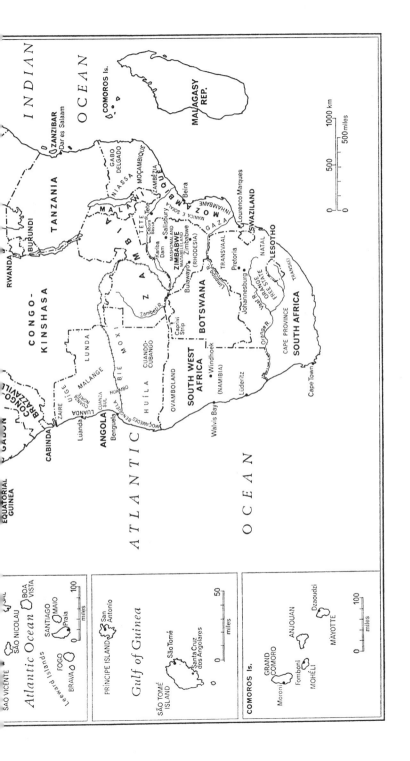

PART ONE:

INTRODUCTION TO THE CONCEPT OF NATIONAL LIBERATION IN AFRICA

Any examination of the development of the struggle against colonial and other forms of white-minority rule in Africa in the second half of the twentieth century must necessarily begin with the attempt to place these complex struggles within their specific geographical, economic, social, and historical context. Inherent in the concept of national liberation is the existence of an historically constituted national entity (even if it is subjugated by an external power) or the coming into existence of such an entity—through popular aspirations, forged in the struggle against an oppressive and irreducibly alien 'Other'. In such sense, Algeria was never really French, but there were moments when a sizeable minority of its Moslem population believed that it possibly might be; the bloodshed and suffering endured in the battle for independence between 1954 and 1962 removed all such illusions and branded the consciousness of their nationhood upon all classes of the Algerian people. Moreover, even before gaining their own liberation, the Algerian nationalists had obliged France in an effort to avoid insurrections elsewhere to grant at least nominal independence to almost all French-speaking Africa south of the Sahara.[1]

In English-speaking Africa, British colonialism was prepared by its previous experience in India and Burma for the granting of independence to Ghana in 1957 and, over a relatively short period, to most of the remaining African territories under British rule where white settlers were not sufficiently strong to thwart the transfer of power to the black majority. In Kenya, settler interests were sacrificed to more important British economic and political interests. A combination of factors— Mau Mau, land hunger, a strongly developing national consciousness among the bulk of the population that found political expression in the Kenya African National Union (KANU), and the relative weakness of the settlers and their lobbying in Westminster—led to African majority rule and eventual independence. Further south, the break-up of the settler-dominated Central African Federation brought independence to Zambia and Malawi, and the abandonment of Rhodesia to its local white masters.

[1] See Roland Oliver and J. D. Fage, *A Short History of Africa* (Harmondsworth, Penguin, 1962), p. 248.

One of the areas where political progress had long been systematically denied to Africans was the Belgian Congo. Yet, when faced with the upsurge of Congolese nationalism—despite its fluid and contradictory nature—Belgium hastily ceded independence. The subsequent civil war in the Congo, as well as the tribal massacres and conflicts in Belgium's other ex-protectorates of Rwanda and Burundi, was only part of the heritage of the Belgian colonialists.

Elsewhere, in what had been British Africa, only in Rhodesia, the Republic of South Africa, and South West Africa[1] did white minorities stem the tide of majority rule. Democracy, banished from metropolitan Portugal under the Salazar dictatorship, was hardly likely to be permitted the Africans of Angola and Cabinda, Guiné and the Cape Verde Islands, and Mozambique. In addition, the rulers of an impoverished Portugal greatly profited from the super-exploitation of their 'Overseas Provinces'. In the hope of countering African nationalist demands, they willingly sustained the myth that, whereas other European powers were 'real' colonialists, Portugal had somehow brought into being a multiracial, 'Lusotropical' civilization. And Western military and economic assistance enabled Portugal—which otherwise could not have afforded the luxury—to arm the ever-mounting numbers of troops needed to repress urban unrest and resist spreading revolutionary warfare in the African countryside.

In other parts of Africa, other European powers fought rearguard actions against African independence. Pleading a variety of special reasons for these exceptions, France held on to a number of African islands, such as Réunion and the Comoros, where the demand for independence assumed a national character. Similarly, Spain rejected even the notion of autonomy for the Canaries. In the Horn of Africa, France hastily renamed French Somaliland the 'Coast of Afars and Issas' in an effort to frustrate Somali irredentist demands upon Djibouti and equally insistent Ethiopian claims upon the vital Red Sea port.

Where white minorities were entrenched, African nationalists were left no course but armed struggle to achieve liberation. In South Africa, all hopes for political progress to a non-racial democracy were systematically crushed by the ruling whites; instead, the doctrine of apartheid

[1] The U.N. General Assembly terminated South Africa's League of Nations Mandate over South West Africa in October 1966 and called on South Africa to quit the territory, permitting it to become an independent state. The South African Government ignored this and subsequent U.N. resolutions and has virtually annexed the country. For the background to the dispute, see Ronald Segal and Ruth First, *South West Africa: Travesty of Trust* (London, Deutsch, 1967), and Barbara Rogers, 'South West Africa: Whose Responsibility?' *Race Today* (January 1971).

was promulgated as an ideological cover for the maintenance of the black man in the status of a beast of burden. Here was constitutional regression from meagre, limited rights for some non-whites to a total racist rejection of citizenship rights to black and brown helots. Non-violent protest was repressed with such violence on the part of the white regime that recourse to violence by Africans seems more a measure of self-defence and survival than arbitrary defiance of an unjust but 'peaceful' social order. In South Africa and South West Africa, violence is the cohesive element in a society which would otherwise disintegrate. And European rule in most of Africa would have been impossible but for violence, the encroaching whites having, over the centuries, not only plundered the natural resources of the land but also seized millions of African people as slaves.[1] Primary African resistance was almost always organized by isolated tribal groups. Although repeated appeals for unity were made in various places by the more clear-sighted African leaders, what unity was achieved was ephemeral. These ancient battles for freedom still echo in the background of contemporary liberation struggles. However, the nationalist parties have by now, at least in principle, replaced tribal-based action with struggle based on an evolving national consciousness. While to the westernized elites this appears not only natural but necessary, the transition often means a difficult process of adjustment for the masses, especially in the country-side where the battle has to be launched and fought out. In a few places as we shall see, the transition has hardly been made, and stagnation of the struggle within ethnic boundaries is the inevitable price paid for this failure. On the other hand, we shall also see externally-based westernized elites meeting equal failure as a result of their inability to sink roots into the tribal societies that dominate the countryside of Africa—as though the evolving national consciousness could only be an extension of their essentially urban viewpoints.

In these pages I am concerned solely with the national liberation movements of Africa directed against colonial ar   direct forms of white-minority rule. I follow the guidelines c   of African Unity as put into practice by its African although some of the organizations under discu by the A.L.C. Unfortunately, this means t¹ some quite genuine revolutionary struggles regimes. They remain outside the pale of ¹ president of the outlawed Sawaba Party of ℕ that the O.A.U. could easily degenerate ir

¹ See Basil Davidson, *Black Mother* (*l*

men in power striving to bolster each other in order to resist popular currents'.[1] But non-interference in the internal affairs of other states is a proclaimed—if often violated—principle of good international relations. No matter how apparently well-founded the denunciations by African revolutionaries of African rulers (whether they be denounced as agents of neo-colonialism or tyrants imposing central rule over formerly autonomous or independent regions—broadly, as between Zaïre, formerly Congo-Kinshasa, since the fall of Patrice Lumumba or Haile Selassie's Ethiopia in relation to Eritrea) the O.A.U. has scrupulously avoided giving the complainants the slightest assistance and has given them precious little encouragement. In January 1969, the Basutoland Congress Party of Lesotho learned that, despite its impeccable African nationalist stance and glaring proof of the seizure of power by the South African-backed regime of Chief Leabua Jonathan, the O.A.U. had no intention of encouraging the restoration of democracy in Lesotho through revolutionary struggle. In any case, these domestic struggles fit into a pattern of social revolution throughout independent Africa and, although they are by no means unconnected with the liberation struggle against white-minority rule, their complexity makes impossible their inclusion in a work of limited size and scope such as this. One can only hope that reporters and scholars will devote more attention to recording and analysing these convolutions.[2] I shall only glance at the tragic history of the *Union des populations du Cameroun* (UPC), the first party to launch the armed struggle against colonial rule in sub-Saharan Africa.

The UPC was originally founded in 1947 as the Cameroun section of the French West African interterritorial *Rassemblement démocratique africain* (RDA). Despairing of constitutional progress to independence from France, and prompted by France's losing battle against Algerian nationalists, the UPC went into the maquis on 12 July 1956. Its secretary general, Ruben Um Nyobé, was killed by French troops in 1958. Its president, Félix Moumié, was murdered by a French agent in Geneva in 1960. By that time, France had already granted formal independence to the Cameroun, but the UPC remained in the maquis and some of its leaders tried to direct the struggle within the country from exile headquarters in Conakry and Accra. Needless to say, the UPC got no support from the O.A.U., among whose member states was

akary Djibo, 'For Revolutionary Unity', *Revolution* (Vol. 1, No. 1, May 1963).
t Verhaegen has already done an extraordinary service by his studies of the
dence struggle in Congo (K). See especially *Rébellions au Congo*
.P., 1966).

that headed by President Ahmadou Ahidjo of Cameroun. The UPC had split into two factions: a pro-Soviet faction headed by a so-called 'Revolutionary Committee' composed of Woungly-Massaga and others, and a militant pro-Chinese wing—the *'Comité Directeur'*—headed by Osendé Afana. A brilliant economist, Afana joined the Revolutionary Armed Forces inside Cameroun, headed by another historic leader of the UPC, its Vice President, Ernest Ouandié, who had been in the maquis since 1961. Afana was killed by government troops on 15 March 1966, and Ouandié—whom many had believed dead since 1963—was captured on 18 August, 1970. Also arrested, on 29 August 1970, for participation in the rebellion, was the Roman Catholic Bishop of Nkongsamba, Monsignor Albert Ndongmo.[1] Ouandié and two lower-ranking UPC leaders—Raphaël Fotsing and Gabriel Tabeu—were sentenced to death for high treason and rebellion. They were publicly executed by firing squad in the town of Bafoussam, in what had once been the heart of rebel territory, on 15 January 1971. Also sentenced to die, Monsignor Ndongmo's condemnation was commuted to life imprisonment. It appeared that the revolutionary nationalist party had been crushed by the neo-colonialist regime that was nevertheless solidly based on certain ethnic groups within the country. But the reality was even more complex and the reasons for the successive defeats of the UPC were difficult to ascertain.[2] Yet no one can deny the UPC the merit of having launched the struggle for the independence of the Cameroun and having persisted in its obviously unequal battle for the establishment of a democratic socialist regime.

Such is not an objective, however, of the O.A.U.'s African Liberation Committee. The A.L.C. limits its aim to obtaining formal independence for African territories still under the yoke of white-minority rule. Even this restrained ambition was openly contested by some African states, led by conservative powers, mainly French-speaking, headed by President Félix Houphout-Boigny's Ivory Coast. He demanded frank recognition of the South African white regime and abandonment of the black freedom fighters, while advocating the softening of South African apartheid policies through diplomatic contacts, trade with South Africa, and the pressure of benevolent African and world opinion on the white rulers of South Africa. This growing divergence of views has meant that only a small amount of the A.L.C.'s liberation budget,

[1] See *Le Monde* (22–3 November 1970, and 17–18 January 1971).
[2] See Gérard Chaliand, *Lutte armée en Afrique*, (Paris, Maspero, 1967), pp. 127–8, where Chaliand accuses the UPC leaders of failure to relate and act according to the social realities of their own country. For the origins of the UPC, see Ronald Segal, *African Profiles* (Harmondsworth, Penguin, 1962), p. 188.

reportedly set at £750,000[1] in 1968–9, has been paid in. Although the budget was supposedly secret, a disaffected South African Coloured exile disclosed that £504,000 was allocated for materials and equipment, with a further £61,000 for 'Administration and Propaganda' purposes.

Administered by Tanzanian Executive Secretary George Magombe, the A.L.C. operates from headquarters in Dar es Salaam. Originally, the A.L.C. was the formal *raison d'être* for African unity and was used to justify all the compromises needed to bring the Organization of African Unity into existence in Addis Ababa in 1963. A number of African states, especially Ghana, Algeria, and the United Arab Republic, had already been giving substantial assistance to some liberation movements. PAFMECA[2] (the Pan-African Freedom Movement for East and Central Africa, and later Southern Africa) was also attempting to aid some liberation movements. The original member nations of the A.L.C. were Algeria, Zaïre (Congo-Kinshasa), Ethiopia, Guinea, Nigeria, Senegal, Tanganyika, Uganda, and the U.A.R. Later, Zambia and Somalia were added.

The O.A.U. had given the A.L.C. two specific objectives: first, the establishment of a liberation budget to finance the struggle for African freedom; and second, the co-ordination of the struggle on a territorial and interterritorial basis, beginning with the elimination of rival parties and the formation of united fronts. All efforts to impose unity on the squabbling, even fratricidal, movements of various countries have so far ended in dismal failure. And, as we have already seen, the fund-raising efforts met less than signal success. In 1966, the A.L.C. was nearly abolished after bitter criticism by the rightist states who alleged that the bulk of disbursements was on administration and expense account travel by movement leaders. Only the determined efforts of President Julius Nyerere of Tanzania succeeded in halting the attack on the A.L.C., but its enemies within Africa and abroad have never ceased hoping for its eventual dissolution. As matters stood, most of the liberation movements that received its aid maintained they could not survive long if they did not also receive direct financial and material assistance from China, the Soviet Union, Cuba, and even Algeria and the U.A.R.[3]

The most serious challenge to the authority of the A.L.C. was made

---

[1] See *Sunday Telegraph* (4 May 1969).

[2] Composed of Tanganyika, Kenya, Uganda, Northern Rhodesia (Zambia), and Nyasaland (Malawi).

[3] For a discussion of the relationship between the O.A.U. and the liberation movements see Jon Woronoff, *Organizing African Unity* (Metuchen, N. J., Scarecrow Press, 1970).

in 1969 when the Soviet Union indirectly organized a conference in Khartoum of liberation movements under its influence. Officially sponsored by the Soviet-dominated, Cairo-based wing of the Afro-Asian Peoples' Solidarity Organization (AAPSO) and the World Council of Peace, the Khartoum Conference sought unsuccessfully to substitute for the A.L.C.—which continued to support movements considered either pro-Chinese or otherwise escaping of Moscow's control—a purely Moscow-oriented group led by the African National Congress of South Africa. Also participating were the constituent members of the *Conferencia de Organizações Nacionalistas das Colónias Portuguesas* (CONCP), the ANC's junior partner in a formal military alliance, the Zimbabwe African People's Union (ZAPU) and the South West African People's Organization (SWAPO). As we shall see, this was but one of myriad reflections in African liberation politics of the shattering Sino-Soviet split within the world communist movement.

Chairman Mao Tsetung and his followers in the Communist Party of China viewed the struggle in Africa as one of crucial importance for the world revolutionary movement. In fact, their assessment of the primacy of revolution in Africa, Asia, and Latin America was one of the key points in their dispute with the Soviet revisionist communist leaders. In 'A Proposal Concerning the General Line of the International Communist Movement', the Chinese leaders declared the areas of those three continents 'the most vulnerable areas under imperialist rule and the storm-centres of world revolution'.[1] In another document addressed to the Central Committee of the Communist Party of the Soviet Union (CPSU), the Central Committee of the Communist Party of China stated bluntly: 'It is impossible for the working class in the European and American capitalist countries to liberate itself unless it unites with the oppressed nations and unless those nations are liberated.'[2] The Chinese communists believed that the Soviet leadership was willing to sacrifice fraternal support for the revolutionary movements in the three continents as part of a global pact of peaceful existence with the United States and other Western powers. Naturally, the Chinese gave financial and material support to their African friends, but serious analyses[3] of that assistance indicate that its amount was vastly inflated by both Soviet and Western critics, who conjured up a terrifying spectre

---

[1] In *The Polemic on the General Line of the International Communist Movement* (Peking, F.L.P., 1965), p. 13.

[2] Ibid., p. 14.

[3] See Paul M. Whitaker, 'External Aid and the Portuguese African Liberation Movements', *African Report* (Vol. XV, No. 5, 1970).

of the hoary Yellow Peril, in more modern gear than in its last appearance on the world stage. The fact of the matter was again much more complex. Simplistic notions about Chinese assistance and counsel have all proved wholly incorrect. What the Chinese seem quite openly to have done is to demand that revolutionaries re-examine the modalities of their struggle, which must inevitably be an armed struggle, within the specific frame of the national realities of their respective countries. And while giving money and arms, the Chinese communists, remembering their own long revolutionary experience, have never ceased to remind their friends in Africa that the first virtue of successful revolutionary struggle is self-reliance.

The ideological programmes of African liberation movements betray a mixture of influences in language and ideas, ranging from eighteenth-century European and North American bourgeois democracy to the Communist Manifesto and the latest accents of the Sino-Soviet dispute. Not only is there a genuine radicalization of many movements when they discover that all roads of constitutional progress towards independence are blocked, but, even without radicalization, there is often recourse to full-blown revolutionary rhetoric. Looking over their shoulders at Western capitalism, some parties were initially reluctant to proclaim a commitment to socialism. In 1963, Amilcar Cabral, Secretary General of the *Partido Africano da Independência da Guiné e Cabo Verde* (PAIGC), merely stated that the African Revolution meant 'transformation of the present economic life in accordance with the movement of progress'. He envisaged, but did not name, 'new forms of economic, political and social existence . . . developing throughout the continent'.[1] Only the densest of capitalists, of course, would have failed to sense the thinly veiled threat behind the words. Earlier, on 1 November 1954, in the first proclamation of the Algerian National Liberation Front (FLN), there was not even the veiled threat. The Algerian nationalists declared their aim solely to restore the 'sovereign, democratic Algerian state within the framework of the principles of Islam', while 'respecting the basic rights of man without distinction of race or creed'.[2] Eight years later, on the eve of independence, the FLN at last dared openly to espouse socialism—although not without serious internal opposition—in the Tripoli Programme of May–June 1962. This commitment remained tenuous until, in April 1964, the Charter of

[1] Amilcar Cabral, 'The War in "Portuguese" Guinea', *Revolution* (Vol. 1, No. 2, June 1963).

[2] Quoted in Arslan Humbaraci, *Algeria: A Revolution That Failed* (London, Pall Mall, 1966), p. 48.

Algiers was adopted by the first post-independence congress of the FLN.[1] The particular conditions which, on independence, obliged the new Algerian state to take over abandoned European farms and the operation of stalled industries gave concrete substance to this option.

A more anodyne version of socialism, grandly labelled 'African Socialism' by Léopold Senghor of Senegal, enjoyed considerable esteem in less rigorous climes. Senghor's brand of socialism, stripped of its African 'spiritual' overtones, boils down simply to 'rational dynamic planning' that does 'not scorn private capital'. In so far as the accumulation of capital is concerned, 'there is no difference between a capitalist and a socialist state', declares Senghor.[2] In Jomo Kenyatta's Kenya, African Socialism was soon to become frankly synonomous with the 'encouragement of African businessmen, entrepreneurs and independent farmers rather than on co-operative, collective or other forms of communal effort. . . . Nationalization of enterprises already in private hands has generally been rejected as unnecessary, costing too much in compensation and harmful to Kenya's congenial investment image.'[3] This devalued concept of 'socialism' obviously threatened no interests except those of the masses. Small wonder then that by the seventies, regardless of where their leaders actually stood in the political spectrum, all self-respecting African liberation movements readily proclaimed their faith in the principles of socialism as well, naturally, as demanding national independence. Consequently, little attention will be given in this work to details of the published programmes of African liberation movements. Rarely does analysis of their contents reveal much of significance about the organizations themselves and the use to which they plan to put their eventual conquest of state power.

Nor should it be assumed that all the liberation movements discussed are engaged in armed struggles. National liberation is not immediately synonymous with guerrilla warfare or any other form of revolutionary war. The African Liberation Committee grants its assistance to a number of organizations that have never so far raised a gun. In fact, all the movements described in this book have commenced their struggle with non-violent political demands. Subsequent escalation is generally caused by unyielding white-minority regimes. Almost always, it is the

[1] Ibid., p. 67, and David C. Gordon, *The Passing of French Algeria* (London, Oxford University Press, 1966), p. 77.

[2] Leopold Sedar Senghor, *African Socialism*, translated by Mercer Cook (New York, A.M.S.A.C., 1959), p. 40.

[3] A. J. Hughes, *East Africa: Kenya, Tanzania, Uganda* (Harmondsworth, Penguin, 1963), pp. 232–3.

white policeman or his black auxiliary who strikes the first blow. But, after recovering from that stunning blow, armed struggle is almost inevitable and, considering the relationship of forces, implies guerrilla warfare or People's War. Clausewitz declares that five conditions are required for effective pursuit of this form of struggle:

1. That the War is carried on in the heart of the country.
2. That it cannot be decided by a single catastrophe.
3. That the theatre of War embraces a considerable extent of country.
4. That the national character is favourable to the measure.
5. That the country is of a broken and difficult nature, either from being mountainous, or by reason of woods and marshes, or from the peculiar mode of cultivation in use.[1]

It is the second condition that was most often only dimly understood by those who launched the struggle. Early hopes of bringing their enemies swiftly to a conference table to arrange the transfer of power faded only with time and in blood. In South Africa, the myth of a massive, almost spontaneous, uprising of the black masses sweeping white oppression aside in one blow did not perish in the Sharpeville massacre of 1960. But the endurance of even a feeble modern state, such as Portugal, and its ability to wage limited warfare are far greater than has been generally believed. Mao Tsetung's concept of protracted war essentially answers the question how a seemingly weak force can defeat a strong enemy by gradually reducing that enemy's advantages and aggravating his shortcomings—as in the case of China's War of Resistance against Imperial Japan. Victory depends on active support of the population, mobilized by a revolutionary party or movement.[2] While many have learned that 'Political power grows out of the barrel of a gun',[3] far too many would-be revolutionaries anywhere have failed to heed Mao's corollary injunction: 'The revolutionary war is a war of the masses; it can be waged only by mobilizing the masses and relying on them.'[4]

There is a growing body of studies on every aspect of irregular warfare, but on these pages we shall be more concerned with the political struggles within the movements themselves. By seeking to

[1] Roger Ashley Leonard, ed., *A Short Guide to Clausewitz on War* (London, Weidenfeld and Nicolson, 1967), p. 224.

[2] See Mao Tsetung, *Selected Military Writings* (Peking, F.L.P., 1963), pp. 111–12 and p. 208.

[3] Mao Tsetung, 'Problems of War and Strategy'. *Selected Works* (Peking, F.L.P., 1965), Vol. II, p. 224.

[4] Mao Tsetung, 'Be Concerned with the Well-Being of the Masses, Pay Attention to Methods of Work', *Selected Works*, Vol. I, p. 147.

unravel sometimes obscure intrigues of rival claimants for the leadership and examining the greater or lesser contradictions of every sort within the structures of organizations, I hope to be able to determine broadly the dynamics of these groups within the context of their specific national reality.

Any examination of the problems of African liberation leads inevitably, as we have already seen, to the question of unity, whether on a national or continental scale. I shall be forced to examine against aspirations for unity, the existing disunity. Throughout his distinguished career, Ghana's exiled President Kwame Nkrumah has fought for African unity, urging black men to join in a continent-wide struggle for liberation. It was largely because of Nkrumah's insistence that the Organization of African Unity came into being. But writing in his *Handbook of Revolutionary Warfare*,[1] from his refuge in Guinea, Nkrumah expressed bitter disappointment with the O.A.U. for its hesitations, doubts, and obvious lack of enthusiasm for an all-out commitment to the bloody business of removing the last vestiges of colonial and white-minority rule from the African continent. It is worth noting that the Ghanaian leader did not, as many others have done, try to make the administrators of the African Liberation Committee the scapegoats for what is essentially an African political failure. In any case, Nkrumah abandons all hope for the O.A.U. and envisages the creation of an All-African People's Revolutionary Party to replace it. Directed by an All-African Committee for Political Co-ordination, the fighting instrument of this continental party would be the All-African People's Revolutionary Army, organized in five regional divisions: northern, western, southern, central, and eastern. Clearly, Nkrumah's army would be taking on adversaries in territories far beyond the white redoubt in Southern Africa and the Portuguese Colonies.

However desirable, Kwame Nkrumah's All-African People's Revolutionary Party and its Army obviously do not yet, and may never, exist. Not only is the African liberation struggle being pursued within the confines of colonial territorial borders, but violently antagonistic, rival organizations in nearly every territory consume considerable energy and often human lives in fighting each other. To report these clashes, whether mere squabbles or blood feuds, is sometimes held as inimical to the cause of African freedom, as though silence would alter the unpleasant reality. All too often, important developments within the liberation movements thus go unreported, either due to lack of interest on the part of editors of foreign journals or the self-censorship

[1] Published in London, by Panaf Press, in 1968.

of the few veteran observers of the scene who know full well what is happening. The author is nevertheless convinced that these contradictions can only be resolved in blood or, more happily, through debate in the forums of Africa and the world.

In most cases originally formed as broad movements, in principle grouping nearly all classes of African society in a national democratic revolutionary struggle, in practice, the liberation movements now much more closely resemble traditional sectarian political parties, with contending programmes and personalities whose rhetoric often only partly masks long-standing tribal rivalries and class antagonisms. The Sino-Soviet dispute, as we will see repeatedly, has enormously sharpened the hostilities between rival groups, although rarely is any movement completely homogeneous in ideological orientation. Apparent commitment is often determined and shifted by the size of the financial and material assistance thereby to be obtained from the donor Great Power. It was reported that Dr. Eduardo Mondlane (first president of FRELIMO, and later assassinated), somehow managed the rare feat of obtaining simultaneous support from the Soviet Union, the United States, and China.[1]

Securing victory in Africa depends upon more than technology and advanced weaponry. Not that the freedom fighters cannot put to good use an abundant supply of arms and munitions. Victory depends upon winning masses of people to a cause that is both material in an immediate political, economic, and social sense, and moral in the highest sense in directing man's efforts to give his existence dignity. The African liberation struggle is indeed a profoundly moral struggle. To fail to realize the vast difference between black freedom fighters—despite all their internecine squabbles—and dehumanizing, fascistic white rulers who would indefinitely repress and exploit millions of blacks, and whites, under their domination is, in the author's opinion, to lack simple human decency and the vaguest awareness of what is of enduring value in the history of mankind. Racism is only a lame alibi. As André Gide discovered a half-century ago: 'Moins le Blanc est intelligent, plus le Noir lui paraît bête.'[2]

In the following pages, I shall examine country by country the development of each of the major African liberation movements. I will not confine myself to those organizations recognized by the African Liberation Committee, but will be guided by the sole criterion of the effective existence, however embarrassing, of each group. First,

---

[1] Whitaker, 'External Aid and the Portuguese African Liberation Movements'.

[2] André Gide, *Le Voyage au Congo, Retour de Tchad* (Paris, 1928).

I shall examine the specific geographic, economic, social, and political conditions in which each national struggle evolves. Secondly, I shall survey the history of African resistance to white encroachment and rule in each territory under consideration and trace the efforts at reformist solutions. Finally, I shall chronicle the development of the movements until 1972.

PART TWO:
SOUTH AFRICA (AZANIA)

African National Congress (ANC)

Unity Movement (UMSA)

Pan Africanist Congress (PAC)

The Background

Although the Portuguese were the first whites to land on the shores of South Africa, they had little interest in the country itself; rather, they were preoccupied in the sixteenth century with their monopoly of the sea route around Africa to the Orient. The explorer Bartolomeu Dias first discovered the Cape of Good Hope in 1488. Nine years after Dias had returned to Lisbon with news that the route was open, Vasco da Gama set sail. He erected a landmark on the Cape in 1497, but soon continued eastwards on his epoch-making voyage. The natives had been less than welcoming; after the death of d'Almeida in a skirmish with some Khoikhoi in 1510, the Portuguese generally avoided the Cape, preferring seemingly easier and richer lands to conquer, especially Mozambique, which also became their main re-victualling station *en route* to the Far East.[1] Disputing the Portuguese monopoly in the seventeenth century, the Dutch sought to seize Mozambique, but were driven off by the entrenched Portuguese. The Dutch then decided upon the Cape, almost midway on the direct sea route to the Straits of Sunda, between Sumatra and Java.[2] Favoured by warm sun, an agreeable, partly sub-tropical climate and Mediterranean-type agricultural land, the Cape was eminently suitable for European colonization, and the sparse groups of Khoikhoi could not oppose a well-armed settlement.

On 7 April 1652 the first Dutch colonists, under Jan van Riebeeck, were established at Table Bay to 'provide that the East India ships . . . may [procure] . . . herbs, flesh, water, and other needful refreshments'.[3] By 1682, thirty years later, 700 Europeans were living in the settlement, producing wine and wheat for export, as well as re-victualling the ships.[4] The Dutch settlers were joined before the end of the seventeenth century by Huguenots, fleeing religious persecution in France.

[1] See Monica Wilson and Leonard Thompson, *The Oxford History of South Africa*, Vol. 1 (Oxford, The Clarendon Press, 1969), p. 187.
[2] C. R. Boxer, *The Portuguese Seaborne Empire* (London, Hutchinson, 1969), pp. 106–27.
[3] Quoted in Wilson and Thompson, op. cit.
[4] Walter Fitzgerald, *Africa* (London and New York, Methuen and Dutton, 1957), p. 187.

Serious British occupation began in 1806, but did not really develop until the nineteenth century with the discovery of diamonds and gold. The Dutch-style pastoral life, which also depended to a great extent on African labour, ceased to be the mainstay of the economy. Massive investments were made in the mining companies that extracted the precious minerals from the sub-soil, employing black workers under conditions of intense exploitation.

Finally, with the First World War, the basis of a modern industrial state was created. Iron and steel mills were set up, using local ore and coal. According to the statisticians of the United Nations, by 1960 South Africa was producing 2,000,000 metric tons of steel. I.S.C.O.R.P., the government-owned iron and steel corporation, supplied two-thirds of the country's requirements. Highly diversified secondary industries provide a great variety of goods, many of which are exported to the north, to Rhodesia, Zambia, the Portuguese colonies of Mozambique and Angola, as well as the nominally independent former British High Commission Territories of Botswana, Lesotho, and Swaziland bordering the Republic.

South Africa is wealthy; it is the richest, economically most developed country on the continent. It possesses vast natural resources: the most important of these remains the underpaid African, whose labour provides the ruling European minority with the highest *per capita* income in Africa and one of the highest in the world. Only the United States, Canada, and Sweden have a higher *per capita* income than White South Africa.[1] Against this, it has been estimated[2] that the cash earnings of an African worker in the gold mines were no higher in real terms in 1966 than in 1911. The wages of Africans in industry are somewhat higher, but they hardly share in South Africa's much-touted economic 'boom'.

Only 13 per cent of South Africa's 472,347 square miles has been allocated by the white-minority regime to Africans, who comprise nearly 70 per cent of the population. The so-called 'Bantu' (i.e. African) areas are impoverished rural ghettos; these form a fragmented horse-shoe shape around the Transvaal and Orange Free State. Within these areas, there are no industries and no major towns or cities. Communications are poor, despite the high density of population in the north and south east. African agriculture is mainly subsistence farming of maize and sorghum on poor, eroded soils. In apartheid theory, these 'Bantu

[1] Brian Bunting, *The Rise of the South African Reich* (Harmondsworth, Penguin, 1969).
[2] Ibid., p. 513.

homelands' are supposed to become eight viable black states—'Bantu-stans'—enjoying separate development from white South Africa. According to Allister Sparks, a reporter for the *Rand Daily Mail* (23 March 1968), 'in practice they will amount to little more than a chain of labour reservoirs to which white South Africa will send requisition orders for workers.'

Farm products, especially fruit, wine, and wool, still rank very high among South African exports. Agriculture on a commercial basis is entirely in the hands of European farmers. There are three main farming areas: the Cape, the High Veld of the Orange Free State and Southern Transvaal, and the semi-tropical coastal strip and the middle belt of Natal. Commercial farming depends closely upon available water resources, and more than half South Africa's high plateau and coastal borderlands suffers scarce rainfall. Whereas the Cape receives Mediterranean-type winter rains, the interior plateau is dry in many places and rainfall is elsewhere unreliable. Droughts are frequent. South Africa can make good use of Lesotho's sole natural resource—water—for irrigation and possibly hydro-electric power; this explains in part the continual intervention of the Republic in the domestic affairs of this mountainous, landlocked, nominally independent, black African country totally surrounded by South African territory.

To the west of the Drakensberg mountains, in the High Veld—a region varying from 4,000 to 6,000 feet in altitude—ample pasturelands permit large-scale raising of cattle and sheep. On a ridge of this undulating plateau lies the Witwatersrand, the greatest gold field in the world. Ignorant of the fortune under their feet, the Dutch 'Voortrekkers' settled here in the 1830s, having migrated from the Cape to escape British rule and establish their own independent Boer republics of the Orange Free State and the Transvaal. Today, the 'City of the Rand', the big conurbation of Johannesburg and its satellite towns, with nearby Pretoria, the administrative capital, is a mushrooming symbol of white prosperity and South African industrial growth.

This growth has meant rapid urbanization of both the African and European populations, although the apartheid laws were later designed to prevent the increase of blacks in the white areas. However, the shortage of white workers to do semi-skilled and some skilled jobs has led to the greater use of African industrial labour. Nevertheless, the Government is committed to keeping the Africans at the level of migratory workers with one-year contracts in the white areas, thus blocking the development of an urban black proletariat. Even the number of black domestic workers must be reduced, say the more extreme proponents of apartheid. In the Western Cape, all Africans are eventually to be cleared out and sent to the 'Bantu homelands', leaving manual and semi-skilled labour to the large Coloured population who will remain to serve the Europeans. Cape Town—like Durban and Port Elizabeth/Uitenhage, a major centre of secondary industry—will be inhabited only by Europeans and Coloureds, but Pretoria is still the only city in which the whites outnumber all non-whites combined. About one-third of the African population lives in urban centres, despite the apartheid restrictions.

There are serious doubts, even among some Afrikaner Nationalists, of the feasibility of such relocation schemes. Admittedly, in the final analysis, the division of the black population on tribal grounds is intended to protect the white minority from united black resistance to apartheid and to prepare the way (if ever such an eventuality must be faced) for the creation of numerous—in theory, eight—fragmented black independent states bordering an all-powerful, highly industrialized, easily defendable, white redoubt. This powerful white hub would ultimately control its weakened black perimeter.

According to the Minister of Statistics and Planning, J. J. Loots, the 1970 census revealed that South Africa had a total population of 21,282,000. Of these, 69·7 per cent or 14,893,000 were Africans. Europeans comprised 17·8 per cent of the population, altogether 3,800,000 persons. The Coloureds, i.e. persons of mixed race, numbered nearly 2,000,000 or 9·7 per cent. And Asians (mainly Indians) numbered 614,000 persons, 2·8 per cent of the population.

The Africans are mainly Negroid peoples who moved from the north into South Africa many centuries before Europeans set foot in the country. In the eighteenth century, the Dutch settlers clashed with Bantu-speaking Africans along the Great Fish River in the Eastern Cape. Historians now generally reject the Afrikaner contention that no Bantu-speaking Africans lived west of the Fish River. White propagandists have claimed the land around the Cape was 'empty', except for the Khoisan peoples. Archaeological findings now indicate that there was significant population for that epoch (Britain's sixteenth century population was only 3,000,000). Carbon dating of finds revealed that the Buispoort and Uitkomst cultures of iron-using blacks flourished around A.D. 1100.[1]

In the Western Cape, the Europeans found large numbers of Bushmen and Khoikhoin (contemptuously named Hottentot by the Dutch). The

[1] See Wilson and Thompson, op. cit., and B. Fagan, *Southern Africa* (London, Thames and Hudson, 1969).

settlers exterminated many, pushing the others into the wastes of the Kalahari Desert. The women were often taken as servants and used sexually as well, founding the Coloured, or mixed population. Later, the racial mixture was further added to by Asians, Malagasies, and peoples from other parts of the African continent. Because of their Islamic faith, the Cape Malays have maintained a distinct social and ethnic character. Nearly 90 per cent of the Coloureds still live in the Cape, and more than half speak Afrikaans, the Dutch-based language of the descendants of original Dutch and Huguenot settlers.

According to the South African Government's census, the African population divided by tribal origin was as follows:

Xhosa	3,907,000
Zulu	3,970,000
Southern Ndebele	230,000
Northern Ndebele	180,000
Swazi	487,000
Shangaan	731,000
Venda	360,000
Southern Sotho	1,416,000
Northern Sotho	1,596,000
Tswana	1,702,000
Other	314,000

The main groups are Xhosa, Zulu, and Sotho. It should be emphasized that South African population figures for Africans are only approximate, as little care is taken to register properly the vital statistics of the black population. Moreover, to give tribal statistics only is misleading, considering the growing numbers of detribalized Africans in urban areas and on farms.

More than a third of the African population lived in urban centres. P. K. Leballo, Acting President of the Pan Africanist Congress of Azania (South Africa), argued that any liberation struggle should take this fact into consideration, despite 'leading guerrilla strategists for whom we have the deepest respect and admiration (who) have consistently pointed out that guerrilla warfare is extremely dangerous in the cities.'[1] He added:

The black population in the cities number close to $5\frac{1}{2}$ million. They are the power-house that drives all industry. There is no part of the industrial life

[1] Pan Africanist Congress of Azania (S.A.), *Report of the National Executive Committee Meeting, Moshi, Tanzania, 19th to 22nd September, 1967* (Lusaka, PAC, 1967), p. 18.

of the cities that is not completely dependent on us. Without us these cities
will die. For decades these workers, teachers, students and professionals have
been engaged in political struggles and have been exposed to political philoso-
phies of a most revolutionary kind. They have organized trade unions, participated in strikes, defiance campaigns, armed clashes with the police, and
more strikes. They have sabotaged and killed for freedom. They have died
for freedom.

An uncommitted academic observer, J. E. Spence, is of a somewhat
similar opinion. Commenting on Dr. Verwoerd's Bantustan scheme,
Spence wrote:

The fact remains that however rapidly Dr. Verwoerd develops the Bantustans,
he cannot hope to reverse the movement of African labour of the 'white'
urban areas which already have a large settled African population. The links
binding many of these urban Africans to their tribal 'homelands' are exiguous
if indeed they exist, while the development of common economic and political
interests has made the towns and cities a forcing-house for the growth of an
African nationalism cutting across traditional ethnic barriers.[1]

The sinister purpose of apartheid regulations is to remove from the
African population even the dignity of their African nationhood,
dividing them by tribal origin and labelling them 'Bantu'. Social
control by tribal division is a time-honoured colonial practice, but in
South Africa it is extended to ludicrous and vicious extremes in the
hope of preserving white supremacy for ever.

The term 'Bantu' is merely a linguistic, not a racial one. However, it
is the Ministry of Bantu Administration and Development that regu-
lates without consultation and consent the lives of South Africa's
nearly 15 million blacks. This is not the place to attempt to describe in
detail the fascist-type constraint and repression of the African people, or
to chronicle the continuing high toll in human misery and suffering.
Fortunately, this has been well documented by numerous writers and
investigatory bodies, such as the United Nations Sub-Committee on
Apartheid and Racial Discrimination, the South African Institute of
Race Relations, the African liberation movements and allied bodies, and
countless other groups in every field of endeavour.

The Asian population of South Africa is mainly of Indian origin,
descended from coolie labourers brought from India to work in the
sugar plantations of Natal. The white-minority government continues
without much success to seek to repatriate the Asian population, and
offers financial assistance for those who agree to leave. Nevertheless,
Durban retains a large Indian population, despite the intention of the

[1] J. E. Spence, *Republic Under Pressure* (London, Oxford University Press for the
Royal Institute of International Affairs, 1965), p. 120.

Group Areas Act to remove all non-whites from the centres of all towns and cities for resettlement in rigorously segregated ghettos on the outskirts. At the beginning of the twentieth century, there were also some 55,000 Chinese labourers who had been brought to South Africa to overcome the chronic shortage of labour in the gold mines. However, nearly all were repatriated by 1910 and further immigration of Chinese was banned. Since then, gold has been brought to the surface entirely by the sweat and blood of African contract workers, many of whom are recruited in Lesotho, Botswana, Swaziland, Rhodesia, and the Portuguese colonies. Confined to mine compounds in prison-life conditions, the workers are not allowed to bring their families with them during their fourteen months under contract. They are afterwards sent back to their homes.

Among the oddities of South African racial laws is the glaring admission of the country's dependence on trade with Japan. While Chinese are classified as non-whites, visiting Japanese businessmen are held to be white and thus entitled to all the many amenities of European life in the Republic. During the Second World War, when the Chinese were considered allies, it was just the reverse.

South Africa's European population is the largest anywhere in Africa. A million more than the Jewish population of the State of Israel, the 3·8 million Europeans, and especially those of Dutch origin, maintain they are now a nation and have nowhere else to go if the African majority should come to power in the Republic. Only a handful of whites, mainly in exile, can envisage living in a democratic state with an African majority. And even the South African Communist Party (SACP) views its support of the African liberation struggle as offering the sole possible guarantee for future settlement by Europeans. In his statement from the dock in the Supreme Court at Pretoria on 28 March 1966, the South African communist leader Abram Fischer declared his conviction that:

Over the past two or three decades it has been the Congresses and the Communist Party who have demonstrated in practice that men and women of different races can work together without difficulty on the basis of complete democracy and who have produced leaders prepared to sacrifice everything —even their lives—to achieve this ideal—people who have hammered out a policy, the Freedom Charter, in terms of which there will be room for all to exercise their rights. With these leaders no one need fear that he will be 'driven into the sea'.[1]

[1] Abram Fischer, Q.C., *Statement from the Dock*, Supreme Court, Pretoria, 28. March 1966 (London, Mayibuye Publications, 1966), p. 24.

Significantly, the Freedom Charter mentioned by Fischer, which was adopted at a so-called Congress of the Peoples, convened by the SACP and the African National Congress and allied groups at Klip-town on 26 June 1955, makes no pledge of the customary 'One man, one vote' but rather promises, 'All national groups shall have equal rights'!

Not only are South Africa's Europeans the largest settlement on the African continent, some of them are descended from the Dutch and Huguenot settlers of 300 years ago. It should be noted that no major African liberation movement proposes to drive the Europeans into the sea or exterminate them in any other fashion. But the Republic of South Africa is an African country and the overwhelming majority of its population are black Africans, who are ever more closely drawn together by common sufferings and aspirations, overcoming long-standing tribal divisions that are maliciously aggravated by the apartheid regime.

Europeans of Dutch origin, the Afrikaners (which means 'Africans', hence the insistence on the term 'Bantu' for the blacks), make up more than 55 per cent of the white population and now firmly control the political life of South Africa through their Afrikaner Nationalist Party. More and more of the Europeans of British origin are also voting for the Nationalist Party as the safest party of white supremacy. Tradi-tionally, the English-speakers, who now make up somewhat less than 45 per cent of the European population, voted massively for the United Party, the party of the British imperial connection.

Like the Civil War in the south of the United States, the Boer War in South Africa is virtually contemporary history. For the dispossessed African majority looking on, the dispute has been largely of academic interest. The original constitution of the Boer Republic of the Transvaal declared: 'There shall be no equality between black and white either in Church or State.' The Dutch farmers justified their exploitation and oppression of Africans by reference to the gloomy tenets of their Calvinist religion, which doomed even the bulk of white mankind to eternal damnation.

Invoking the economic rationale of imperialism, the later British colonialists were equally devoted to racial segregation. Cecil Rhodes, the then Premier of the British Cape Colony, declared when introducing a 'Native Bill for Africa' in 1894: 'My idea is that the natives should be kept in these native reserves and not mixed with the white men at all.'[1] He added:

[1] Quoted in the Unity Movement of South Africa's *The Revolutionary Road for South Africa* (Lusaka, Unity Movement, May 1969).

'I prefer to call a spade a spade. Let us boldly say: in the past we have made mistakes about native representation. We intend to change all that. . . . We are going to be lords of this people and keep them in a subject position. . . . They should not have the franchise because we don't want them on an equality with us. . . . These are my politics on native affairs and these are the politics of South Africa. . . . We must adopt a system of despotism, such as works so well in India, in our relations with the barbarians of South Africa.

The 'liberal' consciousness of so many English-speaking Europeans in South Africa is belied by both present and past, as though the choice between segregation and apartheid were not the merely slight one of degree. As far as the majority of the people of South Africa are concerned (i.e. the Africans), South Africa is virtually a slave plantation. The African has no political rights, either direct or indirect: he is denied the vote and parliamentary representation of any kind. He is banned from all overt political activity and from organizing as a worker: to strike is illegal and trade unions are prohibited. The manifold restrictions on his education, movement, and even his right to maintain his own family clearly justify any and all remedial measures.

The Resistance

South Africa was a far from empty land when van Riebeeck landed in 1652. The Bushmen and Khoikhoin who sparsely populated the Cape did not at first understand the menace of the white men. It did not take them long, however, to learn that the Europeans were indeed enemies. These hunter-gatherer, pastoral peoples were no match for the superior firepower of the settlers and they were either exterminated, assimilated through legitimate and illegitimate sexual unions with the women-hungry Dutch, or reduced to slavery. The survivors fled northwest into the Kalahari and Namib deserts—where a few of their descendants still remain. Those who did not escape from the Dutch and their British successors are represented today in the 1·9 million Coloureds, and invisibly present in the coloured genes carried knowingly and unknowingly by hundreds of thousands of 'white' South Africans.[1]

It is enough to note here that under apartheid a person's racial group is 'determined by his appearance and by general acceptance and repute'. It is generally believed by South Africans of all races that many leading Afrikaner families who profess strong racialist views and

[1] Paul Fordham, *The Geography of African Affairs* (Harmondsworth, Penguin, 1965), p. 210. See Bunting, op. cit., Ch. 9, pp. 158 ff, for a discussion of 'South Africa's Nuremberg Laws'.

receive 'acceptance and repute' as persons of pure European stock are nonetheless of Coloured origin.

At the beginning of the eighteenth century, the expanding Dutch colony in the Cape had a series of violent clashes with the better or-ganized African tribes that they met along the Great Fish River. By this time, the Dutch had completed the almost wholesale massacre of the Khoisan peoples who had originally inhabited the South Western Cape. Those who were not killed were reduced to servitude.

Dutch colonial rule, however, was also imperilled by the Napoleonic wars in Europe, and the British first occupied the Dutch settlement in 1795. In the general agreements between the European powers after the wars in 1814, Holland relinquished the Cape Colony to the British, although permanent British occupation began in 1806. However, British sovereignty was not firmly established until 1814, and was to the obvious distaste of the slave-holding Dutch Boers (farmers).

As David Livingstone observed during the 1850s:

The great objection many of the Boers had, and still have, to English law is that it makes no distinction between black men and white. They felt ag-grieved by their supposed losses in the emancipation of their Hottentot slaves, and determined to erect themselves into a republic, in which they might pursue without molestation the 'proper treatment of the blacks'. It is almost needless to add that the 'proper treatment' has always contained in it the essential element of slavery, namely, compulsory unpaid labour.[1]

Finally, in 1836, the Dutch settlers organized a mass exodus from British rule in the Cape. They undertook the 'Great Trek', transporting some 10,000 people and their chattels 500 miles north-east. This migra-tion was opposed by successive African leaders. Chaka, Dingaan, and Moshoshoe led armies against the invaders, but their resistance ended in defeat. The victorious Dutch were able to create the independent Boer republics of the Orange Free State and the Transvaal. Others went as far as Natal, but were dislodged again by the British in 1844. Wherever the Dutch moved, they were determined to expropriate African lands and subjugate the indigenous peoples. Their expansion was constantly met by African resistance, but the European rifle and superior military tactics overcame the courage and determination of the blacks, who were also weakened by tribalism.

The discovery of diamonds in Kimberley in 1870 and gold in the Transvaal in 1886 sealed the fate of the Boer republics. British imperial-ists headed by Cecil Rhodes were driven on from the Cape by greed and

---

[1] David Livingstone, *Missionary Travels and Researches in South Africa* (London, 1857), p. 29.

ambition, provoking the Anglo-Boer War of 1899–1902. Despite cunning and fanaticism, the Dutch Boers were now obliged to yield before Britain's imperial might. Thus almost all of South Africa became British colonies in 1902.

Thousands of British gold-seekers and other adventurers poured into South Africa. While the Dutch on their isolated farms brooded over their defeat, the new British colonists gathered in urban centres and used all their skills to amass wealth, ruling firmly over black and Boer alike. But the threatening demographic mass of the blacks inevitably prompted a truce between the formerly warring Europeans. In 1910 the British Government granted internal self-government to the white minority, creating the Union of South Africa, with an all-white parliament. It was essentially a union of the two factions of Europeans for the more secure exploitation of the African people. But the Dutch were definitely the junior partners in the firm and remained so until their Africaner Nationalist Party, which was established in virtually its present form by the Boer General J. B. M. Hertzog at the beginning of 1914, came to power—first in 1924 and again in 1948. Dr. D. F. Malan, the leader of the party in 1948, declared triumphantly: 'Today South Africa belongs to us once more. For the first time since Union, South Africa is our own. May God grant that it will always remain our own.' The history of South Africa reveals a remarkably consistent effort by the Afrikaners to assert their numerical dominance against the English-speaking Europeans and, having become the senior partners in the limited company, to exploit the blacks together in peace.

African armed resistance lasted for more than 200 years, ending with the defeat of the Bambata Rebellion of 1906. Led by Bambata, a Zulu chief, Africans rose in arms against the expropriation of Zulu lands and onerous taxes in Natal. Bambata died in battle along with some 4,000 other Africans. Only twenty-five whites were killed. The crushing military superiority of the Europeans was demonstrated again in the shedding of African blood.

However, even before the Sharpeville and Langa massacres in 1960 proved the futility of non-violent action, small-scale African violence against Europeans persisted throughout South Africa. Despite its immense and efficient police and military apparatus, South Africa has generally been considered one of the world's most violent societies. Not only confined to shanty towns and locations surrounding the 'white' cities, but in their very midst, clashes between blacks and whites, seemingly irrational, often brutish and sudden, were endemic. Europeans lived, as they continue to do, with their guns perpetually at their sides. The master and servant relationship between white and black was often transformed into that of victim and killer. As a result, according to United Nations statistics, more than half the world's annual executions are carried out in South Africa. Between July 1963 and June 1965 alone, 281 death sentences were passed by white judges and 194 Africans were executed. This amounted to an average of two executions every week.

The first African political organizations of a non-violent nature date from 1886, when the *Imbumba Yama Afrika*, the Union of Africans, was formed in the Eastern Cape, part of the British Cape Colony. The Africans still hoped that British liberalism and its code of values would eventually be extended to include them. Meanwhile, Mahatma Gandhi, a young Indian lawyer with pronounced non-violent views, arrived in South Africa and organized the Natal Indian Congress among his own people, most of them indentured labourers, in 1894. Later, in the Transvaal, 'Gandhi originated the method of passive resistance when he organized Indians against an attempt to force them, like Africans, to carry passes.'[1]

It is clear that for most Africans non-violence was not a deeply-held commitment: rather, it was a tactical necessity in view of the superior weapons of the Europeans. In addition, many—especially the professionals, who had been able to benefit from the meagre educational facilities for Africans—had serious illusions about British intentions. And these illusions were reinforced by both liberal and radical whites. Even in 1966, speaking before the judges of the regime who were enforcing horrors of apartheid on the African masses, the communist Abram Fischer[2] declared his passionate conviction that the consequences of war between African and European—which he termed 'civil war'—would be 'horrifying and permanent'. He pleaded for a gradual, non-imposed solution to South African problems, based on co-operation of white and black, which 'is what the Communist Party has stood for'. 'Clearly', Fischer said, 'it is imperative than an alternative "solution" be found, for in truth civil war is no "solution" at all.' Nevertheless, he declared he was convinced that 'such a civil war can never be won by the whites of this country.' The majority of blacks believed this as well and they at least did not fear the consequences of a war of liberation.

The detribalization of the African through urbanization and common political struggle against oppression continues apace, despite apartheid.

[1] Mary Benson, *The Struggle for a Birthright* (Harmondsworth, Penguin, 1966), p. 19.
[2] Fischer, op cit., p. 23.

Nevertheless, there remain many vestiges of tribalism. It has been maintained that no African has yet been completely detribalized.[1] This process of 'Africanization' was powerfully assisted initially by messianic, nativistic religious movements of a Pan-African character. Although none in South Africa attained the violence and clarity of political vision of John Chilembwe's Church of Christ uprising against British rule in Nyasaland in 1915, the movements developed in South Africa long before they did elsewhere on the African continent.[2]

The movements were either 'Ethiopian' or 'Zionist'. The first was Mangena M. Mokone's Ethiopian Church, founded in 1892. A former member of the Methodist Church, Mokone created his African church after a futile struggle against racial discrimination among the Methodists. Overt in its nationalism, the Ethiopian Church's main tenet was 'Africa for the Africans'. Reinterpreting the Christian Bible purely in terms of African resistance to white rule, Mokone was able to voice the 'yearning of the natives for liberty'.[3] The successful military resistance of the Ethiopian Empire against Italian colonial occupation in 1896 profoundly impressed blacks in South Africa. The Ethiopian churches, despite many tribal breakaways, were already Pan-Africanist in outlook and established ties with independent Afro-American churches in the United States, such as the African Methodist Episcopal Church of America.

From America too came 'Zionism', after the original Christian Catholic Apostolic Church in Zion, founded by J. A. Dowie and W. G. Voliva at Zion City, Illinois, in 1896. Africans, many of whom had already practised ritual bathing in their tribal religions, accepted the Zionists' emphasis on baptism and readily joined in their quest for the New Jerusalem on Mount Zion, seeking the concomitant gifts of physical and spiritual health. According to Lanternari:

The principal difference between the Zionist and Ethiopian churches is in the fulfilment of their messianic hopes: the Ethiopians promise a united Christian Africa ruled by the Lion of Judah, King of Kings, whereas the Zionists look to the Judeo-Christian land of Palestine, to which Moses and John the Baptist will lead them. The Ethiopian churches are governed by men who fulfil the traditional role of king in an aristocratic hierarchy, whereas the Zionists, rejecting the concept of aristocracy, choose their religious heads from among preachers, healers, clairvoyants, or sworn enemies of witchcraft.[4]

[1] J. C. de Ridder, *The Personality of the Urban African in South Africa: A Thematic Apperception Test Study* (London, Routledge, 1961), p. 160.
[2] Vittorio Lanternari, *The Religions of the Oppressed* (New York, New American Library, 1965), p. 39.
[3] Ibid., p. 40.
[4] Ibid., p. 45.

In either case, these nativistic churches were wholeheartedly subversive in respect to European rule. Many efforts to suppress them were made by the white authorities, who fully realized their encouragement of African defiance and resistance. In 1906, the Ethiopian churches were found to have given support to the abortive Bambata Rebellion. The 'separatist' and 'independent' churches (African breakaways from European religious movements and their missionaries, and purely African syntheses of Christianity and tribal religions) have provided numerous militants for the African liberatory struggle until the present day.

The Bambata Rebellion, according to Edward Roux,

> may very well be taken as the turning point between two periods in the history of the black man in South Africa: the early period of tribal wars and fights against the white invaders, which ended in the loss of the country and the reduction of the Bantu to the status of an internal proletariat; and the second period, one of struggle for national liberation and democratic rights within the framework of present-day South Africa, where black and white intermingle in complex economic and political relationships. During the first period the Bantu fought as isolated tribes and on military lines. Though they did not meet the whites on equal terms, but opposed shield and assegai to the rifle and machine gun, at least they met them as members of the independent tribes or nations having their own territory and military organization.[1]

Thus, although the tribes and nations who made up the primary resistance against European settlement exhausted their capabilities by the beginning of the twentieth century, there are few Africans who have not heard of that heroic and bitter struggle. No matter how crushed by repression and the difficulties of day-to-day survival, Africans still can look back with pride to the fight of their tribal forefathers against the whites. And yet there can be no doubt that the contemporary African mass movements are based mainly on at least partially detribalized urban blacks. 'Tribal bonds in the rural areas, with its accompaniment of conservatism and resistance to change, were an effective brake on Congress development both in the countryside and in the cities', says Edward Feit.[2] Nevertheless, the tales of African tribal resistance to European encroachment provide a potent ideological element in legitimating present-day armed resistance to the white-minority regime.

[1] Edward Roux, *Time Longer Than Rope* (Madison, University of Wisconsin Press, 1966), p. 91.
[2] Edward Feit, *South Africa: The Dynamics of the African National Congress* (London, Oxford University Press for the Institute of Race Relations, 1962), p. 61.

In contemporary conditions, only a social movement on a national scale could effect any significant change. According to Hans Toch, social movements are groups,

which are relatively *long-lasting* and which have a clear *programme* or *purpose*. They are viewed as forms of collective behaviour nevertheless, because they are large groups and because they *arise spontaneously*. The key element in most definitions of social movements is the requirement that they must be *aimed at promoting or resisting change* in society at large. . . . A psychological definition of social movements could read: *A social movement represents an effort by a large number of people to solve collectively a problem that they feel they have in common.*[1]

The Industrial and Commercial Workers' Union (the ICU) was the first such mass organization of the black proletarian in South Africa. It flourished during the 1920s and became a powerful force. Both its strengths and weaknesses have been transmitted to the contemporary liberation movements, and no account of the background to today's struggle could overlook this militant black working-class organization. 'Like many other African mass movements, the ICU succumbed to the diseases of lack of policy, poor leadership and bad organization', says Feit.[2] 'It nevertheless stands out as the greatest African mass movement in South Africa,' he adds.

The ICU was founded in Cape Town in 1919 as a union of dock workers by Clements Kadalie, a clerk from Nyasaland. It spread, in Kadalie's own words, 'like a veld fire' across South Africa. Spreading first to other ports, East London and Port Elizabeth, it then gathered adherents throughout the Cape, Orange Free State, Natal, and later the Transvaal. It even jumped the boundaries of the Union to form branches in South West Africa, Basutoland, Bechuanaland, Southern Rhodesia, Mozambique, and Kadalie's native Nyasaland.

Beginning with twenty-four members, who had each contributed one shilling, the membership swelled to 250,000 in 1928,[3] with an annual income of £15,000. Led by the dynamic, courageous firebrand Kadalie, the ICU concentrated on the material demands of South Africa's black workers, above all a minimum wage for Africans. For practically the first time, Africans put aside tribal differences and united as an oppressed, exploited people.

Kadalie declared in a speech in Heilbron in 1926: 'I will simply go

---

[1] Hans Toch, *The Social Psychology of Social Movements* (London, Methuen 1966), p. 5. Italics in original.

[2] Feit, op cit., p. 64.

[3] Roux, op. cit., p. 167.

from dockyard to factory and with a single word, "STOP", the white people will be held at ransom, the railways will lose over £2,000,000 a day and while the trouble is on I will be looked upon as a Prime Minister.' Although European workers in South Africa generally viewed the ICU as a threat to their privileged position, Kadalie had close connections with some European leftists and, according to Roux, it was they who drew up the preamble of the first ICU constitution along the lines of the American Industrial Workers of the World (IWW). This anarcho-syndicalist heritage and the myth of the general strike somewhat transformed has played an important role in the ideological orientation of the liberation movements that followed. Otherwise, there is no explanation for the widespread African conviction after 1960 (the year of massive African entry into the United Nations) that national liberation would be achieved, almost miraculously, in a matter of days, by a general uprising of the African people.

The first African strike occurred in 1918, when sanitary workers in Johannesburg went out in support of demands for sixpence a day more. One hundred and fifty-nine were arrested and sentenced to two months' hard labour. Later, in Bloemfontein, when African workers demanded four and six a day instead of two shillings, martial law was declared and the strike attempt was crushed.[1]

The ICU called its first major strike in December 1919, at the Cape Town docks. White workers rejected the appeals of the blacks for support and the strike was broken after three weeks. Troops were sent in to remove the striking Africans from the port, while police kept ICU leaders under constant harassment.

In October 1920, South African police in Port Elizabeth killed twenty-four Africans and wounded fifty others when a crowd of people gathered outside the Baakens Street police station, protesting against the arrest of Samuel Masabala, the local leader of the ICU, who had been jailed for calling a strike in support of a demand for ten shillings a day minimum wage for Africans. Earlier the same year, more than 40,000 black miners had struck in the Rand. Police broke the strike, killing a number of Africans. In 1925, the police and other whites killed five Africans and wounded twenty-five others in action in Bloemfontein against the ICU.

This pattern of open violence against Africans has remained constant in South Africa. Just as constant has been the refusal to grant black workers the right to organize in order to secure better wages and improved working conditions. The ICU had no official recognition, and the South African Trade Union Congress, a white racist body, only

[1] Benson, op cit., p. 38.

begrudgingly and fleetingly had any contact with it. But the fledgling South African Communist Party (SACP), formed in 1921 under the leadership of Sidney Bunting, gradually took an interest in the ICU. Previously, the Communist Party, which was and still remains overwhelmingly white, had based its revolutionary hopes almost exclusively on the organized, privileged white workers of South Africa. Bunting, who had come to the Party from the International Socialist League, had an outstanding record of contacts with Africans, gradually seeing in them the only genuine revolutionary hope in the country. He was responsible for the founding of the League of African Rights, which was dissolved on Comintern orders in 1929, shortly after its formation, and Bunting himself was expelled from the Party as a 'rightwing deviationist'. George Padmore has called Bunting 'the foremost European champion of the black man'.[1] A member of the British upper middle class, Bunting differed greatly from the majority of SACP members at its founding in 1921, most of whom were Eastern European Jewish immigrants. Bunting himself arrived in South Africa as a young man during the Boer War and settled in Transvaal as a lawyer. Despite his aspirations to give his own party at least a black skin and to build ties with the ICU, Bunting clashed increasingly with Clements Kadalie.

This struggle culminated in 1926 with the expulsion of the communists, all blacks, who held leading positions in the ICU. Kadalie had become irked with the communists' mounting criticism of his leadership and was not prepared to bow to their demands for a drastic reorganization of the ICU, giving them greater control over the leadership and the finances.

Even William Ballinger, the British Labour Party adviser who was to join ICU headquarters in 1928, made numerous criticisms of Kadalie's erratic, demagogic behaviour and lack of interest in administrative and organizational matters. Kadalie liked to think of himself as a 'platform thunderer', and he was indeed a master of oratory, but this was not enough to maintain an organization of the size and growing complexity of the ICU. Politically, although himself defying the South African pass laws, Kadalie had no programme for sustained political action, and doubts about his management of finances, abetted by personality clashes, led to the decline of the ICU. Branches, such as George Champion's in Natal, broke away to form a plethora of local, sometimes even tribal, groups. Champion, a Zulu, played heavily on Zulu nationalism in his clash with Kadalie, stressing his former leader's

---

[1] George Padmore, *Pan-Africanism or Communism?* (London, Dobson, 1956), p. 347.

origins in Nyasaland. The decline of the ICU is described by Roux in these terms:

Secretaries were bolting with cash, the union's furniture was being sold to pay lawyer's fees. . . . The events that led up to the final debacle were full of drama and tragedy. Anarchy prevailed. Individual leaders competed for power. They fought to obtain control of the ICU. And as they fought, the ICU vanished before their eyes until there was nothing to fight over.[1]

The communists naturally viewed the breakup of the ICU as just confirmation of their criticism of Kadalie and his followers.[2] Later, the communists were to maintain that Kadalie had allowed himself to be used by a white anti-communist 'network' headed by the white South African novelist Ethelreda Lewis, who had connections with the Independent Labour Party in Britain, and Winifred Holtby, who had visited South Africa as a journalist and lecturer in 1926 and had met Kadalie. Teresa Zania even goes so far as to claim Ethelreda Lewis's letters to Winifred Holtby make Lewis seem 'like a very naive C.I.A. agent'.[3] Despite this sectarian anachronism, there is little doubt that Kadalie received considerable European encouragement to break with the communists. However, African fears of communist control of their organizations, added to the suspicion that the mainly white SACP was only the most cunning detachment of their European settler enemies, bent on tricking them out of their African nationhood, have remained a constant theme in the history of the liberation movement in South Africa over the past fifty years. Unfortunately, accusations of financial mismanagement, dictatorial and erratic behaviour by leaders, and administrative anarchy also remain a recurring theme.

George Padmore believed that Sidney Bunting's League of African Rights might have been able to retrieve the mantle of the fallen ICU, had it not been for the new instructions from the Comintern, after its Sixth Congress, which forced dissolution of the League. Padmore comments:

Instead of agitating for racial equality and equal citizenship for Africans, they were (after dissolution of the League) to be offered a 'Native Republic' along the lines of the 'Black Belt State' for Negroes in the Southern States of America. Africans had never demanded any such nonsense. Consternation was therefore great when the new Comintern directive was received, ordering that

[1] Roux, op cit., p. 177.
[2] A communist point of view of the ICU can be found in Teresa Zania's 'The ICU', the *African Communist* (No. 38, Third Quarter 1969).
[3] Zania, op. cit., p. 77.

'the party must determinedly and consistently put forward the slogan for the creation of an independent Native Republic, with simultaneous guarantees for the rights of the white minority, and struggle in deeds for its realization'.[1]

Bunting and many other white party members opposed this suicidal change of policy, but they were purged upon orders from Moscow. Padmore adds that Africans overwhelmingly rejected this policy. He says:

They, like the Negroes in America, while opposed to all forms of racial disability have never demanded separatism, either in the form of Apartheid or 'Native Republic'. Rather, the Africans have always demanded full citizenship rights within a multi-racial society. They therefore looked with deep suspicion upon the new Communist slogan of a 'Native Republic', which they interpreted as an attempt to segregate them into some sort of Bantu state, for they knew that Europeans—even those calling themselves Communists—would resent living under an all-African Government.

Contradictions between Europeans calling themselves 'communists' and the African liberation movements would in themselves take an entire book to describe. Regardless of their criticisms of its leader, Clements Kadalie's ICU performed a pioneering task in uniting black workers, making them conscious of their strength, and demonstrating that only their African national unity across tribal lines could withstand European exploitation.

Thus, the essential elements of black resistance in South Africa, the foundations of present-day movements, are to be found in three phenomena. Firstly, the heroic tradition of armed military resistance to white encroachment that began in the seventeenth century and continued until the first decade of the twentieth century. Although generally organized on tribal lines, this armed struggle survives as an example today in the memory of all Africans. Secondly, the influence of the independent and separatist African churches, whether Ethiopian or Zionist, in resisting the European ideological instrument of repression, Christianity, as practised in South Africa. The African churches, despite their messianic prophetism and fruitless searches for the New Jerusalem, had a remarkably accurate view of the society in which Africans were forced to become hewers of wood and drawers of water for alien whites. The revolutionary inclinations of the nativistic churches also spread far beyond the European-imposed boundaries within Africa and extended across the seas to wherever black people were in struggle, in America and elsewhere, establishing a precedent for Pan-Africanism. Thirdly, in Clement Kadalie's Industrial and Commercial Workers' Union,

[1] Padmore, op. cit., p. 351.

despite its short-lived success, Africans demonstrated their understanding of their role in the capitalist, white-controlled society of South
Africa and organized the first strikes of a growing black proletariat
across all tribal lines. In these phenomena, and the constant struggle
against European mastery, the national consciousness of the African
people of South Africa found its first tentative existence. This new
nationalism was not to find full-fledged, self-assertive form until the
middle of the Second World War when Anton Muziwakhe Lembede,
demanding that Africans rely on themselves for liberation, founded
with some other young men the Youth League of the African National
Congress.

The African National Congress of South Africa (ANC)

The African National Congress can easily claim to be Africa's oldest
liberation movement. Founded in 1912 as the South African Native
National Congress, it predates even the National Association for the
Advancement of Coloured People in the United States, which it greatly
resembled during most of its legal existence within South Africa.
However, to call it a 'liberation movement' at that time is to abuse the
generally accepted definition of what constitutes a liberation movement.
The ANC was essentially a reformist, elite-led association for the better-
ment of African economic, social, and political conditions within a non-
violent legal framework. The professionals, many of them lawyers, who
ran the organization, regarded their primary task to be 'more to speak
for the people than to speak to the people'.[1]

The lengthy history of the ANC can conveniently be divided into
four major periods. First, its founding as an elitist social movement of
limited membership, enjoying mixed fortunes. Second, after a brief
decline and near eclipse by the All-African Convention, the revival of
the organization by its Youth League, which was committed to a more
nationalistic, activist programme and its transformation into a mass
movement. Third, the failure of the passive resistance campaign and the
split of the ANC, with the most active nationalists leaving to form the
Pan Africanist Congress. Fourth, its banning by the white minority
regime, followed by the transfer of its leadership abroad and the belated
adoption of the principle of armed struggle as the sole effective means
of creating a democratic, multiracial state in South Africa.

---

[1] 'Memorandum on the *Programme of Action* adopted at the Annual Conference
of the ANC, December 1949'. This typewritten, undated, unpublished document is
quoted in Feit, op. cit., p. 1, and *passim.*

1. The Beginnings (1912-35)

The ANC was not the first political organization formed in South
Africa. That distinction belongs to the *Imbumba Yama Afrika*, the Union
of Africans, organized in 1886 in the Eastern Cape. Around the same
time, the first African Christian Church was founded and the first
African newspaper published. In the British Cape Colony a handful of
Africans even had the vote, although they were opposed by the majority
of white settlers as a threat to European hegemony in the colony. The
British Colony of Natal, on the other hand, treated Africans with the
same harshness as did the Boers in the Orange Free State and Transvaal
republics.

Incidentally, in Natal, Mahatma Gandhi set up the Natal Indian
Congress in 1894. Here, Gandhi was to work among the Indian 'coolies'
on the sugar plantations and develop his theories about passive resistance, which were later to prove successful in India, while failing utterly
in the harsher conditions of southern Africa.

In 1902, Coloured people in the Cape founded the African People's
Organization. This was a forerunner of many Coloured organizations,
culminating fifty years later in the South African Coloured People's
Organization, later to become the South African Coloured People's
Congress, within the Congress Alliance, which in principle at least was
led by the ANC.

These early organizations generally confined their activities to petitioning their white rulers for some measure of social justice. The Peace
Treaty of Vereeniging between the British and their defeated Boer
enemies had already laid the foundations for joint domination over
the blacks. The partnership was sealed in the Act of Union of 1910.
It firmly imposed in South Africa a colour bar which was subsequently
improved upon as a general system of segregation, before reaching the
pervasive totalitarian confines of apartheid.

The Act of Union and the election of an all-white Parliament deeply
shocked Africans, and in fact all non-whites, in South Africa. African
political associations had protested even before Union, but their pleas
went largely unheard in London, where politicians of the day were more
concerned about reconciliation with the vanquished Dutch.

At the instigation of Dr. Pixley Ka Izak Seme, an African lawyer,
who had been sent by missionaries to study in the United States and
Britain, a few hundred educated Africans gathered in Bloemfontein on
8 January 1912. They came from all tribes and from all parts of South
Africa, led by lawyers, clergymen, and teachers. From this meeting was
born the South African Native National Congress.

The new body was influenced by American Negro self-help groups and was committed to constitutional means to redress African grievances. Seme and his associates hoped to educate less fortunate Africans and to win the respect and support of Europeans in their demands for political, economic, and social justice.

One of the curious features of SANNC was its alliance of new elites—the professionals and self-made men—and the old tribal aristocracy. The organizational structure was based on a bicameral parliament, with an Upper House of chiefs and a Lower House of commoners. Each house had its own President. The unanimously elected Honorary Governor, head of the Upper House, was Letsie II, Paramount Chief of the Basuto, whose determined resistance to the expansion of Dutch settlers had preserved a portion of their kingdom from alien rule until 1884, when they were obliged to seek the protection of Britain to resist renewed Boer expansionist pressures. (Under a clause in the Act of Union, Basutoland, and the other 'Protectorates' of Bechuanaland and Swaziland, could ultimately have been incorporated into South Africa. All three became nominally independent countries—respectively, Lesotho and Botswana in 1966 and Swaziland, or Ngwane, in 1968—but one apartheid scheme still foresees their absorption into the Republic as Bantustans.) Elected as first President-General of the body was the Reverend John Langalibalele Dube, an American-educated teacher and clergyman. Pixley Seme was elected Treasurer-General and the Secretary-General was a self-taught clerk from the Cape, Solomon Tshekiso Plaatje.

The mouthpiece of the SANNC was *Abantu-Batho* (The People), founded later in 1912 by Seme with financial backing from the Queen Regent of Swaziland, Natotsibeni. This journal was published in English and three African languages and was the first national newspaper for Africans.

Politically, the SANNC devoted all its efforts to a campaign against the Government's Native Land Bill, which in fact prohibited Africans from freely buying land except in 'native reserves', 7·3 per cent of the country. This Bill was successfully sought by European farmers who wanted the African reduced to a virtually landless rural proletarian. A deputation headed by J. L. Dube was sent to London in the vain hope of getting the British Government to defend the land rights of Africans. Hardly had the Congress delegation returned empty-handed to make its report at a special meeting in Bloemfontein, when the First World War broke out.

The beginning of that war was also the signal for the Boer Rebellion, the effort by a group of Dutch once more to create their own independent republic. General Manie Martiz, an officer of the Union Defence Force, disobeyed orders to attack the German Imperial forces in German South West Africa and instead joined them, setting up a 'Provisional Government of South Africa'. However, by the end of October 1914, the rebellion was crushed by Louis Botha and J. C. Smuts, generals who remained loyal to the British.

No African troops were used against either the Germans or the rebellious Boers, although the Germans had no reluctance about making use of trained native troops in their encircled African colonies. Africans in South Africa were used solely for menial tasks, and neither Britons nor Boers wanted them trained in the art and science of modern warfare, learning to kill white men.

After the war, a black deputation headed by Selope Thema, Secretary-General of Congress since 1915, went to Versailles to lobby the peace conference on behalf of the unrepresented South Africans. The Boers had sent a deputation to lobby for a white republic. While in France, Solomon T. Plaatje, who was a member of the African delegation, attended the first Pan-African Congress, which had been organized in Paris by Dr. W. E. B. DuBois of the United States.

The Congress had no visible influence upon the peace conference, but it established lasting fraternal bonds between men of colour in Africa, America, and elsewhere. The principles of Pan-Africanism far exceeded any slogan of 'African for the Africans!' although that was a most justifiable ambition for subjugated black men. Pan-Africanism implied a struggle for human dignity as well as national freedom, a recognition of the community of interests and necessity for mutual assistance and co-operation between men of African descent wherever they may be found in the world. Ultimately, it is a vision of the united struggle of all the world's impoverished, oppressed peoples, expanding in scope to cover the peasants and workers of Asia and Latin America as well as the blacks of the Caribbean and North America.

The depths of racist feelings among European workers was violently demonstrated in 1922 when white miners struck to protect their privileges, which they feared would be threatened if the colour bar were lowered to allow Africans to do more semi-skilled jobs on the Rand. To their later shame, the South African communists supported this reactionary strike, which was marked by white rioting and unprovoked attacks on Africans, in which seven were killed and thirty-seven wounded. Thousands of black miners lost their jobs and were sent back to the reserves despite the crushing of the strike by the Government, now headed by J. C. Smuts. Today the 'White Revolt on the Rand' still greatly embarrasses and divides the scattered members of the SACP,[1] although Sidney Bunting later did his best to wipe the naturally distasteful memory from African minds.

Initially, leaders of the SACP, which was founded in 1921, took a very dim view of the small, elitist SANNC and devoted the bulk of their efforts towards mobilizing European workers or influencing through the efforts of black communists the flourishing ICU. The expulsion of the communists by Clements Kadalie in 1926 was a blow to Bunting's hopes. This setback might nevertheless have been overcome if the Comintern had not ordered the dissolution of Bunting's League of African Rights, set up by the SACP to replace the disappearing ICU in 1929.

Communists took another look at the Congress, despite its steady decline and general ineffectualness during much of the twenties. In 1925, the SANNC had modified its name to African National Congress and went so far as to adopt an anthem, *Nkosi Sikelel' i-Afrika* (Lord Bless Africa), and design a flag of black, green, and gold horizontal bars. The communists found a friend in James Gumede, a Roman Catholic who was elected President-General of the ANC in 1927. The same year, Gumede attended the communist-organized Brussels conference of the League Against Imperialism, which drew together leaders of national groups from Africa and Asia. After the conference, Gumede was invited to tour the Soviet Union. He returned to South Africa greatly impressed by what he had seen in the Land of Lenin, but Gumede's turn to the left did not find support with the majority of Congress members. They rejected the overtures of the SACP for a variety of reasons, ranging from religious objections against the atheism and dialectical materialism professed by the communists, to deeply nurtured fears of being outmanoeuvred by such strange, wily whites. In any case, Gumede was replaced by the founder of Congress, Pixley Seme.

For a while, the communists turned away from the ANC, whose leaders were often violently hostile to the SACP. Economic crisis during the early 1930s, with lower standards of living for Africans, failed to halt the decline of the ANC. Not even the outburst of African nationalism on behalf of beleagured Ethiopia, which had been invaded by fascist Italy, could instil new life in Pixley Seme's tired organization.

[1] See F. Meli, 'Class versus Colour in South Africa, a Reader's View', *Sechaba*, official organ of the ANC (Vol. 4, No. 6, June 1970).

2. Further Decline and Revival (1935-51)

When the Government of General J. B. M. Hertzog, the first Afrikaner Nationalist regime, proposed to eliminate existing African voters from the common rolls in the Cape and set up instead a Natives' Representative Council, a purely advisory body, the ANC was unwilling to respond vigorously to this challenge, or to the equally obnoxious Native Trust and Land Bill that deprived Africans in the Cape of their right to buy land outside the reserves. This provoked bitter criticism of its leaders.

Finally, Pixley Seme agreed to call a mass conference of African organizations, jointly with Dr. D. D. T. Jabavu, from Fort Hare College, who was the leading African educationist in the country. This conference was held in Bloemfontein on 16 December 1935, Dingaan's Day (now called the 'Day of the Covenant'), which commemorates the defeat of that African chief by the Europeans. Some 500 persons attended, including representatives of Indian and Coloured groups, making the occasion the broadest gathering of non-whites in South African history.

The initial results of the meeting were far from spectacular. Repudiating a minority call for demonstrations and strikes, the All-African Convention decided to plead with the Government for a limited African franchise and improvement of the situation of non-whites in general. In addition, an appeal on behalf of African people was sent to London to the King and the British Parliament.

Hertzog, realizing that his original proposals to amend the entrenched clause in the constitution would not receive the necessary two-thirds majority,[1] then turned to the All-African Convention urging a 'compromise', i.e. African acceptance of his Native Representative Council. Many leaders of the AAC favoured acceptance, despite last-ditch resistance from a group of Coloured leftists who were attacked by the communists as Trotskyites. A number of ANC leaders were elected to the Native Representative Council and it joined with the AAC and the Cape Native Voters' Association in backing candidates to become the three white Members of Parliament and four white senators, who would now ostensibly represent African interests in the all-white parliament in Cape Town.

The N.R.C. quickly proved ineffectual to all but the leaders of the ANC. The white representatives of African interests often spoke well for their constituents but were never successful in diverting the racist course of white-minority government. They worked closely with the ANC, which organized what broad black support it had. But it was

[1] See Bunting, op. cit.

natural that not many Africans had much enthusiasm for the institution after their early and rapid disillusionment.

The All-African Convention had led the resistance to the N.R.C. and now declared its intention of becoming a permanent body, which would eventually (it proved, unsuccessfully) challenge the ANC and the PAC for leadership of the black masses. We will examine elsewhere the subsequent history of the AAC and its related organizations. It only needs noting here that this group, with its vehement Marxist ideology, has had a greater influence than its numbers might lead one to expect. Traces of its views, generally denounced as 'ultra-leftist' by the SACP, can be found in the declarations of African leaders who were never its members.

The beginning of the Second World War in 1939 found the ANC at low ebb. Africans were not so eager to enlist to carry out menial tasks for the white army as they had been in the First World War. Also, although repelled by Adolf Hitler's Nazi doctrines of racial superiority, which naturally found a ready audience among the Afrikaners, Africans and Asians were stimulated by the Japanese challenge to Western hegemony in the Pacific. Within a short time, however, came equally heady Anglo-American promises of new freedoms, a global New Deal, after victory over the Axis Powers. When the Japanese forces seemed poised to strike into British-held India, even General Smuts had found occasion to encourage wartime solidarity of all races, promising economic and social improvements for all and quoting the Four Freedoms of the Roosevelt-Churchill Atlantic Charter. The pass laws were relaxed briefly, until the Japanese menace was repulsed by the Allied fleet in the Pacific.

While Professor Z. K. Matthews and other older intellectuals were drafting an African Bill of Rights at Fort Hare College, demanding an end to racial discrimination and white-supremacy government, another group of younger intellectuals was evolving a philosophy of national revival for African people. It is at this point that one might say that the real history of the contemporary liberation movement begins, with the formation of the Youth League of the African National Congress.

The focus of this development was an extraordinary young man studying law, Anton M. Lembede, who is generally considered the fountainhead of 'Africanist' ideas behind the Youth League, the consequences of which eventually led to the breakaway of the Pan Africanist Congress a little more than a decade later. After teaching at Heilbron High School, Lembede became associated with other young nationalists who were then forming the League at Fort Hare and in Johannesburg's

Orlando location. Among them were Oliver Tambo, Mangaliso Robert Sobukwe, Walter Sisulu, Nelson Mandela, and Peter Roboroko. The League formally came into existence at Easter 1944, although Roboroko claims to have convened an earlier meeting in October 1943.[1]

According to Roboroko, the Youth League came into being at this particular time as younger people were discussing whether to establish another organization completely independent of the ANC or to attempt to revive the moribund organization. As it happened, they decided it would be better to try to put life into the old body.

The principal criticism directed against the ANC leadership at that time concerned their alleged 'collaboration with the oppressors'. ANC support for the N.R.C. was bitterly resented. Another criticism, Roboroko added, was that the ANC leaders were not sufficiently outspoken on the issue of nationalism, or that they were not sufficiently nationalist. The Youth League was to come out plainly with the declaration that it rejected all forms of white domination. 'In fact, they did not say white,' Roboroko commented, 'but "foreign domination and foreign leadership". They stood for Africa for the Africans!'

Members of the Youth League were especially critical of communist influence over the ANC. Many were particularly incensed at the turnabout of the SACP concerning the war. Dr. Yusuf Dadoo, a leader of the South African Indian Congress—later its president—and also a member of the SACP, won considerable acclaim from Africans when he urged non-Europeans not to get involved in the war because it was 'an imperialist war'. Dadoo was sent to jail for six months because of his anti-war stand, of which many Africans as well as Asians wholeheartedly approved. But immediately after the Soviet Union entered the war, Dadoo switched his line, declaring it a 'People's War', requiring the full support and mobilization of all the world's people. Even this might have been accepted by the blacks if Dadoo and the SACP had declared willingness to press on with the fight against fascism and racism in South Africa as well as abroad. The situation of the SACP, turning away from domestic struggle in order to give full support to the war effort, was duplicated in the United States; there, the CPUSA lost Afro-American support when it refused to continue the fight for civil rights during the war years, rejecting the slogan of 'Victory at home and abroad', put forward by militant Negro leaders, who saw in the war an opportunity to redouble efforts against racial discrimination in all fields of American life. In any case, the communists lost broad support

---

[1] From an unpublished interview between Peter Roboroko and the author in Dar es Salaam on 11 March 1966.

among blacks in both the Union of South Africa and the other U.S.A. after 1941.

The ANC had itself been virtually dead until 1940, when Dr. A. B. Xuma, after participating in the All-African Convention, began efforts to revive it and to transform it into what it had never yet been—a mass organization. Despite this, Dr. Xuma was no hero of the Youth League because of his accommodationist attitudes towards the white-minority government and commitment to gradualism in obtaining full rights for Africans. On 16 December 1945, the ANC, which had sent delegates to the historic Fifth Pan-African Congress in Manchester,[1] unanimously adopted a list of 'African Claims'. They demanded adoption of the democratic principle of one man, one vote. They demanded the lowering of all racial barriers: repeal of the hated pass laws, equal education and equal opportunity, equal pay in employment, and equal rights to purchase land. In 1946, Dr. Xuma was to travel to New York to present the newly-formulated 'Claims' to the United Nations, thus beginning the long and mainly futile history of U.N. lobbying by South African petitioners.

The strong feelings among Youth League members about collaboration with whites were in part also due to the influence of the All-African Convention. Captured by Coloured Trotskyists in 1935, at the moment when it had been expected to dissolve, the AAC, under the leadership of Dr. I. B. Tabata, worked effectively as an organ of propaganda, denouncing vehemently any form of collaboration with the rascist enemy in segregated councils or other bodies, which they claimed would be used by the Government like the village *Bungas* to impose more effectively iniquitous legislation upon the blacks. Although there is no trace of black chauvinism in the documents of the AAC, the fact that Tabata was believed to have broken with white Trotskyists around the time that his group took over the leadership of the AAC only contributed to his appeal to the burgeoning Africanists.

Another organization that influenced the formation of the ANC Youth League was the African Democratic Party, led by Paul Mosaka, an articulate young member of the N.R.C. who ceaselessly used his position within that body to denounce it as a 'dismal failure'. Mosaka formed the ADP when he found that the ANC was unable or unwilling to encourage the mass actions that he hoped for. He was assisted in

---

[1] Among those attending this Congress were Kwame Nkrumah, Jomo Kenyatta, George Padmore, and Hastings K. Banda, as well as Dr. W. E. B. DuBois. See *Documents of the Fifth Pan-African Congress* (London, Hammersmith Bookshop, 1963).

this endeavour by Senator Hyman Basner, a leftist lawyer who had defended many Africans in the courts. Although nominally a communist, Basner's views differed greatly from those held by the leadership and he was expelled from the SACP in 1948 for 'individualism'. Unfortunately, the presence of a European, Basner, at Mosaka's side was alarming to many Africans and the ADP never gathered a mass following.

From these and other varied influences and the experience of life itself for black people in South Africa, the Youth League developed into a 'coherent group with a definite programme'.[1] The charismatic figure that inspired this effort was Lembede's. Understandably, he failed to win much sympathy from either white radicals or liberals. Mary Benson describes him as 'an intriguing personality—arrogant and aggressive yet with an unusual ability to laugh at himself. Though not a fluent speaker, sometimes stammering, his swing from pedagogic to demagogic utterances could be spellbinding.'[2]

Lembede was the sickly son of Zulu farm workers and, although plagued by poor health throughout his life, he was seized at an early age by a passion for learning. A hard worker, he won a scholarship to Adams Teacher Training College. Later, while teaching at Heilbron High School, he took by correspondence a B.A. and an L.L.B. in Philosophy and Roman-Dutch law. He completed his studies, moved to Johannesburg in 1943 and was articled to the law firm of Dr. Pixley Seme, the founder of the ANC. Within four years, this visionary of African nationalism was dead, at the age of thirty-three, worn out by illness and toil. His legacy was the victory (although short-lived) of the Africanists at the ANC conference in 1949, and the enduring Africanism that continues to animate so many of the rank and file of the ANC, as well as providing the ideological foundation of the action of the rival Pan Africanist Congress. Just as enduring has been the resistance to these views by some white liberals and, naturally, the South African communists—especially after their wholehearted alignment with the whites of the Soviet Communist Party leadership in the dispute with the Communist Party of China, headed by Chairman Mao Tsetung.

In 1949, the Youth League was at last able to make its bid for leadership, not only because of the hard work it had already done to give new life to the ANC, but also because it had by then worked out its programme around the clear concept of African nationalism. There was also the clear warning of the grim future after eighteen months of the new Afrikaner Nationalist government, headed by Dr. D. F. Malan, who had promised every effort to make South Africa's government

[1] Roux, op. cit., p. 403.   [2] Benson, op. cit., p. 81.

forever white. Although he had a majority of only five in the House of Assembly (the Government was actually in the minority in the Senate), Malan immediately began securing its power by eliminating Indian representatives in Parliament and restricting the number of Coloured voters. Mixed marriages were made illegal. Indian land tenure was further limited and new restrictions were imposed upon the flow of African workers to the towns. In South West Africa, still a separate League of Nations Mandate territory, the Europeans, almost all staunch supporters of the Afrikaner Nationalist Party, were granted six seats in the Assembly and four in the Senate, relieving Malan's fears for his majority.

In the new situation, the Programme of Action proposed by the Youth League provided a cogent and reasonable plan for militant action. The programme aimed at the attainment of 'National Freedom', which was defined as: 'freedom from white domination and the attainment of political independence. This implies the rejection of the concept of segregation, apartheid, trusteeship or white leadership, which are all in one way or another, motivated by the idea of white domination or the domination of white over black.'

Two candidates were put forward for the President-General of Congress, Dr. Xuma, the incumbent, and Dr. James S. Moroka, an African surgeon trained in Edinburgh and Vienna. The Youth League and many others voted for Moroka, and he was elected. Chosen as Secretary-General was Walter Max Sisulu of the Youth League, a Xhosa born in the Transkei in 1912. Largely self-educated, he had learned of white oppression and exploitation at first hand as a mine boy and in other menial jobs. He later became an estate agent, but abandoned this occupation to become the first full-time Secretary-General of the ANC and hastened to find ways of putting into action the militant programme of the Youth League.

A call for a one-day work stoppage and mass demonstrations by African workers in May 1949 brought the rejuvenated ANC into immediate conflict with the SACP. The Youth League was infuriated by obvious communist efforts to take over the 1 May demonstrations and the quarrel between them ended in physical violence. Only the greater brutality of the South African police, who killed eighteen Africans and wounded more than thirty others in breaking up the May Day demonstration, briefly reconciled them.

In conjunction with the communists and the Indian Congress, which was now under communist control, the ANC issued a call for a national work stoppage on 26 June. This time there was no conflict and Indians joined Africans and the handful of Europeans in a spectacular demonstration. But the Youth League had also demanded a total boycott of elections and the N.R.C. However, neither the new President-General of the ANC, Moroka, nor other leading older members, such as Professor Z. K. Matthews, showed any inclination to comply. They remained in the N.R.C. until the end of 1950, just months before the Government itself abolished the Council as a useless body. A new stream of discontent within the ANC was slowly growing.

The Suppression of Communism Act in July 1950 actually made SACP influence greater than ever within the ANC. This legislation was written around a ludicrously broad definition of 'communism' which permitted the Government to 'name' an organization or individual who 'aims at bringing about any political, industrial, social, or economic change within the Union.'[1] This definition was clearly intended to be applied to more than the SACP. In any case, the Party dissolved itself before the Bill became law on 22 June 1950. The dissolution was announced in Parliament by Sam Kahn, a communist M.P. The Central Committee issued a statement explaining that the decision to dissolve the Party was made in order to protect members who otherwise would have been liable to imprisonment for up to ten years. Roux reports that the decision to dissolve was 'not unanimous and that W. H. Andrews and a number of others recorded their vote against it.'[2] Probably the largely petty bourgeois social composition of the SACP dictated this hardly courageous action, but its mainly white, professional European members had too much to lose otherwise. Also perhaps, like the liberals, the white communists could not really conceive that they were now facing a fascist government that would halt at nothing in abrogating any and all opposition. In any event, the communists ceased to exist as an overt body and devoted their attentions to building the Congress movement. Within the ANC, now debating the form its militancy was to take, the communists plumped successfully for non-violent action. As Abram Fischer continued to believe in 1966, 'civil war is no "solution" at all.'[3] Basically, there was still faith in Gandhian methods and the appeal to reason, decency, and humanity as a means of changing the racist course of the white-minority regime.

[1] See full definition in Bunting, op. cit., p. 199.

[2] Roux, op. cit., p. 380. H. J. and R. E. Simons in *Class and Colour in South Africa, 1850–1950*, (Harmondsworth, Penguin, 1969), p. 607–8 state that only Andrews and Michael Harmel voted against dissolution. Moses Kotane and I. O. Horvitch, the national chairman, then visited each party district to explain the decision, which was accepted without dissent.

[3] Fischer, op. cit., p. 23.

It was in these circumstances that Walter Sisulu planned the Defiance Campaign that was supposed to demonstrate non-violently the desire of Africans for freedom in the land of their birth. The ANC had almost reached its highest point as a mass movement, and yet not all the members of the Youth League were happy at the developments in Congress.

3. Failure and Schism (1952-9)

Dr. Moroka, the President-General, called for 10,000 volunteers to come forward from Congress ranks to defy the Government, beginning with a massive work stoppage on 26 June 1952. The volunteers came forward, were given an impressive pledge to swear, and had a non-violent code of discipline dinned into them. The campaign began with prayers, quickly followed by arrests. By October, despite thousands of ANC members behind bars, new volunteers joined the campaign and the general membership was the highest it was ever to be—more than 100,000. However, by December, harsher repressive measures by the Government prompted the ANC leadership to call it off, while hailing it as a triumph.

The Defiance Campaign had been directed at six specific laws: the pass laws, the Group Areas Act, the Separate Representation of Voters Act, the Suppression of Communism Act, the Bantu Authorities Act, and the compulsory cattle culling policy.[1] In addition, as in the American sit-ins, the volunteers were to protest against the colour bar by entering public facilities intended for Europeans only.

Benson, who viewed the Campaign as 'an amazing success', sums up the situation well:

Of the 10,000 volunteers called for, more than 8,500 had gone voluntarily to jail despite the intimidating effect of police action, of dismissal by employers, and the propaganda of the bulk of the Press and of the radio; some teachers who had done little before had thrown up their jobs to defy; the United Nations had been inspired to discuss apartheid and the Press of the world had taken the non-white challenge to oppression more seriously than ever before. Even the Government—instead of talking about *Baaskap*—began to talk about Bantustans and self-government for the Bantu. Congress prestige was enhanced; its membership greatly multiplied to more than 100,000. Yet the unjust laws remained intact: indeed, they had been augmented.[2]

Undaunted, the ANC leadership pressed on with a new campaign. Congress was now headed by a dedicated and devout non-violent Christian, Chief Albert J. Lutuli. He had been elected President-General at the ANC conference at the end of 1952, while Sisulu was

---

[1] Feit, op. cit., p. 27.   [2] Benson, op. cit., p. 160.

re-elected Secretary-General. Lutuli, who had many white friends despite his obscure rural chieftainship, was a pacifist and a democrat, but his political views were far from the African nationalism of Anton Lembede. It was perhaps inevitable that he would be moved by the offers of assistance and alliance from the white ex-communists and others who had formed the Congress of Democrats. This was supposed to be an organization of progressives who would organize whites to work with the ANC. Despite an initial rebuff, the COD pressed on the Africans offers to join with the ANC in an alliance similar to the so-called Xuma-Dadoo Pact of 1945, which was reaffirmed after the Durban riots between Africans and Indians in January 1949. This Indian connection remained, waxing and waning in importance, yet, despite instruction in Gandhian techniques and other encouragement from the Indian Congress, many Africans never felt enthusiastic about it. Only a small fraction of the Indian community in South Africa actually belonged to the SACP-controlled Indian Congress. Although the Indians had themselves often been brutally exploited, especially in the Natal sugar plantations, they gradually came to include a merchant class that came in daily contact with impoverished Africans across shop counters. Indian racial, religious, and caste exclusivism also did not enhance their relations with the African majority, despite there being many individual Indians who were friends and supporters of African political, economic, and social advancement.

By 1953, the ex-communists had succeeded in pushing through their proposals for a broad alliance. To the Indian Congress were added the European Congress of Democrats, the Coloured People's Organization (later to be labelled the Coloured People's Congress) and the non-racial South African Congress of Trades Unions—all under the theoretical leadership of the African National Congress. Through equal representation of each body on co-ordinating committees, the thousand or so Indians and few hundred Coloured and white 'progressives' were, in effect, able to influence the vastly larger ANC. It should be noted that these co-ordinating committees were supposedly only advisory bodies, but there was considerable authority behind their advice and African former members of the SACP could be relied upon to exert all their efforts inside the ANC to further the policies suggested from outside.

For the Youth League, the Congress Alliance, as it was known, divided former friends and comrades. The League split into two factions; the Africanists who remained loyal to Lembede's African nationalism, and those who were willing to work closely with the white 'progressives', however few their numbers. For the Africanists, the

Alliance was a betrayal and they voiced fears of a white takeover of the leadership of the ANC. The Alliance may have seemed to some as uniting all races within South Africa in opposition to Afrikanerdom, but it divided the Africans more than ever, and the cleavage between the factions was made permanent by Z. K. Matthews's suggestion of a 'National Convention, a Congress of the People, representing all the people of this country, irrespective of race or colour, to draw up a Freedom Charter for the Democratic South Africa of the future.'[1]

A Freedom Charter was duly drafted by the National Council of the Congress of the People, a Congress Alliance co-ordinating committee. The short document bears strong traces of European influence, both in its vehemently egalitarian multiracialism, putting the European and Indian communities on the same plane as the African majority, and its lengthy and detailed demands for socialist economic measures. While the Africanists had no objections, and in fact also called for nationalization of South Africa's mineral resources and an equitable land-tenure system, they were appalled to note the complete lack of any reference to African liberation, inter-African co-operation, and the doctrine of Pan-Africanism. Instead the Charter called for 'peace and friendship' within South Africa and pledged South Africa to 'world peace and the settlement of all international disputes by negotiation—not war'. The Africanists could not object to this, but they very much objected to the omissions, and especially to the opening paragraph of the Charter, which declared:

We, the People of South Africa, declare for all our country and the world to know:
that South Africa belongs to all who live in it, black and white, and that no government can justly claim authority unless it is based on the will of the people.[2]

In the 1959 Pan Africanist Manifesto, the Africanists commented that behind the democratic proposals of the Freedom Charter, which at no time mentions One Man, One Vote—which would have reduced European, Asian, and Coloured votes to near insignificance—these groups were actually using the Congress Alliance to fight for 'constitutional guarantees' or 'national rights'. The Manifesto charged that a portion of the black leadership of South Africa, i.e. the ANC, had been 'captured' by a 'section of the leadership of the white ruling class'.

These 'leaders' consider South Africa and its wealth to belong to all who live in it, the alien dispossessors and the indigenous dispossessed, the alien robbers

---

[1] Quoted in Benson, op. cit., p. 160.
[2] As published in *Revolution* (Vol. 1, No. 6., 1963).

and their indigenous victims. They regard as equals the foreign master and his indigenous slave, the white exploiter and the indigenous oppressed. They regard as brothers the subject Africans and their European overlords. They are too incredibly naive and too fantastically unrealistic to see that the interests of the subject peoples who are criminally oppressed, ruthlessly exploited and inhumanly degraded, are in sharp conflict and in pointed contradiction with that of the white ruling class.[1]

By the time this Manifesto was written, the debate over the Charter had raged for four years. There was no debate at all at the Congress of the People, held at Kliptown, near Johannesburg, on 25 and 26 June 1955, to ratify the Charter. A blend of political rally and folklore spectacle, under the surveillance and humiliating intervention of the South African police, the 3,000 delegates, 2,000 of them Africans who had responded to the call of the Congress Alliance, acclaimed the Charter. The real debate began when leaders of the ANC moved the adoption of the Freedom Charter as official policy of the ANC.

The leadership and the rank and file of the ANC was now split between Charterists and Africanists. In virtually every branch fights between the two factions dominated all activity. The fights were followed by expulsions and/or resignations. After the Congress of the People, the National Action Committee became the National Consultative Committee. African fears of domination by the white 'progressives' seemed more real than ever. The Congress of Democrats was clearly the driving force in the Congress Alliance. Benson writes:

Always the first to volunteer, offering abundant energy and a readiness to suffer, the COD played a leading part in committee despite their small numbers. Though not all were Marxists, on occasion their forcing forward of extraneous issues was sharply divisive—for instance the Korean War was pushed during discussions planning the Congress of the People—making co-operation difficult.[2]

Despite the determination of the leaders of the Alliance, their comrades within the ANC leadership were unable to ram through approval of the contested Charter at the National Conference of the ANC in 1955. Jordan Ngubane, a founder of the Youth League and leader of its anti-communist right wing, launched a bitter attack on the Charterists and Chief Lutuli who, he claimed, was allowing himself to be made a tool of the European and Indian ex-communists in the Congress Alliance. Ngubane later resigned from the ANC and joined

---

[1] Quoted from *The Basic Documents of the Pan Africanist Congress of South Africa* (Lusaka, PAC, March 1965), p. 21.

[2] Benson, op. cit., p. 202.

the Liberal Party which, while gradualist concerning a common voting roll, affirmed the equality of black and white and demanded the creation of a genuinely democratic state in which all would participate. Years later, a leading liberal, Patrick Duncan, son of a former Governor-General, was to become the first white member of the Pan Africanist Congress.

For the Africanists, the duplicity of the Europeans and their determination to become the white head on a black body were demonstrated by the underhanded methods finally used to secure ANC ratification of the Freedom Charter at a special conference in April 1956. The meeting was packed by the Charterists with non-members, who were allowed to vote without having their credentials checked. 'The check on members was only done during the Sunday afternoon session. The Charter had been adopted on Saturday evening. Everybody present in the hall participated in the voting. It was impossible to distinguish members from non-members of the African National Congress.'[1] This undistinguished victory of the 'progressives' was really the kiss of death for whatever hopes of a united ANC may have remained. It should be emphasized that this strange, divisive behaviour took place at a moment when J. G. Strijdom's government was intensifying its repression of African protest, banning leaders of the ANC from public life and visibly preparing to crush African nationalism in South Africa, if possible, for ever. It was in fact the Government's arrest of 156 persons of all races and all ideological tendencies, who were allegedly part of a 'treasonous conspiracy on the part of international Communism to overthrow the government of South Africa', that held the divided Congress together a little longer. The so-called Treason Trial opened on 19 December 1956, and dragged on, as the Prosecution and Defence ploughed through mountains of evidence that itself constituted the most complete, if often tendentious, documentary record of the long history of the ANC and its more recent allies and advisers. When the trial finally ground to a halt on 29 March 1961, the accused—whose numbers had dwindled from 156 to 30—were found not guilty and discharged. However, by this time the split in the Congress had become overt and permanent, and both the ANC and the new Pan Africanist Congress had already been declared banned organizations for nearly a year by a white-minority government that had no intention of relying on the doubtful processes of justice in carrying out its white-supremacist policies.

The actual split had its immediate cause in the squabble over the

[1] P. L. Tsele, Letter to the Editor, the *Bantu World* (28 April 1956). Quoted in Feit, op. cit., p. 17.

failure of the 1958 'stay-at-home strike'. To the Africanists, this again seemed an example of the white tail wagging the black dog. The Congress Alliance had determined upon a one-day work stoppage on the day of the all-white parliamentary elections. This proposal was initially rejected by the ANC, but was forced through by the Europeans and Indians in the Alliance. When the strike, which had been opposed by the majority of the provincial divisions of the ANC, failed, the vexed Alliance leaders demanded disciplinary action against the Africanists who had actively opposed it. A vast purge of the ANC leadership and rank and file was begun, under Nelson Mandela, now in the Charterist camp. Entire branches with Africanist leadership, such as in the Transvaal, were under attack. Strong-arm tactics and arbitrary expulsions of members at the Transvaal Congress of the ANC on 2 November 1958, resulted in a final walk-out by the Africanists as a group, led by Potlako Kitchener Leballo, a World War II veteran and activist during the Defiance Campaign. With the Africanists went Johannesburg's Orlando Branch, the largest and most dynamic in the ANC. The Africanists held their own meeting nearby and sent a final message to the Charterists who were now in control of the Congress. They declared: 'We are launching out on our own as the custodian of ANC policy as formulated in 1912 and pursued up to the time of the Congress Alliance.'[1]

Nevertheless, the Africanists did not form their Pan Africanist Congress until 6–7 April 1959. They had not really wanted the split, nor had they been completely prepared for it. Time was needed to rally their forces scattered throughout the country and to begin intensive mobilization of the black masses.

4. From Illegality to Liberation Movement in Exile (1960 till the present)

Within the ANC, the Charterists quickly consolidated their now un-contested control of the organization. But they had no plan of action and drifted from day-to-day resistance to the regime.

In December 1959, the annual conference was held in Durban. Chief Lutuli sent a message from his place of banishment, warning against hasty decisions that might lead to rash action.

Actually, the momentum had already shifted to the PAC. At its first annual conference, held a week after the ANC conference, the new organization had decided upon its plan of militant action: a non-violent campaign against the pass laws. Calling for massive disobedience and

[1] See Benson, op. cit., pp. 206–7.

mass arrests, the PAC hoped to disrupt the entire life of the country, under the slogan of 'No bail, no defence, no fine'.

The ANC could not help but follow, although separately. It announced the organizing of an anti-pass day on 31 March 1960, with subsequent demonstrations to be held in May and June. But the initiative remained with the PAC, whose leaders toured the country to galvanize the masses. Mangaliso Robert Sobukwe fixed 21 March as the date for the opening of the anti-pass campaign. That day's events marked a turning point in South African history and sounded the death knell of non-violent action.

Sobukwe and many of his aides were arrested after they had presented themselves at police headquarters in Orlando. However, they were held only after news arrived of the shooting at Sharpeville and then they were charged with incitement to violence under the Public Safety Act. At Sharpeville, thousands followed PAC instructions and gathered at the local police station. The white police panicked at the sight of the massed, although unarmed, Africans, and opened fire. Altogether, 69 persons were killed and 180 wounded.

Elsewhere, at Langa, 60 police clubbed and shot at a crowd of African protesters, killing 5 and wounding 49. Africans were brutally assaulted in Nyanga and Vanderbijl Park as well, the police killing 2 persons in each place. Official sources claimed there were no fatalities and admitted only two dead in Langa.

The stunned ANC at first blamed the violence on the precipitate action of its young rivals, but a week later, on 27 March Chief Lutuli burned his pass. Both ANC and PAC joined in mourning the dead, and huge funerals were held. For a few days, the pass laws were suspended, but were then reimposed with greater vigour as the Government declared a state of emergency throughout the country. Mass arrests of African leaders were carried out by the Special Branch of the South African police, who ruthlessly beat striking black workers back to their jobs in Cape Town.

Finally, on 8 April the Verwoerd Government declared the African National Congress and the Pan Africanist Congress 'unlawful organizations' and a 'serious threat to the safety of the public'. The ban was ratified by the overwhelming racist all-white Parliament, by 128 votes to sixteen. The handful of opposing votes came from the four Native Representatives, themselves whites, and the recently-formed Progressive Party.

Oliver Tambo, the ANC Vice-President, had slipped out of the country just before the ban, while the remaining leaders still at large awaited arrest or went underground. Virtually their last gasp was a call for a National Convention of all South Africans to create a democratic republic. Once more, instead of appealing to African nationalism, the Congress Alliance fell back on multiracial formulae that had little chance of mobilizing the black masses for action. Yet the leaders of the Alliance must have been aware that only the millions of blacks could possibly have brought a change of course in South Africa. However, it should be added that nothing in the history of white-minority rule, especially since the Boer Nationalists had come to power, indicated that the Government would be moved by anything but gunfire. Nevertheless, even PAC leaders were commited to tactical non-violence and non-collaboration.

Forty African leaders gathered for an All-In African Conference in Pietermaritzburg in 1961. The ANC's Nelson Mandela, who had recently been released from successive bans, addressed the meeting, renewing the call for a multiracial National Convention. He proposed a three-day work stoppage if the Government refused to comply with the demand. Naturally, the regime replied with the same force as had worked so well in the past. The strike, which was opposed by the PAC, was set for 29 May 1961. Response was so poor, except among Coloured workers in Cape Town and some Indians in Durban, that Mandela, who was in hiding, had to call it off on the second day. He conceded partial failure.

Even the Congress Alliance now doubted the wisdom of non-violence. Nelson Mandela met with a few other leaders in June 1961 and reluctantly agreed to limited violence: a sabotage campaign that would be directed only against property, not persons. There were to be no efforts to seize power by force, or attacks on the hated South African Army and Police, or assassinations of Europeans. It was feared that any 'indiscriminate violence' might provoke a racial blood bath in South Africa, so great was African hatred of whites and the power of the whites to reply with mass destruction and killings of Africans and other non-whites.

Mandela himself left the country undetected and went on a tour of African independent countries. He addressed the Pan African Freedom Movement Conference in Addis Ababa and visited the Moroccan border headquarters of Colonel Houari Boumedienne's Algerian National Liberation Army, where he observed at first hand the concrete results that a protracted armed struggle against minority rule could achieve. In July 1962, the Algerian army, under its National Liberation Front (FLN), successfully won independence for Algeria, ending 132 years of French colonial rule and exploitation by a large and long-established settler community. Before returning secretly to South Africa, Mandela visited London, where he met with some British political leaders and sympathizers. Returning to South Africa, he tried to direct an underground network, but was captured by police in August 1962 under suspicious circumstances, following reports of serious differences with the SACP.

The sabotage group set up by the Congress Alliance called itself *Umkhonto we Sizwe*, 'Spear of the Nation'. Again, the accent was placed on multiracialism. A tract announcing the new underground organization declared:

This is a new, independent body formed by Africans. It includes in its ranks South Africans of all races. . . . We hope that we will bring the government and its supporters to its senses before it is too late, so that both the government and its policies can be changed before matters reach the desperate stage of civil war. We believe our actions to be a blow against Nationalist preparations for civil war and military rule. In these actions we are working in the best interests of all the people of this country, Black, Brown and White, whose future happiness and well-being cannot be attained without the overthrow of the Nationalists.[1]

However, Umkhonto did not have the honour of striking the first platonic blow against the regime. The first sabotage attempt was made in October 1961 by a group of white liberals calling itself the National Committee of Resistance. This name was later changed to African Resistance Movement (ARM), but the group remained overwhelmingly white despite its desire to strike a blow on behalf of oppressed blacks. Most of the ARM's leaders later fled the country, while the remainder were arrested for sabotage and sentenced to prison, the group's one Coloured member—Edward Daniels—receiving the heaviest sentence of 15 years. The whites received from 2 to 10 years in jail.

Umkhonto set off its first bombs on Dingaan's Day, 16 December 1961, the day celebrating the Dutch victory over the Zulu Chief Dingaan at the Battle of Blood River. Ten bombs in Johannesburg and five in Port Elizabeth damaged some electric pylons and government offices. One of the inexperienced saboteurs was killed by his own bomb.

Only a few days earlier the Government had made a gesture towards world opinion by permitting the elderly Chief Lutuli to leave his place of restriction to travel to Norway to accept the Nobel Peace Prize for 1960. Reaffirming his devout Christian pacifism, the old leader pledged himself to a policy of non-violence and multiracialism. He then returned to

---

[1] Quoted in Bunting, op. cit., p. 216.

South Africa and never escaped virtual imprisonment until his death in 1967.

In any case, the multiracial Umkhonto—which initially was described as an 'independent body', having no direct ties with the ANC, though acknowledging its political leadership—was later to be described by an ANC Executive Committee member as the 'nucleus of the future national army of our people'.[1]

In 1961 and 1962, as the repression was intensified and hopes of a return to legality faded, hundreds of South Africans of all races began to leave the country. By far the largest group first to go into exile were Europeans, both communists and liberals. Next in number were Africans prominent in the ANC and PAC who were wanted by the police. After a while, the ANC seemed to encourage this stream of black exiles, most of whom left South Africa clandestinely via Bechuanaland (now Botswana). Perhaps because the strategy of the PAC was developing rapidly in another direction, PAC militants who left were far fewer in number and many remained to await a call to action on the border of South Africa in the relative safety of the British Protectorates of Basutoland (now Lesotho), Bechuanaland, and Swaziland. In all these countries, the leading nationalist parties also tended to be more sympathetic to the Africanism of the PAC than to the multiracialism of the ANC.

Despite these differences, the representatives of the ANC and PAC were able to create overseas a brief United Front. The most visible consequence of the new unity in action was the appearance together at the United Nations of Oliver Tambo of the ANC and Vusumzi Make of the PAC, who made an impressive pair. The mild-mannered, reflective Tambo was able to present the case against the apartheid regime calmly and without undue passion before critical European and American audiences, while the fiery Make vehemently insisted upon the Pan-African obligations of the growing number of independent African delegations at the United Nations and enthralled Afro-American audiences with first-hand accounts of the black freedom struggle in South Africa. Eventually, the United Front foundered on the unresolved contradictions between ANC and PAC, especially as greater number of Europeans left South Africa and began a lengthy and ultimately successful campaign to reconstitute the Congress Alliance, tying the ANC to the exigencies of the Sino-Soviet split. Moreover, as the numbers of African refugees in Black Africa mounted, many of them from the ANC rank

---

[1] Joe Matthews, 'Armed Struggle in South Africa', *Marxism Today* (September, 1969).

and file, the Alliance leaders began to fear their infection by 'black chauvinism' and urgent steps were taken to isolate them from the PAC.

Oliver Reginald Tambo, the leading representative of the ANC overseas, who had been sent abroad by the ANC Executive Committee in March 1960, after the Sharpeville-Langa massacres, found his own authority often contested. Although later designated the Acting President-General of the ANC, Tambo was threatened with removal on several occasions by his restive allies. They had not forgotten his friendship with Anton Lembede and that he was a co-founder of the Youth League. Lembede had been elected National President of the League, while Tambo held the post first of National Secretary and later National Vice-President. Born in 1917 of a peasant family in the Eastern Cape, he was later fortunate to attend primary and secondary schools and enter Fort Hare College. He first obtained a Bachelor of Science degree and took a diploma in education in 1943. He returned to his own St. Peter's Secondary School, were he taught from 1943–7. Expressing a desire to study law, he was helped to become articled to a law firm in Johannesburg by another member of the Youth League, Walter Sisulu. He became a member of the National Executive Committee of the ANC in 1949 and was Secretary-General from 1955–8, when he was chosen as Deputy President-General of the ANC. In the split between Africanists and Charterists, Tambo had eventually sided with the Charterists and the leaders of the Congress Alliance, but his continuing personal friendship and contacts with Africanists were to bring him reproach from some associates and allies for years afterwards. Personally a political realist, Tambo appears to have endured successive rebuffs and humiliations from these circles because he believed that no other practical course was offered the South African liberation movement.

Inside South Africa, overt political activity by blacks had been banned and Umkhonto's sporadic sabotage attacks failed to have any effect except to justify the Government's tightening of repression through the use of systematic torture in the interrogation of black suspects, and a series of Acts permitting house arrest and detention without trial for lengthy periods. The ANC, or rather the Congress Alliance, was nevertheless to retain considerable mobility for action *outside* the African locations and reserves because of the white and Indian communists who, despite their small numbers, did not suffer the physical restrictions and and pass laws that bound the Africans.

The Congress of Democrats was not banned until September 1962, while the Indian Congress and the Coloured People's Congress remained untouched as organizations, although individual leaders suffered every form of harassment and repression. The CPC's President Barney Desai and Chairman Cardiff Marney, themselves exiled in London, dissolved the organization in March 1966 and joined the PAC. The interracial Liberal Party was obliged to dissolve in 1968. Under the Prohibition of Political Interference Act of that year, persons belonging to different racial groups were not allowed to belong to the same political party. Addressing a final meeting in Durban, the National President of the Liberals, Alan Paton, declared: 'We could have re-formed as separate Liberal parties, each committed by law to having nothing to do with any other. But we came into existence to oppose apartheid and separate development and therefore we have no alternative but to decline to re-form.'[1]

As time passed more ANC tracts were found outside than inside the African locations, which the underground whites were far too conspicuous to penetrate. The Indians were somewhat more mobile and useful to the stricken Alliance as, in their capacity as traders in large areas of South Africa, they could at least pursue normal direct contact with African clients. The last area of white-black contact—except between black workers in field, factory, and home and their white masters—was in the English-speaking universities. And the Government was soon to eliminate all but a handful of Africans from these institutions, while holding out the shabby substitute of higher 'Bantu education', which would retribalize the African and prevent, as Hendrik Verwoerd had declared in 1953, 'wrong expectations on the part of the native'.

Towards the end of 1962 came another development that was almost as much deplored by white South Africans in exile as feared by the Government—the launching of the armed struggle inside the country by Poqo, the military wing of the PAC. On the night of 21 November 1962, an armed group of Africans attacked the Paarl police station, killing two Europeans and wounding several others in the vicinity. Five Africans lost their lives in the clash and hundreds of others were arrested by the police.

The SACP, now coming to life again abroad, condemned this 'senseless violence'. Rather the hopes of the Congress soon to be dashed—were for controlled sabotage as a 'demonstration' to make the European in South Africa 'reconsider his whole attitude', as Abram Fischer declared. He added:

If it had succeeded in that it would have succeeded without loss of life or injury to persons, the very things which stimulate race antagonism. It might

---

[1] Quoted in Bunting, op. cit., p. 145.

in addition have the effect of deterring extremists, whose numbers and influence were growing at an alarming rate, from undertaking precisely that kind of terrorism which we have fought to prevent. It may in fact have succeeded in this respect if one remembers that but for Umkhonto the pattern of the future in this country may have been set by the Paarl riots and the Bashee River murders. [On 2 February 1963, when a Poqo unit attacked a road camp and killed four Europeans.][1]

For the PAC, 1963 was to be the Year of Freedom, when that organization promised major action. This is not the place for an account of that action, but numerous black and white observers record the promise of freedom that was in the air in South Africa. The South African Institute of Race Relations conducted a poll among Africans in 1963 and found that the PAC enjoyed 57 per cent of African support and the ANC 39 per cent. The Government was bracing itself for trouble and its police were active.

On 11 July 1963, the Special Branch scored a coup. Walter Sisulu, Govan Mbeki, Denis Goldberg, Arthur Goldreich,[2] Harold Wolpe, Bob Hepple, Lionel Bernstein, and others—almost all of the whites were communists—were arrested while allegedly planning further activities by Umkhonto we Sizwe. The raid took place at Lilliesleaf Homestead, in the Rivonia area, Johannesburg, a farm secretly bought by the SACP. Goldreich and Wolpe managed to escape by promising a bribe to a guard. Bob Hepple, who was supposed to have been a prosecution witness, also managed to flee. But Nelson Mandela, who was already behind bars, was implicated in disclosures within some 250 documents, including Mandela's diary of his secret tour abroad, which had naively been kept at the house and fell into the hands of the police. Altogether nine persons were eventually tried and convicted as a result of the police operation. Mandela, Sisulu, and Mbeki were sentenced to life imprisonment on the bleak Robben Island.

Although diminished, Umkhonto was nevertheless able to cling to life and sporadic sabotage continued after the Rivonia trial, to the annoyance of the police but always without causing serious damage or loss of life. More classical terrorism was attempted in the bomb blast at the Europeans Only concourse of the Johannesburg Railway Station on 24 July 1964. The time bomb, which killed an elderly woman and maimed a child, was planted by John Harris, a white activist in the Liberal Party and organizer of the South African Non-Racial Olympic Committee

[1] Fischer, op. cit., p. 29.

[2] Goldreich, a staunch Zionist, eventually went to Israel. He visited the ANC in Tanzania after the June Arab-Israeli War in 1967, to lecture the ANC on the 'lessons' of the Israeli victory for African freedom fighters.

(SANROC), a body of sportsmen who fought against racial discimination in sport and called for the barring from the Olympics of unfairly selected South African teams. Terrorism is always horrifying because it generally strikes the innocent or marginal in society, but its justification usually lies in the contribution it makes to panic and loss of public morale as a revolutionary movement tries to seize power. Unfortunately, Harris, a white member of the ARM, was acting alone, making a courageous if bloody protest against white South Africa's oppression of the African. For his crime against Afrikanerdom, Harris died on the gallows on the morning of 1 April 1965—one of the rare whites in South Africa willing to take white lives in the cause of African liberation. He was not a member of the Congress Alliance. And he was shown no mercy by his white judges, who had really found him guilty of treason against the white race.

By 1965, the ANC had ceased to show any appreciable strength under the fascistic conditions of South African life. From time to time an ANC or SACP leaflet would be hurriedly scattered in the streets of the cities, but sabotage attempts were rarer and as ineffectual as ever. 'Meetings were almost impossible to hold'; Bunting writes, 'and if held merely exposed the organizers to reprisals. Special Branch police and informers swarmed everywhere, harassing, spying and intimidating.'[1]

It was abundantly clear that during its ten years as a mass movement the African National Congress had failed in its efforts to find a strategy that would oblige the white-minority regime to yield to African demands. Feit believes that this failure can be summarized under three main headings:

First, the Government had set its face against the changes demanded by the Congress and in a clash between them the forces of the Government were immeasurably superior to those that Congress could muster. Second, by taking other Congresses into an alliance with it, the African National Congress created dissention in its own ranks, confused the African masses, and gained nothing of sufficient value in return. Third, the gap between what Congress leaders wanted and what the masses wanted was too great to be bridged. Masses and movement, consequently, never really came together.[2]

It should be stressed that the ANC's allies imposed upon it an ideology and strategy that were alien to the requirements of South African life. Certainly, as has been proved in China, Marxism-Leninism as a method need not be alien to the revolutionary movement within any society, but the alleged Marxist-Leninists of the SACP, with rare exception, did not

[1] Bunting, op. cit., p. 242.   [2] Feit, op. cit., p. 60.

and were apparently incapable of Africanizing Marxism-Leninism to deal with the problems of their country. In contrast, Mao Tsetung perfectly adapted the Marxist-Leninist revolutionary method to China's peasant and worker upheaval. The maverick Marxists of the Unity Movement at times seem to have greater feeling for South African reality than the theorists of the SACP.

Gandhian tactics were equally out of place in South Africa, whose history is one continuous record of white brutality against black. The Afrikaner Nationalists might indeed be bigoted, racist fanatics, but, unlike their African adversaries, they had a remarkably clear vision of the goals they sought and had no scruples about the means they would use to reach them. Multiracialism as a concept, offering guarantees to the minority against arbitrary and discriminatory rule by an African majority, could only have been justified if there had been—as there was not—a substantial number of Europeans and Indians who were prepared to close ranks with the oppressed majority. As it was, the paltry numbers of European, Coloured, and Indian allies that came forward under the Congress Alliance blunted the driving force of African nationalism, the only ideology likely—as the subsequent history of the PAC demonstrates —to appeal to the broad masses of the black proletariat. In addition, while non-violence might have been acceptable in the short term as a tactic, nothing in the record of African struggle against European encroachment indicated that it could have any deep, long-term appeal to the African people, who passed their daily lives in conditions of often extreme social violence and brutality, harassed by white bosses and anti-social black thugs, as well as the ever-vigilant and violent South African police. Only a political programme of counter-violence on a massive scale, decided upon years earlier by an African organization, might have mobilized the masses and permitted them to force an early clash with the regime before its repressive apparatus had been installed. The want of such action should not be blamed only on the Christian pacifists of South Africa and the white liberals with their illusions of justice and democracy, but principally on the leaders of the SACP, whose reformist, revisionist views and naive faith in their ability to provoke a crisis of conscience among the white minority, bringing about the restoration of some form of democracy, prevented them from ever taking a revolutionary road inside South Africa.

Abroad, the story was not completely different. The communists continued to argue among themselves concerning the necessity of the armed struggle later than most of their African protégés. As editor of the English-language edition of an African revolutionary journal, *Revolution*, the author had first-hand experience of that debate in London in 1963 and 1964. Perhaps the mainly white, middle-class social composition of the SACP accounts for the extreme reluctance of this party to countenance an armed struggle in South Africa. However, according to Joe Matthews, a black communist, the decision to resort to armed struggle was taken after the failure of the strike to protest the proclamation of the Republic of South Africa in 1961. Matthews says the major considerations were:

(a) There was no prospect of achieving liberation by the methods of the previous fifty years.

(b) The struggle of the previous period had created big mass organisations and a leadership capable of gaining the allegiance of the people for armed struggle and with the ability to carry out the planning, preparation and overall conduct of the struggle.

(c) The independence movement in Africa had, particularly in 1960, swept across the continent and by 1961 stood close to the borders of the unliberated white-controlled countries in the South. This was a vital factor for it meant that the opportunity now arose which had not existed before of bases at which our people could obtain the training and facilities for conducting armed struggle.[1]

In any case, the ANC and SACP were powerless within the country. Now, from external bases, the Congress Alliance would seek to wage a liberation war.

The flood of South African political refugees provided the manpower base for the movement in exile. Initial contacts with Algerian revolutionaries and other African leaders by both ANC and PAC representatives abroad had demonstrated the existence of a willingness to assist the struggle. Through the long-standing ties of the SACP with the Communist Party of the Soviet Union (CPSU), the ANC was assured of the material support of the Soviet Union and other socialist countries. Numerous African armies, led by the Algerian National People's Army and the Army of the United Arab Republic, were ready to provide military instructors in the art of guerrilla warfare. These were to be supplemented, and in some cases replaced, by instructors from Eastern Europe, Cuba, and China. The arms began flowing immediately from African countries and from the Soviet Union and China. Of course, none of this would have been possible without the hospitality of Tanzania and Zambia, which provided the bases and in so doing exposed themselves to possible South African retaliation, not to mention the active annoyance of some Western interests, more concerned with anti-communist orthodoxy and maximum profits than social justice.

[1] Matthews, op. cit., p. 271.

Tanzania gave forthright assistance to the liberation movements, in keeping with the Pan-African policies of President Julius K. Nyerere's Tanganyika African National Union (TANU). The ruling party's one-time Secretary-General, Oscar Kambona, who was Foreign Minister for a period, also served on the Organization of African Unity's African Liberation Committee whose administrative headquarters was established in Dar es Salaam, after the first meeting of the Committee there from 25 June to 4 July 1963. The A.L.C. sought to channel assistance, both financial and material, to the movements under its charge, from a common treasury and arms pool. The ANC was to become one of the major beneficiaries of A.L.C. assistance, while also receiving substantial aid from elsewhere. Nevertheless, relations with the A.L.C. have been far from completely harmonious, and at the Khartoum Conference in Support of the Peoples of the Portuguese Colonies and Southern Africa, a purely Moscow-run affair, a determined, if abortive, effort was made to supplant the tutelage of the O.A.U. and create a closed shop of liberation movements recognized by the Soviet Union.

Naturally, military security has kept journalists from freely visiting most of the camps in Tanzania and Zambia. It should be noted that many of the exaggerated reports concerning alleged camps refer, if to anything real, to the camps housing South African and other African refugees in Tanzania and Zambia. In 1970, military training was confined to a few special areas around Kongwa, Mbeya, Bagamoyo, and Morogoro in Tanzania and the well-known Nkomo Camp in Zambia.[1] The training courses lasted from three to nine months, and the recruits were taught general military skills, the use of firearms and explosives, sabotage, and the principles of guerrilla warfare, as well as receiving political idoctrination.

Zambia's economic and political circumstances made her assistance to the freedom fighters more circumspect. This landlocked Central African country still depended heavily on her imports and exports entering and leaving through South Africa or Angola. Not until the Chinese-built Tanzam Railway from Dar es Salaam to Lusaka was completed would Zambia be capable of offering the same kind of refuge to South African guerrillas that Tunisia and Morocco gave the Algerian revolutionaries during the Algerian War. The railway would remove Zambia from South Africa's economic sphere of influence, linking the country firmly to the independent black African countries of East Africa.

[1] A somewhat fanciful list of camps was published in the *Sunday Telegraph* (11 May 1969), under the title of 'Black Liberators Made in Moscow'.

However, the railway was not scheduled to be completed until around 1975.

The provisional headquarters of the ANC was eventually established in Tanzania at Morogoro, a small town west of the capital. Heie, in theory, the political and military leaders could plan their strategy and supervise the administration of the movement, far from prying eyes in Dar es Salaam. Difficulties seemed to mount as the ANC pressed ahead with the training of its armed forces. For one thing, there was nothing for them to do after their training. Some of them were probably the world's most highly-trained guerrilla fighters, having received military instruction under varying personal pseudonyms in Algeria, the U.A.R., the Soviet Union, and Cuba. As the Sino-Soviet dispute developed, China ceased to accept ANC men for training. Those who returned from China were often kept under surveillance by their pro-Moscow leaders for suspected Maoism.[1] Ideological feuds, personality clashes, and boredom gradually disrupted life in the camps as the number of trained men mounted.

Massive infiltration of insurgents into the Republic of South Africa will be no easy task. To a certain extent, the ANC would need closer, politically more reliable springboards. Botswana, independent in 1966, refused use of her territory, and Zambia was not prepared to permit raids against South Africa from her territory at the time. Hence, the ANC found itself reduced to waiting upon the success of the liberation movements in the Portuguese colonies of Mozambique and Angola and in Rhodesia. In 1963, no one had imagined that the struggle might last more than a few years. Now, the struggle is clearly seen as one of decades.

The problem of what to do with trained men was solved by the ANC's fondness for alliances. This time, the partner was the Zimbabwe African People's Union of Rhodesia. ZAPU, headed by Joshua Nkomo, who is held in jail by the white-minority regime of Ian Smith, was directed abroad by James Chikerema, a tough political veteran from Salisbury who had set up his exile headquarters in Lusaka.

On 22 August 1967, *Le Monde* reported that Oliver Tambo and Chikerema had held a joint press conference in Lusaka a few days earlier to announce an alliance between their two movements. Henceforth, ANC troops would be sent into the fight inside Rhodesia, which in principle was the first stage of a long battle that would eventually bring them within South Africa. The main action in this first large-scale

---

[1] See the statement by ANC deserters in *Black Dwarf* (London, 26 November 1969).

incursion across the Zambezi River took place in the Wankie National Park. Reports were conflicting, but it seems that at least 200 heavily armed members of the ANC, guided by a smaller group of ZAPU fighters, had crossed into Rhodesia from Zambia. Later, the ANC denied that they were carrying heavy machine guns and mortars, but admitted they were equipped with Soviet-made anti-tank guns. In any case, the large concentration was quickly spotted by the Rhodesian police and army or given away to them by informers. South African forces later joined the two-week long battle to wipe out the invading Africans. In the end, a few survived to escape back into Zambia, while the rest were either killed or captured. The *Guardian's* John Worral reported from Salisbury on 28 August 1967: 'They fought ferociously with their deadly Russian and Chinese weapons, but many were killed or captured and the others put to flight by the highly mobile Rhodesian forces. Those who got across the Botswana border were captured by Sir Seretse Khama's police.'

Actually, it appears that the fighting was not completely over until September 1967. Superior numbers and arms and superior strategy sealed the fate of the ANC–ZAPU guerrillas, who fought courageously but failed to heed the basic principles of guerrilla warfare. They abandoned mobility—perhaps because they were overloaded with heavy weapons—and engaged in conventional positional warfare, at which their more numerous adversaries would inevitably win. If nothing else, however, the courage and tenacity of the Africans proved that black men could and would give their lives in the struggle for freedom. This signal demonstration was not lost on either the Rhodesian or South African regimes, which subsequently intensified their already massive arms build-up.

Besides the fatal choice of conventional tactics and reliance on heavy weapons, the ANC–ZAPU strategy had other serious flaws. First, the propaganda of the alliance, which was controlled by the ANC, was maladroit. Obviously, exiles saw in the battle proof that their cause was not hopeless, and in the fighting additional sanction for fund-raising among sympathizers throughout the world. Hence, Tambo himself was to exaggerate the limited nature of the incursion and announced to a London rally: 'Today fighting is in Rhodesia, tomorrow it will be in South Africa.' The ANC–ZAPU leaders also announced a 'fight to the finish' in Rhodesia, leading their adversaries to suspect further incursions and to prepare for them by a general mobilization of their troops. Second, far from its being a classic People's War, there seems to have been no contact with the local African population. Third, there was a surprising lack of unity between the two allies. Later, there were nasty recriminations between ANC and ZAPU, which of course were broadcast widely by ZAPU's rival organization, the Zimbabwe African National Union. ZANU claimed in February 1968 that the ZAPU guides led the ANC men to a thicket near the town of Wankie and left them, on the pretext of going to neighbouring villages to collect food and information, 'only to return a few hours later at the head of an enemy contingent'. In any case, when the captured South Africans went on trial in Bulawayo, their former ZAPU guides were among the principal witnesses against them.

Besides various local publications of ANC missions, and *Sechaba*, a monthly magazine edited in London, the SACP's much more serious quarterly, the *African Communist*, also edited in London, the Congress Alliance uses the Anti-Apartheid Movement in Britain, with its *Anti-Apartheid News*, a monthly, as part of its widespread propaganda machinery abroad. (Both *Sechaba* and the *African Communist* are now printed in the East German Democratic Republic.) Although sponsored by prominent members of the British Labour and Liberal parties, the AAM depends essentially on its numerous white South African supporters in exile, headed by Mrs. Ethel De Keyser, the Secretary.

On 29 June 1969, the Anti-Apartheid Movement completed a decade of existence, campaigning against apartheid, mainly in support of the ANC. Naturally, the AAM hailed the claims of ANC–ZAPU as an 'historic new phase of armed resistance when the principal African liberatory organizations announced their freedom fighters engaged the the Rhodesian colonial troops.'[1] Representatives of other liberation movements have often complained of discriminatory treatment by this mainly white body, which claims nevertheless to be non-sectarian and non-partisan. There were alleged to be 50,000 South Africans living in Britain in 1969, although this figure has been strongly contested.[2] Certainly, the vast quantity of ANC propaganda in Britain and elsewhere is due in part to the highly-educated, politically conscious white exiles who used to stand discreetly behind the ANC through the Congress Alliance and who later took their places in the ANC leadership, in the spring of 1969. Blacks and Indians from South Africa were found to make up no more than 200 of the total. Ironically, many of the 'progressives' from South Africa, including ex-communists, were discovered to be deeply involved in the property business in Britain, where

---

[1] *Annual Report of the Anti-Apartheid Movement*, October 1967/July 1968, published in London in 1969.

[2] Brian Lapping, 'Unromantic Exiles', *New Society* (24 July 1969).

there have been repeated complaints about landlords rent-gouging the country's growing coloured communities.[1]

Though Africans have repeatedly criticized[2] the Anti-Apartheid Movement, many have nothing but praise for the International Defence and Aid Fund, set up by Canon John Collins, Precentor of London's St. Paul's Cathedral, in 1956, to provide legal assistance for the 156 defendants of the Treason Trial in South Africa. After the trial ended, the Fund remained in existence, providing humanitarian assistance for Southern Africans of all races, although it is not allowed under its constitution to subsidize political organizations. There have been occasional complaints that sums given for humanitarian purposes have been used by various dissidents from the movements to continue their struggle against the leaderships.

Finally, the world's Moscow-orientated 'revisionist' communist parties greatly assist the propaganda effort of the ANC. Either directly or through the SACP, these parties recognize the ANC as the sole 'authentic' liberation movement in South Africa. Representatives of the PAC generally receive chilly receptions from these parties, as does anyone not provided with an ANC seal of approval. In a few cases, this attitude has been communicated to other political parties and groups, such as the Socialist International and the international Socialist Youth Movement, which have recently begun viewing the Moscow communists in a more friendly light as the policy of peaceful coexistence between East and West develops from international relations to domestic political life in some countries. Moreover, the ANC has a well-developed network of missions scattered throughout the world and considerable sums of money are devoted to tours of leaders to present the ANC's point of view on South Africa and win friends and supporters. In Scandinavia alone, such a persistent campaign has paid off handsomely, particularly in Sweden, where the governing Social Democratic Party maintains warm, fraternal relations with the ANC.

In 1968, more evidence of dissidence within the ANC came to light, when Lawrence Makhubu, the former secretary of the Orlando West Branch inside South Africa, later of the ANC National Committee in the Soviet Union, led a group of ANC guerrillas from their camp in Tanzania to political asylum in Kenya. In a statement issued in Nairobi in 1969, four dissident ANC men—Omar Bamjee, Amin Cajee, Hoosain Jacobs, and Maurice Mthombeni—assured their South African

---

[1] See Brian Lapping, 'Unromantic Exiles'.

[2] See Jariretunda Kozonguizi, 'The South African "Left" and the Struggle for Liberation', *Race Today* (September 1969).

brothers they had not deserted the struggle. They pledged themselves to 'struggle and resist all attempts to make South African revolutionaries tools of the lukewarm South African Communist Party or the Communist Party of the Soviet Union.'[1]

The ANC dissidents accused the leadership of strong-arm tactics in the camps, stifling free discussion of the Sino-Soviet dispute in order to favour the Soviet line, tribalism, nepotism, and even unexplained 'murders in a certain Central African State'.

Another ANC top official, James Hadebe, who had been the Congress's chief representative in Tanzania, announced about the same time that he was resigning from the External Mission of the ANC, but not from the party itself. Hadebe told journalists that, although the ANC leadership abroad had claimed he had been expelled, he did not recognize the expulsion as, with the exception of Acting President-General Oliver Tambo, none of the current ANC leaders in exile had a mandate from the people at home to represent the party. And even Tambo had not been granted powers to expel anyone, Hadebe said.

In 1969, four dissident ANC guerrillas who reached Europe revealed the extent of the dissension within the ANC. These men—Omar Bamjee, Hoosain Jacobs, Maurice Mthombeni and Amin Cajee—circulated a lengthy document about their experiences—which was eventually published in *Black Dwarf*. This virtually repeated previous accusations against the leadership—allegations of corruption and tribalism and of struggle between the (as was alleged) mainly Xhosa leadership and the Zulu-Sotho masses. Tribal and ideological opponents were forced to go on suicide missions inside Rhodesia, they claimed, while the leadership was not willing to share in any way the risks of battle. Furthermore, the four claimed that the 1967 Wankie incursion had been staged for two reasons: 'to get rid of unwanted dissenters and to persuade organizations to give more for the heroic cause.'

The document was explicit about the dominance of the Moscow line in the ANC. 'Whoever spoke against the Kremlin and its policies', they declared, 'was branded as a deviate Maoist and revisionist, or alternatively an imperialist, and branded a fifth columnist who was against the liberation of South Africa.' According to the four dissidents, the ANC's Kongwa Camp in Tanzania was a place of incredible corruption, deprivation, and brutality. A 'people's court' sentenced grumblers and other delinquents to be flogged, while the commanders provided themselves with whisky and young girls. Although the troops allegedly went

---

[1] See Omar Bamjee, Amin Cajee, Hoosain Jacobs, and Maurice Mthombeni, *Why We Left 'Umkhonto We Sizwe'* (*ANC in Exile*), undated typewritten statement, p. 7.

ragged, the ANC-run People's Bazaar in Dar es Salaam raised large sums of money by selling textiles sent to the ANC from Eastern Europe.

The ANC's Youth and Students Section in London vehemently denied these charges, which it maintained were part of South African government propaganda. After seven closely printed pages of rebuttal came the frank admission of the existence of certain 'problems and difficulties'; at the same time, *Sechaba* and *Anti-Apartheid News* were still speaking of 'victories' in Rhodesia. The Youth and Students' Section assured its readers that these 'problems and difficulties' had been tackled 'in a responsible, serious and honest manner' at the ANC's Morogoro Conference of 23 April to 1 May 1969.

The ANC's various foreign missions throughout the world were principally dependent upon the propaganda and information disseminated from the London office above a betting shop at 49 Rathbone Street, London, W.1. While they and the vast network of unseen white South African comrades and friends could disseminate this propaganda and collect funds from well-wishers, they could not deal with the rot in the camps in Africa. Sharp clashes between veteran leaders after the death of Chief Lutuli in 1967, opposition to the continuing leadership of Tambo, and widespread rumours of a forthcoming split in the movement, despite its well-oiled administrative machinery and large reserves of funds, made a top-level conference more urgent than ever.

The *African Communist*, organ of the SACP, declared in its Number 38, Third Quarter 1969, that the conference 'was perhaps the most remarkable, critical and decisive in the long history of the ANC which began in 1912'. The first visible results of the gathering were eight brief resolutions, adopted on the final day, 1 May. The most important were the first four, which approved a new administrative structure for the organization; instructed the National Executive Committee to implement this by mobilizing 'all revolutionaries in functioning units of the African National Congress'; unanimously approved the Political Report of the N.E.C. and once again affirmed multiracialism, as expressed in the Freedom Charter, as the 'Programme of the Revolution'. The final four resolutions consisted of fraternal greetings to 'brother fighters for Freedom in Africa, Vietnam, the Middle East and elsewhere'. Separate resolutions hailed 'our brothers of Southern Africa and the Portuguese colonies who have scored and are scoring brilliant victories over the enemy.' Another paid 'unstinted tribute' to the National Liberation Front of South Vietnam and the fourth was to greet the 'peoples of the Arab countries resisting imperialist-backed Zionist aggression, and support the right of the dispossessed Arabs of Palestine to fight for their return to their homeland.' (Apparently, Arthur Goldreich was to be allowed to deliver no more eulogies of Zionism to the troops, as he had done after the June War. Significantly, this also marked a shift by the SACP, which has strong Jewish membership and has always been wary of blanket condemnations of Israel as an alien entity in the Middle East.)

The administrative changes in the ANC were sweeping. A new and smaller National Executive Committee was elected, headed by Oliver Tambo as President-General; the other members elected were Alfred Nzo, Secretary-General, J. B. Marks, M. Mabidha, Moses Kotane, Joe Matthews, T. T. Nkobi, W. Mokgomane, and M. Piliso. In addition, a Revolutionary Council was created, allegedly representative of all 'national groups and revolutionary forces' in South Africa. As the *African Communist* itself noted: 'Present too—for the first time as fully participating delegates and not only as bearers of fraternal messages— were outstanding leaders of the partners of the Congress Alliance; the Indian and Coloured People's Congresses and the revolutionary working class movement [i.e. the SACP; tried] revolutionaries of the calibre of Dr. Yusuf Dadoo, Reg September, and Joe Slovo.' The Alliance had reaffirmed its leadership to the extent of officially and for the first time seating a white communist in the leadership of the ANC itself.

The Morogoro Conference was formerly opened in the presence of O.A.U. Liberation Committee Executive Secretary George Magombe of Tanzania—who on various occasions had been criticized privately by ANC and SACP militants for his generally even-handed attitude towards the rival movements he dealt with—and other Tanzanian and African representatives. Once the formalities were over, the seventy-odd delegates engaged in what the *African Communist* described as 'unrestricted criticism in which all the main aspects of the movement's programme and strategy, its leadership structure and style of work were examined and tested.'

After praising the 'correct policy of the ANC–ZAPU military alliance' and other 'achievements', the delegates turned to the numerous weaknesses of the movement. According to the report of the SACP organ,

Political activity and information was lacking, especially at grass-roots level; the virtual collapse of the old Alliance machinery had left a gap which resulted in a failure to integrate all revolutionaries in the work of the movement; a dangerous chasm was opening up between the leadership and the rank-and-file which provided soil for various divisive tendencies foreign to the spirit of the ANC and its traditional allies.[1]

While this was indeed a frank admission of the acute contradictions

[1] The *African Communist* (No. 38, Third Quarter, 1969).

within the organization, the remedy appeared to be a tightening of Alliance, i.e. SACP, control and the bizarre acceptance of Joe Slovo, a European lawyer from Johannesburg living in exile in London, as representative of an 'oppressed national group' in South Africa. The black sheep were to be herded by a white sheep dog. No wonder then that the conference went on to hail the U.S.S.R.:

The pillars of the anti-imperialist movement are the Soviet Union and other socialist states, in alliance with the progressive states in Africa, Asia and Latin America, the revolutionary liberation movements in countries which are still under colonial or white minority rule, and the democratic forces in the imperialist countries themselves.[1]

Also receiving special praise as 'close friends' were the German Democratic Republic and Poland. Concerning the Soviet-Warsaw Pact invasion of Czechoslovakia, the ANC noted that that country had always been a 'firm friend' and expressed the hope that 'the situation there will soon return to normal'. There was also kudos for Cuba ('far from our country but always very close to our revolutionary struggle') and India ('cemented by Mahatma Gandhi's direct association with our country').

As for China, the ANC Political Report commented tartly: 'We have received much support from China in our struggle. Recently, through no fault of the ANC this support has been withheld.'

Finally, as whenever in time of difficulty in the past, the Alliance leadership stressed the value of the multiracial Alliance and urged its extension to other movements throughout Africa. The ANC–ZAPU military alliance 'must be consolidated and extended to include FRELIMO, MPLA and SWAPO', the conference decided. Of liberation movements receiving substantial Soviet support, only the PAIGC of Guiné was to escape the embrace of the ANC. This was probably because of distance and the stubborn and successful quasi-independent line pursued for years with agility and consummate skill by the PAIGC's Amílcar Cabral, who would hardly have been expected to accept kindly advice and direction from such 'tried revolutionaries' as Yusuf Dadoo, Reg September, and Joe Slovo. Perhaps embittered by the failure of the Khartoum Conference a few months previously to modify in any way the line of the African Liberation Committee, much less to supplant it with a new organization, the ANC conference gave a small parting kick to the A.L.C. for its 'unfortunate sponsorship of the PAC' which 'has not in any way helped the struggle'.

In his closing address, Oliver Tambo who, as Acting President-General had managed to retain the leadership at the price of bringing

[1] Ibid. Italics in original.

his once-silent partners openly into the direction, urged unity and vigilance upon all. 'Beware the wedge driver! Men who creep from ear to ear driving wedges among us; who go around creating splits and divisions.'

Undoubtedly, the leaders of the ANC were deeply frustrated by the failures since 1961. But they had created a large and powerful, if far from stable, organization in exile. Faced with a choice of Pan-Africanism or the Soviet hegemony, they chose without hesitation the Russians, hailing them and not the O.A.U. or African revolutionary regimes as the pillar of their struggle. Likewise regarding the Sino-Soviet dispute, they obediently followed the line laid down by their comrades of the SACP, one of the few communist parties that wholeheartedly and uncritically accepted the CPSU theses at the international meeting called by the CPSU in Moscow from 5 to 17 June 1969. The veteran black communist J. B. Marks, later to become Chairman of the SACP, who headed the delegation, declared that it found the differences of other communists with the Russians 'rather difficult to understand'. Reaffirming the conviction that the U.S.S.R. was 'the citadel and mainstay of the anti-imperialist forces everywhere', Marks condemned the 'sidetracking and disruption of various international solidarity organizations by Chinese delegations who persisted in dragging into gatherings of non-communists their alleged "ideological" campaign against the CPSU and the world communist movement.' He claimed Chinese assistance to the ANC had been withdrawn 'without reason or explanation', adding 'instead we find the Maoists subsidizing and actually preserving from complete collapse a group of right-wing renegades from our struggle whom documentary evidence now proves to have been started at the instance, and with the support, of the CIA.' Thus, perhaps to make his own personal position clear, his former PAC drinking companions in Dar es Salaam were described as mere tools of the Central Intelligence Agency and the Chinese communists.

Internationally, since the Moshi conference in 1963 and the Winneba conference in 1965 of the Afro-Asian People's Solidarity Organization, ANC representatives had baited the Chinese delegates—often, oddly enough, in the name of African nationalism menaced by 'alien influences'. These attacks were not made solely by members of the SACP. At Winneba, Robert Resha, at that time of the ANC's National Executive Committee, made such implicitly racist denunciations of the Chinese communists that Oliver Tambo had to intervene to apologize before the conference broke down completely. Whatever Resha's personal feelings about the Chinese, which hardly seem friendly, it was abundantly clear that the anti-China line adopted by the ANC was itself motivated from external sources and probably was the counterpart to continuing or increased Soviet material assistance.

Having proved its loyalty and quelled rebellion in the ranks, where there always remains a danger of Africanism among working-class blacks, the ANC took other steps to restore discipline and order, if not to heal its divisions. The ANC–ZAPU alliance was in serious trouble. Apparent ANC interference in ZAPU's internal affairs had encouraged a violent split in ZAPU ranks and for the time being there could be no question of further major raids across the Zambezi. The troops, now idle, were packed off once again for 'training', reportedly to the Soviet Union this time, so prompting new desertions of the disgruntled and disillusioned, who fled to Nairobi and other havens. Despite this, throughout 1970 the ANC strategists made ever more insistent demands that their troops be allowed to go into action in other countries: Mozambique, Angola, and South West Africa. The leaders of the organizations in those lands did not express great joy at the prospect of such reinforcement, but how long they could successfully resist the overtures of the ANC, backed by the authority of the Soviet Union, was problematical.

The Unity Movement of South Africa (UMSA)

Unrecognized by the African Liberation Committee and without any visible forces, the Unity Movement of South Africa need not have appeared in this work if it were not for the surprising vigour and influence of the mainly Coloured intellectuals who have directed it since the forties. The Unity Movement proclaims itself a Marxist movement. A UMSA publication declares: 'Only the weapon of Marxism can cut a clear path through the ideological jungle with which imperialism so skilfully trammels up the unwary.'[1]

The Unity Movement is the direct descendant, greatly diminished in numbers, of the All-African Convention. This *ad hoc* body was created in 1935, under the leadership of Dr. D. D. T. Jabavu of Fort Hare Native College, at a period of great decline and inactivity of the ANC. Among those who participated in its founding was Dr. A. B. Xuma, a young doctor who had been trained in the United States and Europe and who was later to become President-General of the ANC. The AAC was set up expressly to fight two racist measures put forward by the white-

---

[1] In a pamphlet, 'The Revolutionary Road for South Africa' (Luska, Unity Movement, May 1969).

minority regime, led then by General J. B. M. Hertzog. One called for the gradual elimination of the existing African vote in the Cape. Africans were to be allowed instead to elect indirectly four white Senators through electoral colleges based on the chiefs. A Natives' Representative Council, which was purely advisory, was to be set up—as indeed it eventually was—composed of elected Africans, Chiefs, and nominated government representatives. The second proposal, the Native Trust and Land Bill, was to debar Africans from buying land outside the Native Reserves. Throughout the country, Africans were not allowed to own more than 13 per cent of the land, and that generally the most impoverished.

More than 150 organizations, including the ANC, were represented by 500 delegates at the meeting of the All-African Convention in Bloemfontein on Dingaan's Day, 16 December 1935. This was the largest and broadest based gathering of non-whites in the history of South Africa. As was to be expected, the AAC completely rejected the Government's two proposals, but was divided on the question of what action should be taken.

A minority wanted militant action—demonstrations and strikes—while the moderate majority preferred to petition the Government for a change in policy. General Hertzog played upon these internal contradictions, inviting a deputation from the Convention to meet him, urging them to be 'reasonable'. Eventually, even despite considerable European opposition, the disenfranchizement of Africans was voted into law, as were the racist restrictions on land tenure.

In spite of this affront, the moderates, backed now by the South African Communist Party, decided to accept the creation of a Natives' Representative Council and the indirect election of whites to Parliament. Backed by the ANC and other moderates within the AAC, three white Members of Parliament and four white Senators were eventually elected.

At this time, a group of young African and Coloured intellectuals, many of them teachers, joined the AAC. These young leftists were immediately accused of Trotskyism by the SACP and branded as 'ultra-leftists'. There seemed considerable justification for both accusations. The AAC leadership were far more thoroughgoing and revolutionary, at least verbally, than the overtly reformist SACP, and there were indeed definite links between them and the Trotskyist Fourth International. These links were at least made less visible, however, when Dr. I. B. Tabata, the leader of the group, broke with his former white Trotskyite associates in South Africa. This break created a good impression on fledgling African nationalists and such acquaintanceship with Marxism as many acquired at the period came from the AAC rather than the SACP.

In 1943, the organization of the Cape Coloured teachers, which had been called the Anti-Coloured Affairs Department in opposition to the white regime's discriminatory Coloured Affairs Department, eventually merged with what remained of the ACC to become the Non-European Unity Movement. This was later to be called simply the Unity Movement.

The presence of a preponderance of Coloureds in the organization created serious difficulties. All Coloured groups in South Africa had to contend with the same problems, arising from the mixed origin of the Coloureds and their relative privileges in relation to the black masses. In the Cape, the Coloureds enjoyed for a time considerable political rights and they were hardly encouraged to look upon the Africans as brothers. Rather, they were put on a par with the Indians. Both were half way between the European masters and the Africans. In every field, they received somewhat better treatment than the Africans. For instance, the South African Institute of Race Relations reported in 1965 that salary scales of Indian and Coloured teachers were nearly the same. While Coloured male teachers received 77·4 per cent of those of white male teachers, and Coloured women teachers received 80·2 per cent of white women teachers' pay,[1] both were vastly higher than African teachers' salaries. As Marxists, the leaders of the Unity Movement realized that the sole genuine hope of a revolutionary upsurge in South Africa lay with the vast African proletariat, and they acted accordingly. But occasionally their publications betrayed a certain hesitation, and even fear of the African national struggle. One commented:

Thus the national liberation of the Non-White oppressed people in South Africa for freedom and liberty must be understood within the framework of its material development. To declare categorically that it is a purely national struggle or even to go to the extent of enunciating a new brand of racialism to the effect that it is a struggle of one colour against another and therefore the main task is to fight segregation or the doctrines of apartheid, namely Verwoerdism, is completely unhistorical, demagogic and worst of all, fatal to the understanding of the real issues at stake.[2]

Rejecting legalistic reformism, which viewed the struggle as essentially a battle for full and equal rights for Africans and all races in South Africa, the Unity Movement insisted upon an historical materialist analysis which downgraded the national and racial aspects of that struggle.

[1] Bunting, op. cit., p. 278.
[2] From *APDUSA*, 'We Build a Nation', Special Edition (Vol. II, No. 12, June-September 1967), published in Lusaka.

The main battle of the Unity Movement was centred around a ten-point minimum programme of non-collaboration. Developed during the forties, this non-collaboration programme remains the strategic guideline of the organization right up to the present. The leaders of the UMSA have bemoaned the failure of their fellow South Africans to grasp the 'significance and potency' of the programme. 'Unfortunately, even amongst revolutionaries there are very few who seem to comprehend its full import.'[1]

At its origin, the non-collaboration programme referred to the Hertzog proposals for a Natives' Representative Council and all the other *Bungas*, village councils, and other Advisory Councils, used by the Government for the indirect control of the African masses, and acceptance by them of their own oppression and exploitation, reinforcing the myth of the black man's inherent inferiority. From its origin, the Unity Movement was to place great emphasis on fighting the 'slave mentality' of many non-whites in South Africa. In time, non-collaboration was to mean not only inaction and abstention but also such direct action as strikes and boycotts. This programme and other views of the Unity Movement were originally expressed in their publication, *Torch*, which was finally forced out of existence by the Government in 1963.

Commenting on the pervasive influence of the UMSA, Leo Kuper wrote:

The Unity Movement exerted an influence out of proportion to the small number of its members not because it reflected the political views of the student body [among non-European students at the University of Natal] but because it crystalized in emotion and slogan the underlying resentment and intimidated the nonconformist.[2]

The All-African Convention was an *ad hoc* federal body, originally supposed to represent 150 separate non-white groups. The subsequent Unity Movement was alleged to be an even wider federal body. Nevertheless, the component organizations were rarely visible to outsiders and were then ephemeral and minute in size.

In 1961, the Unity Movement launched a new organization which was called the African People's Democratic Union of South Africa (APDUSA), 'a mass unitary body which individuals could join directly.'[3] A year later, when both ANC and PAC were outlawed inside South Africa, the APDUSA held its inaugural conference in Cape Town under

---

[1] From 'The Revolutionary Road for South Africa'.

[2] Leo Kuper, *An African Bourgeoisie* (New Haven and London, Yale University Press, 1965), p. 161.

[3] *APDUSA*, 'We Build a Nation'.

Tabata's leadership. Unity Movement spokesmen later hailed the new affiliated body as an 'instantaneous success'[1] among peasants and workers, especially in Sekhukhuniland and Pondoland.

Relying essentially on boycotts and the concept of rural self-defence, the Unity Movement deplored the non-violent campaigns, sabotage, and terrorism of the ANC and PAC, which it maintained were caught between 'the two vultures' of the SACP and the Liberal Party. The UMSA insisted that there could be no revolutionary road, no anti-imperialist struggle, unless that struggle were explicitly directed to the overthrow of capitalism, which was ultimately responsible for the South African situation.

The concept of self-defence, as used by the Unity Movement, did not imply the creation of any military forces as such, but arming of the people, naturally under the direction of a party with a 'conscious leadership'. Eventually, there would be an armed uprising of the population against their capitalist oppressors, but nothing indicates that the UMSA ever began organizing such an uprising in South Africa.

Now, still led by Dr. Tabata and some of his long-time associates, the Unity Movement operates from modest quarters in Lusaka. It receives no assistance from the African Liberation Committee and it is generally considered a relic from the distant past by both ANC and PAC. Despite a visit to China by Tabata in 1969, the UMSA has apparently still not broken all its Trotskyist international connections, although the name of Trotsky never appears in its recent publications. Official Trotskyist organizations such as the Socialist Workers Party of the United States and small Trotskyist groups elsewhere have shown great sympathy for the Unity Movement and have tried to assist it. The Movement had its unofficial martyr in Dr. Neville Alexander, a Coloured teacher who, with four associates, was arrested and tried in Cape Town in 1964 for allegedly studying various ways of ovethrowing the Government. Alexander and the others were sentenced to four years in prison. Appeals on his behalf came overwhelmingly from Trotskyist groups in many countries. Frantz Lee, a Coloured student in West Germany and member of the Unity Movement until his later split with Tabata, travelled widely in Europe and America, lecturing on behalf of Alexander and the UMSA. In America, he was sponsored by the SWP—as was Tabata himself when he later visited the U.S.A.—although black militant groups also showed great interest.

In 1971, fourteen other members of the UMSA were put on trial in Pietermaritzburg under South Africa's Terrorism Act. Many of the

[1] Ibid.

accused were professional men, especially lawyers and teachers, and students, but there were also some farm workers from the Transkei, where the UMSA has long claimed to have a peasant following, despite vehement denials of this by both the ANC and the PAC. In any case, clashes between police and peasants in the area had been frequent at the beginning of the seventies when the police forcibly moved the peasants off farms they had worked for years.[1] The charges in Pietermaritzburg were wide ranging, however, and covered the period 1963 to 1970, alleging that the accused 'endangered the maintenance of law and order and sought to overthrow the government by force of arms'.

The most surprising thing about the Unity Movement was the respect that its Marxist analyses of the South African situation had earned among Africans and others. Echoes of its pronouncements come from unexpected sources. Undoubtedly, this was due above all to the ideological weakness of the SACP, which for years had been extremely careful to couch its own declarations in the conventional language of liberalism, stressing the struggle for democratic rights. Hence, Dr. Tabata was for many the most outspoken practitioner of Marxist theory in South Africa.

Organizationally, despite its broad beginnings in the AAC, the Unity Movement has shrunk and has confined itself to a sectarian, self-perpetuating style of work, so that it resembles more an extended family around the leader than a political party. Proud of their intellectual achievements and self-conscious of their duty to instruct the masses, the teachers in the Unity Movement eventually discovered they had no pupils in their classrooms. The influence of Trotskyite doctrine alone is not responsible for this; its cause is also the failure of the UMSA to grasp sympathetically and develop the national question—as Lenin and Stalin had done so successfully in the Russian revolution—responding creatively to the aspirations of the African majority in South Africa for a liberated African homeland. As we have already seen, the Unity Movement was not the only organization to fail to perceive the importance of these national aspirations. However, but for this failure, it might have become a far larger and more relevant body in the panoply of African liberation movements.

The Pan Africanist Congress of Azania (South Africa) (PAC)

Since Clements Kadalie's ill-fated ICU faded away, no African organization in South African history has enjoyed such massive support—if not

[1] For an account of South African resettlement practices, see Cosmas Desmond, *The Discarded People* (Harmondsworth, Penguin, 1971).

in formal membership, at least in active sympathy—as did the Pan Africanist Congress during the hectic early years of its existence. It is not really accurate, however, to describe the PAC as a new organization; rather, it was the resurgence of an historic, deep-rooted tendency in the ANC—that of African nationalism. Congress had never been hostile to the white man, as Roux noted.[1] However, within the first decade from its founding, its leaders became conscious of the bonds of colour and common sufferings and aspirations that linked the peoples of African descent in Africa and America. Solomon T. Plaatje attended the First Pan African Congress, organized in Paris in 1919 by Dr. W. E. B. DuBois, in the hope of influencing the Versailles peace conference. Plaatje was later to lecture in America about the hardships of African life in South Africa. Although limited means and distance prevented these ties from being developed extensively, they were never completely broken.

The Second World War had brought the edifying spectacle of Japan, an allegedly backward Asian country, even challenging for a time the might of the Anglo-Saxon powers. Victory over the Axis brought promises of new freedoms. In October 1945, the ANC delegates attended the Fifth Pan African Congress in Manchester, where they met African leaders like Kwame Nkrumah and Jomo Kenyatta, who were already thinking of lifting the colonial yoke from their respective countries. Significantly, it was in Manchester that the ANC delegation revealed their own illusions about the state apparatus they would increasingly have to challenge, by proclaiming their conviction that Gandhian non-violent campaigns were the most effective means of persuading European rulers to grant concessions to their black subjects without the bitterness of civil strife and racial conflict.[2] Given the name of Positive Action and with the element of passivity greatly reduced, this non-violent tactic was adopted and successfully used in the Gold Coast by Kwame Nkrumah's Convention People's Party in wresting power from the British in 1957 and creating Ghana, the first African state in the post-war world to achieve independence through the efforts of an active nationalist movement. But situations in the British-ruled Gold Coast and the Afrikaner laager of South Africa were vastly different, as the South Africans were to learn belatedly and to their dismay.

The immediate roots of the PAC were in the Youth League of the ANC, the group of young activists who after 1943 gathered around the charismatic figure of Anton Muziwakhe Lembede in Johannesburg. As we have already seen in our discussion of the ANC, this group was deeply

[1] Roux, op. cit., p. 402.   [2] Benson, op. cit., p. 90.

dissatisfied with Congress and critized the older leadership for 'collaboration with the white oppressors' and submitting to the 'foreign domination and foreign leadership' of white radicals and liberals. Ideologically, the Youth League had been influenced also by the All-African People's Convention, which later became the Unity Movement, and Paul Mosaka's African Democratic Party, as well as by the example of the heroic tribal resistance of the African inhabitants against white encroachment and settlement, beginning in the seventeenth century and not ending until the Bambata Rebellion of 1906. However, the Youth League's brief victory at the ANC annual conference of 1949 was swiftly subverted by the right wing of the ANC, the moderates who feared conflict with the Government, and those who clung to the multiracial concepts being put forward by the SACP and its front organizations. Lembede died in 1946, having laid the foundations of Africanism and personally rallied its first adherents. After his death, the Youth League was increasingly divided between two opposing factions; these were later labelled 'Africanist' and 'Charterist' respectively, during the battle over the 1956 Freedom Charter, making multiracialism the official policy of the ANC.

Again, as we have seen, the formal rupture of the ANC was prompted more than anything else by the high-handed, undemocratic methods adopted by the Charterists in their determination to impose their views and to manipulate the black masses of the ANC through the 'advisory' co-ordinating council of the Congress Alliance, composed of the ANC, Indian Congress, Coloured People's Organization, SACP, and SACTU. The split was made inevitable by the punitive expulsions of leading Africanists after the failure of the 1958 'stay-at-home', which had been forced on the ANC by its allies.

The actual parting took place at the Transvaal congress of the ANC in the presence of Lutuli and Tambo. Led out of the stormy meeting on 2 November 1959 by Potlako Kitchener Leballo and Peter Molotsi, the Africanists gathered nearby within minutes to declare their loyalty to the principles—which they believed to have been essentially Africanist—that had guided the ANC from 1912 to the time of the Congress Alliance.

The PAC was not formally constituted until 5–6 April 1959. During the intervening months, the scattered Africanists throughout South Africa rallied round another extraordinary man—Mangaliso Robert Sobukwe. He was known to most of his associates as 'Prof'. After being dismissed from a teaching post during the 1952 Defiance Campaign, he had gone on to become a lecturer at Witwatersrand University. Sobukwe was born in Graaff-Reinet in the Cape in 1924. He studied at Lovedale and Fort Hare College, where he was extremely popular and was elected president of the Student Council. His personal warmth, natural dignity, and steadfastness in adversity have won the praise of people in all corners of the world; admired by the South African people as a genuine leader, he was praised even by many who feared his African nationalist ideas.

The Africanists had hoped to have some prominent African leader— either Kenneth Kaunda of the Zambia African Nationalist Congress or Dr. Hastings Kamuzu Banda of Nyasaland (now Malawi)—address their inaugural convention. Both were 'detained' at the time by the British rulers of their respective countries and it was Sobukwe himself who spoke. The relatively short address was an expression of moderate African national aspirations, typical of African thought at the end of the fifties when many African territories were visibly on the verge of independence. The influence of Nkrumah's successful bid for power in Ghana is very striking, especially in Sobukwe's reaffirmation of positive neutrality and non-alignment between the American and Soviet world blocs and commitment to Pan-Africanism. Sobukwe declared:

We honour Ghana as the first independent state in modern Africa which, under the courageous nationalist leadership of Dr. Nkrumah and the Convention People's Party, has actively interested itself in the liberation of the whole continent from white domination, and has held out the vision of a democratic United States of Africa.[1]

Sobukwe pledged PAC to work for African unity and the eventual creation of 'a union of free, sovereign, independent democratic states of Africa' to which South Africa would eventually belong.

Many South Africans had been profoundly influenced by George Padmore's *Pan-Africanism or Communism?*, published in 1954, which seemed to speak to their own difficulties with the South African Communist Party and to offer a way forward that skirted vulgar anti-communism. In later years, the example of the Communist Party of China under the leadership of Chairman Mao Tsetung was to demonstrate that a communist party could be quite different from the SACP and successfully lead a revolution of peasants and workers in a 'backward', non-European country. This, as well as Chinese material and moral support, explains the gusto with which some PAC members have castigated the 'modern revisionism' of the mainly white communists of South Africa. However, at the founding of the party, Padmore's

---

[1] *The Basic Documents of the Pan Africanist Congress*, p. 12.

influence was predominant. And Sobukwe specifically mentions him in his inaugural address and quotes from his book.

Padmore was a disillusioned West Indian communist who had formerly worked for the Comintern. His concept of Pan-Africanism meant 'the attainment of the government of Africans by Africans for Africans, with respect for racial and religious minorities who desire to live in Africa on a basis of equality with the black majority.'[1] He was convinced that no sane African would freely choose to continue to live under imperialism and hence believed that the only real ideological struggle in Africa would eventually be between the opposing forces of Communism and Pan-Africanism. 'Pan-Africanism offers an ideological alternative to Communism on the one side and Tribalism on the other. it rejects both white racialism and black chauvism. It stands for racial co-existence on the basis of absolute equality and respect for the human personality', Padmore added.[2] He thought that colonialism could only be maintained from outside by military force. He declared:

The white man in East and Central Africa has forfeited the loyalty and good-will of the Africans, who no longer have illusions about professions of 'trusteeship' and 'partnership'. These British settlers, to say nothing of the fanatical racialists and rabid defenders of *Apartheid* in South Africa, have made it abundantly clear to the Africans that they regard them merely as hewers of wood and drawers of water in their own countries.[3]

Politically, Padmore transmitted to the Africanists of South Africa a high regard for individual liberties under law, the Declaration of Human Rights and the Four Freedoms of the Atlantic Charter, while stressing the necessity of 'Democratic Socialism, with state control of the basic means of production and distribution.'[4]

All these themes are to be found in Sobukwe's brief inaugural address to the founding conference of the PAC. Concerning socialism, Sobukwe was to point out China in particular. 'We are not blind to the fact that the countries which pursue a policy of planned state economy have out-stripped, in industrial development, those that follow the path of private enterprise,' he declared. 'Today, China is industrially far ahead of India.' But, loyal to Padmore, he was to add immediately:

Africanists reject totalitarianism in any form and accept political democracy as understood in the West. We also reject the economic exploitation of the many for the benefit of a few. We accept as policy the equitable distribution of wealth, aiming, as far as I am concerned, to equality of income which to me is the only basis on which the slogan of 'equal opportunities' can be founded.[5]

[1] Padmore, op. cit., p. 21.   [2] Ibid., p. 379.   [3] Ibid., p. 21.
[4] Ibid.   [5] PAC, op. cit., p. 12.

Sobukwe rejected all theories of racial superiority. 'The Africanists take the view that there is only one race to which we all belong, and that is the human race,' he said, but went on also to reject explicitly multi-racialism. He declared:

Against multi-racialism we have this objection, that the history of South Africa has fostered group prejudices and antagonism, and if we have to maintain the same group exclusiveness, parading under the term of multi-racialism, we shall be transporting to the new Africa these very antagonisms and conflicts. Further, multi-racialism is in fact a pandering to European bigotry and arrogance. It is a method of safeguarding white interests irrespective of population figures.[1]

On the other hand, Sobukwe said that anyone who 'owes his basic loyalty to Africa and who is prepared to accept the democratic rule of an African majority' would be regarded as an African. But he cautioned, 'We guarantee no minority rights, because we think in terms of individuals, not groups.'

In general terms, Europeans were 'a foreign minority group which has exclusive control of political, economic, social and military power', thereby humiliating and degrading the indigenous African people. Although Indians came to South Africa 'not as imperialists or colonialists, but as indentured labourers', Sobukwe accused members of this group of becoming a 'merchant class', 'tainted with the virus of cultural supremacy and national arrogance.' 'The down-trodden, poor "stinking coolies" of Natal who alone, as a result of the pressure of material conditions, can identify themselves with the indigenous African majority in the struggle to overthrow white supremacy, have not yet produced their leadership. We hope they will do so soon', he declared. (In fact, not many years were to pass before Ahmed Gora Ebrahim and others of Indian and Pakistani origin were to take their places in the ranks of the PAC.)

The programme of action for the national liberation of South Africa was essentially the same as for elsewhere in Africa, Sobukwe claimed, denying the 'fashionable doctrine' of African exceptionalism. Rather, it was the contention of the Africanists that:

True democracy can be established in South Africa and on the continent as a whole, only when white supremacy has been destroyed. And the illiterate and semi-literate African masses constitute the key and centre and content of any struggle for true democracy in South Africa. And the African people can be organized only under the banner of African nationalism in an All-African Organization where they will by themselves formulate policies and programmes

[1] Ibid., p. 16.

and decide on the methods of struggle without interference from either so-called left-wing or right-wing groups of the minorities who arrogantly appropriate to themselves the right to plan and think for the Africans.[1]

This was the essence of Africanism and the foundation stone of all PAC policy. Under Sobukwe's energetic leadership, the fledgling PAC also believed that it had a practical plan of action and it set about creating a formal organization to implement that plan. The inaugural conference ratified a party Constitution, a Disciplinary Code governing the behaviour of individual members and the party as a whole and a Manifesto, which spelled out the ideology of Africanism, 'the third social force in the world', which serves 'the material, intellectual and spiritual interests of Africa and does not in any way serve the spiritual interests of either the Eastern or the Western powers.'[2] Today, such optimism and underestimation of the pervasive, insidious influence of Western interests, not to mention every aspect of the West's 'Pop' culture—not only in Africa but even in Eastern Europe itself—would be generally rejected as naïve, but not in those heady days of African resurgence in the fifties; Africans were yet to see the spectre of neo-colonialism behind the shaky façade of their independence.

The ANC had been organized along provincial lines. This structure was rejected by the PAC's founding conference, which adopted in its place a regional structure. Originally, all of South Africa was divided into six regions, but later these were found to be too large and eventually the party settled on seventeen regions, divisions being made solely on a geographical basis.

Each region has a chairman, who sits on the National Executive Committee with the national officers of the party, headed by the National President and the National Secretary, the Treasurer, and secretaries for various departments—Foreign Affairs, Publicity, Education, Economic Affairs, Culture, etc. Orginally, there were sixteen officers in all, plus the regional chairmen.

The Constitution stipulated the creation of a central committee, called a National Work Committee, to expedite current business. Supposed to have been composed of the President and four other members of the National Executive Committee, according to report it was usually enlarged to the President and six other members.[3] Obviously, these constitutional niceties were often overlooked in the heat of the struggle, although because the strong-arm tactics and arbitrary treatment meted

[1] PAC, op. cit., p. 16.   [2] Ibid., p. 25.
[3] Interview with Peter Roboroko, Dar es Salaam, 11 March 1966.

out to them by the Charterists while they were still in the ranks of the ANC were fresh memories, the PAC usually made considerable efforts to observe the letter and spirit of their democratic constitution.

The Pan-Africanist position was to be denounced as 'black chauvinism' and alleged to be the expression of 'agents' of the U.S. Central Intelligence Agency. The Pan-Africanists were also, it was later alleged, in the employ of Mao Tsetung and the Communist Party of China. The party's subsequent decision to give South Africa the 'African name' of 'Azania' was repeatedly mocked as unhistorical and another symptom of black chauvinism. Of course this was partially true, but the same could be said of Botswana, Ghana, Malawi, Mali, Zambia, and even Lesotho—all countries which for nationalistic reasons had wished to replace their old colonial names.

No less a personage than the late Professor I. I. Potekhin, leading Soviet specialist on African questions, was to set his sights at the PAC. His arguments sum up most of the numerous denunciations of the organization made by the SACP and other European 'progressives', which can still be heard in some quarters, and bear repeating here:

A wide range of historical experience convincingly shows that racial considerations have always been introduced into politics by reactionary forces (slave-owners, colonialists, German fascists, Japanese militarists, etc.) to justify their repugnant anti-popular policies. History shows that popular movements having a racial basis have always arisen as a reaction to racial oppression. Although in the first instance these movements are usually progressive, they always have some features which can be and in fact are used to a reactionary end. A member of such a movement may make up his mind, or may be persuaded, that all people of another race are his enemies and the enemies of his people. The case of the Pan Africanist Congress in South Africa is an instructive example. For a number of years before it was banned by the Government, the Congress of Democrats in South Africa grouped together English and African supporters of the progressive, anti-imperialist organizations of the non-European population—the African National Congress, the South African Indian Congress, and the Coloured People's National Union [sic]. When all these organizations formed a common front of struggle against Verwoerd's fascist policies, a small group of ANC members split away, complaining that the ANC had fallen under white influence, and set up their own organization, the Pan Africanist Congress, as a purely racial organization allegedly 'free' from white influence. The PAC leadership immediately came out with violently anti-communist statements and soon attracted the support of the white Liberal Party also engaged in vicious anti-communist propaganda. The leader of its Right Wing, Patrick Duncan, a rabid anti-communist, became a particularly enthusiastic champion of the PAC. After having left the ANC for the alleged reason that it cooperated with progressive whites, the PAC fell into company with white reactionaries. This is, of course, quite natural: the main contradiction in bourgeois society is not between races but between antagonistic classes, between the forces of progress fighting for the socialist transformation of society and the forces of imperialist reaction striving to save the outlived decadent capitalist system. The PAC leaders are no exception. There are political figures in other African countries who counterpoise black to white, and with the same result: in turning their back on friends, they find themselves bound in a shameful alliance with the enemies of African freedom.[1]

Potekhin sets up a straw man. Of course it is not true that the PAC was at any time a 'purely racial organization'.

Interestingly enough, these same misguided black tools of reaction, to paraphrase Potekhin, admittedly became overnight the driving force of the liberation movement in South Africa and were to win recognition from Marxist-Leninist revolutionaries in China and other lands. As Mao was to declare in 1963, in his first statement on the Afro-American struggle, 'In the final analysis, a national struggle is a question of class struggle.' This was only one among many issues that were soon to divide the international communist movement.

Between April and December 1959, the cadres of the new PAC concentrated on recruitment and structuring their organization. They had been fortunate in having the Orlando branch of the ANC, in Johannesburg, the largest and most dynamic of Congress branches, come into their party immediately, led by its president, Mangaliso Sobukwe. The party was soon building itself in many other parts of the country, especially where conflict between Africans and the white-minority regime was at its most intense, as in the Western Cape and the Southern Transvaal. With this work moving ahead rapidly, the PAC was able to call its first national conference in Johannesburg on 19–20 December 1959.

Sobukwe and his associates announced their plan of action, beginning with a campaign of defiance of the pass laws and mounting through unspecified steps to 'freedom and independence' by 1963. Demanding tactical non-violence of his followers, Sobukwe called on them to leave passes at home and accept arrest and imprisonment, filling South Africa's prisons and, more important, halting work in field and factory. No compromises were to be accepted. The slogan would be: No bail, no defence, no fine.

The ANC, which had also announced a demonstration against the pass laws on 31 March 1960, was in consternation at the plans of the PAC. Duma Nokwe, an African member of the SACP, spoke on be-half of the ANC, categorically rejecting PAC proposals for the two

---

[1] I. I. Potekhin, *African Problems* (Moscow, Nauka Publishing House, 1969), p. 117.

movements to join in the anti-pass campaign. Nokwe said that the ANC would not join in 'sensational actions that might not succeed'.[1]

Sobukwe announced that the opening day of the unlimited Positive Action campaign would be 21 March. Throughout the country, intensive organizing of the people went on. They were asked to leave their passes at home and to surrender themselves at their nearest police station as violators of the pass laws.

Early on the morning of the 21st, Sobukwe himself led a group of militants to the police headquarters in Orlando, where they were eventually taken into custody. There was no violence, but in Sharpeville, thirty-five miles away, the panic-stricken white police opened fire on the thousands of unarmed Africans who had gathered around their station. Sixty-nine Africans died in the hail of bullets and 180 others were injured. In Evaton, South African Air Force planes dived at and made low passes over a huge crowd of some 20,000 protesters in order to disperse them. In Langa, where at least 10,000 had gathered, the police battered hundreds of Africans with their clubs and then opened fire, killing five and wounding forty-nine.

Thus, the myth of the efficacy of peaceful, non-violent protest died in South Africa. Not a single European had suffered at the hands of the unarmed blacks during the day. That night, there were to be some burnings of segregated schools and other inferior facilities for Africans, but even this violent reaction was pathetically limited. Nevertheless, South African stocks and bonds plummeted on the world's exchanges. Panic seized the money markets and stock exchanges of the West. Values were all later regained and surpassed, but the fear of another Sharpeville disaster still haunts speculators in South African investments. For the SACP, the day meant the ruin of a lengthy patient process of gradualism, based more on illusion than results. Leaders of the Congress Alliance have since sought to present the Sharpeville martyrs as part of their following, counting on the world's ignorance to prevent exposure of their opportunism. In 1960, however, the Alliance leadership quite rightly saw in the killings of Sharpeville and Langa the collapse of the strategy and tactics they had so carefully elaborated. And, at the time, their ire at the PAC was not hidden, but the popular temper forced them to get belatedly into step. Chief Lutuli even burned his own pass on 27 March, six days after the massacres, and both parties joined in honouring the dead in elaborate funeral ceremonies.

For the first time in the history of the white-minority state, the pass laws were suspended. A young student in the PAC, Philip Kgosana,

[1] Benson, op. cit., p. 222.

deputizing for detained regional leaders, demonstrated African power by leading 30,000 Africans in a march on the Parliament in Cape Town. He was tricked into dispersing the crowd and later arrested, but Europeans were more frightened than they had been since their conquest of this African land. One Government Minister—Paul Sauer—even expressed misgivings about apartheid, but in general the hard-headed Boers who ruled South Africa were determined to prevail, using greater force, greater violence, if necessary. No mists of liberalism penetrated this determination—there was no need to compromise with unarmed Africans.

Despite the initial reliance of the PAC upon non-violence, the Africanist leaders had few illusions about pacifism. When the PAC and ANC were both banned on 8 April 1960, leaders of both organizations put into action plans for underground organizations. The ANC was favoured in that none of its allies in the Congress Alliance was then outlawed, as it was itself, although individual leaders from all member groups were being put under ban or arrest by the Government. Whereas many of the ANC's activists were well-known, middle class professionals, those of the PAC were, fortunately, ordinary black folk from the locations and townships who were hardly known outside their own communities. These militants began organizing the PAC for an armed struggle, the next stage on the march towards the Freedom Year of 1963.

The PAC sent a picked handful of militants abroad, especially to Ghana, the United Arab Republic, and Tanganyika (now Tanzania), to receive military training and establish missions of the party. The ANC did likewise, although their strategy was vastly different. It is doubtful, even today, if the ANC leaders really believe it possible to seize power through armed struggle in South Africa. They do not say as much; but a significant portion of their propaganda is aimed at liberal opinion in the West and stresses United Nations action, boycott, and the political quarantine of the apartheid state as a world outlaw. Such measures have had little success. In Europe, the boycott of South African fruit was a miserable failure—as the PAC predicted it would be. ANC's military build-up and sporadic raids into Rhodesia seem to be all part of a programme of demonstrations of power, intended to persuade the adversary to negotiate concessions. Unfortunately, the adversary has only strengthened his own military forces and has never engaged in any talks whatsoever with the petitioning Congress Alliance.

On the other hand, the PAC appeared to have an almost anarcho-syndicalist vision of a massive, generalized uprising throughout the country, led by a relatively small number of cadres, that would paralyse the industrial state and sweep away an impotent regime. This almost mystical belief in the efficacy of the general uprising is not unique to South Africa. Much later, in field interviews with Zimbabwe freedom fighters in Tanzania and Zambia in 1966, the author was forcefully impressed by their confidence that such a co-ordinated, generalized mass uprising would bring down the oppressive white regime—though 'uprising' is almost too strong a word for the essentially peaceful action that they envisaged. Perhaps such a conviction was encouraged by the legacy of Kadalie's ICU, which also had a Sorellian faith in the general strike, and that of the Ethiopian and Zionist churches with their apocalyptic vision of history.

The end of 1962 marked the beginning of violence, a sort of preparation for the major uprising. Groups of Africans, in the past generally docile and non-violent, even when not law-abiding, in their dealings with Europeans, mercilessly struck down individual whites in a number of localities. The attacks began on the night of 21 November 1962, when a black group attacked the police station in Paarl. The apparent object of the attack was to eliminate the police and seize their arms, but this was thwarted by police reinforcements, so the group turned its fury on nearby whites. Armed only with pangas, machete-like knives, the angry Africans killed two whites and wounded many others. Five of them in turn were killed by police, who arrested several hundreds.

This Fanonist violence—oppressed masses finding catharsis in the killing of their enemies—continued until 1963. On 2 February a group of fifty Africans attacked a road camp near the Bashee River Bridge in the Transkei and killed five Europeans. On 8 February a white businessman was murdered in Langa. There were other attacks in Queenstown, Qamata, and Krugersdorp. It seemed that the South African powder keg was at last exploding.

While much of this violence was spontaneous and its sole achievement was to increase terror among the hitherto all-powerful white minority, it was definitely encouraged, and later controlled to a certain extent, by the PAC. Directing the opening of the armed struggle as far as he could was P. K. Leballo, the National Secretary of the PAC. Born in 1925 just inside the border of Basutoland (now Lesotho), Leballo had been educated at Lovedale. During the Second World War, he had served in the Army and was sent to North Africa, where he quickly earned notoriety as a black troublemaker. After his discharge from the forces, he returned to school, and later taught in Ladybrand and Pretoria. Virtually a founding member of the Africanist group of the Youth League, he participated actively in the 1952 Defiance Campaign and was dismissed from school as a result. Expelled (or resigning, as he maintains) from the ANC in 1958, he had rallied the Africanist forces at the ANC's Transvaal Congress against the Charterists. He was elected National Secretary at the inaugural conference of the PAC, and since 1963 it is he who has led the group in the absence of Sobukwe. As we have seen, Sobukwe was arrested on 21 March. Leballo, who had also been jailed, but was released, settled in Basutoland (still under British rule) and assumed control of the PAC underground from headquarters in Maseru, preparing the mass uprising.

Sobukwe himself was also supposed to have been freed on 3 May, after serving his sentence for the pass offence, but the Government passed a special law on 1 May, permitting indefinite detention of political prisoners. This repressive measure is now known as the 'Sobukwe clause' and is still in effect in South Africa, although after his seven years in solitary confinement on Robben Island the South African Government made a gesture to appease world opinion and transferred Sobukwe to Kimberley, 300 miles from his home in Johannesburg, where he was held under house arrest. Living in a government-selected house, he was kept under intensive police surveillance and was not allowed out of the house twelve hours of the day. A former university instructor, who had even continued his studies during his imprisonment on Robben Island, Sobukwe was now banned from entering any university, college, school, or other educational institution. He was also prohibited from publishing or assisting in the publishing of anything, and banned from both political and social gatherings. Furthermore, he was ordered not to communicate with anyone on the Government's lengthy list of banned persons. Early in 1970, the Government refused to allow him to leave South Africa to accept a teaching post at the University of Wisconsin in the United States. His health was reported to be poor, but it was clear the white regime still feared him.

The name given the angry gangs that attacked whites was *Poqo*. According to Leballo, as reported by a former PAC official, the belief that they were part of a completely independent organization was false. The word *Poqo* was part of a PAC slogan: *Um Africa Poqo*, which meant 'unadulterated African nationalist', and had been used as a code name by the Western Cape Region of the PAC as far back as 1960.[1] A Government Commision of Inquiry into the Paarl riots had speculated that

[1] Matthew Nkoana in *Crisis in the Revolution* (London, Mafube Publications, 1969), claimed it began in Port Elizabeth in 1961, but Bantu Methodists were using the term when they broke with the white Church in the thirties.

Poqo was another name for PAC. Leballo not only confirmed this, but reportedly disclosed at a press conference the approach of a massive uprising, which he claimed would be led by 150,000 PAC underground fighters throughout South Africa who were impatiently awaiting the signal from Maseru. Leballo was later sharply criticized for these disclosures, which were considered by some PAC men to have been totally uncalled for in the circumstances. Nevertheless, it was just at this time that the PAC acquired its first white member, the formerly Liberal activist Patrick Duncan, son of a former Governor-General of South Africa. Announcing that he had abandoned all hope of change in South Africa through peaceful means, Duncan was to work selflessly until his death in 1967, organizing on behalf of the PAC and publicizing its stand abroad.

PAC members had been quietly leaving South Africa since 1961, although not in numbers as large as those of the ANC, which had wholeheartedly decided upon the formation of an organization in exile. Moreover, once their mission abroad was terminated or training completed, the PAC men usually settled as close to the borders of South Africa as possible, awaiting the call to return. Within the mountainous enclave of Basutoland (now Lesotho), which had successfully resisted the full fury of Boer expansionism in the nineteenth century, the PAC also built up its forces. It was fortunate perhaps in Leballo's birth within the borders of the tough little kingdom and in the close ties that had developed between PAC leaders and equally nationalist and Pan-Africanist-oriented leaders, such as Nstu Mokhehle, of the Basutoland Congress Party. Mokhehle was anathema to the Congress Alliance, which wasted large sums in creating the Maremathlou Freedom Party to oppose the BCP. The summit of absurdity, however, was the formation of a minuscule Moscow-backed Lesotho Communist Party, headed by the SACP–ANC stalwart Joe Matthews, the son of Professor Z. K. Matthews who had issued the fatal call for the Freedom Charter and the Congress of the People. In any case, although the BCP remained quite separate from the PAC, whose exile headquarters were in Maseru, there was no question about their sympathy for their fellow Africans fighting against the Pretoria regime.

Inside South Africa, regional chairmen and other officers were organizing under cover for the day of the uprising. Co-ordinating their efforts and acting as chairman of the Presidential Council in the absence of Sobukwe was Leballo. By now fully alerted to the activities across the border, the South African Government demanded action by the British Government in the territory under its rule. On 2 April 1963,

British police—aided by South African policemen in plain clothes— raided PAC headquarters in Maseru, arresting thirteen members of the party and seizing all documents. The wily Leballo escaped, however, and after pressure had been put on the British Government and the warrant for his arrest was withdrawn, in September 1964, he was able to reach Tanzania, where the PAC had another external mission. Meanwhile, thousands of suspected African militants were rounded up throughout South Africa in a bid to crush any efforts at a generalized uprising. Undoubtedly, the material seized in Maseru aided in these massive arrests, but the amount of the information found in the Basutoland office of the PAC has since been greatly exaggerated by the ANC and other adversaries of Leballo, who repeatedly castigate him, and the PAC in general, for 'irresponsibility'.

The March 1963 raid in Basutoland did not, however, suppress all PAC activities there. The headquarters simply went underground, transferring its activities to more remote areas of the rugged country. A 'Presidential Council' was formed to handle the work of the National Executive Committee and National Working Committee. However, since the police raid, the highest powers of the PAC were actually exercised by the party's main external mission in Dar es Salaam. The presence of Leballo in Tanzania or neighbouring Zambia gave these decisions authority, but nevertheless they had only the force of recommendation when they were transmitted secretly to Basutoland for ulterior retransmission inside South Africa. Couriers were able to pass successfully through the Republic of South Africa, despite the surveillance of the Special Branch and military intelligence.

Only against this background can we understand the frenetic decision of Chief Leabua Jonathan, backed by Pretoria, to cling to power by a coup on 27 January 1970, rather than accept the democratic victory of the BCP in the general elections. The action brought violence to nominally independent Lesotho itself, but police measures to crush the BCP and PAC mountain strongholds were far short of decisive. The BCP was solicited to join in a coalition with Leabua Jonathan's minority National Party, with the proviso that the PAC exiles be either expelled from the country or compelled to cease their political activity.

In any case, from 1963 on there could no longer be any question of Africans seizing power in South Africa suddenly, almost magically, through a massive uprising. With reluctance and resignation, the leadership of the PAC turned to the concept of protracted struggle which had been brilliantly developed by the Communist Party of China during twenty-five years of revolutionary combat.

Inside South Africa, the PAC's seventeen regions continued to function, although with extreme difficulty. Real activity was organized around cells within the framework of branches. Each branch had a minimum of fifteen members, which indicates the reduced dimensions of the once vast mass movement. According to the region, the individual cells could have up to ten or twelve members, generally far less. They operated on a layer system for security's sake, so that members of one cell had no knowledge of the identity of members of another cell.

The intensity of the PAC's efforts can best be measured in the numbers of its members who were apprehended by the police. By 1970, more than 13,000 PAC militants were reported held inside South African prisons. And a total of ninety-seven freedom fighters had been hanged for their opposition to the apartheid regime.[1]

Throughout history, exile movements have been noted for their internal dissension and splits. Lack of funds and the indifference, even antipathy or hostility, of outsiders—including sometimes their hosts—and increasing isolation from the masses and the realities of the struggle at home, encourage every sort of personality conflict, loss of morale, and progressive fragmentation of the exile movement. None of the South African liberation movements has been an exception to this rule. However, the PAC was able to keep in closer touch with the realities at home through its Maseru headquarters, literally buried in the midst of South Africa. The rundown of morale and confidence after the failure to keep the grand appointment of 1963 was much more serious and had other causes. Some even wondered if now anything could ever be done in their lifetime to reverse the regime in South Africa, and their part-time studies and other employment in various parts of the world appeared more permanent than transient. Surprisingly, ideology played a far less important role—on the surface at least—than the clash of personalities, the charges and counter-charges of personal corruption and violation of a revolutionary code of behaviour. The continuing penury of the movement was the great stimulus to these quarrels, sometimes over petty sums of money and other favours from outsiders. Unless steeled by firm conviction that their cause is just and can achieve victory, poor men under any banner are for ever tempted and perhaps swayed.

Ironically enough, the influence of these feuds led at one point to the growth rather than decline of the PAC. The Coloured People's Congress, once part of the Congress Alliance, became increasingly out of step as its

---

[1] David Sibeko, 'Sharpeville, the Turning Point', in *10th Anniversary of Sharpeville* (Dar es Salaam, PAC, 1970).

President, Barney Desai, issued vehement appeals for revolutionary action. As a result of negotiations in London and clandestine contacts with leaders in Maseru and Cape Town, the Coloured People's Congress dissolved itself and its members joined the PAC. A communiqué announcing the move was issued in London in March 1966, negotiations having been conducted by Matthew Nkoana, then PAC representative. As Nkoana had long been at loggerheads with Leballo—who was later to be referred to in Nkoana's publications as the 'Monster'[1]—it was natural that Leballo should view with great suspicion the entry into the PAC of the former CPC leaders. Three of these—Barney Desai, Cardiff Marney, and Kenneth Jordaan—were given seats on the PAC's National Executive Committee. But instead of adding their votes to those of the beleaguered Leballo's enemies, the CPC-ers for a while supported Leballo, even against their original sponsor, Nkoana.

Ultimately, the entry of the CPC into the PAC was to have little practical importance. They were not the first Coloureds to belong to the PAC but, in accepting their entry, the Maseru headquarters reaffirmed in the name of the party's underground masses the principle that Sobukwe had pronounced at the formation of the party, viz. that Coloureds should be considered fully African. Unfortunately, many Coloureds had been tempted into believing themselves superior to blacks because of their semi-privileged (though perilous) position in the South African hierarchy of racism. Even the many Trotskyite-inclined radicals among them were not always able to overcome this attitude. And it soon appeared that at least two of these Coloured radicals in the PAC believed so much in their superior wisdom that they envisaged the PAC as, eventually, a black body with a Coloured head. Without resort to racism or character assassination, this take-over bid was firmly squelched by Leballo and his associates in 1969. Nevertheless, the entry of the CPC had not been without moral value to the party and many honest revolutionary Coloured South Africans continued to look to the PAC.

In 1969, the extent of active Coloured support for the PAC was dramatically demonstrated by the arrest and mysterious death in Cape Town police station of Imam Abdullah Haroun. Imam Haroun was taken into custody in May after police claimed that he was recruiting Muslim pilgrims going to Mecca for training as PAC guerrillas in China. He was alleged to have been an active PAC militant and to have been setting up a terrorist unit inside South Africa. He died in September,

---

[1] Nkoana, op. cit., p. 50 ff.

before he could be brought to trial. The police claimed he had fallen down a flight of stairs. The post mortem disclosed that his body had twenty-six bruises, haematoma of the back, and a broken seventh right rib; but there was not a mark on the buttocks of the man who was supposed to have fallen down a flight of stairs. PAC spokesmen claimed that the Imam had died under torture.[1]

After the entry of the former CPC-ers into the PAC, the ANC was once again, obliged to similar initiate action to that taken by the PAC. Reg September, former Secretary of the CPC, who had not gone with Desai to the PAC, was hired as 'Coloured Affairs Officer' of the ANC's London office. September was not considered a member of the ANC, however, as the more nationalistic Africans protested that the Congress Alliance existed only *inside* South Africa. Their protests were not directed against September personally, but mainly against the white South Africans, especially the SACP-ers, who believed it their destiny to lead the black masses. Eventually, as we have seen, the Alliance was reaffirmed and extended abroad. September was even to become official representative of the ANC in London.

As for the PAC, persistent internal strife resulted in the creation of a 'Revolutionary Command' around Leballo and a re-examination of the organization's strategy. This reorganization followed a take-over bid in 1967 by the Treasurer, A. B. Ngcobo, and Educational Secretary, Peter Roboroko, and resulted in the elimination of these two from the leadership.

The PAC office on Mkwepu Street, in Dar es Salaam, near the cable office, was temporarily closed as the opposing factions clashed. African Liberation Committee Executive George Magombe quickly restored a semblance of calm and organized a meeting of the PAC National Executive Committee in Moshi from 19–22 September. This crucial meeting reaffirmed Leballo's leadership, and afterwards Leballo was received personally by Tanzanian Second Vice-President Rashidi Kawawa.

According to the communiqué issued by Leballo following the Moshi meeting, the gathering had been marked by 'brutally frank discussion' and 'rigorous but healthy self-criticism'. In his main address to the meeting, Leballo mentioned the transfer of PAC external headquarters from Tanzania to Zambia. He praised the Zambian Government for 'keeping with the true Pan Africanist solidarity'.[2] The move to Lusaka—which was to be short-lived—was not platonic. The PAC leadership were

[1] *Azania Combat* (Vol. I, No. 5, 1970).

[2] PAC, *Report of the National Executive Committee Meeting, Moshi, Tanzania, 19th to 22nd September, 1967* (Lusaka, PAC, 1967).

hoping to use Zambia as a springboard for direct action against South Africa.

In his Moshi speech, Leballo outlined his plan of action. Gone were the sweet dreams of the general uprising of oppressed blacks and quick victory. 'The masses are ready for a long Revolutionary war', he now declared.[1]

As this 'Revolutionary Message to the Nation' remains the most authoritative and complete outline of the PAC's strategy, it is worth examination at greater length. Leballo first asserts the necessity of violent struggle to bring social change in South Africa. Although it has been maintained that revolution is impossible in well-armed, industrialized South Africa, Leballo denies, 'a thousand times over that our position is helpless. On the contrary, we contend that it is our business to make revolution—that is to persevere in our efforts to spark off the all-embracing spirit of revolt that is simmering just below the surface.' He praises both the revolutionary experience of China and Cuba, and the 'glorious example' of Vietnam for 'those colonial and ex-colonial peoples who dare to struggle for the expulsion of the invader from their countries'.

'But', say the liberals and reformists, 'the South African terrain is not suitable for guerrilla warfare. Where are your mountains and jungles? It is indeed revealing that the descendants of the Boers who fought a guerrilla war against British imperialism at the turn of the century—and held them at bay for three years—have not as yet put forward this proposition to subvert the incipient people's armed struggle.'

The basic requirement of guerrilla warfare is neither terrain nor weapons but 'complete integration of the guerrilla forces with the suffering of the masses'.

Mountains and jungles help the guerrilla—they don't in themselves become an indispensable requirement for armed struggle. Even so, an elementary knowledge of the physical geography of Azania (South Africa) reveals the existence of extensive mountain ranges—on a rough estimate they have a basic area of approximately 2,700 miles. There are large forests and dense bushes.

Because it is so industrialized, Leballo says, South Africa is in fact more vulnerable. 'Let there be no mistake about the fact that no industrial economy can stand a prolonged civil war without collapsing. South African industry, agriculture, as well as the country's highly exposed power and communications network, lie within range of the black revolutionaries.

Unlike classic guerrilla strategists of the past, Leballo insists on

[1] Ibid., p. 6.

carrying on the armed struggle in the cities as well as in the countryside. 'The strategically well-placed Azanians in the cities must be geared to act at the very earliest stages of the revolution. The revolution thus opens up a second front in the cities,' Leballo declares.

The PAC is well aware that this view does not fit in with the views of certain 'leading guerrilla strategists for whom we have the deepest respect and admiration'—undoubtedly none other than the leaders of China's protracted revolutionary war, and Mao Tsetung himself. Leballo boldly argues that the black fighting forces need the assistance of the urban masses who must open a second front in the cities 'to PIN DOWN THE ENEMY IN THE CITIES AT THE OUTSET'. Among the forms of urban action he stipulates are the general strike— a 'great traditional political weapon . . . employed on the eve of the overthrow of white tyranny'—the elimination of all known traitors and spies among the African population and the organization of illegal trade unions with military wings to carry out industrial and military action.

Leballo declares that the cities and towns must belong by night to the black masses, who will harass the white enemy with bombs and sniper fire, as many Afro-American communities have done in similar conditions. He pays tribute to Robert F. Williams, the black American revolutionary leader then living in China, who had sketched an apocalyptic vision of revolutionary violence and destruction in U.S. urban centres. 'The black insurrections in the American cities will show the Azanian masses in the cities of South Africa the potential strength they possess to terrorize, destroy and demoralize and defeat white supremacy,' Leballo argues.

Using the Maoist distinction between enemy and friend, Leballo opens the door to collaboration to all who in deeds will oppose the South African white-minority state, including the white liberal who, 'disgusted with the brutality of the system of apartheid, completely identifies himself in word and deed, with the aspirations of our people.' Leballo quickly adds there is no place for outsiders who 'insist on *imposing their* values on us in an effort to sidetrack our revolution. The white liberal comes into our struggle on *our own terms and accepting our* values.'

One of the reasons for the split that led to the Moshi meeting was the PAC stand on the possibility of United Nations intervention in South Africa. Roboroko and Ngcobo, along with delegates of the ANC, had presented a paper at the U.N. Seminar on Apartheid in Brasilia in August 1966, endorsing the notion of U.N. intervention. This appeal to the U.N. was denounced by Leballo as 'a deviation from PAC policy'. In his speech Leballo declares that revolutionaries have to rely above all on their own efforts, and in any case 'the U.N. is being used as the instrument of the U.S. foreign policy to crush or blunt revolutionary movements all over the world. We cannot therefore countenance the call for such U.N. intervention when we are dedicated to the proposition of an anti-imperialist, revolutionary struggle.'

Another cause of the split had been sordid squabbling over money raised by the party's external missions. Repeating his call for greater self-reliance, Leballo comments:

A party that therefore looks to the outside world for assistance, financially and militarily, before it has shown what it has achieved by relying on its own efforts, is not practising revolutionary self-reliance. This must be repeated for the benefit of those who regard the work of external missions as the *sine qua non* for the initiation of guerrilla war in their respective countries. These external missions, to be sure, use up much needed monies to support themselves outside their countries, when the people at home cry out for finances to help build up the movement. Thus external missions unavoidably tend to consume the very money they collect to support the armed struggle back home. This is especially the case where the external mission is in operation for a number of years during which time its personnel and administrative network have become considerably enlarged. The perpetuation of external missions is finally a confession of lack of faith in the creative powers of the people to overcome all obstacles and solve all difficulties which the armed struggle presents.

This comment of course could be applied to other liberation movements, especially the rival ANC, perhaps better even than the PAC.

In conclusion, Leballo reiterates the call for 'protracted armed struggle as the only way to obliterate all traces of white supremacy and imperialism! In such a struggle there are no dirty compromises against the best interests of the people. It needs therefore to be categorically asserted that the PAC does not believe in a *six-day-wonder-guerrilla war on unfamiliar territory and amongst politically ill-prepared population groups.*' Thus, relying on an ideological arsenal extending from Chairman Mao to Frantz Fanon, the PAC Acting-President and head of its Revolutionary Command criticizes the joint raids of ANC–ZAPU into Rhodesia and commits his own party to a necessarily lengthy, self-reliant armed struggle inside South Africa, conducted simultaneously in the cities as well as in the countryside.

Stifling their own internal dissensions and announcing their strategic plans, the PAC leadership also announced their organization's readiness to accept 'in principle' a united front with 'all forces fighting for liberation' of South Africa. In a memorandum presented by the PAC to the O.A.U.'s African Unity Conference in Kinshasa, also in September 1967, the PAC announced it was prepared to work together with rival organizations. The memorandum had also obliquely criticized the ANC's disastrous Rhodesian raids, declaring: 'Problems of language, terrain and the cardinal requirement of mass support make it difficult, if not impossible, for guerrillas to operate in territories from which they do not originate.' The ANC did not take the advice nor did it even agree to discuss the possibility of a united front with the PAC.

Less than a year after the Moshi meeting, the PAC gave tragic proof that it intended to carry the struggle into South Africa. In June 1968, the organization confirmed Portuguese military reports that a PAC military unit had been discovered several hundred miles inside Mozambique while attempting to cross the Portuguese colony in an effort to reach South Africa. In Dar es Salaam, PAC spokesmen admitted the unit had been wiped out and its 27-year-old leader—identified as Gerald Kibwe Kondlo—killed with several of his men. Several others were captured, while a few lucky survivors eventually made their way back to Zambia, their jumping-off point.

Zambian Government officials, who claimed not to have been informed of the PAC thrust towards South Africa, were furious. Zambia's President Kenneth Kaunda had repeatedly declared his opposition to a war against South Africa at a time when Zambia was heavily dependent upon the apartheid republic. On the other hand, Kaunda had far fewer objections to attacks against the Smith regime in Rhodesia.

For the PAC, the discovery of its guerrillas in Mozambique was an embarrassment and a tragic setback, but the group's leaders insisted their men were only transiting the Portuguese colony, not going there to wage a substitute war for the one they could not fight at home. The unit that had been caught by the Portuguese was merely an advance party, trained in China and other countries in guerrilla warfare techniques and the science of making weapons and munitions from locally available materials. It had hoped that such a unit could set up the nucleus of a liberated zone in rural South Africa and there begin training an indigenous Azanian Liberation Army. Although this first effort had failed, PAC leaders were convinced that their strategy was the only one that might work at the early stage of the struggle, when black freedom fighters would have to rely entirely on their own skills and limited local resources.

In any case, the Zambian Government expressed its displeasure by withdrawing all facilities from the PAC. Its military camp was closed, as well as the Lusaka office, and all its personnel were bundled out of the country, most of them rejoining their comrades in Dar es Salaam. Officially, the Zambian Government said it acted as it did because of renewed feuding between the PAC top leadership. Another set of leaders had denounced Leballo—this time, T. T. Letlaka and Z. B. Molete—and went so far as to announce that he had been 'expelled' from the PAC because he was a 'non-citizen of South Africa' (he had been born in Lesotho). Once again the A.L.C.'s George Magombe intervened and Leballo's leadership was reaffirmed. His rivals left Tanzania.

There is nothing unique about the dissension within the PAC, except that it has often received extensive publicity while other liberation movements, particularly the ANC, have been more successful in hiding their inner-party struggles. However, as we shall see, the Mozambique Liberation Front (FRELIMO) ruling triumvirate was to tear itself apart after the murder of Eduardo Mondlane. And there were similar splits between leaders of numerous other organizations. In the PAC, the feuds have almost always centred around the personality of Leballo, who sometimes inspires as much revulsion among contenders for the PAC leadership as apparent admiration and respect among the party's rank and file in the difficult conditions of the camps. Perhaps also important for his continued leadership has been Leballo's close working relationship with T. M. Ntantala, former PAC regional chairman in the Western Cape and military commander of the party's fighting forces.

The most consistent, tireless campaign against Leballo has been conducted from his London exile by Matthew Nkoana, a former regional chairman in South Africa and later representative in London. Himself a convinced idealistic Pan-Africanist, Nkoana envisages an all-African united struggle against the white-minority regimes in Southern Africa, and he has sharply castigated both the PAC and the Zimbabwe African National Union for their criticism of the ANC–ZAPU alliance which he believes is based on a ' "my country" type' of mentality. '*A decisive halt must be called to the squabbles among the rival organizations, so they can get on to serious discussion and planning. Don't let the chauvinistic tail wag the revolutionary dog.*'[1] Amidst worldwide conflicts of the second half of the twentieth century whether overt or covert, such an appeal for unity seems both naïve and unrealistic. While Nkoana's own determined campaign against Leballo—with later attacks on Leballo's supposed mentor, A.L.C. Executive Secretary George Magombe—has not provided the example of how to create unity even inside one organization.

Styling himself Secretary/Treasurer, Nkoana set up a 'Reorganization

[1] Nkoana, op. cit., pp. 78–9. Italics in original.

Convention Co-ordination Committee' from his North London home to rally the anti-Leballo forces. Relying mainly on contacts with disillusioned South African students in Europe and America, he sought to displace all the 'warring factions of the PAC leadership' and set up a convention of the PAC in exile to restructure the party. Nkoana has received little encouragement from Africa for his project; but clearly a means of bringing back into the struggle the numerous disaffected elements scattered about the world would be a great boon and source of strength, especially as the years advance and younger leaders are needed.

Even without prodding from Nkoana, the PAC under Leballo has established warm fraternal relationships with certain other liberation movements such as ZANU and the National Union for Total Independence of Angola (UNITA). So far, however, there has been neither desire nor necessity for formal alliance with any other party. When making the attempt to reach South Africa through Mozambique in 1968, the PAC worked both with the Mozambique Revolutionary Committee (COREMO) and its rival FRELIMO. Its men benefited from informal assistance from both organizations' local field commanders. However, FRELIMO leaders in Dar es Salaam rebuffed feelers from the PAC for a formal working arrangement that would assist the South Africans in reaching their own country.

Nkoana took an uncritical view of the 1969 Khartoum conference sponsored by the Russians, and preferred to ignore Soviet political purposes in organizing the gathering in the hope of seeing its promise of unity extended to other groups. Unlike him, the PAC leadership reiterated their appeal for a united military command of all groups fighting against the Pretoria regime, but condemned the Khartoum meeting as 'splitist'. Those who attended the conference—Russians, Eastern European and pro-Moscow communists, and 'progressives' from elsewhere, who outnumbered African freedom fighters—were accused of seeking to further 'Soviet ambitions of sharing world domination with the U.S. imperialists, strangulating the socialist republics of Albania and China, genuine friends of the African liberation struggle, and boost puppet regimes in Africa, Asia and Latin America.'[1] In any case, there was no question where the PAC stood in regard to the Sino-Soviet dispute. Even the fractious Nkoana repeatedly quoted from Chairman Mao in his lengthy polemics with Leballo.

In 1970, Leballo was again the object of criticism from some quarters because of his involvement in the Tanzanian treason trial of seven associates of former TANU Secretary-General Oscar Kambona.

[1] Sibeko, op. cit., p. 6.

Kambona was accused of seeking from his exile in London to over-throw the regime of President Julius Nyerere. The prosecution's main witness was no other than Leballo, who allegedly had been in close secret contact with Kambona and his friends, reporting the entire plot to the Tanzanian authorities. While some saw this as unwarranted interference in Tanzania's domestic and political affairs by a foreign political party, Leballo defended his action vigorously. He claimed that Kambona was 'anti-China' and under the influence of both Western and Eastern blocs and would have halted all Tanzanian assistance to the PAC and other troublesome liberation movements that might not fit into some Washington–Moscow agreement on Africa. Whether or not this was fanciful, it was clear that Leballo would remain loyal to those he believed were aiding his struggle, whether President Nyerere of Tanzania or the ousted President Kwame Nkrumah of Ghana, who still remains a hero to the Pan-Africanists. For his part, Nkoana again called for an examination of the workings of the office of A.L.C. Executive Secretary George Magombe, who had accompanied Leballo to London on one of the trips on which Leballo allegedly secretly met Kambona.

The biggest problem for the PAC, however, remained how to reach the borders of South Africa and merge with the black masses within in a revolutionary struggle. The obstacles were distance, lack of material and money, and faint-heartedness on the part of governments whose territory would provide the initial operational bases. Key to the puzzle was Zambia, and it was believed that only the completion of the Tanzam Railway by the Chinese would change the negative attitude of its Government. The personalities of the PAC leaders naturally have considerable bearing on the conduct of the struggle, but essentially the appeal or lack of appeal of this movement will depend on the attach-ment of the African majority of a future black South Africa in arms to the values of African nationalism. Even if the PAC abroad were to collapse, it is hard to believe that the oppressed, exploited black masses would accept readily the multiracial vision of South Africa proposed by the Congress Alliance, with its insistence on class, not race, in that land in which oppression and exploitation are based on gross racial distinc-tion.

In the struggle between white and black in South Africa, the PAC has clearly great objective and subjective potentiality as the revolutionary party of the blacks, no matter how small or divided the party may remain in exile.

PART THREE:
SOUTH WEST AFRICA (NAMIBIA)

South West Africa National Union (SWANU)

South West African People's Organisation (SWAPO)

The Background

To the Portuguese sailors, who first landed there and hastily left in 1484, and the other European adventurers who followed them, the arid wastes of the Namib Desert, waterless, uninviting dunes that stretched as far as the eye could see, were the 'coast of death' or the 'skeleton coast'. Only the discovery of diamonds in quantity attracted human beings to this sandy strip of land, although not all of South West Africa was so uninviting. The whites arrived belatedly nevertheless, literally hundreds of years after European settlement in South Africa to the south or the Portuguese colony of Angola to the north. The first Europeans to stay for any length of time were British missionaries at the beginning of the nineteenth century. The most important of these—the London Missionary Society—transferred the cultivation of black and brown souls in 1840 to the Bremen-based Rhenish Mission Society, thus paving the time-honoured path to full German colonial rule by May 1885.

The British, who had been divided about the profitability of colonization of South West Africa, had already acquired the best natural harbour on the bleak coast, Walvis Bay, in 1878. The Germans had to content themselves with the second-best harbour, named Luderitz after the German trader from Bremen who had wangled patronage in the form of a proclamation of imperial protection and a gunboat from Bismarck. Bismarck was host to the Berlin Conference of 1884–5, at which the European imperialists carved up the map of Africa under the guise of philanthropy, equally desirous of bringing the native the benefits of Christianity and commerce.

The indigenous peoples of South West Africa had been weakened by tribal divisions and especially the ruinous wars of Herero and Nama peoples. They were to prove nonetheless capable of unity in the unequal struggle against German colonial troops and their Krupp weapons.

South West Africa, covering 318,216 square miles, is larger than France and Britain put together, nearly as large as Nigeria, but, with a population estimated in 1966 at less than 700,000, it is the most sparsely populated country south of the Sahara. Europeans, more than a quarter of them still German-speaking, constitute only 15·73 per cent of the total population. About 67 per cent of these whites are Afrikaans-speaking descendants of the Dutch settlers in South Africa, while only 10 per cent are English-speaking.[1]

More than 44 per cent of the African population is made up by the Ovambos, a large tribal group who by South African law are confined to the northern area of the country, along the Angolan border—and in fact the tribe, as in other parts of Africa arbitrarily sliced up by ignorant and unconcerned whites, is divided by the border: its members are found on both sides. The Ovambos are farmers but, without irrigation, their flat, malarial, tsetse fly infested, grassy lands produce only subsistence yields in good years, and the men must emigrate to support their families. By law, none can leave his area without a work contract and a pass. Labour recruiting offices provide these contracts for twelve to eighteen months of virtual indentured servitude, and ship the men off to the mines in the south.

The mines are all white-owned, run from South Africa if not from Europe or America, and are among the most profitable enterprises of their kind in the world. Consolidated Diamond Mines of South West Africa Ltd. is controlled by De Beers and produces 99·6 per cent of South West Africa's diamonds.[2] The American Newmont Mining Corporation and American Metal Climax are among the biggest shareholders in the giant Tsumeb Corporation and, along with the South West Africa Company Ltd., General Mining Corporation, the Canadian Rio Tinto, West German, and even Japanese interests, exploit the rich sub-soil, bringing to the surface copper, lead, zinc, tin, manganese, chrome, lithium, gold, and anything else of value on the world's markets. Without cheap black labour, as in South Africa, the exploitation of this wealth would not be as profitable as it is.

After the Ovambo, the next largest tribal group are the Hereros, a Bantu-speaking people who, in the past—at least five centuries ago—immigrated to South West Africa from somewhere west of Lake Tanganyika. A portion of the tribe fled to what is now Botswana, after or during the Herero-Nama-German war of 1904–7. Mainly pastoral by tradition, the Herero were a rich, cattle-raising people when the first missionaries settled among them. After their catastrophic defeat by the Germans in the Herero-German war of 1904–7, the Hereros were banned by law from raising cattle in order to make them available as manpower for the European farms and mines. Yet somehow the

[1] Muriel Horrell, 'Aspect géographique du Sud-ouest Africain', *Civilisations* (No. 3, 1967).
[2] Ruth First, *South West Africa* (Harmondsworth, Penguin, 1963).

cattle-raising tradition survived among the Herero in South West Africa which—below the parched farmlands of Ovamboland, where millet is the chief crop—is excellent ranching country. While the Ovambo were lucky enough to live virtually untouched in their northern area, the Hereros and their traditional tribal enemies, the Namas (a Khoisan people, who were labelled Hottentot by the Dutch) came into bitter conflict with the European invaders. Eventually, the happiest result of this was the fostering of unity between Herero and Nama in battle against the German colonists.

Other peoples are Damara, or Berg-Damara—8·23 per cent of the population—whose more negroid features and darker skins make them slightly different in appearance from other tribes. These suffered in the past from both their stronger neighbours, Herero and Nama, who held them as slaves or drove them to the west of the country.

Also to be found—forming about 1 per cent of the population—are a small group of Tswana, who predominate in neighbouring Botswana, and Bushmen—2·18 per cent of the population—a hunting-gathering folk of simplicity who, by flight into the Kalahari, managed to survive massacres by Dutch settlers, or slavery.

Finally, there are two groups of Coloureds, persons of mixed African and European origin. The most remarkable of these are the so-called 'Rehoboth Basters', Afrikaans-speaking descendants of Boer farmer and Nama women who trekked up from the Cape in the latter half of the eighteenth century to form an independent, half-caste—or 'Bastard'—territory, the Rehoboth Gebiet. They acquired their land in what is now South West Africa through negotiations with a Nama chief, later approved in 1870 at a meeting of Herero and Nama at Okahandja. When the Germans landed, the Rehobothers concluded a treaty with them that granted German protection to a sovereign Rehoboth community and left them their own criminal and civil law. The other half of the Coloured population is composed of Coloureds from South Africa who have migrated to South West Africa, where they hold skilled and semi-skilled jobs. The Rehobothers constitute 2·24 per cent, and the Coloureds from South Africa 2·52 per cent of the population.[1]

Although some Afrikaners in South Africa came over to the German side at the beginning of the First World War, as we have seen, their rebellion was quickly crushed by the loyal Boer generals Botha and Smuts. The German masters of South West Africa were completely vanquished by 1915. Except for German officers and functionaries, the

---

[1] All population figures from Horrell, op. cit.

vast majority of German settlers were allowed to remain in the colony, which was placed under League of Nations Mandate and administered directly by South Africa. International interest in South West Africa has been great since 1946, when the fledgling United Nations refused South Africa permission to annex the territory completely into the Union. In due course, the white-minority regime in Pretoria was to go ahead regardless of the world organization and the legal squabble has been resounding ever since in the various Councils of the U.N. and the International Court of Justice at the Hague. The South African Government claims that the Mandate of the League gave it rights to administer South West Africa as an integral portion of South Africa and that full responsibility for South West Africa devolved solely upon South Africa, rather than the new United Nations, after the dissolution of the League in 1945.

An elaborate challenge to South African rule, presented by Ethiopia and Liberia had been argued before the International Court of Justice for nearly six years when, in 1966, the Court held by a majority of one that neither of these two states had established any legal right or claim in the subject. The Court specifically stated that it was not pronouncing on the merits of the case or on continuing South African rule over South West Africa, but the decision was generally considered as a major victory for South Africa. A strong dissenting opinion was voiced by Judge Philip C. Jessup of the United States, and the independent black African states who had supported the Ethiopia–Liberia case (because, of all the African members of the U.N., only Ethiopia and Liberia had been members of the defunct League of Nations) were bitterly disappointed.[1]

This decision and the subsequent impotence of the U.N. to do anything more than vote platonic resolutions concerning the illegality of continuing South African rule naturally gave strong impetus to the organization of the armed struggle against the usurping South African regime.

On 21 June 1971, the International Court of Justice rendered an 'advisory' opinion that backed up the decision of the United Nations that the mandate of the Republic of South Africa over South West

[1] Voting for the majority decision was the President of the Court, Sir Percy Spender (Australia), who also gave the casting vote that broke the tie among the fourteen judges on the Court. Also voting for the decision were the judges from Britain, Greece, Italy, France, South Africa, and Poland. Mr. B. Winiarsky, the Polish judge, later retired in the West rather than return home. The dissenting votes came from the United States, U.S.S.R., Japan, Nationalist China, Mexico, Senegal, and Nigeria. See *The Times* (19 July 1966).

Africa should be revoked and that the territory should be administered, pending full independence, by a U.N. commission. The Court's ruling was a thirteen to two decision, with negative votes cast by the British and French judges. On the other hand, the United States Government had strongly supported revocation of the South African mandate. The Court's ruling declared:

The continued presence of South Africa in Namibia [the name given the territory by the United Nations] being illegal, South Africa is under an obligation to withdraw its administration immediately and thus put an end to its occupation of the territory.

In an editorial on 23 June 1971, the *New York Times* hailed the Court's decision as a 'clear verdict' for an end to South African rule. Despite U.S. political support for the decision, the American newspaper ruefully noted that 'Washington is not prepared to support economic sanctions, let alone military action' against South Africa to enforce the decision of the World Court. South African Prime Minister John Vorster accused the Court of anti-South African bias and rejected its verdict, which left the African nationalists still obliged to conduct an armed struggle for their now internationally recognized right to eventual independence.

Consistent with its policies within its own undisputed boundaries, the South African Government has gradually introduced into South West Africa all the racist refinements of the apartheid system. The mainly Afrikaner and German white population was quickly given representation in the South African Parliament after the Afrikaner Nationalists took power under Dr. Malan in 1948. The Nationalists needed the votes of the white electorate of only 24,000 at that time, who were given six seats in the lower House of Assembly and four Senators in the upper house. All have been staunch supporters of apartheid ever since.

In addition, the Europeans of South West Africa elect a Legislative Assembly of eighteen members, which sits in Windhoek, the capital. Pretoria directly controls defence, security, foreign affairs, 'Bantu affairs', immigration, and customs, while the territorial assembly governs all other domains. Executive powers are exercised by an Executive Committee composed of the Administrator, who is president of the Legislative Assembly, and four members elected by the Assembly. Coloureds elect members to an advisory Coloured Council, while the Africans are left to their tribal councils and the mercies of the Ministry of Bantu Affairs in Pretoria.

As a leading South West African, Mburumba Kerina, declared in 1965 before the U.N. General Assembly's Fourth Committee:

The catalogue of atrocities perpetrated by the South African Government against our people is well known to this Committee and to many of the distinguished representatives who have kept the light aflame at the United Nations on the South West African problem for the past 20 years. Although apartheid and oppression is evident in many parts of the colonial countries, nowhere is it so lustily pursued as in South West Africa. Our people are enslaved and penned like beasts of burden in the land of their birth. Yet their determination to free themselves from South African colonialism remains as firm as the 'Rock of Gibraltar'.[1]

Even if the United Nations could never do anything effective to remedy the sufferings of the Africans, it did at least provide their representatives with a rostrum to air their woes. The same was also done for representatives of the black majority in South Africa, but, while the South African regime could argue that its peculiar Bantu affairs were purely domestic and hence beyond the pale of the world body, the very history of the Mandate, regardless of the strange decision of the world court, implied that South West Africa was an international question that eventually grew into a dispute pitting Pretoria against the United Nations, exposing the white-minority regime as an international outlaw over South West Africa. As Fordham notes: 'It is thus a far more significant country than its population, resources, and state of development alone would warrant.'[2]

But if only one thing were to be remembered about South West Africa, it ought to be more than obvious to anyone that it is *not* South Africa. No matter how closely it is integrated into the white Republic, geography and the history of the peoples of what some South West Africans and the United Nations itself now choose to call 'Namibia' proves the separate national existence of this land. Their growing unity in struggle against their oppressors should eventually lead to the creation of an African state, independent of its neighbours to the south. Despite the massive build-up of white troops and police in the country, South West Africa is clearly a weak link in Pretoria's racist empire.

The Resistance

The Germans in South West Africa behaved very much like colonists everywhere but, because they were antagonists against Britain in the

---

[1] U.N. Document 65-44476, *Statement Made by Mr. Mburumba Kerina at the 1565th Meeting of the Fourth Committee* (23 November 1965).

[2] Fordham, op. cit., p. 227.

great imperialist struggle of 1914–18, their record of atrocities was gleefully made known to the world by their victorious enemies. However, the British did not have to embellish the sordid record. Here was a clear-cut case of mass extermination if ever there was one, even perhaps genocide, but the world had not yet invented the word.

The early years of German colonization had been marked by efforts under the direction of an Imperial Commissioner—a Dr. Göring, whose son Hermann was to become notorious as the Nazi leader—to sign treaties of protection with the tribal leaders. Those who would not sign were attacked by German troops without warning, like the Nama Chief Hendrik Witbooi in 1890. Witbooi escaped to fight on against the encroaching whites. But others, like the Bondels people, a small tribe, were crushed by superior force. Nevertheless, it seemed for a while that as soon as the rapacious Germans had stifled one people another rose in rebellion against alien rule.

Of course, the German plan of colonization implied the removal of the tribes from their lands so that German settlers could have them. When they arrived in South West Africa, the first whites had noted the immense herds of cattle of the Herero. By fast trading and unmitigated theft, the Germans had taken more than half of the Herero cattle by 1903. Similar 'deals' were also depriving the Hereros and other tribes of much of their lands.

The spark of rebellion was set off by the Nama in 1903. The Nama war, following a period of inactivity after Witbooi's defeat, broadened into a nationwide Herero war by 1904, when 7,000 warriors under Chief Samuel Makarero—most of them without firearms—delivered a stunning blow to the Germans, who retreated into their coastal strongholds to await the arrival of reinforcements from home. They eventually arrived and began a campaign to exterminate the outgunned Hereros. A German colonial specialist, General von Trotha, was ordered to South West Africa. Experienced in the killing of non-whites in crushing the Boxer Rebellion in China and at the beginning of the Maji Maji War in Tanganyika, von Trotha issued a *Vernichtungsbefehl*, an order for the extermination of the defeated Hereros, men, women, and children. An estimated 60,000 Hereros were slaughtered by the German troops, while 2,000 Germans died in the fighting.

Chief Hendrik Witbooi led the Nama and most of the other southern tribes against the Germans. After a year of desperate, unequal battles, Witbooi was killed in battle, but the war continued despite his loss until 1907, under Chief Jacob Marenga. The bloody campaign reduced the 80,000 Herero to 15,000 starving refugees. Half of the Nama and

Damara had been exterminated also by the time of the complete German triumph. Then, the Herero were stripped of their lands and forbidden to raise cattle, thus transforming them into cheap labour for the Germans, who were already settling on their lands. The high period of German immigration began. The discovery of diamonds and the start of copper mining added to the prosperity of the 'pacified' colony. Railways were built and the harbours at Luderitz and Swakopmund developed. Many of the German troops remained behind as settlers on the lands taken from the Africans.

In the north, the Ovambos had escaped direct clashes with the Germans. To prevent any, the German Government had banned outsiders from entering Ovamboland unless they had received the special permission of the Governor. The well-armed, strongly organized Ovambos were obliged instead to ward off Portuguese encroachment from Angola in 1885 and 1902. The peoples of the central and southern areas of the country bore the brunt of German rapaciousness and were herded into impoverished reservations known as 'Native Reserves'.

The brutal facts about German colonization of South West Africa were published in a Blue Book in 1918 by a British Special Commission of Inquiry into German rule. Crammed with horrors, all quite true enough, the Report of the Commission was intended to convince world opinion that the defeated Imperial Germany was unfit to carry the white man's profitable burden in Africa and elsewhere. Had similar commissions been appointed in Indochina, North Africa, or the West Indies, they would have produced similar findings. Yet, the Germans— late starters in the race for colonies—had hardly been more frenzied in their greed or more cruel in their methods than the older European imperial powers had generally been in the past.

In any case, the First World War ended Germany's colonial ambitions. British troops from South Africa occupied South West Africa and, after the defeat of the outnumbered German force, it was ruled by martial law from 1915 to 1920. Under terms of Article 119 of the Versailles Treaty, the German Government ceded South West Africa to the principal Allied and Associated Powers. They passed on the country to Britain, which in turn handed administration of South West Africa to the Union of South Africa under the Class 'C' Mandate from the League of Nations to Britain.

This meant that, because of particular conditions of small population or remoteness or size, a territory was to be administered as an integral part of the mandatory power, subject to guarantees for the interests of the indigenous peoples. But for South Africa, the mandate was seen as a first step towards eventual annexation. In fact, South West Africa had secretly been promised to South Africa by the British Imperial War Cabinet, in which General Smuts was a member in 1914. Made before the United States entered the war, this agreement was bitterly opposed by President Woodrow Wilson of the United States.[1] But Wilson finally acquiesced on this as he did on many other issues. Officially, however, South Africa's mandate did not confer sovereignty over the territory, but merely the responsibility of administering it, in trust, on behalf of its peoples.

These administrative powers were entrusted by the South African Governor-General to an Administrator in South West Africa. European settlers were given the right in 1925 to elect Members to an all-white Legislative Assembly. One European member of the Administrator's Advisory Council was selected on the so-called grounds of his 'thorough acquaintance with the *reasonable wants* and wishes of the non-European races in the territory.'[2] The German settlers were given automatic naturalization and equal representation in this Assembly. General Smuts was personally very eager to unite all whites in the country to prevent any upsurge of African rebellion.

But rebellion there was. A Nama tribe, the Bondelswarts, infuriated by a dog tax that had been imposed upon them to oblige them to work for European settlers, protested against this tax. South African troops and planes crushed the protest in five days, killing a hundred men, women, and children. In 1917, King Mandume of the Ovambo, after fighting off Portuguese encroachment with heavy losses to his people, was forced to submit to the 'protection' of a South African force. The Portuguese and South Africans settled their dispute over the undefined border by tracing a line through the midst of the Ovambo people. But Mandume and his people refused not to cross the artificial border and they were attacked by the Europeans at Ondjiva. However, the king and his bodyguard escaped and allegedly committed suicide. According to a popular account, his head was later cut off as a trophy by the South Africans and taken in triumph to Windhoek where it was buried in a park which no African is still allowed to enter.

The mandate system provided for annual reports to be submitted to the League's Permanent Mandates Commission, composed of delegates from four non-mandate states and four from states holding mandates. The system was incredibly vague and weak, as P. T. Moon pointed out:

[1] U.N. Document 65-44476 (Kerina), op. cit., pp. 4–5.
[2] Ibid.

Charged with the responsibility of ensuring administration of the mandates in harmony with the humane principles of the Covenant (of the League of Nations), the League is nevertheless inadequately equipped with specific powers for the fulfilment of its task. It cannot, or does not, issue orders for the improvement of conditions, or injunctions to check objectionable practices.[1]

The Commission was found by First, who examined its working over a quarter of a century, to have been 'well enough informed, but finally powerless'.[2] The truth concerning conditions in the mandated territories emerged slowly through the patient questioning of South African representatives, and clause by clause examination of their report. But the Commission could not receive other reports or hear petitions from the aggrieved African population, or make on-the-spot investigations of its own and, most important of all, it could not publish a report of its findings concerning the situation in the territory.

Thus, the years passed in growing distress for the Africans until after the Second World War. A young generation of South West Africans came to the fore, joining the traditional tribal leaders, demanding justice for the black masses. Some young men, like Jariretundu Kozonguizi, had been educated in Fort Hare College and other South African schools and were caught in the upsurge of the Youth League that briefly revitalized the ANC. Others managed to go abroad through the help of missionary educators, or by devious means. As the United Nations had taken over from the defunct League and the members of the U.N. considered that South West Africa had now automatically become a trust territory under the Charter, Africans looked hopefully to the U.N. for relief.

At first, South Africa—while maintaining that South West Africa had not automatically become a trust territory—appeared to bow to the world body. But in 1950, when the International Court of Justice found that South West Africa was still a territory held under international mandate, the South African representatives announced their Government's decision to ignore this ruling and to treat the country as incorporated into South Africa. A host of angry Africans managed to find their way to New York to testify before the U.N.'s Fourth Committee, led by Mburumba Kerina in 1957—joining the Reverend Michael Scott, who had already been lobbying vigorously on behalf of the Africans. A Rehobother, Hans Beukes, was smuggled out of South West Africa by three adventurous Americans, Sherman Bull, Emory Bundy, and Allard Lowenstein. In 1959, Kozonguizi was sent by the

[1] P. T. Moon, *Imperialism and World Politics*, quoted in First, op. cit., p. 173.
[2] First, op. cit., p. 174.

Herero Chief's Council to speak for their people at the U.N. The Reverend Marcus Kooper had also made his way to New York, after an escape through Bechuanaland, to testify about the situation in Hoachanas. Beginning in 1946 with a single petition from the Herero and Nama Chiefs, a total of 120 petitions were sent to the Fourth Committee in 1960 alone.[1]

Thus, we have seen that a flame of resistance was kept alive by the tribal chiefs and their councils. Pressing ancient and all-but-forgotten claims and pointing to clauses of long-violated treaties with the Europeans, the tribes achieved nothing in the face of white determination to lay hold of their land and reduce them to virtual serfdom. But they were allowed to talk, if only to themselves, and their talking kept alive their peoples' feelings of the injustice done them and led them to seek other remedies.

The germ of modern political organization in South West Africa is to be found in the South West African Student Body, set up by South West African students in South Africa in 1952, and reconstituted in 1955 as the South West Africa Progressive Association (SWAPA). All later nationalist groups in the country have their roots in this student organization. Three names stand out among its members: those of Kerina, Kozonguizi, and Zedikia Ngavirue. In Cape Town, Kozonguizi also met Toivo Herman ja Toivo, an Ovambo ex-serviceman who was then working in South Africa and had gathered around himself a group of like-minded South West African expatriates of nationalist inclinations.

Active political organization within South West Africa began in 1958 and, although the South West African students in South Africa had hoped to see the formation of a truly national party, the organizations that came into existence were eventually all tribal-based. According to Kerina:

1. The Ovambo people found the Ovamboland Peoples' Congress, which later became known as the Ovamboland Peoples' Organization and finally changed into the South West Africa Peoples' Organization (SWAPO).
2. The Herero people together with the Mbanderu people found the South West Africa National Union (SWANU).
3. The Nama people found the South West Africa United National Independent Organization (SWANIO).
4. The Damara people found the South West Africa Democratic Union (SWADU).
5. The South African Coloureds living in South West Africa formed the notorious South West Coloureds Organization (SWACO).

[1] First, op. cit., p. 195.

6. The Rehoboth people formed the Rehoboth Burgers' Association, often referred to as the Bastersraad.
7. The Herero people also worked through the powerful chief's Council of the Honourable Hosea Kutako, which has played a vital role in the political awakening of the peoples of South West Africa before the appearance of political organization in the Territory.[1]

All these groups, with the exception of the South West Africa Coloureds' Organization (SWACO), opposed apartheid and the white-minority regime that ruled South West Africa from Pretoria. The Coloured group, under complete control by the South African Government, demonstrated the low political consciousness and confusion of the Coloureds who had settled in South West Africa and who appeared to believe promises from across the border that they would share in the exploitation of the unfortunate country.

Numerous abortive attempts at unity were made inside the country and abroad. In 1965, Kerina announced to the U.N. Fourth Committee the formation of a 'united, non-tribal revolutionary organization which will become the major national liberation party of our country'. Called the National Unity Democratic Organization (NUDO), and backed by such prominent personalities as Hosea Kutako, S. H. Witbooi, Clements Kapuuo, Hans Beukes, and by Kerina himself, NUDO nonetheless never came to life. An energetic lobbyist and spokesman on behalf of South West Africa, Kerina settled in New York with his Afro-American wife and their children. On one occasion he decided to return home to South West Africa, but was thwarted by numerous factors and got no farther than Botswana, from which he was eventually expelled. He went back to New York and soon announced the formation of yet another 'unity' movement, this one being called the South West Africa National United Front (SWANUF). It too withered on the vine, and Kerina settled more into the role of an expert and adviser on South West Africa to African delegations at the United Nations.

Of the seven tribal-based organizations listed by Kerina in 1965, only two remain vigorous enough to interest us here: SWANU and SWAPO —and one of them appeared at the beginning of the seventies to be barely clinging to life.

The South West Africa National Union (SWANU)

At the beginning, the roots of the two leading liberation movements of South West Africa were virtually the same. They could have been

[1] U.N. Document 65-44476 (Kerina), op. cit., p. 48.

merged into a single, nationwide body, if the young men had had their way, but tribal politics intervened. Chief Hosea Kutako of the Herero had been the leader of his people since 1904 and he remained in the leadership until his death at the age of about 100, in 1970. The petitioning to the United Nations had been initiated by the Herero and eventually all the African tribes joined, but their ancient tribal rivalries still left them suspicious of each other and rendered formation of a single national party impossible.

In schools in South Africa, the young men had belonged to a single South West African Student Body and at home they and others formed the South West Africa Progressive Association, led by Uatja Kaukuetu. This Association had made repeated efforts to create a unified national movement throughout South West Africa. When Toivo ja Toivo, the dynamic Ovambo expatriate leader, was expelled from South Africa in 1958 for having sent a tape-recorded petition to the United Nations to Mburumba Kerina, he and Jariretundu Kozonguizi travelled back to South West Africa together. There, they had talks with older leaders, such as Hosea Kutako and Clements Kapuuo, concerning the formation of a national movement. Kozonguizi was to organize in Windhoek, while Toivo continued north to his own people in Ovamboland, where he was kept under constant surveillance for years.

Kozonguizi was at this time delegated by the Herero tribe to join the Reverend Michael Scott at the United Nations as a petitioner. Since 1956, while the English missionary Scott had vigorously presented the African case, the only South West African petitioner had been Mburumba Kerina, who left South Africa with a passport under the name of Eric Getzen, and went to the United States where he obtained a scholarship to Lincoln University. Kerina had been in correspondence with Toivo in Cape Town and he offered to represent the new organization at the United Nations, where he already was a petitioner on credentials given by the South West African Student Body and Hosea Kutako for the Herero tribe.

Kozonguizi left for New York, via Bechuanaland, in February 1959. In April of that year, Sam Nujoma and Jacob Kuhangua set up the tribal-based Ovamboland Peoples' Organization (OPO), while the first South West Africa National Union came into existence in May, with Uatja Kautuetu as President. In September, SWANU's leadership was broadened and Nujoma and other OPO leaders were elected to the executive of what was to be the national organization.

Rivalry at home and abroad, however, prevented the consolidation of SWANU as a united national movement. In New York, there was tension between Kerina and Kozonguizi. Kerina wrote to Nujoma, demanding the extension of OPO into a national organization. 'The name SWAPO (South West African Peoples' Organization) was founded here in New York by Dr. Kerina in an attempt to make OPO a national organization,' one of his associates, Nathanael Mbaeva, told the U.N. Fourth Committee in 1965, when the ebullient Kerina had later broken with SWAPO.[1] Perhaps, because of the tribal squabbling at home, Nujoma did not need the hint from New York. In any case, Nujoma found himself in exile after the shooting at Windhoek's Old Location on 10 December 1959. Seeking to remove Africans to a new apartheid township called Katutura, police killed thirteen Africans, including a brother of Kerina, and wounded forty-two others. This carnage occurred five months before the Sharpeville-Langa massacre in South Africa itself.

Kozonguizi, who had been elected President of SWANU in the September elections, despite his absence, met Nujoma in Monrovia, Liberia, and the two young leaders jointly signed a letter calling for a merger of their two organizations at home. But nothing came of this gesture and the two organizations continued their separate courses, sometimes friendly and co-operative, but increasingly divided by ideological and personal conflicts as well as tribalism. Both groups continued to operate in quasi-legality in South West Africa, as well as functioning in exile.

Simplistic notions that SWANU is merely a Herero party are belied by a much more complex reality. At one point, the Herero Chief's Council, urged from New York by Kerina, virtually disowned SWANU. And the young men who built up SWANU in Windhoek and other centres of South West Africa repeatedly disavowed tribal politics. Yet SWANU leaders continually found themselves being involved in tribal politics.[2]

Abroad, SWANU became identified with the personality of Kozonguizi. At first, he played the role intended of him as petitioner at the United Nations and emissary to independent African governments. A SWANU office was established in Dar es Salaam and another in Cairo, where a number of South West African exiles had gathered.

Like its rival, SWAPO, SWANU originally pleaded for U.N. intervention in South West Africa. The legal case seemed so obvious to the Africans, they could not believe that the U.N. could fail to act on

---

[1] U.N. Document 65-44477, *Statement Made by Mr. Nathanael Mbaeva at the 1565th Meeting of the Fourth Committee* (23 November 1965).

[2] First, op. cit., gives a detailed account, Part Five, Section 4, pp. 196–208.

their behalf, if it wanted to keep faith with its Charter. But, led by Britain, which dreaded any racial conflict in Southern Africa that might harm the vast British interests in South Africa, the U.N. has never gone beyond voting platonic resolutions, and the long-awaited U.N. police force, 'with troops drawn from Afro-Asian and other uncommitted countries',[1] according to one SWANU programme, never materialized.

Kozonguizi appealed in vain for action. He declared:

The reformist approach to the struggle for liberation, reformism has had its time—fifteen years of petitioning, of 'Native conferences' with Native Commissioners, of deputations to the Secretary of South West Africa, of appeals to Macmillan. . . . We also reject the idea that our deliverance should rest entirely with the Big Powers. We appeal to all the states of the U.N. and particularly our brother states in Africa to *act* against South Africa but the right to *decide* remains vested in the people of South West Africa. It is for us to find the most effective methods to liberate ourselves.[2]

Kozonguizi, who had been a member of an African National Congress student branch during his days at Fort Hare College, tended to be sceptical of the Africanists and more sympathetic to the South African communists who, he felt, offered hope of action: hence his willingness to explore contacts with socialist countries. Ironically, it was SWAPO leaders who strongly objected when Kozonguizi spoke over Peking radio during a visit to China. Under Kozonguizi's leadership SWANU was to build close ties with the East, and especially with China, but this was before the Sino-Soviet split had burst into the open. At that time, SWAPO was attacked by SWANU for allegedly maintaining close connections with the American Metal Climax Corporation, which has large interests in South West Africa and reportedly had given grants to SWAPO members abroad. Thus, as a militant progressive group, SWANU became a member of the Afro-Asian Peoples' Solidarity Organization and attended the founding conference of the Tricontinental Organization in Havana on 3 January 1966.

When the Organization of African Unity was founded, SWANU welcomed the new body, but declined to create a military force under the sponsorship of the African Liberation Committee. Rather, Kozonguizi ridiculed the growing battalions of other liberation movements and predicted that in time they would become a headache to the O.A.U. and the movements themselves, in so far as the political situation did not permit the use of these freedom fighters in combat against South Africa. Another consideration perhaps that caused Kozonguizi to spurn the O.A.U. invitation to train South West African

[1] First, op. cit., p. 206.   [2] Quoted, ibid., p. 204.

freedom fighters was the quasi-legal nature of his party. SWANU still operated, despite growing difficulties, as an overt formal political movement inside South West Africa. South African authorities had not banned either SWANU or SWAPO at the time of the outlawing of the ANC and PAC and other groups in South Africa.

Whatever the reason for this decision, it was to prove a tactical mistake and the eventual cost to SWANU was the loss of O.A.U. support. The office in Dar es Salaam was closed and SWANU written off as a defunct organization, although SWANU continued to maintain an office in Cairo and to receive some limited support from the U.A.R. government. SWANU students and ex-students were scattered from Eastern Europe through Western Europe to North America.

Around Zedekia Ngavirue, a former social worker who had fled South West Africa after the shooting in 1959 at Windhoek Old Location, and Charles Kauraisa, a former school teacher, a group of SWANU members gathered in Sweden. There, with the backing of Swedish Social Democratic and other political and social groups, SWANU's External Council was formed, headed at first by Ngavirue. Later, in 1968, Kauraisa was to become Chairman of the six-man Council. Kozonguizi, the President of SWANU since September 1959, was never among its members.

When he had the time to spare from lobbying the U.N. and other travels, Kozonguizi studied law desultorily in London. Like almost all South West African exiles, he followed closely his country's case at the International Court of Justice at the Hague and often visited the Court. Despite the many bitter words about U.N. inaction, he and his comrades seemed convinced that the Court would have to find in their favour, and South Africa, pressured by world opinion, if not U.N. troops, would regurgitate their rugged homeland.

Differences which are not yet clear to outsiders, perhaps due more to personalities than politics, developed between Kozonguizi and the mainly Swedish-based External Council. Nevertheless, it was Kozonguizi who represented South West Africa at the Havana Tricontinental Conference in January 1966. SWANU had been invited because it was still a member of the Cairo-based Afro-Asian Peoples' Solidarity Organization, but the workings of this body were increasingly hampered by echoes of Sino-Soviet conflict. Some would-be delegates to the Havana gathering never got there. They complained that invitations and visas had been deliberately held up or 'lost' by pro-Russian elements in Cairo. (Delegations of the PAC and the Unity Movement— somehow managed to reach Havana, but were never admitted to the conference. Treated as simple tourists, they were lodged in the distant Habana Riviera Hotel, far from the conference at the Habana Libre Hotel in the heart of Vedado.)

The conference was dominated by a three-way struggle between the militant pro-Chinese groups, the pro-Russian groups and pro-Cuban organizations from Latin America and elsewhere. The strife was so evident that the leader of the Ghanaian delegation, John K. Tettegah, pleaded for calm, cautioning fellow delegates, 'It will serve us no purpose through our words to disarray and disrupt the very unity we are fighting for.'[1]

The pro-Russian elements, led by the ANC of South Africa, the Indian delegation, and the U.A.R. delegation, argued for unity based on maintenance of Soviet hegemony over the world's revolutionary movements. They rejected attacks on the concept of 'peaceful co-existence', the keystone of Soviet foreign policy in the Khruschev and post-Khruschev era. Khaled Mohiedin of the U.A.R. declared, 'Africa is well aware that peaceful coexistence is also a means of realising peace based on justice.'

On the other hand, the chief of the Japanese delegation, Shizuma Kai, insisted: 'We can never agree . . . to use "peaceful coexistence" as a pretext for suppressing the national liberation struggle in the countries under imperialist domination and subjecting it to the policy of "peaceful coexistence".'

As for unity, the head of the Chinese delegation, Wu Hsueh-tsuen, declared:

There are some people who maintain that they stand for 'united action' to wage a 'common struggle against the enemy'. But their actual deeds cannot but oblige us to raise the following questions:
With whom do they really take united action? And unity against whom? Why do they regard U.S. imperialism, the mortal enemy of the people of our three continents, as their principal ally, proclaiming that their policy of all-round co-operation with the United States will never change?
Why do they sabotage people's war and why do they preach here and there that 'a tiny spark can cause a world conflagration'?

At no time was there any opposition to the creation of a new international organization, although a number of Afro-Asian delegations, led by China, refused to discuss dissolution of the Cairo-based AAPSO or its simple merger into a new tricontinental solidarity organization.

---

[1] Conference document 64A-12-16. Unless otherwise stated, all following quotations in this section are taken from official documents of the Tricontinental Conference.

On the other hand, the Sov:et delegation originally fought for the new body to be located in Cairo. This position was strongly supported by the U.A.R. delegation, which maintained that Cairo was the 'natural capital of the Third World', and the ANC delegation, which protested vehemently that Havana was too far and too difficult to reach for representatives from Africa and Asia.

The matter was eventually solved by the personal intervention of Cuban Premier Fidel Castro, who talked with a number of African delegations and paid a call on the Chinese delegation. The Chinese voted for the Havana site. Faced with mounting opposition, the Soviet delegation abandoned the Egyptians and the ANC and agreed that Havana should be the headquarters of the new tricontinental organization. AAPSO would continue its independent existence in Cairo, at least until its next conference scheduled for some time in 1967—no exact date had been set—in Peking. That meeting was never to be held.

Clearly, the Russians had imagined that if the African, Asian, and Latin American Peoples' Solidarity Organization (OSPAAAL) were located in Cairo, near AAPSO, it would soon absorb the fractious smaller body, and all would come under Soviet control, thanks to a large, mainly pro-Moscow, Latin American element in the tricontinental organization. If it had been the intention of the Soviets when they came to Havana to replace AAPSO with a more docile body to bring the revolutionary movements of Africa and Asia under their control, they failed badly. The battle for control had to be fought again and again on other terrain.

SWANU was to play an important role in these battles. At Havana, Kozonguizi had shocked many delegates, even friends, by his unvarnished words. 'Contrary to the expectation of many,' he said, 'we think . . . that the revolutionary forces, at least in our view, are today in disarray all over the world.' He added, 'It will be useless to go away from here with one of those general, watered-down, so-called "unanimous" declarations which later become open to many interpretations.'

Instead, Kozonguizi joined in the condemnation of 'Soviet-American collusion under the guise of peaceful coexistence'. The sole path of salvation for the world's oppressed people, he declared, was the path of armed struggle. 'The independence of Africa today is not complete,' he added, 'because the armed struggle in that continent of my birth is not complete. Asia will never see peace unless the imperialists are driven out by force. Latin America, except Cuba, will always remain in

U.S. hands without an armed struggle. The Afro-Americans in the U.S.A. will always be in chains unless they take to guns,' Kozonguizi declared.

In his speech, Kozonguizi hinted briefly that he personally was fed up with words and would soon turn to direct action. In any case, his fiery, disabused words to the conference were not soon forgotten or forgiven in many quarters. Later, he was to complain that four of the six members of SWANU's External Council had expressed disapproval. The long latent conflict between Kozonguizi and the Council came to a head a few months after his return to London from Havana.

In an open letter to friends and associates on 4 July 1966, Kozonguizi announced his resignation as President of SWANU. He said he would henceforth be neither 'president, representative nor member' of SWANU. But he insisted that his position in 'the struggle against colonialism, imperialism and neo-colonialism throughout the world . . . remains unaltered.' Shortly afterwards, in an interview with the author, he vehemently denied any plans or hopes of creating yet another liberation movement inside or outside South West Africa. He confided however that his resignation had been prompted by a long series of clashes with the External Council, which he claimed was not supporting his militant anti-imperialist stand. Members of the External Council were said to have complained that such strong talk embarrassed them in their relations with the U.S. and other Western governments, as well as with the U.S.S.R. and other Eastern European countries and pro-Moscow communist parties.

Kozonguizi said the conflict would have led inevitably to a split if he had not decided to resign. But he maintained that his militant, clearly pro-Chinese position was fully supported by the militants in South West Africa, and that, regardless of the recalcitrant members of the External Council, SWANU could never abandon that position without losing vital support at home and abroad. He expressed the hope that, at home, led by Vice-President Gerson Veii and other members of SWANU's still functioning fifteen-member National Executive Committee, SWANU would remain a major factor in the struggle against South African rule.

Kozonguizi received a cable and a letter from Windhoek from the N.E.C., 'rejecting *in toto*' his resignation. Moses Katjiuongua, then SWANU representative in Cairo and a member of the External Council, and another member, Bamba Uirab, in Sweden, reportedly also urged Kozonguizi to reconsider his resignation. But he would not resume the presidency, although he agreed to consider himself a SWANU member once again. He even appeared in that capacity before the United Nations.

SWANU was represented by Charles Kauraisa at the next round of the battle for control of AAPSO. Meeting under the protection of U.N. troops at the Cyprus Hilton in February 1967, the AAPSO Council meeting was convened by the Russians with the express purpose of cancelling the selection of Peking as the venue of the scheduled 1967 AAPSO conference. The smaller council meeting, which was to precede the conference, was originally scheduled to be held in Tanzania but the Tanzanians sent their apologies when confronted with Russian demands for a change of venue and an eventual split with the Chinese. The Russians then moved the council meeting to Cyprus.

Ten days before the session was to begin, the Chinese Afro-Asian Peoples' Solidarity Committee denounced the Council meeting as an attempt by the 'Soviet revisionists' to set aside the previous decision to hold the conference in Peking and to complete 'preparations to cause a final organizational split of the Afro-Asian Peoples' Solidarity Movement.' This view was echoed by a number of member organizations.

Nevertheless, the organizers of the Nicosia meeting were able to announce shortly after the opening that delegates from sixty groups were present, as well as observers from OSPAAAL in Havana and the League of Arab States in Cairo. Only five members—China, Ghana, Guinea, Indonesia, and Japan—of the fifteen-nation AAPSO Permanent Secretariat, based in Cairo, had refused to attend the Nicosia council meeting, although delegates from Kenya and Tanzania indicated that they were present only under protest at the way the meeting was organized.

Heading the pro-Soviet faction among AAPSO members had been the ANC, which had written to AAPSO Secretary-General Yussef El Sebai, an Egyptian, to urge a change in venue from Peking because of the 'circumstances' in China due to that country's current 'Proletarian Cultural Revolution'. El Sebai maintained an air of impartiality, while going ahead with preparations for the Council meeting, despite protests from the Chinese and others.

El Sebai declined to deny the quite untrue stories in the Cyprus press that delegates from the Botswana (Bechuanaland) People's Party (BPP), Swaziland Progressive Party (SPP) and SWANU had been provided with tickets to Cyprus by the Chinese. All three were long-standing members of AAPSO and had indeed received their fares from AAPSO funds. SWANU was even a member of the thirty-nation AAPSO Executive Committee.

There was also a frigid greeting in Nicosia for representatives of the PAC and the Zimbabwe African National Union (ZANU), whose applications for membership had been pending since AAPSO's Winneba conference in 1965.

The fight inside the Council, although hopeless for the adversaries of the Moscow line, was led by SWANU's Kauraisa and the BPP's Bobby Mack. Kauraisa strongly protested against the lack of freedom of speech at the meeting, held entirely behind closed doors. He ridiculed the talk of 'unity' in such conditions.

However, the ANC's Robert Resha, a well-known anti-China figure at previous Afro-Asian meetings, savagely attacked SWANU as a virtually non-existent 'student group' that was seeking to undermine AAPSO in word and deed. He pointedly referred to Kozonguizi's speech in Havana as an example of the negative attitude of SWANU and called for the expulsion of SWANU from AAPSO. Kauraisa retorted that such a move was unconstitutional, but a vote was called. Dr. Vassos Lyssarides, the Cypriot chairman of the meeting, claimed twenty-five votes to nil for SWANU's expulsion. Some delegates accused Lyssarides of counting six votes from the Russian delegation and four votes from the ANC as though they were votes of separate delegations. In any case, the SWANU delegation immediately left the meeting, followed by a number of African delegations. They were never to return and AAPSO was permanently split, with the Russians hanging on to the Cairo secretariat.

Through Kauraisa, who was not then its Chairman, the SWANU External Council had made a strong impression at Nicosia and taken its place among the ranks of pro-Chinese militants. After the SWANU conference in West Berlin in August 1968 (a gathering of South West African exiles, at which Kauraisa was elected Chairman), the dispute with Kozonguizi boiled over once again, and in a spectacularly sordid fashion.

The May/June 1969 issue of the *Windhoek Review*, a mimeographed publication put out by Moses Katjiuongua, who had now moved from Cairo to Sweden, appeared with a photo of 'Fanel Jariretundu Kozonguizi' and the headline 'KOZONGUIZI—A SOUTH AFRICAN SPY?' The *Windhoek Review* said it was making public some ' "interesting" documents' which had come into its possession 'in the interest of the security of the Liberation Movement of the peoples of Africa in general, and those of South West Africa in particular, and in the interest of the militant friendship between the people of South West Africa and the people of various countries.' Readers were invited to 'draw their own conclusions', but the headline had already indicated the conclusion that was supposed to be drawn.

The two documents that followed were alleged to be reports 'by the gentleman in question to an AGENT of White South Africa. Document B seems to be a summary of "K's" activities by this AGENT to his employers or "superiors".' Later, in the July/August issue of the *Windhoek Review*, a letter was published from the South African Consulate in London concerning an application or request for a passport or visa.

How these documents fell into the hands of Katjiuonga and the *Windhoek Review* is not clear, although Kozonguizi's unhappy marital life in London at the time was generally believed to provide the ultimate explanation. Kozonguizi himself was clearly shaken, but vehemently rejected the insinuations. Characteristically, he fired off a cable to the U.N. Fourth Committee, demanding an official inquiry, but it was obvious that the U.N. members had other more pressing matters to deal with than the squabbles of the SWANU leadership.

This seemed to be the attitude of some of the rank and file as well. One wrote in an open letter to the External Council and SWANU members, 'I am not denying that Kozonguizi might not be a spy. If he is a spy let all the evidence speak for themselves loud and clear, but don't feed us with inconclusive evidence.'[1] The evidence was hardly conclusive, but Kozonguizi did not press his counter-attack. He passed his final law examinations in the spring of 1970 and as a barrister began looking for some way of making a living.

External Council Chairman Kauraisa, who in September 1969 had finally stated that the 'treacherous revelations' in the *Windhoek Review* had been published with the *full knowledge* of the External Council, also seemed eager to rebuild the badly shattered organization. He toured Eastern Europe to try to improve the situation of some forty SWANU students there, who had been complaining of prejudicial treatment because of their party's stand on the Sino-Soviet dispute, and once more testified before the U.N.

Inside South West Africa, the quasi-legal existence of SWANU led in 1967 to the arrest and trial of Gerson Veii, the former SWANU Vice-President who took over as President after Kozonguizi's resignation. Veii was charged with having urged the murder of Europeans, but was actually found guilty under South Africa's Suppression of Communism Act and sentenced to five years' imprisonment. The new

---

[1] Duplicated typewritten letter by Ewald Tjotuku Kanguatjivi, of 19 September 1969, from Philadelphia, Pa.

Vice-President and Acting President, Gerson Kangueehi, was criticized with others for faulty leadership when, in the final act of the Katutura Affair in 1968, he and Foreign Secretary John Muundjua had left Windhoek Old Location. The battle over the move had begun in 1959, as we have seen, when the police killed and wounded a number of resisting Africans. The affair lay dormant for years, but South African determination to create Bantustans in South West Africa was not diminished. Tactics changed, however. As a result of more subtle pressures, SWAPO's National Chairman David Meroro announced their decision to move to Katutura. Clements Kapuuo, speaking on behalf of NUDO (which was virtually the Chief's Council led by Kapuuo), also urged people to leave for Katutura. Then SWANU Propaganda Secretary Hiaseve Kazongominja issued a statement to the *Windhoek Advertiser* of 11 September 1968, drawing the moral of the situation, which he claimed should teach the African community:

(a)   what kind of leadership to follow;
(b)   to bury and forget the toothless bulldog UNO;
(c)   that our salvation rested in our hands and the solution had to be found by the people themselves;
(d)   to think seriously and act to advance unity amongst the Africans. [1]

SWANU Acting-President Kangueehi and his Foreign Secretary then moved to the Aminuis Reserve, followed by some people, while the remainder moved finally to Katutura. The *Windhoek Review* commented caustically, 'They thought press statements and political speeches would be sufficient to deter the government. They failed to realize that a new strategy was called for.' There followed a quotation from Chairman Mao on 'self-reliance' and the necessity for revolutionaries strategically,

. . . to despise the enemy, dare to struggle against him and dare to seize victory; at the same time, tactically, with regard to each part, each specific struggle, they must take the enemy seriously, be prudent, carefully study and perfect the art of struggle and adopt forms of struggle suited to different times, places and conditions in order to isolate and wipe out the enemy step by step.

By mid-1970, the London-based External Council Secretary for International Relations and Information, Tunguru Huaraka, assured friends and associates that the internal squabbling was finished and SWANU should be expected in due course to surprise the world with its action in Africa and elsewhere. But whether they had digested the lessons of Chairman Mao remained to be seen.

[1] As quoted in *Windhoek Review* (May/June 1969).

The South West African People's Organization (SWAPO)

Founded in April 1959 by Sam Nujoma and Jacob Kuhangua as the Ovamboland Peoples' Organization, the OPO had no pretensions to being more than a tribal group. Nujoma and other OPO members had participated in the SWANU conference in September 1959 and he and Louis Nelengani and other OPO members were elected to the National Executive Committee of that organization, which it was hoped would become a united South West Africa national party.

Inner-tribal bickering, especially among the Herero, as well as traditional rivalries between the varied African groups, made the formation of a united movement extremely difficult. The divisions at home were amplified by divisions abroad. At the United Nations, where Mburumba Kerina, who was in conflict with the newly arrived SWANU President Jariretundu Kozonguizi, wrote letters to Nujoma, urging him to abandon SWANU and transform OPO into a rival national party.

The name SWAPO was in fact bestowed in New York by Kerina, who became Chairman of the new body, to wipe away the traces of the organization's tribal origins. Thanks to the dynamic efforts of Toivo ja Toivo on the spot, made despite surveillance of reactionary tribal leaders and South African authorities, the tribal base in Ovamboland was never lost. This was to prove of vital importance when the movement in exile decided upon armed struggle as the only path left open for the liberation of South West Africa.

Despite its Ovambo origin, perhaps due to Kerina's connections, the newly formed SWAPO had the blessing of the Herero Chief's Council. Moreover, the tribal leaders actively feared the radical young men in SWANU, who were believed to be opposed in principle to the chieftainship. The elders had been the sole seat of tribal authority and they had initiated petitioning to the U.N., so they had no feelings of inferiority whatsoever about their role in the national struggle.

SWAPO had the same illusions about the U.N. as SWANU. Its representatives have repeatedly called for a U.N. police force to intervene in South West Africa to expel the encroaching South Africans. The organization continues to look towards the world body for some sort of action. In October 1969, a five-man SWAPO delegation, headed by Gottfried Hage Geingob, the party's representative in the United States, testified before the U.N. Fourth Committee. Geingob summed up SWAPO demands, calling for:

1.   U.N. recognition of the legitimacy of the struggle in Namibia[1] [the name
     given South West Africa by SWAPO and accepted by the U.N.] and the
     granting of material assistance;
2.   action by the Security Council to enforce Resolution 269 (1969) calling
     upon the Government of South Africa to withdraw from Namibia;
3.   action by the U.N. Council for Namibia to amend the laws of the
     territory with respect to corporations doing business in Namibia, taxing
     them in order to fulfil its obligations and 'to award a larger number of
     scholarships to Namibians';
4.   recognition by all states of the laws adopted by the Council for Namibia
     as is normally given the laws of other sovereign States.[2]

Sam Nujoma, the young President of SWAPO, began his personal
career of petitioning before the international organization in 1960. He
had fled from South West Africa after the Katutura affair, when South
African police shot and killed thirteen Africans and wounded forty-two
others, on 10 December 1959. The massacre was immediately brought to
the attention of the Fourth Committee, which duly deplored the
incident and went on to other business. Nujoma himself was immediately
deported from Windhoek to Ovamboland, whence he eventually left
the country. Nujoma met Kozonguizi, who was then touring Africa,
in Monrovia, and the two reached an agreement for the merger of their
two organizations. But from abroad, they were unable to enforce the
implementation of their decision and another chance of unity appeared
lost because of the opposition in New York.

Eventually, Kerina was to denounce SWAPO as an Ovambo tribalist
organization, claiming that the South African Government was deliberately cultivating Ovambo separatism in the hope of creating a Bantustan
in the northern area. He declared:

A deadly doctrine of Ovambo separateness has been evolved out of Pretoria
and it is being exploited by certain imperialist powers abroad to provide the
political basis in the minds of the people for Ovambo Bantustan or
'Ovambostan'.... Because of the peculiar circumstances of isolation, colonial
indoctrination and oppression forces upon inhabitants of Ovamboland, our
people from the North, perhaps more than any other tribes, are susceptible to
tribalistic political demagoguery. Meanwhile, Namas, Hereros, Damaras and
Coloureds are goaded into attitudes of intellectual and cultural superiority
over Ovambo fellowmen and incited to act against them. National liberation
movements cannot exist as such in this environment under the influence of
tribalist orientated leadership. In the long run, under the inevitable stresses

---

[1] In 1965, Mburumba Kerina was already referring to his homeland as 'Namib',
after the great coastal desert, rich in diamonds, but SWANU has ridiculed such
names and they never appear in its publication except in derisive use.
[2] *Namibia News* (London, July/December 1969), Vol. 2, Nos. 7–12.

and strains of the struggle, the interests of the broad masses are subordinated to opportunism and sacrificed upon the altar of tribal domination as we have seen so tragically in our country.[1]

Whatever the tribal rivalries at home, SWAPO leaders abroad, and especially Nujoma, have repeatedly denied that theirs is a tribal organization. They point to non-Ovambo members of the leadership as proof of this. Suspected initially by South African communists and other white 'progressives' as something of an Africanist, Nujoma clearly demonstrated a national consciousness in his personal dealings with other South West Africans. He long remained on terms of close personal friendship with Kozonguizi, his supposed rival, and even offered Kozonguizi a post in SWAPO if he cared to join after his (Kozonguizi's) much-publicized resignation from SWANU. (Kozonguizi replied that ideological considerations would have made his presence in the Moscow-leaning SWAPO impossible and only have embarrassed Nujoma.)

In 1960, SWAPO's programme betrayed the influence of the Africanists who had created the PAC in South Africa, although among the small European population of South West Africa there were no visible white revisionist communists, or even white liberals, to threaten the black leadership of the national struggle. Nevertheless, the Positive Action Campaign of the PAC was felt across the border. It was more than chance that SWAPO set 1963 as the Year of Independence, just as the PAC had done in South Africa. Despite later external constraints due to their replacement of SWANU in the Russian-controlled AAPSO and other bodies, individual members of SWAPO continued to maintain friendly personal relations with members of the PAC and other groups disapproved of in Moscow.

The ANC, which had early protested against South African annexation of South West Africa, had established contacts with South West African students in Fort Hare College and elsewhere. These contacts continued after the split of the organization and the formation of the PAC, but it seems clear that the hopes of the Congress Alliance were initially pinned on the radical SWANU. Events were to prove that SWANU was too radical for the tastes of the reformist communists of the SACP, staunchly loyal to the CPSU, and Kozonguizi and his associates were finally accused of being in the 'pay of the Chinese'. On the other hand, the SWANU leaders, pointing to the activities of Kerina in New York and alleging handouts to SWAPO from American mining firms with interests in South West Africa, hinted heavily at the 'imperialist' orientation of their rivals.

[1] U.N. Document 65-44476 (Kerina) op. cit., p. 30.

Nevertheless, another attempt at unity between SWAPO and SWANU was made on 1 October 1963. The executives of the two organizations decided to merge into the South West Africa National Liberation Front (SWANLIF). Nujoma and Kozonguizi jointly presented the new organization to the African Liberation Committee on 6 December. By 2 January 1964, SWAPO's Vice-President Louis Nelengani wrote from Cairo to the SWAPO representatives in Dar es Salaam, rejecting *in toto* all the decisions taken for unity. Nelengane asked, 'What do we want in this so-called Front, which we can not get in SWAPO?'[1]

Nathanael Mbaeva claimed that tribalism was the main cause of SWANLIF'S failure to come to life. The Ovambos reportedly felt that, since they were the biggest tribe in South West Africa, SWAPO had to be accepted as the main organization and they should have the leading positions in the new body. They also feared the tradition of Herero leadership, developed in petitioning the U.N. and earlier stages of the national struggle. About the same time, the brief united front between PAC and ANC in exile also broke up and the moment was hardly propitious for unity.

In due course, Kerina and Mbaeva, who had testified before the Fourth Committee on behalf of SWANU, created in New York yet another unity movement, called the South West Africa National United Front (SWANUF). This appeared as luckless as previous creations of this sort and, although it was said to be a merger of SWAPO and SWANU, the leaders of both groups denied any merger, and SWANU suspended Mbaeva. SWANUF's life appeared to be confined to the corridors of the U.N. headquarters and interminable correspondence between Kerina and tribal and other political leaders in South West Africa. NUDO, an earlier creation, continued a limited existence as an extension of Clements Kapuuo's Herero Chief's Council.

After the disappointment of 1963, when hopes of easy victory over the white supremacists were dashed, the SWAPO leadership adjusted its tactics. Taking advantage of the sponsorship of the African Liberation Committee, SWAPO began training guerrilla forces. Although South African authorities refused to issue passports for foreign travel to Africans, the sparse policing at that time along the lengthy border with Bechuanaland (now Botswana) made it relatively simple for eager young men to leave the country. Encouraged by their leaders, hundreds left and eventually found their way to Zambia and Tanzania. Some were trained there, while cadres went on to Algeria, the U.A.R.,

[1] U.N. Document 65-44477 (Mbaeva), op. cit., pp. 2–3.

the Soviet Union, and elsewhere for military instruction. Eventually even, until discovered by South African authorities, a training camp was functioning at Ongulumbashe in Ovamboland. The police raid on the camp netted thirty-seven guerrillas, who received long terms of imprisonment in South African jails.

In 1966, before any action commenced, a curious incident occurred that has not yet been sufficiently clarified. After some tension in the exile leadership of the party, Sam Nujoma suddenly flew back to South West Africa in a chartered plane. There was speculation that Nujoma was planning to step down from political activity, especially as his leadership was often subjected to the rudest criticism from some of his colleagues. According to reliable reports, when Nujoma's plane touched down at Windhoek Airport the baffled South African Immigration officials refused to believe that he was really the President of SWAPO. He was taken overnight to security police headquarters in Windhoek, where he was again questioned, awaiting a decision in Pretoria. The next morning, the hapless African leader was driven back to the airport and put aboard his aircraft. South African authorities warned the pilot to take off and fly as swiftly as possible out of South West Africa with his passenger who, as far as they were concerned, could be President Nkrumah in disguise.

The entry into action of the SWAPO guerrillas was announced before the South African Parliament by John Vorster (then Minister of Justice) on 26 August, 1966. Vorster said that there had been a clash early that morning between a detachment of South African police in Ovamboland and a group of infiltrators. He said that the Government had received information, 'some time ago' that a group of sixteen Africans had crossed the border 'with the object of murdering Ovambo chiefs, other well-disposed Bantu and whites, and training members of certain subversive organizations with the object of instigating murder and an armed uprising.'[1]

Vorster claimed that two of the guerrillas had been killed and eight others, some of them wounded, taken prisoner. In Dar es Salaam (now become SWAPO's Provisional Headquarters), several days later, SWAPO representative Peter Nanyemba accused Vorster of not mentioning South African losses. SWAPO claimed fifteen policemen had been killed in the firefight, although Vorster had said that no policemen had been hurt.

Further incursions were reported during the rest of the year. South African police with tracker dogs, Bushman trackers, and helicopters

<hr>

[1] The *Star* (26 August 1966).

combed the mountainous, rugged country, killing and capturing isolated groups of guerrillas. In December 1966, one of the bodyguards of Ovambo Chief Jackie Ahipala was shot dead and two others were wounded when SWAPO men attacked his kraal, where a SWAPO leader, Leo Shopala, had previously been killed. By 12 January 1967, the *Windhoek Advertiser* reported that police had apprehended forty alleged terrorists. The newspaper said that about ten of the prisoners would give evidence for the State, leaving about thirty men to face trial in connection with their alleged 'sabotage' under South Africa's so-called Terrorism Act.

The *Windhoek Review*, the 'personal' publication of Moses K. Katjiuongua, a member of SWANU External Council, claimed that SWAPO Vice-President Luis Nelengani had turned State witness when he had been apprehended in 1968 and had divulged the guerrillas' plans to the South African authorities in order to save his own life. Considering the extensive, systematic use of torture in interrogation in South African jails, it is hardly surprising that the security forces should not eventually have wrung precious information from their captives.

Despite these setbacks, the guerrillas continued their raids, coming from their base camp in Zambia, entering South West Africa either through the rugged but exposed Caprivi Strip or, with somewhat less initial risk, through southern Angola. In 1962, considerable publicity was given a short-lived agreement between SWAPO and the *Govêrno Revolucionário de Angola no Exilío* (GRAE). GRAE's Holden Roberto personally negotiated the alliance with Jacob Kuhangua of SWAPO. SWAPO wanted assistance in passing through the Cuanhama region of Angola and clearly Roberto was hoping for support for his movement, which had been virtually confined to the north of Angola along the Congolese border, among the Ovambos who are found on both sides of the artificial frontier.[1]

Portuguese colonial authorities established co-operative relations with their fellow white rulers in South West Africa. In addition, the *Polícia Internacional e de Defensa do Estado* (P.I.D.E.), the Portuguese secret police, began close co-operation on a continental scale in Africa and Europe with the South African intelligence and their junior partners in Ian Smith's Rhodesia. Police and troops of South Africa and Portugal worked together in anti-guerrilla operations along the border of the Caprivi Strip and Ovamboland. In fact, a SWAPO leader in Lusaka in 1968 reported to the author that South African helicopter units were

[1] See John Marcum, *The Angolan Revolution* (Cambridge, Mass. M.I.T. Press, 1969), p. 310.

flying patrols deep inside Angola, while South African ground units often replaced Portuguese troops in this part of the contested colony.

In July 1964, Jonas Savimbi and his associates split away from Holden Roberto's GRAE, later, in March 1966, forming their own *Unaião Nacional para a Independência Total de Angola* (UNITA). SWAPO worked out more satisfactory arrangements with UNITA. More than that with GRAE, this informal alliance was to bring down the wrath of the MPLA on SWAPO for allegedly collaborating with Savimbi, who was variously described as a 'CIA agent' and 'Maoist thug'. More important for SWAPO—which had been recognized by the A.L.C. and was receiving substantial material assistance from it—the *Movimento Popular de Libertação de Angola* (MPLA) sought to have this aid suspended unless SWAPO promised to cut all ties with UNITA and instead help MPLA to establish its forces in southern Angola. SWAPO leaders warned that fighting between rival Angolan liberation movements could only assist the Portuguese and South Africans, but the MPLA, which had also turned to the ANC for help in bringing SWAPO into line, increased its pressure and multiplied threats against the alleged interlopers. These pressures were crudely applied at the 1969 Khartoum conference of Moscow-line liberation movements, attended by a SWAPO delegation. Here, in addition, leaders of the ANC called privately for an alliance with SWAPO similar to their party's tie-up with ZAPU. As failures mounted in Rhodesia, the ANC were increasingly keen to extend their alliance to other movements. The Morogoro Congress of the ANC laid special stress upon this. 'The ZAPU/ANC alliance must be consolidated', wrote the *African Communist*, organ of the SACP, 'and extended to include FRELIMO, MPLA and SWAPO'.[1]

Although the leaders of SWAPO reportedly were sharply divided concerning this issue, most felt that any formal alliance with the ANC of South Africa would only serve as an alibi for the ANC's military failures elsewhere and provide the ANC with a dumping ground, if not final resting place, for its inactive and increasingly demoralized guerrilla forces. Although, as South African press reports indicated, not all SWAPO guerrillas were Ovambos, the tribal base still had great importance if SWAPO was ever to establish a liberated area somewhere in South West Africa, and intruding South Africans with no knowledge of the country or its customs and languages would not help at all.

Moreover, from the international legal point of view, SWAPO forces had a certain moral backing from the U.N., especially as that body

[1] The *African Communist* (No. 38, Third Quarter, 1969), p. 27.

would not take action on its own against South Africa. But the presence of South African guerrillas in South West Africa would obviously provide the Pretoria regime with a precious excuse for maintaining its unwanted presence north of the Orange River. On the other hand, some ANC leaders secretly accused SWAPO of trying to make deals with Pretoria, via the U.N. and 'the imperialists', that would grant South West Africa some sort of nominal, if guided, independence, that naturally would prevent the ANC ever using South West Africa as a staging point on its march south. Ironically, some black South Africans repeated arguments used by the Europeans in their country, to the effect that South West Africa with its small population, vast size, and economic integration with South Africa had inevitably become a part of South Africa and would so remain, regardless of whether the government was white or black. Naturally, these unpleasant quarrels were not publicized, but reliable reports of the extent and bitterness of the debate continued to reach outsiders well into 1970.

In principle, SWAPO's Namibia Liberation Army has divided the country into four regions:

1. Northern Region—Ovamboland and Okavango
2. North-western Region—Kaokoveld
3. Grootfontein District in the Central Region
4. North-eastern Region—the Caprivi Strip.

Most activity has been reported in Ovamboland and along the Caprivi Strip, which South African helicopters, ground patrols, and radar have turned into a death trap for many brave freedom fighters. Hence the importance of the Angolan passage.

Addressing the Khartoum Conference, Sam Nujoma reported:

We do not, for the time being, claim to have liberated areas, but we do have large areas which are under our control. These areas contain hundreds of thousands of peasants. In these areas our fighters are running some semi-administrative functions such as medical and social services and as yet at a small scale they teach the people to read and write. It is true also, that up to now, the enemy does send its superior number of forces into these areas. But since it cannot maintain forces there permanently, it naturally will leave a much weaker number behind which soon becomes an easy target of the guerrillas.

Unfortunately, as *Namibia News* later reported, 'easy targets' were difficult to find in 1968 and 1969. Although on 1 July 1968, Al Venter of London's *Daily Express* reported from Johannesburg that: 'Some South Africans were killed and two police helicopters crashed during the chase through semi-desert bush country' of a SWAPO guerrilla unit that had attacked the Caprivi Strip. The Africans struck at the large South African air base at Katimo Mulilo and the South African administrative centre of Runtu, some miles to the west. The guerrillas were eventually cleared from the Strip, but not before John Vorster, now Premier of the apartheid Republic, had reiterated his threats to strike at the guerrilla bases in Zambia, if necessary.

The pattern of South African counter-insurgency tactics had become clear:

Guerrilla activities lead to mass-arrests, detentions of innocent civilians, brutal retaliation and victimization of the Namibian population. Some will argue that we bring unnecessary suffering to our civilian population by continuing our guerrilla struggle. We do not accept this. Time and again we have pointed out that there are many parallels between Vorster's South Africa and Hitler's Germany, but it does not seem to register. The atrocities performed by the South African Government are as brutal and inhuman as those performed by Hitler's henchmen. However, they are not performed just outside the European front door, they are performed far away, in a part of the world where people happen to be black, happen to be exploited victims of international indifference. By taking to arms in order to free ourselves, we know that we not only fight for our freedom, we also combat a force which is threatening world peace.[1]

The price paid in lives and lengthy prison sentences by the hapless guerrillas who fell into South African hands continued to mount through 1971.

Meanwhile, SWAPO perilously hung on to its threatened organizational independence, wary of would-be allies and mentors. Namibia was not South Africa, they protested. In June 1970, Sam Nujoma declared while on a visit to Nigeria, 'We don't need to be liberated by outsiders.'[2] He appealed for arms and other material support for SWAPO, while ruling out the possibility of Nigerian or other foreign troops going to South West Africa to aid SWAPO forces.

But clearly SWAPO's struggle depended upon complex factors in African and world politics. Unless they could find some of the self-reliance demonstrated by their controversial comrades in UNITA, SWAPO faced political defeat at the hands of aggrandizing would-be allies far from the borders of Ovamboland and the Caprivi Strip, and assimilation into the ranks of Moscow's hard-pressed devotees in the Congress Alliance.

Indications grew stronger that at least some SWAPO leaders were beginning to question past policy and look in other directions for

[1] *Namibia News* (July/December 1969), Vol. 2, Nos. 7–12, pp. 1–2.
[2] Agence France-Press dispatch No. 1684 (12 June 1970), from Lagos.

assistance. On 15 September 1970, the Chinese Hsinhua News Agency published a statement from Dar es Salaam by Hiuanua Shihepo, SWAPO chief representative there, 'warmly hailing' the Chinese people 'in their struggle against imperialism' under the leadership of Chairman Mao. But one robin does not make a Red Spring.

PART FOUR:
ZIMBABWE (RHODESIA)

Zimbabwe African People's Union (ZAPU)

Zimbabwe African National Union (ZANU)

Front for the Liberation of Zimbabwe (FROLIZI)

The Background

The Africans of this landlocked Central African country are divided among themselves about many things, but one thing about which they all agree is that they do not want it to be called Rhodesia. The name of Cecil Rhodes, the arch-imperialist, plastered across their land is resented as a daily insult and humiliation. When they broke away from the short-lived Central African Federation, which would have imposed white-minority rule from Salisbury on the three component territories, the more fortunate Nyasaland became Malawi and Northern Rhodesia hurriedly changed its name to Zambia after independence in 1964. As for Southern Rhodesia, whose white settlers had been granted, since 1923, the right to govern their domestic affairs and those of the African majority as well—it remained under white-minority rule, with its name shortened simply to Rhodesia, after its white founder. But to Africans of all parties their land, long ancient beyond Rhodes's schemes, is known as Zimbabwe.[1]

The country's 150,820 square miles make it nearly three times the size of England. Of the three main geographical regions, the most important is the High Veld 'island', a belt of land 4,000 to 5,000 feet above sea-level, generally not more than 50 miles wide, from below Bulawayo in the south-west to Salisbury in the north-east. The soils are good and the rainfall is more than adequate for agriculture. In addition, some mineral deposits are to be found. With the majority of the population concentrated in the High Veld, throughout the country Africans outnumber European settlers by nearly twenty to one. At 31 December 1969, the total population was estimated at 5,119,000, of which 4,930,000 were Africans, 234,000 Europeans and 24,000 Asians and persons of mixed race.[2]

Lying within the High Veld is Salisbury, capital and largest city, with some 390,000 inhabitants. Bulawayo, second largest city and

[1] As this book is written from the African point of view, I shall refer generally to Zimbabwe, rather than Rhodesia. In other sections, such as South Africa, I have not done likewise because the various liberation movements are not in agreement in accepting the proposed 'African' name.

[2] Central Office of Information, British Information Services, *Rhodesia*, R.5864/70 (London, April 1970).

railway centre, lies to the south-west, in the Middle Veld. Rail lines connect the country with South Africa and Mozambique, main avenues for import and export—often clandestine, since Ian Smith's white-minority regime proclaimed its illegal Unilateral Declaration of Independence (U.D.I.) on 11 November 1965. Another rail line connects the country with Zambian railways and the Benguela railway through part of Zaïre, formerly the Congo (Kinshasa), and Angola.

Below the healthy, inviting High Veld lies a considerable area of Middle Veld, covering nearly half the country's total surface at an altitude of 3,000 to 4,000 feet. Here, too, soils are good and the rainfall is fairly reliable, but this area is less developed and much of it is farmed by Africans. In the north, bordering Zambia and the Zambezi River, and in the south running along the Limpopo River and South Africa, is the Low Veld, a hot, malarial, tsetse-infested area. It is in the northern portion of this sparsely-populated region that guerrilla activity has been most intense.

The blacks have ample reason to fight. Long before Ian Smith, Europeans made clear their intention of adding Zimbabwe, the country of Africans, to the White Dominions under the British Crown, although the Portuguese from neighbouring Mozambique were the first Europeans to visit, making three expeditions to the country in the sixteenth century. Impressive ruins at Zimbabwe testify to the development of the African kingdom, ruled from there between the eleventh and fifteenth centuries. Zimbabwe lies in Mashonaland, in the north-east, which was settled in antiquity by Bantu-speaking peoples from the north. Their descendants make up the tribes known collectively as the Shonas.

From the south, a part of the Zulu nation called the Ndebele—or, more commonly but incorrectly, 'Matabele'—migrated and settled in the southern portion of the country, which was later called Matabele-land. Their king, Mzilikazi, established his kraal near what is now Bulawayo. A warrior people, the Ndebele carried out frequent raids on their northern neighbours, and it was in fact the conflict of the two African peoples that facilitated European conquest. Although Ndebele and Shona were belatedly to stand and fight together against the common enemy, continuing tribal enmity bedevils the two main rival national liberation movements.

The discovery of minerals, particularly, gold, and Rhodes's ambitions to run a railway under the British flag from the Cape to Cairo, prompted his interest in the country that was to bear his name. In 1888, Rhodes's British South Africa Company enticed Lobengula, King of the Ndebele, into granting the Company the right to mine minerals throughout Matabeleland. British adventurers poured in. The mineral concession, known as the 'Rudd Concession', led Rhodes to form the British South Africa Company, which received a Royal Charter in 1889 'to promote, under the supervision of the High Commissioner for South Africa, trade, commerce, civilization and government'. In other words, the Rudd Concession was interpreted as licence to seize the entire African country. Hypocritically deploring past Ndebele incursions against the Shona, British colonists in 1890 themselves moved into Mashonaland and occupied it.

From the African point of view, this is naturally seen as treachery and aggression. For the imperialist pioneers, the Africans constituted merely another natural obstacle to their right of expansion—and, later, a source of cheap labour for their farms and mines. Despite various constitutional niceties, Africans tend to view whatever government was imposed by Europeans without their consent as a 'British settler dictatorship'.[1] Resistance to this encroachment, which took violent form from 1890 to 1900, was considered rebellion by the British and punished as such. The so-called 'Matabele Rebellion' of 1893 ended the following year with the death by smallpox of King Lobengula, and the 'Mashona Rebellion' of 1897, despite heroic leaders such as Mgandane and Nehanda, also ended in Europeans crushing the Africans.

Until 1923, Southern Rhodesia—as it was then known—was administered by Rhodes's British South Africa Company. Self-government for Europeans developed swiftly after the formation of Executive and Legislative Councils in 1898 with appointed and settler-elected members. The elected settler representatives were already a majority by 1907, and in 1922 the white electorate was asked to vote on whether the country should be attached to the neighbouring Union of South Africa or become a self-governing white Dominion within the British Empire. By 8,774 votes to 5,989—largely votes of English settlers, who have always constituted the majority of Europeans, against those of Dutch Boer stock from South Africa—Dominion status won. On 12 September 1923, Southern Rhodesia was formally annexed to the Dominions as a colony, and, on 1 October the colony was granted full self-government except for legislation affecting African rights, railways, and international affairs. Significantly, although the British Government had the legal right to veto discriminatory legislation against Africans, it never did so.

Mining and farming, both based mainly on black labour, produce

---

[1] 'Background to the Zimbabwe Struggle', *Zimbabwe Review* (Vol. 1, No. 2, June 1969).

Rhodesia's wealth. Mines are all foreign-owned and highly profitable, exploiting deposits of asbestos, gold, chrome, copper, lithium, nickel, cobalt, iron ore, lead, zinc, uranite, silver, and other minerals. In addition, the Wankie Colliery produces an abundant supply of coal. Hydro-electricity from the Kariba Dam, shared with Zambia, also supplies power for industry. The largest agricultural crop is traditionally tobacco, followed by sugar. Livestock are raised under good conditions in large areas of the country.

Under the 1931 Land Apportionment Act, Africans—mainly rural—found themselves confined to ownership of lands outside the High Veld; those who did live there were obliged to remain landless agricultural workers in the pay of white farmers. The country was divided into European land and African land, plus some Crown land not allocated. The small European population was given 49 per cent of the total area. Under Ian Smith's Land Tenure Bill of 1969, this was increased to more than half the country's cultivable land. Yet this was only one of the settler regime's constitutional devices to maintain white-minority rule for ever: Desmond Lardner-Burke, the regime's 'Minister for Law', assured the Legislative Assembly in Salisbury that, under the discriminatory constitution, 'African majority rule as an aim is no longer constitutionally attainable'. African representation in the Senate and House of Assembly is in democratic terms farcical, with government dominated African chiefs electing all ten African senators, against ten elected Europeans and three persons of any race appointed by the Head of State. In the lower House of Assembly, fifty elected Europeans would face sixteen Africans, eight of whom would be selected again by chiefs. In no case, no matter what the population imbalance, could the number of Africans exceed that of European members.

After the break-up of the Central African Federation of Rhodesia and Nyasaland, due to the resistance of African nationalists in what are now Malawi and Zambia, successive British governments carried on independence negotiations with the settler regime from 1963 to Smith's U.D.I. in 1965. The British position was based essentially on six points:

1. The principle and intention of unimpeded progress to majority rule, already enshrined in the 1961 constitution, would have to be maintained and guaranteed.
2. There would also have to be guarantees against retrogressive amendment of the constitution.
3. There would have to be immediate improvement in the political status of the African population.
4. There would have to be progress towards ending racial discrimination.

5. The British Government would need to be satisfied that any basis for independence was acceptable to the people of Rhodesia as a whole.
6. It would be necessary to ensure that, regardless of race, there was no oppression of majority by minority or of minority by majority.

Although bursting with good intentions, the British proposals clearly left settlers in full control of the country for the foreseeable future. But this was not sufficient for Smith's white supremacist diehards in the Rhodesian Front, the majority settler party. Obviously, African nationalist opinion, although muzzled by legal and political repression, was outraged at what it felt was a 'sellout' of its rights. The unhappy Africans were privately assured that an African majority government might actually reach power in Rhodesia under these proposals within 15 to 50 years.

The illegal declaration of independence called Britain's bluff, and no British Government was found willing to use force against 'kith and kin' entrenched in Salisbury. Undoubtedly, as opinion polls have shown, large numbers of British people clearly sympathize with Rhodesian whites. As a substitute for military force, which could still be promptly used against a rebellious black government, as was proved when British troops and police were rushed to Anguilla in 1969, the British Government proposed economic sanctions against Rhodesia. The U.N. Security Council endorsed these sanctions in November 1965 and December 1966, and called on member states to prohibit trade with Rhodesia. A Royal Navy blockade was established off the Mozambican port of Beira in an effort to halt delivery of oil supplies to Rhodesia. However, thanks to Portuguese and official South African government complicity in aiding Rhodesian triangular trade to circumvent sanctions, the trade embargo proved pitifully ineffective. An indignant Zambian High Commissioner to Britain had to be recalled when he undiplomatically referred to Britain as a 'toothless bulldog', yet his was a view held farther afield than Black Africa.

Testifying on 12 May 1969, before the U.N. Committee on Colonialism, George Silundika, Secretary for Publicity and Information of ZAPU, defended his organization's choice of armed struggle as the sole way to liberate Zimbabwe. He pointed to the Smith regime's record budget of £103 million for the 1968–9 year, with a surplus from the previous budget. 'These surpluses and the consequent record budget', he said, 'are occurring in Rhodesia in the era of worldwide economic sanctions spearheaded by Britain.' He explained:

The measure by measure economic sanctions introduced by the **British Government** at the United Nations have been an exercise not so much to have an adverse effect on the Rhodesian economy than to encourage its diversification so that it could withstand the strains of independence when legalized. The acreage of the plantation of coffee has touched record level resulting in expanded growth of the crop; cotton growth has experienced the same expansion . . . ; wheat growth particularly of the Mkwasime scheme some twenty miles from Chiredzi has increased production of the crop from 16 bags per acre in 1966 to about 20 bags this year [1969]; the production of tea in the Eastern districts of the country has almost trebled in this era of British sanctions, changing Rhodesia from an importer to a net exporter of 2·5 million lbs. Livestock has also increased and the regime has since become self-sufficient in dairy products.[1]

The ZAPU leader reminded his listeners that, under the apartheid-style land act, for every acre held by an African a European settler owned 500 acres, on average four times as fertile as the African holding.

While some African leaders and white liberals outside Africa tirelessly predicted that Rhodesia would become 'Britain's Vietnam', the British Government showed no inclination to become further involved; rather, they gave every indication of desperately seeking total disengagement from the problem. Prime Minister Harold Wilson met Ian Smith aboard H.M.S. *Tiger* in December 1966 and proposed means for the regime to return to legality, which Smith rejected. In October 1968, the British Prime Minister met Smith again, aboard H.M.S. *Fearless* in Gibraltar, but these talks too broke down when Smith rejected any concessions to the African majority. In Salisbury, the regime went ahead with plans to declare the country a 'republic' on 2 March 1970. Looking ahead to general elections in Britain, Smith declared he would be willing to resume talks with the Conservatives, if they were elected, but there could be no going back on Rhodesia's independence and white-minority constitution, with measures to separate the races along apartheid lines. The Conservative victory in June 1970 delighted white Rhodesians, who eagerly awaited gestures of reconciliation and acceptance by the Government of Prime Minister Edward Heath.

The Heath Government, with Sir Alec Douglas-Home as Foreign Secretary, indicated that friendly relations and limited sale of arms to the Republic of South Africa were among its priorities as part of a more 'realistic' approach to Africa, based on Britain's big stake in South African prosperity. On its part, the Pretoria regime was seen to be pressuring its protégés in Rhodesia to come to terms with Britain, if a face-saving formula could be found. South African whites had con-

[1] 'ZAPU before the United Nations Committee on Colonialism', *Zimbabwe Review* (Vol. 1, No. 2, June 1969), p. 13.

sidered U.D.I. as precipitate and unnecessary, but they were bound to prop up any white regime in Southern Africa.

The 'realistic' approach of Britain's Conservatives led swiftly to an agreement, ending the six year old conflict between London and the settler regime. Signed in Salisbury on 24 November 1971 by Sir Alec Douglas-Home and Ian Smith, this accord virtually legalized indefinite white-minority dictatorship, although offering Africans vague promises to reduce racial discrimination and somehow bring about democratic government in the distant future. Africans of all parties, as well as the Labour opposition in Britain, condemned the agreement as a 'sellout' and an abandonment of the six principles originally drawn up for an end to the conflict. In exile in Lusaka, ZAPU voiced the feelings of all three African liberation movements when it declared that the agreement brought Zimbabwe 'to the brink of the inevitable racial bloodbath'. For every voice in Britain calling for a policy of 'Keep Britain White', there is a corresponding call to keep Africa Black. Behind such a call there is a further one—'Get the whites out of Africa, bag and baggage.' Zimbabwe African nationalists commented that they had been left no choice but *Chimurenga*, the armed struggle, if they hoped ever to regain their country.

The Resistance

By 1900, Britain's armed superiority had crushed all African tribal resistance to colonial aggression. The British South Africa Company became a going concern, imposing its rule upon defeated Ndebele and Shona. While the newly-arrived European settlers were preoccupied in exploiting the country's mineral wealth and the rich High Veld land, missionary societies worked to conquer the souls of Africans. In fact, the first British missionaries had preceded Rhodes's adventurers. The famed Dr. David Livingstone had arrived in 1851 and, by 1855, had reached Victoria Falls. The London Missionary Society was active among the Ndebele by 1861. As Bismarck said after Germany turned belatedly to Africa: 'The missionary and the trader must precede the soldier.' In Rhodesia, trade was left to the all-pervasive Company, but Christian missionaries were nevertheless indispensable agents of colonization.

As elsewhere in Africa, missionary-imported religion did not meet the needs of the oppressed African masses. Messianic nativistic religious movements developed in Rhodesia. Most important of these was the Kitawala cult. Founded by a native of Nyasaland, Romo Nyirenda, who proclaimed himself Muana Lesa, the Son of God, this cult 'Africanized' the American Watch Tower movement, also known as Jehovah's Witnesses. Nyirenda first preached his doctrine in Katanga, where Belgian colonial exploitation and repression of Congolese were intense and bitter. Later, he and his followers travelled widely throughout East and Central Africa. Nyirenda himself, accused of killing whites, was eventually hanged in Rhodesia in 1926. The halo of martyrdom increased the cult's attractiveness to many Africans.

Founded in the United States in 1874 by Charles T. Russell, the American Watch Tower movement's apolcalyptic doctrine preached the approaching end of our epoch in the Battle of Armageddon, to be fought between God and the Devil. God's victory in this final struggle between good and evil would usher in an era of justice. More interesting perhaps for the brooding and fatalistic, vanquished Africans, Jehovah's Witnesses condemned both the state and organized religion as works of the Devil and predicted their common destruction. Nyirenda's Kitawala cult added to these elements an intensely nationalistic, Pan-Africanist strain, legitimating resistance to European interlopers and, if that failed, offering hope of a coming Judgment Day when they would at last pay for their crimes.[1]

The first African organization to function within the framework of the new colonial institutions was founded in 1911 when a certain Chirimuhuta[2] formed the Southern Rhodesian Native Association. This was essentially a channel for protest against various arbitrary settler measures, appealing to British authorities against plunder of African lands, theft of cattle, and other misdeeds. In African minds a fictitious dichotomy already existed between settler and local white official exactions and the assumed fairmindedness and benevolence of more distant British officialdom in Cape Town and London. Hence, in 1919, an African Voters League was organized by Jerry Sobantu in the hope of giving blacks a voice in the developing settler democracy. By the May 1965 elections, only 1,781 votes—from an African population of around 4 million—were counted in the 'B' Roll, i.e. predominantly African, election districts. This result was modified by the fact that African voters had widely boycotted these elections. In any case, some Africans in Rhodesia, unlike those in South Africa, have been allowed a regular vote. But there have always been severe property qualifications which, in effect, have disqualified the black masses. Under the Smith

---

[1] See Vittorio Lanternari, op cit., pp. 37–8, and Robert Kaufman, *Millénarisme et acculturation* (Brussels, Editions de l'institut de sociologie de l'Université libre, 1964).

[2] See 'Background to the Zimbabwe Struggle', *Zimbabwe Review* (Vol. 1, No. 2, June 1969), p. 15.

regime's Electoral Bill of 1969, Africans and Europeans were confined to separate electoral rolls. To be eligible to vote, whites have to have an annual income of at least £R 900 or property worth £R 1,800 or four years' secondary education and an annual income of £R 600 or property worth £R 1,200—a very easy requirement in the privileged conditions of colonial life. Africans are required to have an annual income of £R 300, or property worth £R 600, or two years' secondary education and an annual income of £R 200 or property worth £R 400. Black poverty is such that only a few thousand blacks can qualify for the already limited franchise.

The influence of African organizations in South Africa was strongly felt in Rhodesia. Perhaps the most militant influence came from Clements Kadalie's Industrial and Commercial Workers' Union, which had been founded at Cape Town in 1919. The ICU flourished during the twenties, and Kadalie, who had come to South Africa from Nyasaland, set up branches throughout Southern Africa, including Rhodesia. The Rhodesian ICU was officially founded in Bulawayo, second city of the colony, by Masotsha Ndlovu, in 1924. Rapid formation in the mines of a black proletariat and in the countryside of a landless peasantry created ideal conditions for trade unionism, although some of the clashes with colonial authorities and white bourgeoisie were hardly over issues of an industrial nature—such as the battle against a discriminatory law that forbade blacks from walking on settler *stoeps* and pavements.[1]

Kadalie himself was based in South Africa. Nevertheless, the influence of his fiery personality and anarcho-syndicalist notions reached black workers in Rhodesia. Day-to-day management of ICU affairs was left to local leaders, like Masotsha Ndlovu and Charles Mzingeli Moyo. Erratic policies, poor bureaucratic organization, and Kadalie's volatile personality, as we have already seen, led to the break-up of this great African mass movement within a decade of its founding. The South African pattern of splits and breakaways was repeated in Rhodesia, where Moyo attempted to set up his own independent ICU. Despite these vicissitudes, the ICU in one form or another survived in Rhodesia until the Second World War. Its tradition of militant working-class protest provides a major element of militancy in the Zimbabwe national movement's heritage.[2]

Another import from South Africa was the African National

---

[1] 'Background to the Zimbabwe Struggle', loc. cit., p. 15.

[2] For an account of the ICU in Rhodesia, see T. O. Ranger, *The African Voice in Southern Rhodesia* (London, Heinemann, 1970), pp. 148–93.

Congress. Within a few years of its inauguration in Bloemfontein as the South African Native National Congress, similar organizations sprang up elsewhere in Africa. But it was not until 1930, during the struggle against the 'Land Apportionment Act'—with its allocation of 49 per cent of the country's land to Europeans, who made up less than 7 per cent of the population—that a similar body was formed in Rhodesia. Initially called the Bantu Congress, its name was changed to African National Congress of Southern Rhodesia in 1934. Under various leaders, the ANC of Rhodesia was probably even more reformist than its namesake in South Africa. Its action, based on black elites, centred on ceaseless appeals to the white authorities in Salisbury and elsewhere for some measure of justice for the African majority.

In Rhodesia, World War II did not have the immediate, galvanizing effect that it had in many other parts of Africa. In South Africa, the formation of the Youth League of the ANC had been well advanced by 1945. In Southern Rhodesia, comparable young men did not come to the fore until 1956, when the Youth League was formed independent of the withered ANC, which clung to life only in Bulawayo under Joshua Nkomo's chairmanship. A new African National Congress of Southern Rhodesia was created in 1957 out of the two groups—Nkomo's Bulawayo-based old ANC and the Youth League that had been organized in the African townships of Salisbury around two energetic young men, James Chikerema and George Nyandoro.

When the settler regime had first proposed a Central African Federation in the forties and early fifties, the old ANC, the African Voice Association, and the Reformed ICU had participated in combined talks at Fort Jameson with similar African organizations in Nyasaland and Northern Rhodesia to protest against the proposed federation. After this conference, an All-African Convention was formed in Rhodesia to fight the federal scheme, which was nevertheless imposed in 1953. The Convention fell apart in 1954.[1]

Immediate influences on the Southern Rhodesian movement came not from distant South Africa but from Northern Rhodesia and Nyasaland, where African National Congresses also existed, with a stronger tradition of militancy. In addition, both Congresses maintained branches among their migrant workers in Southern Rhodesia. A principal source of guidance and encouragement to Chikerema and Nyandoro had been Dunduza Chisiza of the Nyasaland African National Congress, who lived in Salisbury until expelled by the white

[1] See T. M. Franck, *Race and Nationalism: the Struggle for Power in Rhodesia-Nyasaland* (New York, Fordham University Press, 1960).

settler government in July 1956. Afterwards, despite obstacles raised by an apprehensive government, considerable efforts were made to co-ordinate African nationalist activities. But a planned summit meeting of Secretaries-General from the four main nationalist parties (there were two rival organizations in Northern Rhodesia) in Blantyre in February 1959 could not be held because by that time all but one of these Congresses had been banned by their respective white rulers. In fact, pretext for the ban in Southern Rhodesia was that the ANC there was working with the Congresses of Nyasaland and Zambia, declared by a government commission to be 'subversive organizations committed to a policy of violence'.[1] Sir Edgar Whitehead's Government detained 307 members of Southern Rhodesia's ANC and hastily enacted a series of repressive measures further restricting African political activity.

Describing the Southern Rhodesian ANC's two years of life, John Day wrote:

ANC attacked on a wide front. It had particular success in mobilizing discontent against the Native Land Husbandry Act which the Government was trying to implement at this time (1957). The aim of this Act was to improve African farming practices, but it was carried out without taking account of African resentment at two of its principal parts, the destocking of cattle and transference of communally held land into farms for individuals. Africans often regarded these measures as fundamental attacks on their livelihood and traditional ways of life.

During its whole existence ANC made its onslaughts directly on the laws, policy and administration of the Southern Rhodesian Government. It did not try, like its successors, to apply indirect pressure by enlisting the assistance of foreign governments and international institutions.[2]

Although the ANC may have held up independence with African majority rule as its eventual objective, its activities were confined to efforts to remedy some of the Africans' grievances under the system established in their country in 1923. The radicalism and success of Chikerema, Nyandoro, and Nkomo in rallying blacks across tribal lines in all parts of the country nevertheless were correctly viewed by whites as an ultimate threat.

However, despite detention of ANC leaders, not all avenues of political action were definitively closed. In January 1960, a new African nationalist party, the National Democratic Party (NDP) was formed by many of those who had been active in the banned ANC. Under Whitehead, the Government now attempted to persuade Africans that

[1] John Day, *International Nationalism: The Extra-Territorial Relations of Southern Rhodesian African Nationalists* (London, Routledge and Kegan Paul, 1967), pp. 63–7.
[2] Ibid., pp. 15–16.

their best hope lay in co-operation with the regime. A number of measures, later rescinded by the Smith regime, were taken to limit racial discrimination in public places.

Joshua Nkomo was lucky enough to have been abroad at the time of the ban on the ANC. He had represented the party at the first conference of the All-African Peoples' Organization in Accra in December 1958 and had not returned to Rhodesia. When his colleagues were arrested on 26 February 1959, Nkomo was representing the ANC at the Cairo meeting of the Afro-Asian People's Solidarity Council. Rather than return home to jail Nkomo went to London where he set up, in January 1960, the Southern Rhodesian Congress Committee Abroad. Before doing so, he had lobbied widely in Africa and had toured the United States. He appeared at the United Nations for the first time in October 1960, as an unofficial observer. Nkomo did not return to Rhodesia until after the NDP congress that month had elected him President of the party. Stopping off *en route* in Nigeria and Kenya, he eventually arrived on 20 November, remaining only one week in Rhodesia before returning to London for the crucial Federal Review Conference and subsequent conference on Southern Rhodesia. When this broke down, just before Christmas 1960, Nkomo went back to Salisbury. He was to make numerous other trips abroad, later the subject of considerable controversy.[1]

What seems of greater importance for understanding the development of the liberation movement in Zimbabwe is the pattern it established of appeal to external bodies and institutions in the hope of pressuring the Salisbury regime to grant concessions to the African majority. Under the 1923 Constitution, the British Government had the right to veto discriminatory legislation against the African majority. Although this veto was never used, African politicians appeared mesmerized by Britain's formal sovereignty over the country despite the self-governing settler regime. On the other hand, the Whitehead and subsequent settler governments sought to persuade Britain to grant Rhodesia— especially after the Federation's break-up—full independence without any reserve powers. Both sides lobbied Whitehall and British politicians, but power remained exclusively with the white state apparatus, its police, troops, and air force. There seems to have been no preparation at this time for clandestine political organization or any form of violence against the regime.

Instead of mobilizing the black masses. Nkomo and his associates

---

[1] Day, op. cit., chronicles Nkomo's travels in great detail in Chapter 9, pp. 112–19.

gave full priority to winning support for the African cause in Britain and lining up the United Nations and friendly African and other foreign governments to pressure the British Government into intervening directly in Rhodesia. Offices were maintained in independent African countries and in London and New York. All these pressures failed to stay the British Government in imposing the 1961 Constitution. The constitutional conference was held in Salisbury under the chairmanship of the then British Secretary of State for Commonwealth Relations, Duncan Sandys, with the Whitehead regime and an NDP delegation headed by Nkomo. Nkomo and other NDP leaders' initial acceptance of the terms of the proposed constitution quickly switched to rejection when the strength of African disapproval became known. However, Sandys had already flown back to London. He refused NDP demands to call a new conference. The constitution came into force in November 1962, after winning approval from the European electorate. Africans boycotted this and the general election of 1962—which brought the racist Rhodesian Front to power—despite the pressing advice of British political leaders to try to make the 1961 Constitution work. Under both Conservative and Labour governments, this was to remain in substance the British position in regard to Africans. Day reports that in 1961 the Duke of Devonshire (then Under-Secretary of State for Commonwealth Relations) told an NDP delegation of Nkomo, Moton Malianga, and Enoch Dumbutshena that 'the Africans could not be given control in Southern Rhodesia, because the complex industrial organization there must not be placed in inexperienced hands.'[1]

It is amazing how, despite such rebuffs and signal lack of success, the African leaders persisted in their efforts, never seeming to abandon their hope that, in the long run, world opinion would oblige the British Government to permit an African majority to come to power in Rhodesia. However vigorous the African lobby in London and New York, its leaders had underestimated the extent of British sympathy for their European 'kith and kin' in Rhodesia and the much greater lobbying effectiveness of the powerful financial and industrial interests that were also concerned about the future of Rhodesia.

In December 1961, the NDP was banned by the settler regime, which alleged that it had embarked on a campaign of violence. A new nationalist party was immediately formed, called the Zimbabwe African People's Union, made up essentially of the same people.

---

[1] Day, op. cit., p. 33.

The Zimbabwe African People's Union (ZAPU)

The Zimbabwe African People's Union was the direct successor of the banned NDP, although its leaders were not anxious to stress the point at its founding in December 1961 since they rightly feared government suppression. It had the reputation of being the 'major' of the eventual two rival liberation movements in Rhodesia and of inheriting the legacy of past African militancy and resistance. The former opinion is now much contested and the latter quite tendentious. Both movements share a common past, but, initially, they separated mainly over the failure of the leadership to evolve policies that had any effect on the regime's white supremacist course in Salisbury, or the passivity in London. Their separation was exacerbated by personality clashes.

The guiding personality was Joshua Nkomo. This tireless traveller and lobbyist for the African nationalist cause was born into a Kalanga peasant family in the Matopa district of Southern Rhodesia. After secondary education in Rhodesia, he went to South Africa to attend a college in Natal and the Hofmeyer School of Social Work in Johannesburg. In 1947, on returning to Rhodesia, he was employed as a social worker by the Rhodesia Railways African Employees' Association, which by 1952 had twenty-two branches and over 2,600 members. A Protestant lay-preacher, Nkomo was deeply religious at this time and for a while fell under the conservative influence of Moral Re-Armament. Reviving the moribund African National Congress of Southern Rhodesia, he took part in the All-African Convention that waged a futile campaign against the constitution of the Federation of Rhodesia and Nyasaland. He attempted to win a seat in the Federal parliament in 1953, but was rejected by the overwhelmingly white electorate. Abandoning his job with the railway, he set up in private business as an insurance agent and auctioneer. Elected President of Congress, he was nevertheless unable to develop more than his own Bulawayo branch until he allied himself with James Chikerema and George Nyandoro of the Youth League, with whom he then built up the new ANC of Southern Rhodesia. In December 1958, Nkomo travelled to Accra to represent the ANC at the First All-African Peoples' Conference and later went on to Cairo where, as explained in the previous section, he learned that the settler regime had declared a State of Emergency in Rhodesia and had arrested and detained Congress leaders. Nkomo remained abroad for nearly two years, operating from a London exile office, before finally returning to Rhodesia in October 1960 as President-

General of the National Democratic Party (NDP), which had been formed at the beginning of 1960 to replace the banned Congress.

Shortly after ZAPU was formed, Nkomo and his associates agreed that, if it too were banned, they would not try to form another party but would go underground at home and operate offices in exile. The white Government moved quickly and ZAPU was outlawed in September 1962, after hardly nine months' existence. By now an expert at exile politicking, Nkomo—who had lived abroad from 1958 to 1960, running an office in London—suggested moving the entire leadership out of Rhodesia and eventually setting up an African government-in-exile. His associates reportedly were not convinced of the wisdom of this proposal but, just before the Government banned ZAPU, on 20 September, Nkomo flew to Tanganyika, where he had proposed locating his Zimbabwe exile government. That March, Nkomo and Washington Malianga had appeared together before the U.N. Fourth Committee— ZAPU's first official appearance as a petitioning organization. Garfield Todd, the liberal former Premier of Rhodesia, also testified before the Committee, at the invitation of Nkomo. A sub-committee on Rhodesia was sent to London to investigate the legal status of Rhodesia and reported back to the Committee that Rhodesia was not a genuine self-governing territory, recommending that Britain should expedite African majority independence. This position was approved by the full Committee and ratified by the General Assembly, but the British Government was not to be prodded into action on behalf of Africans. As Day says: 'The British Government took the line that only the British Government had the right to do anything about Southern Rhodesia and it had chosen not to do so.'[1]

Nkomo himself had been present in New York in June when the General Assembly approved the Fourth Committee's findings and recommendation. He was not the only member of the ZAPU national executive committee convinced that the opinions of that world body could not be ignored for ever by the British Government. ZAPU therefore intensified its lobbying of the U.N.

Emergency headquarters of the party in exile functioned in Dar es Salaam under two members of the executive, the Reverend Ndabaningi Sithole and A. Mukhahlera. While in Tanganyika, Nkomo had met Rashidi Kawawa, then Premier, and other top government and Tanganyika African National Union (TANU) party officials, who offered whatever facilities in the Tanganyika capital he needed to maintain ZAPU abroad.

[1] Day, op. cit., p. 49

Nkomo left Dar es Salaam to return to Rhodesia via Lusaka, and it was there that he learned the Government had finally banned his party. He cancelled his flight back to Salisbury and discussed the situation with Northern Rhodesian African officials; then he returned to Dar es Salaam. There, Sithole urged him to return home, despite the arrest of a number of ZAPU leaders, which he finally did at the beginning of October. Nkomo was immediately put under restriction by the Government, but he managed to remain in contact with many of his colleagues and actually held an executive meeting, despite police surveillance. The journalist Nathan Shamuyarira—who later broke with Nkomo—provides us with valuable insights into the operation of ZAPU at this time and claims that Nkomo proposed at this meeting that the executive should flee Rhodesia and set up a government-in-exile in Dar es Salaam. This proposal was rejected by Nkomo's colleagues, who believed that they could still play an important role inside the country.[1]

Nkomo remained under restriction until January 1963. Although the ban on ZAPU was not lifted, a ZAPU delegation led by Nkomo met R. A. Butler, then British Minister for Central African Affairs, when he visited Salisbury. The Africans found Butler personally more sympathetic to their cause than Duncan Sandys had been, but he too refused their demands for another constitutional conference. Butler had at least urged them to send him a document listing their grievances, which they were only too happy to do. Nkomo and his associates spoke to Butler again in March in London, on the margin of the talks there concerning the future of Northern Rhodesia and its relations with Southern Rhodesia. (Nkomo had hastened to Lusaka to speak with Kenneth Kaunda of the United National Independence Party (UNIP), a break-away from the old ANC of Northern Rhodesia.) From London, Nkomo travelled to New York and appeared again at the United Nations. Returning to London, he at last saw Sithole, who was still running the ZAPU office in Dar es Salaam, then went to the Tanganyika capital to meet other ZAPU people.

At the end of March, Nkomo finally went back to Rhodesia. He convened a secret meeting of the illegal ZAPU executive in Bulawayo and persuaded them that other African leaders now thought it wise for the entire executive to leave Rhodesia. Only James Chikerema, released from four years in detention at the beginning of the year, was to remain behind a little longer. According to Shamuyarira, the executive members found when they reached Dar es Salaam that President Julius K. Nyerere had not given his approval to their move. In any case, Nkomo

[1] N. M. Shamuyarira, *Crisis in Rhodesia* (London, Deutsch, 1965), p. 175.

announced to the press that he was not forming a government-in-exile. He then left on a tour of some African countries, and in May headed the ZAPU delegation at the Addis Ababa summit meeting of African heads of State that established the Organization of African Unity.

Nkomo immediately asked the O.A.U. for financial assistance for his party to maintain the leadership in exile. This was flatly rejected and the wandering ZAPU executive committee was urged to return home, despite the ban on its overt activities, to organize further African political activity inside Rhodesia. Later, when the O.A.U.'s African Liberation Committee was set up, action on another ZAPU request for funds was suspended until the party could prove it was functioning within Rhodesia.[1] These rebuffs from fellow Africans intensified the contradictions within the ZAPU executive and led directly to the split of the organization.

Meanwhile, in the middle of 1962, a new development had occurred which was to set the only practical line of action for African nationalists. Thanks to ZAPU's foreign contacts, a group of young Africans went abroad to begin military training in Algeria, China, Czechoslovakia, and Ghana. They were to form the first cadres of the Zimbabwe Liberation Army. By distributing tracts in Salisbury and Bulawayo, the military group began publicizing its existence in September 1962, just before ZAPU was banned. Despite the fact that the military group was covertly directed by members of the ZAPU executive, the party's leaders publicly announced that they had no connection with this illegal, terrorist group. The group initiated various forms of low-scale violence, but it was four years before guerrilla warfare was actually launched. And then it was the rival Zimbabwe African National Union (ZANU) that led the way.

When pressing their requests for financial assistance from the O.A.U., in May 1963 and later, ZAPU did not stress—if it even ventured to mention privately—any preparations for a generalized war of liberation against the settler government in Salisbury. In June, Nkomo—whose executive was still based in Dar es Salaam—lobbied the Victoria Falls Conference at which Rhodesian Front Premier Winston Field failed to obtain British approval for full independence. Nkomo, accompanied by Chikerema, also stopped for talks in Lusaka with Kaunda, who urged the wandering ZAPU leaders to return home, where organized activity, even covert, had virtually ceased. There was mounting dissatisfaction with Nkomo's leadership, which had been criticized as vacillating and

[1] Shamuyarira, op. cit., p. 178.

indecisive, focused almost exclusively on pseudo-diplomacy and lobbying foreign governments and international organizations. In the executive, criticism against Nkomo came principally from Sithole, Leopold Takawira, Moton Malianga, and Robert Mugabe. Ironically, the actual split took place in Dar es Salaam after Nkomo's return to Salisbury, where he found that his critics on the executive had been in contact with local leaders and were broadcasting reports of his incapacity. Nkomo immediately denounced his opponents and sent a cable to Dar es Salaam to suspend the four rebellious executive members. They, in turn, convened a meeting of the seven executive members in Tanganyika, to depose Nkomo. The three members loyal to Nkomo (J. Z. Moyo, C. M. Muchachi, and Joseph Msika) declared the meeting unconstitutional and left. Sithole was elected President to replace him, but the four had no intention of remaining any longer in exile. They decided to return home to organize the new nationalist party that Nkomo had opposed. And on 8 August 1963, the new party, called the Zimbabwe African National Union, was formed.

ZAPU, of course, was still officially banned. But the formation of a new party by his opponents forced Nkomo's hand. Rather than permit them a free hand in organizing among the masses, he had finally to consent to the creation of a new body called the People's Caretaker Council (PCC), which he maintained was not a party, but an 'African interest group'. In fact, it was the old ZAPU—minus the dissidents in ZANU—and abroad its members continued to operate under the ZAPU label. Both ZANU and PCC/ZAPU enjoyed exactly one year of legal existence under the settler regime, during which militants of the two organizations probably struck more blows at each other than at the white regime. Nevertheless, their policies were hardly different, although ZANU was somewhat more militant in tone, as Nkomo clearly did not want to provoke another government ban.

However, rather than strike the party itself, the new Ian Smith Government chose to detain its leaders. In April 1964, Nkomo was sent to a detention camp at Gonakudzingwa, where he was joined by Lazarus Nkala and Joseph Msika: he was still confined there at the beginning of the seventies, having never been formally arrested or tried for any alleged crime.

Many African sympathizers of the Zimbabwe cause deplored the split in ZAPU and numerous efforts were made to effect a reconciliation. But enmities had become bitter, while ideological or opportunistic alliances also intervened. Both Kaunda and Dr. Hastings K. Banda of Malawi urged the rivals to settle their differences. Banda personally tended to support the ZANU leaders in their criticisms of Nkomo, while Kaunda hesitantly backed ZAPU in April 1964 when reconciliation no longer seemed possible. ZANU offices in Zambia were even attacked by UNIP Youth Leaguers, but the growing colony of Zimbabwe refugees in Lusaka and other centres repulsed the attacks and eventually the Zambians resigned themselves to permitting the two rival parties to establish their exile headquarters there.

In continuing contacts with the British and other governments and at the United Nations, there were now two delegations from Zimbabwe where there had been one. Both lobbied—equally without success—to prevent Britain from transferring the Central African Federation's armed forces to the Rhodesian white minority Government. A resolution against this transfer was presented to the U.N. Security Council by Ghana, but was vetoed by Britain.

Both the PCC/ZAPU and ZANU were outlawed by the Smith regime in August 1964. By this time, the Lusaka headquarters was fully functioning under James Chikerema, who became Acting President after Nkomo's detention, assisted by his long-time associate George Nyandoro, the PCC–ZAPU National Secretary. (A conference had been held at Cold Comfort Farm in Rhodesia on 10 August 1963, which dissolved all previous party arrangements, and Chikerema and Nyandoro were sent to Lusaka to run the exile organization. Just what happened at this meeting has become the subject of violent controversy, as we shall see. All that is necessary here is to note that Chikerema and Nyandoro were joined in Lusaka early in 1964 by J. Z. Moyo, the National Treasurer, and T. G. Silundika, National Secretary for Publicity and Information. Initially, their task was not to attempt to direct the struggle inside the country but simply to control the party's diplomatic efforts abroad and conduct a vigorous propaganda campaign.) Although in detention in a remote area, Nkomo was nevertheless presumed to be directing the clandestine party inside Rhodesia—especially as he was still allowed visitors at Gonakudzingwa.

As it became clearer that Smith was about to proclaim U.D.I., so stripping his Government of its constitutionality in British official eyes, Chikerema and his associates hinted that they might proclaim a government-in-exile in such an event. They also predicted wide-scale African violence after U.D.I., but with both PCC/ZAPU and ZANU banned there was no visible African violence when Smith went ahead with his U.D.I. in November 1965. And there was no proclamation of a government-in-exile, whose legitimacy could only have been demonstrated by a reconciliation between the exiled ZAPU and ZANU leaderships. In

November 1968, after the talks on H.M.S. *Fearless* between British Prime Minister Harold Wilson and Smith, Nkomo and his associates were brought to separate and hastily arranged meetings at Sarum Airport, Salisbury, with George Thomson, British Minister Without Portfolio in charge of Rhodesia, and Maurice Foley, Minister of State in the Commonwealth Office. Sithole, and his colleagues, also detained by the Smith regime, met similarly with the visiting British officials. The latter tried to persuade both groups of imprisoned African leaders, who had no previous knowledge of the terms, to rubberstamp British proposals for settling the Rhodesian crisis. Neither Nkomo nor Sithole gave the British any satisfaction, although ZANU sources subsequently claimed that Nkomo had suggested during his two-hour talk with Thomson and Foley that he might be willing to accept if Smith would set up a nominal coalition cabinet with PCC/ZAPU, granting him, in the name of the African majority, a seat.

The clash at Sinoia between ZANU guerrillas and troops of the Smith regime on 29 April 1966, five months after U.D.I., came as a bitter shock to ZAPU. Although ZAPU men had been training in a number of countries, they had yet to go into action, except for the handful that had operated inside the country as the Zimbabwe Liberation Army. This ZANU action was denounced as 'irresponsible' by the ZAPU exiles, perhaps especially as it clearly indicated an effort by their rivals to launch a full-scale guerrilla war. In July 1964, a ZANU 'Crocodile Gang' had killed a European farmer near Melsetter, but this had been an isolated incident. Moreover, Zambian authorities had not approved of violence inside Rhodesia at that time. Now, although the Zambians still maintained official ignorance of the guerrillas' presence on their soil, they were not seriously hindering their operations. ZAPU spokesmen betrayed the apprehensions of their organization and revealed the influence of the growing Sino-Soviet conflict when they referred to the ZANU fighters, who had been trained in China, as 'pro-Chinese extremists'.

Perhaps because of a belief that more was to be obtained from the Russians, or because of increasingly close ties with the ANC of South Africa, whose representatives in independent African countries and particularly in Eastern Europe were introducing ZAPU men to local leaders who might help them, the ZAPU exiles moved closer to the Soviet orbit. Nevertheless, Chikerema had visited China in January 1964 on behalf of the PCC/ZAPU, following up contacts made by previous leaders before the split. In addition to socialist countries and pleas to African countries, such as Ghana and Algeria, ZAPU and

ZANU reiterated in 1965 their requests for A.L.C. financial and material assistance in preparing for an armed struggle.

For reasons which are difficult to appreciate, ZAPU began associating the ANC of South Africa with its military preparations. From the ANC standpoint, the development is easy to understand. As long as Zambia, after U.D.I., depended heavily on South Africa as an avenue for imports and exports, President Kaunda—who had little liking for bloodshed at any time—would not permit his territory to be overtly used as a base for direct attacks against South Africa. A special exception was made in the case of guerrilla raids launched from Zambian bases against South West Africa, the U.N. General Assembly having terminated South Africa's mandate in October 1966. There is considerable evidence to indicate that originally the guerrillas of ANC and ZAPU were trained mainly to blackmail their respective white-minority regimes into nego-tiating with the African nationalist movements—failing that, to con-vince the United Nations that international action was urgently needed in order to avert the threat to world peace that any major conflict in South Africa would potentially become.

On 19 August 1967, only hours after their joint forces had crossed the Zambezi River into Rhodesia, Oliver Tambo of the ANC and Chikerema called a press conference in Lusaka to announce a military alliance between their two movements and to proclaim that their forces were already engaged in a long-term operation that was designed to carry them through Rhodesia and into the Republic of South Africa. The presence in Rhodesia of blacks from South Africa excused the prompt despatch of South African police with helicopters to bolster European and African mercenary forces at the disposal of Smith's regime. Actually, some South African forces were already in the country before the attack. According to African sources, the South African force in Rhodesia in 1969 amounted to 2,700 men, while the illegal white regime had 1,800 white regulars and 1,800 black mercena-ries of its own, plus several thousand white reservists.[1] The Rhodesian Air Force that Britain had given to the Salisbury Government despite protests in the United Nations, went into action against the guerrillas; unfortunately, they were not able to disperse, their heavy equipment and their leaders' poor strategy obliging them to concentrate in the Wankie game reserve area, so providing an excellent target for the strafing and bombing jets.

Even the number of ZAPU-ANC guerrillas who took part in this

[1] *Zimbabwe Challenge*, organ of the Zimbabwe Students Union in Europe (April 1969), p. 20.

first battle is a matter or argument, figures ranging from fifty to 200. What is certain is that the fighters fell into a trap, as John Worrall reported in the *Guardian* from Salisbury on 28 August 1967. The Africans had marched into a 'huge trap', Worrall said, prepared by Rhodesian-South African forces after intelligence reports from secret agents revealed the plans for an attack into Western Matabeleland, not far from the Botswana border. The only undisputed fact in the incident, as Worrall himself reported, is that the blacks 'fought ferociously with their deadly Russian and Chinese weapons, but many were killed or captured and the others put to flight by the highly mobile Rhodesian forces.' Nevertheless, ANC spokesmen throughout the world, and their friends, hailed the Wankie disaster as a 'victory'.

ZANU praised the courage of the fighting men, but denounced the large concentration of forces and the use of the ANC men as a gross blunder. *Zimbabwe News*, the ZANU publication in Lusaka, argued that

... the greatest help we can get from ANC is for ANC to wage intensive guerrilla warfare in South Africa. If ANC can pin down the whole South African force inside South Africa, then Zimbabweans shall be left with Smith alone without South African aid. . . . As it is now, the ANC and PCC (ZAPU) alliance has made it easy for Smith and Vorster to unite and concentrate their forces to slaughter Zimbabweans.[1]

To spell out its distaste for the use of South African blacks in Rhodesia, the ZANU organ added: 'There are four million Zimbabweans and they are enough to defeat 200,000 whites in Rhodesia. To bring mercenaries [the ANC men] to help Zimbabweans is to insult the revolutionary zeal and the ability to fight of every Zimbabwean.'

The PAC of Azania (South Africa) equally deplored the ANC's presence in Rhodesia, in a memorandum presented to the O.A.U. summit meeting in Kinshasa. The PAC claimed that Tambo and Chikerema had no idea of guerrilla warfare and their apparent strategy of direct confrontation with a regular army was doomed to defeat. 'It is wholly unacceptable both in theory and practice, and is the worst bluff and a criminal act of manslaughter,' declared the PAC, because, hoping against hope to effect a breakthrough into South Africa, and drawing world attention to the 'United Front', the ANC's 'apparent belief was that the racist regimes would be frightened and have a "change of heart",' rather than initiate a genuinely revolutionary people's war. 'If for argument's sake, the process was a success, you can well imagine how jubilant the Imperialist world would have been to

[1] *Zimbabwe News* (Vol. 2, No. 19, 30 September 1967).

establish new puppet regimes in Southern Africa, with the system of exploitation left untouched, and run by the same old bourgeois States.'[1]

A year after the Wankie defeat, a ZANU spokesman in Lusaka claimed to have discovered that the ZAPU guides had led the ANC fighters to a thicket near the town of Wankie and left them on the pretext of going to collect food and information—'only to return a few hours later at the head of an enemy contingent.' ZAPU 'is well known to be infested through and through with enemy informers—a fact which explains their utter failure to put up even a minute's battle against enemy forces by themselves,' the spokesman claimed. Whatever the truth about the Wankie incident, it could not be denied that when the captured freedom fighters were put on trial in Bulawayo, their former ZAPU guides were among the principal witnesses against them.[2]

Equally disturbing were reports that African villagers were hostile to the guerrillas. ZAPU appeared to have no political cadres in the area and the tribal chiefs acted as auxiliary police on behalf of the settler regime, reportedly informing authorities of the whereabouts of fleeing guerrillas and their base camps inside Rhodesia. According to Christopher Munnion in the *Daily Telegraph* of 7 May 1968, the well-equipped guerrillas had 'well-hidden bunkers . . . stocked with food supplies and equipment' but they 'are not getting the support and succour they seem to expect from the typical African inhabitants.' Clearly, there had been a political failure in that the guerrillas had not integrated themselves with the people, first principle of classic Maoist People's War.

At least, after Wankie, ZAPU-ANC raids were made by much smaller units, generally crossing the Zambezi from Zambian bases and moving as rapidly as possible through the bush in the valley until spotted by the Rhodesian-South African security forces. These infiltrations appeared to be fairly easily controlled by their adversaries, and successive failures and tensions between ZAPU and ANC men, as well as tribal feuding in both movements, demoralized many guerrillas, and even provoked a number of desertions from ZANU forces.[3]

By the beginning of 1970, Rhodesian authorities claimed that since U.D.I. in 1965 they had killed 'at least 146 guerrillas, for the loss of only

---

[1] *The Wankie Fiasco in Retrospect*, a mimeographed pamphlet (issued by Publicity and Information Secretariat of the PAC, Dar es Salaam, January 1969), p. 9.

[2] The author reported these allegations in detail in a Negro Press International dispatch from Lusaka, published in the *Chicago Daily Defender* (2 March 1968).

[3] See 'From China with Love', the account by a ZANU deserter of his experiences and reasons for abandoning the struggle, by Musosa Kazembe in the *Guardian* (8 April 1968).

14 Rhodesians and South Africans.' However, African spokesmen maintained that the white regime security forces had much higher losses than they were willing to reveal. In any case, African casualties were not excessive in the unequal terms of revolutionary warfare at its initial stages, provided the lives expended had firmly implanted the revolution among the people and created liberated areas for continuing and broadening the struggle. That was clearly not so in Rhodesia.

But the political and military views of ZAPU leadership could be seen in transformation. At last, despite the continuing appeals to liberal public opinion in Britain, ZAPU lost hope of any British Government action on behalf of the African cause. In fact, fear was now expressed that any future British intervention would be aimed at *preventing an African takeover*, if the settler regime should somehow collapse. George Silundika, Publicity and Information Secretary of ZAPU, told the U.N. Committee on Colonialism on 12 May 1969, during the Committee's Lusaka hearings:

We think it is time to put an end to the call on Britain to use force to topple its regime in Rhodesia. Equally the hopes that Britain can solve the Rhodesian problem justly in any other way must no longer be entertained. This is neither an attitude of despair nor a tactless move. It is a question of facing concrete realities and getting away from the hazards of illusions. Firstly, Britain will never use force against her own agency, the Rhodesian settler regime. She has declared this umpteen times. Secondly, if Britain will ever use force in Rhodesia it will only be to frustrate the successes of the armed struggle of the Zimbabwe freedom fighters. So why continue to create a ready excuse for Britain, an excuse she will use at her own time for her own purposes and definitely against the success of the freedom we are striving to achieve.[1]

But the ZAPU leader had not lost hope in U.N. action. He declared: 'We believe it is time the United Nations gave us all-out support through member countries giving us directly the necessary materials and facilities to effect the armed destruction of the British settler racist establishment in Rhodesia.' Given the mechanism of the world organization and the powerful restraints on any action by it, this appeal for U.N. material support to African insurgents demonstrated naïveté equally as great as now-dashed illusions about British benevolence.

Militarily, ZAPU leaders were also changing their views. In a filmed interview with a team from the 'World in Action' programme of the British commercial Granada Television, televised in London on 1 January 1970, James Chikerema, leader of ZAPU in exile, did not

[1] 'ZAPU before the United Nations Committee on Colonialism', *Zimbabwe Review* (Vol. 1, No. 2, June 1969).

contradict his interviewer's contention that 'your people are doing very badly indeed.' He merely replied:

Well, this is really a protracted struggle—we do not intend to finish in a matter of 2, 3, 4 or 5 years—this is a protracted struggle. . . . The type of war we fight depends on—on changes of tactics and I can tell you that we've changed our tactics. . . . We will combine both where they meet us and intercept us—we will stand and fight—we will stand and fight—where they don't see us—we will go to our own areas and infiltrate ourselves in the population and organize our masses.

The British television cameramen were allowed to film a ZAPU camp inside Zambia, as well as to interview Chikerema. But the nearest the cameras got to action was a shot taken on the banks of the Zambezi River, where Rhodesian security forces could be dimly seen on the opposite bank. Significantly, Chikerema and the other ZAPU men in the film did not once mention their ANC allies.

Chikerema had spoken of 'changes of tactics' and held out, as any leader would, the comforting image of inevitable victory. But it was common knowledge in Lusaka and Dar es Salaam that serious tensions had been mounting within the ZAPU–ANC alliance with each successive setback after Wankie. Chikerema's television interview—apparently given without the approval of his comrades or the Zambian authorities, who were greatly embarrassed that the presence of guerrilla bases on their territory should be so blatantly publicized—precipitated an explosion of wrath which shattered the entire ZAPU organization in exile.

Accusations of political degeneration, corruption, tribalism, and cruelty in the camps and ZAPU headquarters in Lusaka were broadcast to the world in three extraordinary documents. Conditions revealed were so appalling that some of the *bien-pensants* abroad who had so faithfully echoed the 'victory' communiqués of the ZAPU–ANC alliance at first claimed the documents were forgeries; when it was proven otherwise, they retreated into offended silence.[1]

The first of these documents, entitled 'Observations on our Struggle', dated 25 February 1970, was signed by J. Z. Moyo, ZAPU's National Treasurer. In it, Moyo complains that since mid-1969 'there has been a steady decline of a serious nature' in ZAPU's military wing. He speaks of 'scathing attacks' on the military command and 'cases of tribal incitement', and cites the desertion of 'five out of the nine comrades'

---

[1] For a rare exception, see François Chenu, 'La difficile naissance de la guérilla rhodésienne', in *Les Temps Modernes* (No. 292, November 1970).

who were in ZAPU's Camp C2. In September 1969, there had been a mutiny at the same camp 'when the Chief of Staff and Headquarters officers were detained pending the arrival at C2 of the Vice President', he adds. In general, the picture is one of indiscipline, which 'is fast approaching dangerous proportions in our Army. Apart from an alarming number of deserters, loose forces are increasing—cadres live anywhere they choose.'

Moyo complains of soldiers demanding beer and spirits from functionaries who visit their camps.

I have no quarrel with the idea as such, but I am concerned with the problems which I have personally encountered when I visited camps without beers and spirits. Questions have always been asked why did you not bring us drinks. If so and so can manage to bring us something, why is it not possible with you? Implications of lesser concern on my part in this respect have been made.

Moyo suggests that, 'to avoid this embarrassment, from time to time beer be purchased for cadres from public funds.'

Next, he criticizes the 'unilateral decision' to permit the British television team to film ZAPU cadres, which compromised the security of cadres, without his knowledge as a member of the National Executive, High Command, and War Council of ZAPU. 'I wish to confess that I regard this concealment of the film which was known to cadres and a selected group of Military Headquarters personnel as an expression of no confidence in me,' he says.

Finally, he cryptically protests against 'an arrangement wherein top leaders of our organization of Intelligence Officers have direct contact' with Zambian Intelligence. This system is 'inimical to our present and future interests', Moyo declares, adding that it renders ZAPU's 'Intelligence system, at its embryonic stage, liable to penetration'.

To remedy these grievances, the ZAPU National Treasurer calls for the implementation of military rules and respect shown to people's rights 'from top to bottom at all levels of the army.' He calls for a review of the strategy of the armed struggle by the Headquarters Military Command and the expansion of the ZAPU War Council 'by the inclusion of three comrades from the Military command [acting on behalf of the three War Council members at Gonaduzingwa] and each member of the War Council should have special supervisory functions to perform.' Noting that 'it is becoming almost impossible to recruit personnel from Zambia', Moyo attaches a suggested programme of recruitment from inside Zimbabwe. 'Preference for training must, as much as possible, be given to personnel who shall be utilised immediately after completion of their course', he urges, in conclusion.

Although the situation depicted in the ranks of ZAPU's military wing was far from ideal, Moyo's suggestions seemed innocuous enough. Nevertheless, on 17 March 1970, there appeared the thunderous 'Reply to Observation on Our Struggle', fifteen cyclostyled folio pages signed by Chikerema himself.

ZAPU's Acting President begins by vehemently denying that there exist such bodies as a 'War Council' or 'National Executive' or even a 'People's Council'. According to Chikerema, the Cold Comfort Farm conference on 10 August 1963, delegated 'full and complete mandate . . . to only one man, our President Comrade Joshua Nkomo.' He declares:

No councils, no Committees were set up, no individuals were elected to any Post by anybody. The mandate was given to one man, to elect to, to appoint, to dismiss from, and post any officer. In the context of the above analysis, I was appointed by this *one man* on whose full shoulders the whole destiny of the liberation struggle of Zimbabwe was deposited, on whose full shoulders the representatives of the five million people of Zimbabwe place their hopes and unquestionable trust to lead them to full realization of their hopes and aspirations.

Rejecting Moyo's suggestions for a five-man 'War Council', which would 'by implication remove my authority over my departments and have them run for me', Chikerema insists that he and Nkomo 'constructed the whole structure of the People's Caretaker Council, appointed all its office bearers comprising of all members of the National Executive, all members of the People's Council, all regional and district officers.' He maintains this structure is directly responsible to Nkomo 'or to his agent specifically delegated authority to exercise his mandate' and 'the man so specifically delegated . . . is me.'

Incidentally, Chikerema denies Moyo's passing remark that the decision to set up an army was made in 1964, claiming rather it was as far back as 1960, although,

not for the purpose of waging guerrilla warfare but the purpose, of carrying out acts of sabotage which were considered relevant to bring forth fear and despondency to the settlers in Rhodesia in order to influence the British Government and the foreign settlers in Rhodesia to accede to the popular revolutionary demands of the people in Zimbabwe.

As for Moyo's grievances concerning the army, Chikerema admits the situation is bad. 'Yes Comrades, the Party and the Army is in dismay. It has no Commander. It has no administration. It has no team spirit. It is corrupt, and therefore not sincere to its objectives.' Nevertheless, he accuses Moyo's document of stating 'from beginning to end . . . a position of calculated hypocrisy, calculated manoeuvres for positions and influence in the Party and the Army. It is intended to protect clans, and tribal corruption in the Party and the Army.'

As for his own examination of the affairs of the army, Chikerema says he found 'a shocking state of affairs, the depth and height of decay, corruption, nepotism, tribalism, selfishness, and gross irresponsibility on the part of the military administration from top to bottom.' He adds:

The army has been divided into tribal factions. The party is divided into tribal factions and clannish empires. There are cadres that are more equal than others in both the party and the army. There are cadres that are given special treatment on tribal and clan considerations in both the party and the army. They have places rented for meeting and sleeping with their girl friends. They are the most smartly dressed. They never run short of money, and in fact some of them have boasted that as long as so and so still holds the position he holds, they will never suffer.

As for the controversial British television film, Chikerema admits his complete responsibility for authorizing it, which he says was his right. Nevertheless, the Zambian Government 'rightly' objected to the film being made without their knowledge, and 'I have apologised to the President of Zambia. As far as I am concerned the matter is over', Chikerema adds. 'It is no longer the subject for celebrations in the Townships to mark the downfall of the Vice-President of ZAPU.'

Given this situation, Chikerema then announces he has 'dissolved the whole military command as presently constituted', appointing a new military administration and a new command structure directly responsible to him 'and to nobody else'. In addition, he declares he is taking over direct control of all foreign affairs from the National Secretary, George Nyandoro; taking over direct control of education of ZAPU cadres from T. G. Silundika and control of all the external accounts of party funds from J. Z. Moyo, the National Treasurer.

Because the Lusaka District Council has been 'the centre of tribal intrigues, conspiracy and the promotion of personality cult for a long time,' Chikerema dissolves the whole Council and suspends seven Council members from holding party office for three years for allegedly attempting 'to assault Comrade National Secretary' Nyandoro.

The third document, headed 'On the Coup Crisis Precipated [*sic*] by J. Chikerema', dated 21 March 1970, was signed by Moyo, Edward Ndlovu, Deputy National Secretary of ZAPU, and Silundika, as Publicity and Information Secretary. In a somewhat more conciliatory mood, the three claim that Chikerema's document was drafted in co-operation with Nyandoro. 'Chikerema's name is a front for power which they hoped to share in running the organization as two people imposing themselves on the whole nation of Zimbabwe,' they declare. They hint that Chikerema and Nyandoro are also involved in tribal factions and claim that the Lusaka District Council discovered that Chikerema himself was holding private meetings with 'groups of his own tribe'. Nevertheless, 'we would have no quarrel with Chikerema if he had presented his worries about the state of the Party and made his proposals, which he has never done before, for consideration and solution by the National Executive.' But Chikerema carried out a coup, like Leabua Jonathan in Lesotho, they argue, 'plunging the only hope of the people, the Party, into the sorry mess of his personal power ambitions.'

The three leaders deny that they owe their party posts to appointment by Chikerema and reaffirm their conviction that ZAPU must be run on the 'principle of collective responsibility of the National Executive. We will not have ZAPU run the way Banda runs the Malawi Congress Party as a personal estate.' On the other hand, they declare they have no wish to take advantage of 'the grave blunders' of their colleague and only wish to help him realize his mistakes. Finally they state:

Any difficulties confronting the Party and the struggle at the present moment, be they of tribalism, nepotism, corruption, and manoeuvres are the collective responsibility of us all in the National Executive including Chikerema and Nyandoro who are trying to jump and pass the buck to others. None of us can escape management or mismanagement of the Party by the simple trick of pointing fingers at others and then descending to use and involve junior officers of the Party by baiting them into a pseudo-military structure. We have to pick up our problems, sort them out coolly and solve them as a National Executive in fulfilment of our responsibility without involving cadres, officers and members as has already been done by Chikerema.

But the conflict within the party had reached all levels and erupted into internecine violence, exacerbated by the lingering tribal enmity between Ndebele and Shona. On 24 April 1970, the *Times of Zambia* front-paged the ZAPU split and reported a running battle outside the ZAPU hostel in the Emmasdale Township of Lusaka. Six men were reported hurt and four others 'missing' in the battle between Shona and Ndebele members of ZAPU.

Strenuous personal intervention by President Kaunda halted the violence. Kaunda warned that ZAPU would be asked to leave Zambia if its leaders could not sink their differences. Following his ultimatum, Chikerema and Nyandoro met for the first time in three weeks with their three dissident colleagues. The enmity between them had shattered ZAPU, halted all military operations and convinced their allies of the ANC, who had discreetly backed Moyo's faction in the dispute, that they could no longer rely on their Zimbabwean junior partners and should seek other alliances.

Far from rejoicing over the convulsions within ZAPU, their rivals in ZANU commented that the struggle of all the people of Zimbabwe was being endangered by the tribal feuding. In the context of ZAPU, they noted the label of 'tribalist' was being pinned on people 'who will not believe that anyone with a Shona name has a right to exercise the function of leadership.'[1] ZANU's National Chairman Herbert Chitebo, in a statesmanly speech on 'Africa Day', 29 May 1970, appealed for national unity. He declared:

We need in Zimbabwe to return to the spirit of 1896, when our forefathers Shona and Ndebele, faced the common threat of white settlement. The workers and peasants of 1970 must unite to overthrow the white settler capitalists and racists. We have a national duty as leaders of the Zimbabwe revolution to bring this about. Those who stand in the way of unity will be condemned by future generations as the betrayers of the revolution of the peasants and workers.[2]

But, in the climate of animosity and suspicion that then reigned in Zambia among the rank and file as well as the leadership of ZAPU, even this appeal was decried as partisan and intended to foster greater disunity.

The Zimbabwe African National Union (ZANU)

Born of frustration over the lack of political activity within Zimbabwe and the manifest lack of success of the strategy and tactics imposed on ZAPU in exile after the party was banned in Rhodesia in September 1962, the Zimbabwe African National Union was formed on 8 August 1963. The President was the Reverend Ndabaningi Sithole, who had formerly run ZAPU's exile headquarters in Dar es Salaam, and who with three other members of the executive had rebelled against Joshua Nkomo's leadership. Nkomo's manifest fondness for foreign travel and psuedo-diplomacy, his erratic temperament, lack of decision, and rapidly fading charisma had prompted mounting criticism of his personality and style of leadership. Above all, Nkomo's decision not to form a new African party in Rhodesia after the white settler Government had

[1] *Zimbabwe News* (Vol. 5, No. 4, April 1970).
[2] Ibid. (Vol. 5, No. 7, July 1970).

outlawed ZAPU infuriated some of his associates, who believed that it was mistaken to cease all overt political organization of the country's African majority. For his part, Nkomo seemed more concerned about the possible loss of more party property and funds inside Rhodesia when the new party was banned, as it inevitably would be. Although he himself denied on several occasions the intention of doing so, there were also numerous indications at the time that Nkomo was seeking Pan-African approval for the establishment of ZAPU abroad as a Zimbabwe government-in-exile.

Sithole and his colleagues returned quickly to Rhodesia from Dar es Salaam to set in motion their plans for the organization of the new party, which was to become ZANU. Sithole summarized the purpose of the party in these words:

African politics in Zimbabwe, as well as in European-ruled Africa, began as 'reformist politics', but now we have entered the phase of 'take-over' politics, as it is impossible for the present white minority to rule Zimbabwe for the benefit of the voteless African majority. We have entered the period of political CONFRONTATION. ZANU represents the fighting spirit which began with an imposed rule in 1890 and shows the unity of spirit between those who have gone on and those who are still living. We have a duty to ourselves and to unborn generations of Zimbabwe, and that duty is to free Zimbabwe. 'WE ARE OUR OWN LIBERATORS.'[1]

Although it seems fair enough to state, as Day does, that there was initially no difference in the policies pursued overseas by ZANU and Nkomo's reluctantly formed PCC/ZAPU,[2] there was at least a sharp difference in the militancy demonstrated by the rival parties. Freed from the restrictions imposed by Nkomo's personality, Sithole and his colleagues made strenuous efforts to recruit members and consolidate ZANU. These efforts in the African townships of Salisbury were often met by physical violence from gangs of ZAPU supporters. On the other hand, the tone of ZANU rhetoric was often more violent than that of their rivals, exhorting Africans to prepare for a confrontation with the white-minority regime.

Abroad, ZANU certainly carried on the tradition of contacts with the British Government, which began long before ZAPU existed. ZANU's Secretary General Robert Mugabe went to London shortly after the split to confer with R. A. Butler, then British Minister for Central African Affairs. Butler had made a more favourable personal impression on the African nationalists than his predecessor, Duncan

---

[1] Quoted in *Mwenje* (Lusaka, a ZANU Department of Political Affairs pamphlet, no date).

[2] See Day, op. cit., p. 22.

Sandys, but Mugabe was still unable to persuade Butler to cancel the planned transfer to the settler regime in Salisbury of the bulk of the defunct Central African Federation armed forces. Replacement of the Conservatives by a Labour government in Britain did not alter attitudes in Whitehall towards Rhodesian Africans. Arthur Bottomley, the new Commonwealth Secretary, refused to see ZANU's then Secretary for International Affairs, Simpson Mtambanengwe, and Secretary for Public Affairs Noel Mukono when they visited London in December 1964. Bottomley belatedly made up for this discourtesy when he visited Rhodesia in February 1965, in an effort to head off the threatened U.D.I., and saw a number of ZANU officials, led by Leopold Takawira, Deputy President. Sithole was already in prison and not allowed to meet the British Cabinet member, who, on the other hand, was allowed to see Nkomo, then under restriction, and other PCC/ZAPU leaders. As U.D.I. grew more certain, Prime Minister Harold Wilson himself flew to Salisbury and met Nkomo and Sithole, seeing them each separately, three times. He urged the rival African leaders not to intervene on behalf of the black majority in Rhodesia in the face of British determination, but to work to effect the 1961 Constitution. Naturally, Sithole and Nkomo both refused what no African nationalist could accept—indefinite white-minority rule over their country.

ZANU appeared to follow the same course as ZAPU at the United Nations. Its leaders expressed the same hopes that the international organization would take action against the settler regime, or at least pressure the British Government into taking action. When ZAPU's George Nyandoro appeared before the U.N. Committee of Twenty-four in April 1964, after the formation of ZANU, he maintained that the rival organization had little popular support in Rhodesia. Sithole himself came to the U.N. a few days afterwards, scornfully rejecting this contention, while making essentially the same demands on the world body as Nyandoro had done.

In September 1964 and April 1965, Nathan Shamuyarira also visited the U.N. for ZANU. He made a controversial proposal for the Rhodesian case to be taken before the International Court of Justice at the Hague. Although there were then many illusions about the Court handing down a judgement favourable to Africans in the South West Africa case before it, anti-colonial delegations at the U.N. considered Shamuyarira's suggestion ill-advised and it was not followed up. Moreover, the suggestion was not even taken up by his own party.

More important for a fledgling nationalist party, at least in principle, was support from independent African states and the Organization of

African Unity. ZAPU's Chikerema had urged the first meeting of the O.A.U.'s African Liberation Committee in 1964 not to recognize or aid ZANU in any way. However, the O.A.U. consistently attempted reconciliation of the divided African nationalist forces in Rhodesia. All these efforts ended in failure, in part because of PCC/ZAPU intransigence during the negotiations with their rivals, in refusing to admit that ZANU had any following inside Rhodesia, and, on the other hand, ZANU's equally stubborn determination never to belong to any political movement that had Joshua Nkomo as its undisputed leader.

In the Afro-Asian Peoples' Solidarity Organization, ZAPU was challenged by ZANU, but the AAPSO Council delayed action on ZANU's formal application for membership until its stormy Nicosia meeting in February 1967. And there, Simpson Mtambanengwe, who represented ZANU, pointedly held himself aloof from the militant pro-Chinese caucus as long as there was any hope of favourable action on ZANU's application. Of course, there was no chance of this, as ZAPU delegates lined up the pro-Russian majority to block entry by their rivals, spreading scare tales about 'pro-Peking extremists' who allegedly made up ZANU. Mtambanengwe, a former law student in London, was much incensed by this campaign and the 'pro-Peking' label stuck on his organization. He rightly maintained that ZANU was not a communist organization, but simply an African liberation movement, forgetting that the groups that had voted against ZANU's admission were overwhelmingly marshalled within the Soviet faction that sought to secure Moscow's control over AAPSO. Moreover, as the ANC of South Africa brought ZAPU firmly inside the Soviet orbit, the Russians had no need to subsidize a rival movement.

Occasionally, ZAPU students have contested this Moscow-line orientation of their party, but without modifying the position of the leadership in any way. In London, in 1968, a group within the ZAPU African Students' Union denounced the then ZAPU representative in Britain, Nicholas Chitziga. In their publication, *Isitlangu Sabantu*, the rebellious students described Chitziga as 'a puppet in the hands of his Soviet masters who manipulate him to the advantage of Revisionism and to the detriment of the only form of Socialism acceptable to all Africans, i.e. Scientific Socialism.' The students added: 'The main reason why our rivals ZANU are gaining ground in the struggle for power in an independent Zimbabwe is their discerning choice of impartial, loyal, strong and disinterested allies.' Nevertheless, the students reaffirmed their support for the imprisoned ZAPU President Joshua Nkomo and gave no indication of joining ZANU's ranks.

ZANU'S militancy moved from words to deeds in April 1965 when the first five-man ZANU guerrilla units, reportedly trained in Ghana, hit a number of European farms. Their mission was to disrupt the May 1965 General Election in Rhodesia. Most of the fighters were killed, or captured and tried before white judges. Two of their number sentenced to death in 1965 were hanged, with another African, on 6 March 1968, on orders of the Smith regime which—not yet calling itself a 'republic' —went ahead with the executions despite commutation of the death sentences by Britain's Queen Elizabeth II, in the exercise of the royal prerogative of mercy. The settler regime thus made clear to its African opponents that the struggle ahead would be merciless, without quarter.

Full-scale guerrilla warfare was launched by ZANU from Zambian bases in April 1966, five months after U.D.I. Due to vigorous repressive measures of the Smith regime and lack of an effective African nationalist political underground movement, the widespread African protest against U.D.I., repeatedly predicted by African leaders in exile, failed to materialize. The first clash of the Zimbabwe African National Liberation Army (ZANLA) with the Rhodesian security forces took place near Sinoia on 28–9 April 1966. ZANU spokesmen later claimed that the guerrillas had killed twenty-five police and shot down two helicopters. Officials in Salisbury denied this, but claimed their forces had killed seven of the thirty freedom fighters, reportedly in the attacking ZANLA unit. As other guerrilla units were discovered operating in various parts of the country, it became evident that ZANU was making a determined bid to start a generalized revolutionary struggle.

This initiative was immediately deplored by the British Government. The Government's position, despite all the massive illegalities of the settler dictatorship in Salisbury, had always been to condemn 'all acts of terrorism, whatever their motives and by whomsoever committed.'[1] The fighting was also condemned by ZAPU, which termed the decision to launch guerrilla warfare 'irresponsible', although ZAPU had itself been sending men for military training 'as far back as 1960' and, more seriously from 1964,[2] as its Acting President Chikerema was to reveal in March 1970. None of these men had yet been into battle and when they did go it was mainly as 'guides' for the more numerous troops of the ANC of South Africa.

Many of the ZANU party leadership inside Rhodesia were detained even before the Government banned both ZANU and PCC in August

[1] Rhodesia, BIS/CIO pamphlet R.5864/70 (London, April 1970).
[2] James Chikerema in duplicated pamphlet, *Reply to Observations on Our Struggle* (Lusaka, ZAPU, 17 March 1970).

1964. ZANU President Sithole, his Vice-President Leopold Takawira, and Secretary General Robert Mugable became prisoners. Only the mysterious death of Takawira in 'diabetic coma' on 15 June 1970, freed him from prison. African Liberation Committee Executive Secretary George Magombe spoke of 'suspicious circumstances' and said that Takawira was known to have 'suffered under torture' in the maximum security prison. E. F. Mukuka Nkoloso, President Kaunda's personal representative at the Liberation Centre in Lusaka, expressed the hope of a no longer hesitant Zambia that this 'noble spirit' would 'spark and signal for a new war for the total liberation of Zimbabwe.'

After U.D.I. in 1965, Takawira, Sithole and Mugabe were transferred from Gwelo detention camp to a maximum security prison. Here they remained without charges being made against them, or trial, until a spectacular coup that infuriated Rhodesian white officials. A remarkable document written by Sithole was smuggled out of the prison and sent to London, where, at the beginning of December 1968, Frank Ziyambi, then ZANU representative in Britain, personally delivered it to George Thomson, the British Minister responsible for the Rhodesia question. The document unequivocally rejected the British Government's *Fearless* proposals as 'hypocrisy'. Sithole declared that ZANU unreservedly rejected the *Fearless* scheme as an 'attempt to sell the inalienable right to self-determination of the 5,000,000 Africans of the country to the 220,000 white settlers. The proposals are unacceptable as a basis for any constitution.'

Thomson and the rest of the British Government were well aware of the position of the imprisoned ZANU leaders, but their staunch opposition was minimized or completely overlooked in official accounts of the attempts by the Wilson Government to reach an agreement with the Smith regime after U.D.I. On 7 November 1968, Sithole, Takawira, and Mugabe were brought to the Officers' Mess at Sarum Airport, Salisbury, for a hastily arranged meeting with Thomson and Maurice Foley, Minister of State in the Commonwealth Office, then visiting Rhodesia. The British Ministers tried in vain to secure ZANU approval of the *Fearless* proposals, of which Sithole and his colleagues had had little knowledge until their meeting with Thomson and Foley. However, after quickly glancing over a copy of the British Hansard of 22 October 1968, and a copy of the Rhodesian White Paper containing a report of the talks between Smith and Wilson aboard H.M.S. *Fearless* in October, Sithole deplored the proposals and the conduct of negotiations concerning the future of the country without the consent of the African majority.

Takawira had ridiculed the Labour Government for its apparent sensitivity to the use of force against the illegal settler regime. According to minutes of the meeting made by Mugabe and also smuggled out of the Salisbury Remand Prison—to the intense irritation of the British Government—Thomson replied:

The reason for not using force is that it would be an invasion. It would have to be done from Zambia if it were decided to use it. We have no near base. We had one in Aden, but we no longer have it. The reason is that the whole of Southern Africa would be plunged in a war. There would be lots of bloodshed. It is easy to start a war. But a war is like a bushfire which once it has started flares up and spreads. You don't know where it will end.[1]

Later, Thomson confessed frankly that Britain did not have sufficient available power and, in any case, that British determination not to use force was a 'moral issue'. And he expressed the conviction that South Africa's white-minority Government would back up the Smith regime if British troops were moved into Rhodesia. 'I have no doubt that they would fight,' Thomson reportedly declared. 'I have had several meetings with South African officials and I am left in no doubt that South Africa would fight.'

Shortly after these documents reached London, Sithole and his associates were moved to another maximum security prison outside Salisbury. The conditions of their imprisonment became increasingly harsh. In a fit of pique, the settler regime finally put Sithole on trial and convicted him of allegedly conspiring—from behind bars—to assassinate Smith and several of his colleagues. He was sentenced to five years in prison and afterwards treated worse than a common felon.

The actual direction of ZANU was in the hands of Herbert Chitepo, Rhodesia's first black lawyer and Director of Public Prosecutions in Tanzania before joining the leadership of ZANU in 1964, when he was elected in absentia National Chairman. He had already been a member of the NDP executive and had practised law in Rhodesia, the country's first African lawyer, until he went to Tanzania in 1962 as Director of Public Prosecutions. While in Rhodesia, he had handled practically all political cases and even from Tanzania returned to Salisbury to defend both Nkomo and Sithole in 1963 and 1964 respectively. He was born in 1923 in Banda, in the eastern part of the country, and was educated there and at St. Augustine's School. He went later to Adams College in Natal and, after matriculation, studied at Fort Hare University

---

[1] As quoted in the typewritten, unpublished manuscript entitled 'Meeting between the ZANU Delegation and the British Ministers' (Salisbury, 7 November 1968), signed and verified as 'substantially verbatim' by Robert Mugabe.

College, where he took a Bachelor of Arts degree. After a period as a research assistant at the University of London, he read Law at Kings College and the Middle Temple, qualifying in 1953 and returning to practise in Rhodesia as a barrister.

ZANU's exile operations were, and still are in 1972, directed from a headquarters in Lusaka. Originally, the liberation movement was run by a sixteen-member Revolutionary Council, headed by Chitepo. As in the case of the ZAPU exiles, personality, tribal, and ideological tensions were felt. The conduct of the armed struggle proved more difficult than many had originally believed it would be. Although there were persistent rumours from student dissidents of secret Israeli aid,[1] lack of 'neutralist' or Western support of any appreciable amount, and the battle lines in Africa of the Sino-Soviet conflict, led some African moderate nationalists to be described by their rivals and enemies as 'pro-Peking fanatics', or by similar horror-provoking stereotypes; this was to the obvious consternation of some of those so labelled, as we have already noted. On the other hand, the revolutionary example of China grew to have more than a purely military and material meaning. Party cadres began to study the tenets of Marxism-Leninism and to treasure the *Quotations of Chairman Mao* more than the Bible. Naturally, this radicalization of leaders and rank and file was eagerly pointed to by the white regimes in Southern Africa and reactionaries elsewhere as proof of their hoary contention that the black revolutionary wave was all part of a communist plot hatched in Moscow or Peking. Yet there is not a single shred of evidence for this, and common sense, which white supremacists clearly do not believe is shared by Africans, indicates that objective conditions of deprivation, exploitation, and oppression by white minorities, rather than any doctrine, eventually led to the formation of reformist, and later genuine liberatory, movements.

Nevertheless, ideological tensions have an insidious influence on many movements, especially since some of them still decline to make any clear ideological commitments and their militants are left with vague platforms and programmes, generally obsolete or obsolescent. On the other hand, it is also true that even right-wingers often use Marxist-Leninist revolutionary terminology to mask a totally different

[1] The charges came from leaders of the Zimbabwe Students Union in Europe, but whether founded or not, by July 1970, ZANU was very visibly in fraternal contact with al-Fatah, the Palestine Liberation Movement, and decidedly anti-Israeli in orientation, as were most other African liberation movements, some of which, like the ANC of South Africa, had earlier had friendly relations with the Zionist state.

content. Ideology is frequently employed to mask conflicts of personality and interest which the adversaries would not care to avow as such.

In ZANU's case, with great emphasis placed on militancy, it was also inevitable that some leaders and rank and file members should feel after a relatively short while that the struggle was not proceeding towards victory at a rapid enough pace. Complaints were raised about alleged 'bourgeois leaders' in Lusaka. In Britain, an anonymous deserter from ZANLA, ZANU's military force, explained in an article by Musosa Kazembe, published in the *Guardian* on 8 April 1968, the reasons for his abandonment of the struggle.

Some of my friends have returned to Rhodesia and been killed; others have been captured. Why do I stand apart? There are two reasons. First, I don't have confidence in the military leadership and organization because boys trained in many different countries are mixed up together in the units. . . . But, most important, I want a revolution, not just a nationalist armed struggle. You can't have it half-way. I am a Maoist. The Party should control the whole movement, military as well as political. If I'm going to get killed in Rhodesia I want to know that I am dying for a real revolution, not just a change in regime like there has been in Kenya.

Such straightforward ultra-leftism bears little resemblance to the political sophistication that step-by-step during a protracted war brought the Communist Party of China to power. This anonymous guerrilla fighter, who had been trained in China, refers to discussion with a Chinese instructor of his objections to the nationalist leaders of his own party, who, he feared, would 'take over the Parliament and the whites could run the whole economy as usual.' He quotes the reply: 'Don't worry. Once you start the revolution they won't be able to control it. It will destroy everything that stands in its way.'

For a while, it seemed to observers in Lusaka that this ideological debate, added to other personality and tribal tensions, might cause serious damage to ZANU. Perhaps because of the physical separation of their respective offices in Lusaka, it looked in 1968 almost as though Chitepo was running one ZANU headquarters from the African Liberation Centre, while fiery Washington Malianga ran another from his Publicity and Information Secretariat in the heart of the city.

Nevertheless, as we have seen, the internal contradictions exploded inside ZAPU rather than ZANU. Before that happened, in March 1969, ZANU closed ranks and Chitepo's leadership was briefly reaffirmed. A Special Review Conference of all members abroad met in Lusaka and approved the reorganization of the party's top leadership. More than a hundred delegates voted overwhelmingly to replace the sixteen-member

Revolutionary Council with an eight-member Supreme Council, which would be chaired by Chitepo. This administrative reorganization, it was claimed, would strengthen the party by facilitating policy-making and military decisions.

Chitepo declared the principal objective at this stage of the struggle was national unity, ever menaced by tribalism and sectionalism. In March–April 1970, Chikerema of ZAPU approached Chitepo with a view to unifying their two movements. The ZANU executive agreed to meet him, but found the tribal and ideological splits within ZAPU too great to bridge and Chikerema without the necessary clear-cut authority. There were reports of an agreement between Nkomo and Sithole, in their Rhodesian prisons, to step down in the interests of unity and call upon Robert Mugabe to head a new organization formed from their two rival parties.[1] But neither Chikerema nor Chitepo were able to confirm these reports, and Chikerema's adversaries, encouraged by the ANC of South Africa and the Soviet Embassy in Lusaka, seemed unwilling to enter into any union that might alter ZAPU's previous pro-Soviet stance.

Front for the Liberation of Zimbabwe (FROLIZI)

The repeated failures of the leaders of the rival ZAPU and ZANU to unite infuriated the Zambian Government. President Kaunda warned: 'They have got to choose between coming together or forfeiting Zambia's readiness to accommodate them.'[2] The threat produced immediate action, and on 1 October 1971, members of the two organizations announced at a Lusaka press conference that ZAPU and ZANU had merged to form the Front for the Liberation of Zimbabwe (FROLIZI).

Named leader and chairman of the new Front was 29-year-old Shelton Siwela, the former ZAPU military commander, while Godfrey Savanhu, formerly of ZANU, was given the post of secretary. Also from ZANU, Nathan Shamuyarira was put in charge of 'foreign research' and financial affairs. Present at the press conference announcing the formation of the Front were also James Chikerema and George Nyandoro, but it was stressed that the two former ZAPU leaders would merely hold junior posts in FROLIZI's 'revolutionary command council'.[3]

Unity, however, was far from complete. Herbert Chitebo of ZANU

---

[1] See Richard Gott's report in the *Guardian* (12 January 1971).

[2] Press communiqué of the Zambian High Commission London (No. 49/1971).

[3] See *The Times* and the *Guardian* (2 October 1971), and *Le Monde* (3 October 1971).

and many others refused to join the new group, as did the J. Z. Moyo faction of ZAPU. Thus, although reduced somewhat by defections, ZANU and ZAPU had definitely not gone out of business, and instead of two rival Zimbabwe liberation movements, there then existed three.

It was nevertheless expected that, after a short period of grace, the two groups of recalcitrants would be declared 'prohibited immigrants' by the Zambian Government and swiftly expelled from the country, while FROLIZI would henceforth enjoy the exclusive backing of both Zambia and the O.A.U.'s African Liberation Committee.

The new organization was granted immediate assistance in order to carry out a military programme to revive the armed struggle inside Zimbabwe, but formal recognition of FROLIZI as a liberation movement was postponed in the hope that ZANU and ZAPU would either willingly or of necessity join in FROLIZI's 'national united front'. On the other hand, ZANU and ZAPU charged that FROLIZI was essentially a 'tribal clique' from James Chikerema's Zezure tribe, a Shona sub-group. Regardless, in the camps in Tanzania and Zambia substantial numbers of former ZANU and ZAPU militants were reliably reported to have entered the ranks of FROLIZI.

The arrival of the Pearce Commission in January 1972, sent by the British Government to sound public opinion in Rhodesia on the Douglas-Home proposals to terminate the Smith rebellion by allowing white-minority rule for the foreseeable future, provoked a mass upsurge inside Rhodesia. Organized by the African National Council, which appeared to have no links with any of the three external liberation movements, the Africans showed plainly what they thought of the sellout in a series of demonstrations and marches. Smith's forces reacted by shooting fourteen Africans and imprisoning 300 activists, including Josiah and Ruth Chinamano, Zacharia Kanyasa, and Garfield and Judy Todd. Some chiefs found themselves forced to follow the lead of the Council. This greatly embarrassed the Pearce Commission, since the pretence of a generally acceptable solution could no longer be maintained. By early 1972, the long-term effects remained uncertain.

PART FIVE
THE PORTUGUESE COLONIES

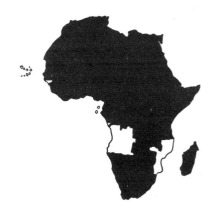

Portugal's involvement in Africa is the longest of any European power; it is also, even when viewed against the meagre achievements and massive plunder of other colonial powers, the most squalid. And yet successive Portuguese leaders have insisted upon the alleged mystical qualities of Portuguese colonialism, the proverbial 'civilizing mission' that Portugal was undertaking in Africa. During the dictatorship of Premier António de Oliveira Salazar from 1928 to 1968, and under his successor, Dr. Marcelo Caetano, the Portuguese corporate oligarchy used the centuries-old imperial mystique as the cornerstone of their fascist *Estado Novo*, the 'New State', in Portugal itself and overseas.

Having driven the Moors from Portugal in the fifteenth century, the Portuguese turned their attention to Africa itself. They captured Ceuta, in North Africa, from the Moors in August 1415, then sent their ships south along the West African coast, searching for the fabled gold of Guinea and the legendary Christian kingdom of Prester John. Thought to be lying to the rear of the Moslem states, the mythical Christian kingdom was hopefully to become the vital second side of a vast pincers movement that would crush the Islamic world. In the meantime, the Portuguese had Papal permission to trade with the Saracens wherever commerce proved more profitable than conquest, provided arms were not sold. The extraordinary personality organizing the Portuguese seaborne quest was Prince Henry 'the Navigator', third son of King João I, who found that the slave-trade also greatly helped to finance the voyages. Slaves and gold dust were generally obtained through barter with coastal chiefs, willing to sell fellow Africans—mainly prisoners of war and condemned criminals—to the European traders. Prince Henry also had a fondness for crusading expeditions in Morocco and occasionally indulged in slave-raiding on the Canary Islands.

After his death in 1460, Prince Henry's trading concession was given to a rich merchant, Fernão Gomes, and in 1475 King Affonso V handed the lucrative monopoly to his son and heir, the Infante Dom João, who when he became King João II in 1481, had developed a keen interest in the African trade. Batholomeu Dias first rounded the Cape of Good Hope in 1488 and, by the end of the fifteenth century, after the voyage of Vasco da Gama, under Dom João's successor, King Manuel I,

Portuguese ships had explored the East African coast and reached India in the quest for spices. Until then, spices and other luxury goods from the Orient had reached Europe via the monopoly of Venetian and Levantine traders, which the Portuguese now hoped to undercut with their new sea route to Asia.

For chroniclers of Portuguese imperial expansion, the century that began with the capture of Ceuta in 1475 was the *século maravilhoso*, the Marvellous Century. The sixteenth century Portuguese poet, Luís Vaz de Camões, who had himself served in the East, composed a great epic, *Os Lusíades*, to celebrate Vasco da Gama's discovery of the sea route to India. A panegyric on the grandeur of Portuguese imperialism, presented as a noble Christian campaign against the heathen, Camões's poem still serves to justify Portugal's tenacious hold upon its overseas possessions. For the hapless Africans along the Guinea coast, the Marvellous Century was the beginning of many centuries of the most unmitigated exploitation of human beings by their fellow creatures. Between 1450 and 1500 alone, it is estimated that something like 150,000 African slaves were taken by the Portuguese in West Africa.[1]

This was only the beginning of a vast slave-trade that was to devastate Africa and leave many areas permanently depopulated. During the first three centuries of Portuguese presence in Angola, from 1550 to 1850, 'a dedicated commerce in black humanity, most of it with Brazil . . . made up more than four-fifths of total exports during this period.'[2] In fact, in Angola, the slave was the only valuable trading commodity. While some slaves were kept for work as labourers and craftsmen in the colony, the vast majority were exported, initially to Portuguese-held African islands such as São Tomé and Príncipe and Cape Verde, and Portugal itself, then to the Americas, especially to Brazil. In the mid-sixteenth century, slaves—mostly African—made up a considerable proportion of the population of Lisbon itself and were well in the majority in the southernmost Portuguese province of the Algarve.[3] It is estimated that about four million black slaves, over three million from Angola alone, were taken from Africa by the Portuguese slavers between 1580 and 1836, when the Portuguese Government officially abolished the traffic. However, the trade was to persist, clandestinely or under various guises such as 'contract labour', until well into the twentieth century.

The Portuguese supplied the Spanish colonies in the New World, as

[1] C. R. Boxer, *The Portuguese Seaborne Empire 1415–1825* (London, Hutchinson, 1969).

[2] James Duffy, *Portuguese Africa* (Cambridge, Mass., Harvard, 1959), p. 49.

[3] See David M. Abshire, 'The Portuguese Racial Legacy' in *Portuguese Africa: A Handbook*, edited by D. M. Abshire and M. A. Samuels (New York, Praeger, 1969).

well as their own, and held a near-monopoly of the trade for a while. They were briefly ousted by the Dutch and then were in fierce competition with the English and French. Despite a late start in the business, the British had outdistanced all rivals by the end of the eighteenth century, transporting in their ships more than half the slaves who crossed the Atlantic.[1]

One of the most revealing episodes in Portuguese early colonial history occurred after the Portuguese discovery of the estuary of the Congo in 1482, when they found themselves in contact with the large Kongo Kingdom, ruled over by a king, the Manikongo, from his capital at Mbanzakongo, the present-day Angolan city of São Salvador. The explorer Diogo Cão returned to their native land four Africans who had been kidnapped a few years earlier and were much impressed by their stay in Portugal. This circumstance gained the Portuguese the confidence of the Manikongo, Nzinga-a-Cuum, who, with the royal family and great chiefs, was converted to Christianity. His successor, Mbemba-a-Nzinga, became the Christian King of the Kongo, Affonso I. He turned wholeheartedly to his brother Christian monarchs, King Manuel I and, later, King João III, for assistance in westernizing his state. Portuguese missionaries, artisans, and traders were welcomed by the Kongo king, but he quickly discovered that most of the Portuguese were more interested in capturing the Congolese for slaves than in converting them to Christianity and introducing them to European science and technology. King Affonso's pleading letters to João III often went unanswered. The belated Portuguese royal decrees against slaving were systematically sabotaged by the Portuguese authorities and plantation owners on São Tomé. Affonso died a broken, disappointed man, and Portugal's 'civilizing mission' in Africa was to remain essentially a cover for the greed of Europeans for black slaves and the exploitation of natural resources.

In comparison with other colonial powers, Portugal failed to exploit the natural resources of the African colonies to the full. Guinea-Bissau, for instance, was never a profitable colony after the slave-trade was brought to a halt. The Portuguese seemed to lose interest in the impoverished, depopulated West African territory. While it might be argued that investment in such an obviously poor area would hardly attract any colonial power, the same pattern is to be found in Portuguese attitudes towards other territories. Only pressure of African nationalism and availability of investment capital from other Western powers in the mid-twentieth century were to alter this pattern.

[1] Ronald Segal, *The Race War* (London, Cape, 1966), p. 39.

For the greater part of the long period of Portuguese involvement in Africa, actual Portuguese control has been nominal and generally limited to the coastal regions; although Portuguese explorers and adventurers pushed deep into the African continent and even crossed it, they showed little interest in settling and ruling over their nominal subjects. Until rival imperialists, especially the British and Germans, contested Portuguese claims to the interior behind their coastal settlements, the Portuguese preferred to remain in their factories and forts on the seashore and maintain from there a profitable monopoly of commerce with the conflicting inland tribes and nations, whose prisoners of war served to swell the slave trade.

During the sixteenth century, Portugal conducted a successful commercial operation along the Guinea coast from such coastal key points as Arguim, Santiago, and São Jorge da Mina. African opposition here also prevented deep inland penetration by the Portuguese, searching for the legendary gold mines of the Ashanti and other African kingdoms. But what force was unable to achieve, bribery and intrigue did, and vast quantities of slaves and considerable gold fell into the hands of the Portuguese. Nevertheless, they were ousted from the Gold Coast in 1642, managing to retain only Guinea-Bissau and the islands of São Tomé and Cape Verde, where flourishing slave plantations existed. The Portuguese were then obliged to divert their slaving operations to Angola and, to a lesser extent, Mozambique.

In these colonies, the principal slave-trader was the Portuguese governor, who made a handsome profit from the sale of licences to contractors, working either as individuals or for a company of investors, and exporting a specified number of blacks over a given period. The slaves were sold to the contractors by local merchants, who sent *pombeiros* (native traders) into the interior to bring in the black captives. A favourite device for securing slaves used by the Portuguese and their agents was the fomenting of local wars between African tribes in order to purchase the prisoners taken by either side. In addition, the Portuguese imposed on local chiefs in areas under their control taxes whose value could be paid in slaves. Even Jesuit and other Catholic missionaries frequently engaged in the slave-trade to cover the costs of their 'civilizing mission'.[1]

By the Berlin Conference of 1884–5, Portuguese colonialism was in ill repute, thanks to the journeys of Dr. Livingstone into the areas of alleged Portuguese control. Livingstone had found signs of illegal

---

[1] James Duffy, *Portugal in Africa* (Harmondsworth, Penguin, 1962), p. 16.

slave-trading and described deplorable conditions of life in the Portuguese coastal settlements, such that there had fallen on the Portuguese the 'same sort of mental stagnation . . . as on the Africans and others'. The Scottish explorer urged Britain to take over Portuguese East Africa, where,

> . . . not a single native has been taught to read, not one branch of trade has been developed; and wherever Portuguese power, or rather intrigue, extends, we have that [slave] traffic in full force which may be said to reverse every law of Christ and to defy the vengeance of Heaven.[1]

Naturally, the Portuguese replied that Livingstone's denunciation of their peculiar colonial methods was designed mainly as a pretext for British aggrandizement in Africa at Portuguese expense. There is no doubt of Livingstone's nineteenth century humanitarianism, but it is also true that Cecil Rhodes, who was anything but a humanitarian, was anxious to seize the inland territory—which was later to become Rhodesia—claimed by the Portuguese connecting their coastal colonies of Angola and Mozambique. Rhodes's own private army and British gunboats forced Portugal to concede the contested corridor to Britain under a treaty signed in 1891. Later, only the outbreak of the First World War prevented Germany and Britain from reaching an agreement on the partition of Angola and Mozambique between themselves.

The Portuguese have remained suspicious to this day of British intentions towards their African possessions, despite the large British financial investment in Portugal and the colonies. A member of the North Atlantic Treaty Organization (N.A.T.O.) since 1949, Portugal has consistently attempted to convince her allies, especially the United States, that she is fighting against communism in Africa and that her purpose there is not colonialism but the creation of a 'Lusotropical civilization' similar to Brazil. This thesis, often exploited by Portuguese propaganda, was developed extensively by the Brazilian sociologist Gilberto Freyre, who maintained that the Portuguese, because of their alleged lack of racial hatred and their willingness to tolerate or even foster miscegenation between whites and blacks, have behaved in a way totally different from, and morally superior to, that of all other European powers in Africa and the New World. Even Livingstone, it must be admitted, had noted that the Portuguese, unlike the European settlers in South Africa, treated 'people of colour', especially *mestiços* (mixed bloods), with 'liberality'. 'The civil manners of superiors to

---

[1] Charles and David Livingstone, *Narrative of an Expedition to the Zambezi and its Tributaries* (New York, 1866), p. 636; quoted in Duffy, *Portuguese Africa*, p. 186.

inferiors is probably the result of the position they occupy—a few whites among thousands of blacks; but nowhere else in Africa is there so much good-will between European and natives as here,' Livingstone wrote.[1]

Against such a view must be weighed the persistent appearance in Portuguese official documents of such terms as *limpeza* or *pureza de sangue* (purity of blood) and *raças infectas* (contaminated races). There is substantial evidence of discriminatory treatment of Africans and Jews, and any other non-Christians or non-Roman Catholics. Moreover, African, Asian, or *mestiço* clergymen suffered humiliations because of their race, to such an extent that a contemporary U.S. historian has found that 'racial prejudice was omnipresent in a Church which ostensibly preached the brotherhood of all Christian [i.e. Roman Catholic] believers' and 'it was inevitably even more obvious in other walks of life.'[2]

Far more important for an understanding of the dynamics of present-day African nationalism in the Portuguese colonies is the role played in colonial life by the *mestiços* and the handful of Europeanized Africans, the *assimilados*. As more Portuguese women settled in Angola and Mozambique, the incidence of miscegenation declined. And, despite the strident propaganda of the Salazar regime and its successor concerning alleged racial harmony in the 'overseas provinces' of Portugal, the new settler element introduced after World War II, often displayed sharp racial antagonism towards blacks and coloureds, similar to that prevalent in Rhodesia and South Africa.

Over the last three decades, nevertheless, a small number of *mestiços* and *assimilados* have received higher education in Portugal, and some have received important positions in government and private life. But many of these realized themselves to be an elite, and became increasingly aware of the gulf that separated them from the bulk of the African people. The frustration and bitterness which accompanied this disenchantment with the Portuguese mystique of racial harmony initially took expression in poetry and prose; later, in the organization of liberation movements against Portuguese rule. A high proportion of the original leaders of the African movements were *mestiço* intellectuals, such as Mário de Andrade, Marcelino dos Santos, Viriato da Cruz, and Amílcar Cabral. The fact that they were not black and had little or no connection with tribal Africans was later to create serious political

[1] Quoted in David M. Abshire, 'The Portuguese Racial Legacy', in Abshire and Samuels, op. cit., p. 102.

[2] Boxer, op. cit., p. 261.

problems for their movements and to complicate their relations with independent black African governments that were often suspicious of the light-skinned cosmopolitan intellectuals whose life-styles were generally closer to those of fellow intellectuals in Lisbon and Paris than the majority of African people in the Portuguese colonies.

Until 1930 Portugal's 'native policy' was mainly, one of exploitative neglect; that is, the Africans were left alone, enslaved, or obliged to work under 'contract', according to fluctuating economic necessity. The economy of the colonies stagnated after the official end of the slave-trade. Occasionally, a Portuguese Army column was dispatched to some outer corner of a colony to 'pacify' Africans who rebelled against Portuguese rule or otherwise displeased their distant rulers.

After the installation of the Salazar dictatorship with its police 'New State' and its mystique of 'neo-imperialism', Lisbon took a much more active interest in exploiting the colonies. With some difficulty, Portuguese farmers were encouraged to emigrate to Angola and Mozambique. After the opening of armed struggle in Angola in 1961, the regime dispatched ever greater numbers of troops to the colonies and belatedly attempted to develop the neglected territories. By 1970, according to United Nations statistics, well over half of Portuguese state revenues went to military expenditures, largely in Africa.

While the Portuguese proved more capable of hanging on to their possessions than many observers had believed possible in 1961, when only weeks or months of survival were predicted, they failed to eradicate the revolutionary movements—even though these might have been much more effective if they had been united. Western capital was increasingly directed into the development of Angola and Mozambique, and N.A.T.O.-supplied weapons significantly augmented Portuguese military resources. Although the United States has strenuously denied that N.A.T.O. weapons are being used outside the N.A.T.O. area for other than N.A.T.O. purposes, there have been numerous detailed reports of N.A.T.O. arms being captured from Portuguese troops in Guinea-Bissau, Angola, and Mozambique. In addition, West Germany and France have openly supplied Portugal with considerable amounts of arms, aircraft, and warships. Even if N.A.T.O. weapons and material do not go to Africa, their supply does permit Portugal to allocate weapons obtained from other sources to be used in the colonial war in Africa.[1]

[1] See *Portugal and NATO*, a pamphlet of the Angola Comité (Amsterdam, October 1969), and David M. Abshire, 'Strategic Implications', in Abshire and Samuels, op. cit., pp. 434–47.

The United States has repeatedly condemned Portuguese policy in Africa, especially at the United Nations, while stressing the strategic importance of Portuguese bases, such as the Azores, to the U.S. armed forces. Secretary of State William Rogers declared in March 1970:

As for the Portuguese territories, we shall continue to believe that their peoples should have the right of self-determination. We will encourage peaceful progress toward that goal. The declared Portuguese policy of racial toleration is an important factor in this equation. We think this holds genuine hope for the future. Believing that resort to force and violence is in no one's interest, we imposed an embargo in 1961 against the shipment of arms for use in the Portuguese territories. We have maintained this embargo and will continue to do so.[1]

On the other hand, a number of reliable reporters have claimed that the United States Government has given covert assistance to the liberation movements. Holden Roberto's GRAE/FNLA in Angola has been persistently labelled as both 'pro-American' and American-backed, despite a visit to Peking by the Angolan nationalist leader. An inquisitive American student of the international relations of the liberation movements claimed in 1969 to have discovered U.S. Central Intelligence Agency covert assistance to all the African movements without exception.[2] A serious American reporter also wrote:

While it was surreptitiously supporting Portugal in its war against guerrillas by allowing it to buy B-26 bombers, the United States was and still is supporting the guerrillas themselves, a fact that is not widely known. In Angola, for instance, it has been supporting Holden Roberto. In Mozambique, also a Portuguese colony, it has been supporting a rebel group led by a pro-West nationalist named Eduardo Mondlane.[3]

Mondlane, the subsequently assassinated first President of the Mozambique Revolutionary Front (FRELIMO), however, was one of the few nationalist leaders who reportedly managed the tricky balancing act of securing aid from Soviet and Soviet bloc, United States and Western, and Chinese sources.

On the other hand, Chinese and Soviet aid was not only often overt; the latter was exaggerated by propaganda media to justify Soviet attempts at political control of the aid-receiving movements, grouped

[1] 'Secretary of State Rogers' Policy Statement on Africa' (London, United States Information Service, American Embassy, 31 March 1970).

[2] Paul M. Whitaker, 'Angola, Guinea, Mozambique: A Comparative Study of the International Relations of the Revolutionary Nationalist Liberation Movements of Portuguese Africa', unpublished B.A. honours thesis, Harvard College (March 1969).

[3] George Thayer, *The War Business* (London, Paladin, 1969), p. 138.

together in the Conference of Nationalist Organizations of the Portuguese Colonies (CONCP). Leaders of most of the movements have frankly admitted that they are not self-reliant and cannot yet hope to conduct a military struggle without substantial external assistance, which must necessarily be sought from the O.A.U., other independent African states, or friendly powers outside Africa.

Fatal illness removed the aged, tyrannical Salazar from the head of the Portuguese dictatorship. Some African leaders had speculated that with this event might come a collapse of the regime and a shift in colonial policy. Nothing of the sort happened, and the 'New State' soldiered on under Marcelo Caetano, a former Colonial Minister and Rector of Lisbon University. Caetano's 'liberalism' proved to be only the most fragile of façades, designed mainly for external consumption, to facilitate Portuguese acceptance within the European Free Trade Area (E.F.T.A.) and eventually perhaps the European Common Market; the latter was already absorbing thousands of Portuguese immigrant workers. Caetano declared unwillingness to meet African nationalist demands in the colonies. Before becoming Premier, he had written of his own colonial experience: 'The blacks in Angola have to be directed and indoctrinated by Europeans. . . . The Africans have not learned how to develop alone the territories they have inhabited for thousands of years.'[1]

How the most impoverished nation in Western Europe could hope to direct and develop an overseas empire when it could not develop its own domestic territory is another question. In 1970, more than 30 per cent of the population of Portugal was illiterate. And according to the *Instituto Nacional de Estatistica* in Lisbon in 1959, after nearly five centuries of the 'civilizing mission' in Africa, less than 1 per cent of the African populations of Guinea-Bissau, Angola, and Mozambique could be classified as 'civilized' by Portuguese standards; that is, could read, write, and speak Portuguese, professed the Roman Catholic religion, had regular employment or a business, and lived according to Portuguese social standards. In 1961, after the upsurge of African revolution, the Salazar Government abolished the *Estatuto dos Indígenas* and conferred the full blessings of the Portuguese police state upon all, regardless of colour. Not even Salazar dared to proclaim that Portugal had fulfilled her 'mission', when Portugal herself lagged behind the rest of Western Europe in every field of endeavour. However, Portugal had built up the strongest land forces in sub-Saharan Africa; over 100,000

[1] Quoted in Duffy, *Portugal in Africa*, p. 182.

Portuguese troops and police,[1] in unofficial but effective alliance with the white-minority regimes in South Africa and Rhodesia, were fielded against a few thousand African guerrillas. By the end of 1971, neither side had managed to strike a decisive blow and the battle became indeed protracted, one in which 'only he who has the greatest patience will win.'[2]

[1] 'Black Man's War', *The Economist* (10 May 1969).
[2] *Le Mois en Afrique/Revue française d'études politiques africaines* (November 1969) p. 94.

I. ANGOLA

Movimento Popular de Libertação de Angola (MPLA)

Govêrno Revolucionário de Angola no Exílio/Frente Nacional de Libertação de Angola (GRAE/FNLA)

União Nacional para a Independência Total de Angola (UNITA)

The Background

Since the nineteenth century, historians of Portuguese colonialism have traditionally categorized Portuguese overseas possessions as either territories of 'conquest' or territories of 'population'. In the latter, Portuguese settlers established themselves, creating vast plantations for the cultivation of sugar-cane or cotton and transporting African slaves to work them. The Cape Verde Islands, São Tomé, and Príncipe are typical territories of population, marked by plantation economies that have gradually moved from slavery to contract labour and slightly less onerous forms of servitude.

Angola is a classic territory of conquest. Although at the end of the fifteenth century Portuguese explorers had sailed down its 1,000-mile long coastline from the River Congo to the River Cunene on the border of what is now South West Africa, effective Portuguese settlement occurred several centuries later and then was confined to the coastal strip, with its ports of Luanda and Lobito. Tropical disease, climatic conditions, and African resistance encouraged the Portuguese to view Angola—a country fourteen times as large as metropolitan Portugal, covering an area of 481,351 square miles—as mainly a source of black slaves, minerals, and ivory. These could all be obtained through *pombeiros* and other African or mulatto traders working for the handful of Europeans in the factories and forts on the coast.

The name 'Angola' is derived from the dynasty of Ngola, chief of the Kimbundu people in what is now the Dongo region. His kingdom was much smaller than present-day Angola, which is bordered on the north and north-east by Zaïre, formerly the Republic of the Congo (Kinshasa), in the east by Zambia, and by South West Africa in the south. Angola is characterized geographically by a low coastal strip some 150 miles wide, with an inland plateau reaching to over 6,000 feet. In general, with some local variation, the seasons are dry from May to September and wet from October to May. Rainfall varies greatly, from near-none in some arid places on the coast to 60–70 inches in the Maiombe forest region of Cabinda, to the north of the River Congo. However, this is exceptional and precipitation is elsewhere moderate or scant.

In the 1960 census, the last before the beginning of the war of liberation, Angola's population, now estimated at 5·5 million, numbered

4,830,499, including 172,529 Europeans. By 1969, the European population was estimated to have grown to around 250,000, due to strenuous Portuguese government efforts to settle white farmers in the contested African land.[1] However, the country remains sparsely populated, with an overwhelming African majority of at least 5 million. *Mestiços* numbered 53,392 in 1960. Although they have certainly become more numerous since then, they can no longer be assumed loyal to the colonial regime.

More than one-third of the European and *mestiço* population live in Luanda, the capital, which has a total population of more than 250,000. Other major urban areas are Lobito, the terminus of the Benguela Railway that brings Zambian and Congolese copper to the Atlantic Coast, and the city of Benguela proper, which is nearby. The area has a total population of around 100,000. Further major towns are Nova Lisboa, in the central plateau, and Sá da Bandeira, in the south-west. Sá da Bandeira and Moçãmedes, on the coast not far away, have long been centres of European settlement and now have more white than black inhabitants. Carmona, in the north, is the centre of the coffee district, and suffered great financial losses in the initial years of the armed struggle when the forces of the *União das Populações de Angola* (UPA) overran the European-owned plantations. Until then, Angola's coffee producers had been enjoying boom conditions. As the guerrilla war dragged on, apparently confined to certain areas of the country, the geographical pattern of the economy was restructured away from the zones of insecurity.

The basis of the economy remains agriculture, with coffee, sisal, sugar, and diamonds the most important Angolan exports. Iron ore and petroleum are now also major exports. A rich oilfield was discovered in the Cabinda enclave, administered from Angola, and is being intensively exploited by Cabinda Gulf Oil. Other foreign oil companies are working elsewhere, but the Cabinda oilfield remains the richest found. West German capital has been invested in the Cassinga iron mines in Southern Angola, which are eventually expected to export 7 million tons of iron ore a year. Not only are other iron deposits being developed nearby, but exceptional gold and copper finds have also been made. An aluminium industry is being set up at Dondo, Cambambe, and Dombe Grande. Overall, industrial production doubled in the decade from 1960, supplied by a growing hydro-electric production. Although most investment in Angola continues to be Portuguese, Western capital has provided the extra development impetus. Another

[1] Abshire and Samuels, op. cit., p. 5.

major source of capital and technological know-how has been South Africa,[1] which has concluded numerous economic agreements with Portugal, as well as tacit agreements for military assistance. Since 1968, reliable sources have reported the presence of South African patrols in southern Angola, striking out from South West Africa against both SWAPO guerrillas crossing Angola and their Angolan African hosts and allies.

As is common in any colonial system, economic development is entirely guided by the necessities and ambitions of the metropolitan power. Africans have only the meagre choice of attempting to continue to survive on a subsistence economy or accepting proletarian status in the colonial market economy. Administrative and legal restrictions and taxation, have rendered the former almost impossible. The black peasant is forced by numerous constraints either to become a labourer for a European enterprise or to work as an 'independent' farmer whose produce and profits mandatorily go into the hands of all-powerful European middlemen. This iron ring of exploitation breaks down ultimately only if the African, either in conscious understanding of his plight or by chance involvement in the revolutionary turmoil and repression, throws in his lot with the nationalist forces of liberation.

The African peoples of Angola are generally divided into four major ethnic-linguistic groups, although there are some hundred tribes in the country. The four main languages, spoken by 70 per cent of the African population, are Umbundu (language of the Ovimbundu people), Kimbundu, Kikongo, and Chokwe-Lunda. These divisions have had direct bearing on the development of the nationalist movement.

The largest group is the Ovimbundu, nearly 1·5 million, who live in the central highlands of Angola around the city of Nova Lisboa. Long in contact with Europeans, the Ovimbundu were receptive to Christianity and have long been energetic traders who often co-operated with the Portuguese. The second largest group, the Kimbundu, about 1·2 million, are found around Luanda and many have been fully assimilated into urban life in the capital.

Far more important than their present numbers in Angola might indicate are the Bakongo (who speak Kikongo). They are the disparate heirs of the ancient Kongo Kingdom, which disappeared in the eighteenth century. The Bakongo were later divided by the colonial boundary between Portuguese Angola and the Belgian Congo. Today, after years of warfare in northern Angola, perhaps less than half a million Bakongo

[1] See Karel Holbik, 'Angola: Economic and Social Reforms', *Inter-Economics* (Hamburg, No. 5, 1969).

remain in Angola, while from 200,000 to 600,000 Angolan refugees, mainly Bakongo, have fled to relative safety across the Congolese border. Bakongo messianic cults, persistent, if unsuccessful, and efforts to restore a state similar to the Kongo Kingdom, have played a vital role in creating modern Angolan nationalism.

The Chokwe-Lunda, who numbered some 360,000 in 1960, are descendants of the Lunda empire of Mwato-Yamvo. They live in north-eastern Angola and extend across the Congolese border as well, into Katanga.

Besides these four groups, there are many smaller tribes. Among them, in the south of Angola, are the Cuanhama tribes, who number only 100,000 people, while another 250,000 Cuanhama-speaking Ovambo live in the northernmost area of South West Africa. A remarkable warrior people, the Cuanhama defeated several Portuguese efforts to conquer them and were finally forced into submission only after allying themselves with the Germans, the losers in the First World War.

The Resistance

Portugal's Angolan wars began in 1575. Rarely has a year passed since when there has not been a Portuguese colonial campaign somewhere in Angola. The current Angolan War began on 4 February 1961, when urban partisans of the *Movimento Popular de Libertação de Angola* (MPLA) attacked São Paulo fortress and police headquarters in Luanda; on 15 March it was spread with greater success throughout the north of the country by the rural guerrillas of another organization, the *União das Populações de Angola* (UPA). The Angolan War has become the longest purely colonial struggle in Africa, outlasting the Algerian War (November 1954 to July 1962) and, except for the decades-long warfare in Vietnam and elsewhere in Indochina, the most protracted guerrilla struggle anywhere in the modern world.

Portugal's failure to respond positively to the appeal of the Christian monarchs of the Kongo Kingdom made inevitable the decline of their African state under the pressures of internal dissension, commercial rivalries, slavery, and foreign enemies. The Portuguese then turned their attention southwards to the Mbundu of Ndongo. These peoples were unfortunate enough to become the first African nation to be subject to European colonial rule.[1]

The capital of the Kingdom of Ndongo was Mbanza Kabassa, located

[1] See Ronald H. Chilcote, *Portuguese Africa* (Englewood Cliffs, N. J., Prentice Hall, 1967), pp. 61–74.

near the present-day Dongo. It was built about the fourteenth century by peoples from Central Africa under Ngola a Nzinga, their chief. In the sixteenth century, the Ngola of that time, prospering from illicit slave trading with the Portuguese in Luanda, declared his independence of the Kongo Kingdom, whose forces he defeated in battle in 1556. The Ngola demanded that an official Portuguese representative be sent to his court. The subsequent detention, after a quarrel with the Portuguese, of the representative, Paulo Dias de Novaes, prompted the Portuguese to attempt the military conquest of the Kingdom.

The 1575 order to Dias to conquer the Ndongo Kingdom opened a century of warfare. African resistance proved more tenacious than Dias had expected, and he died before victory. An alliance of the Ngola with the Kongo Kingdom and the Jagas of Matamba led to major Portuguese defeats in 1590 and 1594. However, the alliance fell apart in 1600. The Portuguese renewed their onslaughts and by 1603 had captured and killed the Ngola. The capital of Ndongo was seized in 1620 and the new king, Ngola Nzinga Mbandi, fled to an island on the Cuanza, where he rallied African forces who were, however, powerless to prevent the Portuguese from devastating the country and enslaving a large part of the population.

In 1621, Nzinga Mbandi's sister, 'Jinga' (who was later given the Christian name of Anna de Souza Nzinga), negotiated a peace treaty with the Portuguese and got them to recognize Ndongo as an independent state. Nzinga Mbandi died three years later and was succeeded on the throne by 'Jinga'. She promptly renounced Christianity. Subsequent Portuguese efforts to remove the apostate failed. The Queen formed an alliance of African kingdoms and successfully resisted the Portuguese forces until they made a treaty with her in 1656, re-establishing trade relations which were then maintained until her death seven years later. The name of Queen 'Jinga' is still today a symbol of African resistance to Portuguese rule.

In 1641, the Dutch challenged the shaky Portuguese hegemony in Angola. Capturing Luanda and Benguela, they forced the Portuguese settlers on the coast to flee inland. In 1648, a Portuguese relief expedition from Brazil joined with African allies to expel the Dutch. After this victory, a Portuguese army of 3,000 African bowmen, 200 European troops, 150 settlers, and 100 African riflemen, led by Luís Lopes de Sequeira, inflicted a crushing defeat on Kongolese forces at Mbwila in 1665.[1] Allied now with Queen 'Jinga', in 1671 the Portuguese defeated Chief Ngola Ari, destroying the African state of Ndongo.

[1] Abshire and Samuels, op. cit., p. 43.

A peace treaty was signed with the Matamba in 1683. It lasted half a century, until hostilities broke out again with the Portuguese attempt to prevent direct access to the slave-trade by European rivals. A Portuguese military expedition in 1744 failed and the Portuguese were forced to leave the Matamba in control of the trade.

In the Benguela Highlands and the south of the country, the pattern of Portuguese penetration was the same—efforts to monopolize the slave-trade, followed by numerous local wars, return to uncertain peace, and further trade. The Caconda fortress was built at the head-waters of the River Lutira as a base for trade and political expansion, but the Portuguese were not able to occupy the African kingdoms and end their independent existence until the second half of the nineteenth century. An Ovimbundu area north-west of Nova Lisboa was to remain in open hostility to the Portuguese until 1904. In Humbe, on the border with South West Africa, African armed resistance continued intermittently until the twentieth century. In 1904, Cuanhama rebels ambushed a Portuguese force at Cuamato, killing 300. The Cuanhama were defeated in 1906 by superior Portuguese forces, but African resistance in the area continued until 1915, at times supported by the German rivals of the Portuguese in South West Africa. The First World War in Europe led to a Portuguese major campaign in the area and the construction of permanent military bases to subjugate the long-rebellious Cuanhama.

As a former Governor-General of Angola, S. Calheiros e Menezes, had remarked in 1861: 'The normal condition of the administration of this colony is to make war, and to prepare itself for war.' The Portuguese military system depended upon large forces of African auxiliaries, called the *guerra preta* (the black war), raised from loyal chiefs, hired as mercenaries or press-ganged into service. Between 1575 and 1925, some 5,000 to 20,000 of these indigenous troops were used to support the 2,000 or less Europeans of the first-line colonial army in Angola.[1] Naturally, in the conditions of sporadic warfare that had prevailed since the fifteenth century, military expenses dominated all other items in the Angolan budget, at one time making 90 per cent of the total.

Until the 'Scramble for Africa' of other European powers menaced Portugal's dominion over her African colonies, the Portuguese were generally satisfied to exercise commercial dominance and exclude rivals. Until the abolition of slavery, they encouraged a merciless slave-trade that depopulated vast areas of Angola. Systematic occupation and

[1] Douglas L. Wheeler, 'The Portuguese Army in Angola', *Journal of Modern Studies* (Vol. 7, No. 3, 1969).

regular, formal settlement of Europeans did not begin in Angola until 1852 and then the initial effort to bring settlers from Madeira ended in failure. After a brief retreat from rebellious interior areas, military expansion resumed in the late 1870s, and received greater impetus after the Berlin Conference of 1884 when British and German rivals claimed that the large areas allegedly under Portuguese rule were not 'under effective occupation.'[1]

Nevertheless, not all Angola was under effective control by Portuguese colonial authorities until the First World War period. Only after 1922 did a genuine administration function, under the programme drawn up by the High Commissioner of the Republic, Norton de Matos. Europeans had been allowed to settle on whatever land they wished, chaotically and with total disregard for African claims. Efforts by Norton de Matos to protect the African population from this and other rapacious exploitation by whites prompted swift expression of settler dissatisfaction and even calls for independence from the metropolitan power. European separatist sentiment was strongest in Benguela where it found a power-base in the Kuribeka, the Angolan branch of Freemasons. Settler separatism has remained an important factor to Angolan whites, who of course enjoy as few political liberties as their relatives in Portugal itself. The settler oligarchy is haunted by fear of being abandoned by Lisbon as the *colons* of Algeria were 'abandoned' by metropolitan France, under de Gaulle. But they have had enough encouragement from the Republic of South Africa to believe that the White Bastion in the south would quickly step in to make up for any loss of metropolitan troops and financial assistance. There might possibly be created a loose confederation of White Southern Africa, grouping the white-minority regimes of South Africa, Rhodesia, Angola and Mozambique, and such black client-states as might be kept in line—Lesotho and some other former British Protectorates, Malawi, and other conservative governments.

Settler separatism played a key role in provoking the awakening of national consciousness among Angolans. At first, this awakening found a purely cultural expression in the *Gremio Africano*, founded in 1929, which later changed its name to *Associação Regional dos Naturais de Angola* (ANANGOLA). Essentially an organization of Angolan-born mulattos, its membership was open to anyone born in Angola, regardless of race. However, applicants were expected to be persons of culture. Initially concerned solely with propagating and defending the values

---

[1] Alfred Margarido, 'Portugais de "provinces d'outre-mer" d'Afrique', *Le Mois en Afrique* (December 1966).

of the white and coloured petty bourgeoisie, the ANANGOLA was later to become the mouthpiece of Angolan cultural nationalism. Around it and Viriato da Cruz's review *Mensagem*, published in Luanda, a generation of mulatto and *assimilado* writers were to protest against the brutalities of colonialism and affirm the uniqueness and value of African culture and the dignity of men of colour.

The concept of the 'specificity' of Angolan society and culture for whites as well as blacks and *mestiços* found widespread acceptance in student circles in Lisbon and Benguela. In 1940, a handful of unemployed graduates, who had been unable to obtain posts in the administration, supported by sympathizers still at school, demonstrated against the practice of appointments being made only by the Overseas Ministry in Lisbon. Protesting also against the sending of forced labour to São Tomé, they were arrested by the *Polícia Internacional e de Defesa do Estado* (P.I.D.E.), the secret political and security police, but later freed by the provincial governor in the face of even wider protest in the settler community.

The P.I.D.E. has always watched for liberal whites almost as closely as for nascent black nationalists. Faithful to Lisbon, it has also always repressed white settler separatism whenever it has come to the surface. The Angolan United Front (*Frente de Unidade Angólana*—FUA) was founded in Benguela in January 1961, growing out of the '1940 Movement' and the white students and other intellectuals who had collaborated with *Mensagem* and its successor *Cultura*. Without accepting the demands of black nationalism, the FUA nevertheless pressed for eventual independence for an 'Angolan nation' composed of all the country's ethnic groups. Many of the FUA members were arrested and deported to Portugal. Some subsequently escaped to France, where they founded a committee in exile in September 1961. While they argued in a petition to the United Nations Sub-committee on the Situation in Angola that the country was not ready for 'immediate independence', they vehemently denounced Portuguese colonialism.[1]

The FUA sought fraternal contacts with African nationalist organizations, but was never able to line them up in a united National Liberation Front under FUA leadership. FUA activities in exile had no echo at home, where the overwhelming majority of whites refused any recognition of African nationalism. The multiracialism of the FUA, like the notional multiracialist ideology of assimilation of the *Estado Novo*, was belied by the increasingly clear racist divisions of Angolan society. Ultimately, the white liberals found themselves in prison or exile

[1] Marcum, op. cit., pp. 280–2.

without white followers at home. Moreover, the guiding role sought by the FUA in the projected united National Liberation Front could not possibly have been accepted by the far stronger African organizations, whose mass support was visible and growing.

The oldest indigenous association in Angola, the *Liga Angolana*, was founded in 1913—a mainly mulatto organization—that voiced demands for African economic and social advancement within the limits of the Portuguese colonial system. Angolan *assimilados* and, mulattos residing in Portugal played a major role in 1923 at the second session of the Pan-African Congress held in Lisbon. The first session, held in London, had been attended by H. G. Wells, Harold Laski, and Lord Olivier and had received a message of encouragement from Ramsay MacDonald. Dr. W. E. B. DuBois decided to hold the second session in Lisbon in the hope of persuading the republican government of the day to carry out urgent measures of reform in the Portuguese colonies. Although two former Portuguese Colonial Ministers promised the Congress they would use their influence to bring about the desired reforms, little or nothing was actually done, especially concerning the brutalities of the system of forced labour.[1]

An inter-territorial group of Africans and *mestiços* had formed the *Partido Nacional Africano* (PNA) in Lisbon in 1921, demanding colonial reforms within the Constitution of the First Portuguese Republic. It was this group of black and brown intellectuals and others in the *Liga Angolana* that Dr. DuBois hoped to strengthen by holding part of the Third Pan-Africanist Congress in Lisbon. With the coming of the Salazar regime in 1926, their activities were stifled by censorship and other police measures. Yet in Angola, the *Liga Angolana* had a rebirth in Luanda in 1929 as the *Liga Nacional Africana* (LNA), another predominantly mulatto organization pressing for economic and social advancement for the educated, and assimilated, within the colonial structure. Later, in the 1950s, the LNA was split between older conservatives and young radicals who demanded cultural, social, and political advancement for the African masses as well as the elites.

Another allegedly cultural association of importance in the growth of Angolan nationalism was the *Sociedade Cultural de Angola*, which had been founded in 1943. Actually more political than cultural, the group provided a rallying point for European liberals and Marxists and permitted them to disseminate their ideas to students and young intellectuals. More radical than the FUA, the Cultural Society's

---

[1] For accounts of the Third Pan-Africanist Congress see Marcum, op. cit., pp. 21–2, and Colin Legum, *Pan Africanism* (London, Pall Mall, 1962), p. 29.

members were also in contact with the nationalist poets of *Mensagem* and *Cultura*, the review that took its place. Some of the most radical members of this group, such as Viriato da Cruz, the courageous *mestiço* editor of *Mensagem*, and Mário de Andrade, another fiery mulatto poet, formed the Angolan Communist Party (PCA) in October 1955. However, the real organizers of the PCA were European civil servants in Angola who were clandestine members of the illegal Portuguese Communist Party.

At the beginning of 1956, the PCA merged with other radical groups to form the *Partido da Luta dos Africanos de Angola* (PLUA)—Party of Struggle of Africans of Angola—ostensibly a united nationalist front. Thus, it was the Angolan Communist Party, despite its smallness, that became the country's first revolutionary party. And the *Movimento Popular de Libertação de Angola* (MPLA), which was set up in December 1956, traces its ancestry and many of its leaders directly to the PCA through the PLUA. A *Movimento de Independência Nacional de Angola* (MINA) was also created in 1957 or 1958, probably as part of a programme of decentralization aimed at bringing together the widest possible united front around the MPLA, with which it later officially merged.[1]

In 1959, the P.I.D.E. moved in the cities of Angola to crush the mounting unrest among radical and liberal Europeans, and *mestiço* and African intellectuals. Hundreds were arrested between March and December, and in January 1960 a secret 'trial of fifty' was held in which the defendants were convicted and sentenced to lengthy prison terms for political subversion. At the same time, the Portuguese Army in Angola began secretly bringing in reinforcements in order to counter a possible nationalist uprising. However, it should be clear that until this time the violence had been initiated solely by the colonial administration in order to repress this essentially urban movement of European separatist-nationalists, *mestiço* intellectuals, and a handful of African *assimilados*. This was the real base of the MPLA. All its subsequent actions must be understood in the light of this.

In the countryside, another kind of nationalism was developing. The tradition of tribal resistance to Portuguese encroachment had not been forgotten, especially in that part of the old Kongo Kingdom whence Christian monarchs had once appealed in vain for Portuguese assistance in modernizing their land. Instead, the Portuguese had permitted it to be ravaged by the slave-trade and eventually sided with the Ndongo Kingdom and other rival states in order to destroy its

[1] See Marcum, op. cit., pp. 26–30.

power and bring it and all the warring African states under Portugal's hegemony and, subsequently, her colonial rule.

Despite the defeat and decline of the Kongo Kingdom, its kings survived and still maintained a semblance of customary rule in and around the city of São Salvador. Mostly disabused of the Roman Catholicism of their late fifteenth and sixteenth century kings, João I and Affonso I, many Kongolese were yet not completely hostile to Christianity from other sources. And in 1878, the reigning king, Dom Pedro V, permitted the Baptist Missionary Society of London to set up a mission in his capital. At the same time, Portuguese colonialism relied upon Catholic missionaries to bolster the ideological defences of the empire. During the First World War, the Portuguese authorities sent troops into the Bakongo area. Within the region, Africans were forcibly recruited into the *guerra preta*, the black auxiliary of the Portuguese colonial army, to fight in the south of the country. Eventually, the Protestant king Dom Manuel Kiditu was deposed and replaced by a Catholic. Many Bakongo fled north to the Congo, then under Belgian rule. This began the Angolan emigration to the Congo that was swelled to massive proportions by tens of thousands of refugees after 1961, as fighting raged throughout the north of Angola.

The Portuguese of course blamed their difficulties in the north on the British and American Protestant missionaries who were active there. Numerous efforts were made to restrict the missionaries or to remove them entirely, but by then the Protestants had established a strong hold over the Bakongo masses. When, after the death of the king Dom Pedro VII on 17 April 1955, a royalist opposition group, composed mainly of Protestants living in the Congo, attempted a modernist takeover, the Portuguese authorities intervened in the succession crisis. A number of the oppositionists were arrested, while others were banned from returning to Angola from exile in the Congo.

When the Catholic Dom António III, who had been placed on the throne by the Portuguese, died on 11 July 1957, the fearful colonial authorities prevented a successor from being chosen until 1962, preferring to let the kingdom languish under the widowed queen regent, Dona Isabela da Gama, keeping her firmly under their control and without great authority among her people.

Across the border, the Bakongo exiles in the Congo gathered together in 1957 in the *União das Populações do Norte de Angola* (UPNA). According to John A. Marcum, the hardcore militants in Leopoldville and Matadi then 'numbered but twelve and nine persons, respectively'.[1]

---

[1] Marcum, op. cit., p. 63.

Basically an Angolan tribal organization with close ties to the Bakongo people, who had been placed under Belgian rule in the Congo by the fortuitous European partition of Africa, the UPNA at first expressed an all-Bakongo nationalism and looked towards a renewal of the ancient Kongo Kingdom rather than the creation of an independent Angolan state.

In November 1957, a UPNA meeting at Cattier, in the Congo, decided to send a representative abroad to lobby in independent Africa and at the United Nations. This was especially necessary because of severe restrictions imposed on political activity in the Congo by Belgian authorities. Characteristically, the UPNA President Manuel Barros Necaca had remained in contact with the Reverend George Hauser, a Protestant clergyman who was executive director of the American Committee on Africa. Corresponding with Hauser in New York on the project to send a representative abroad, Necaca learned of the All-African Peoples' Conference that was to be held in Ghana in 1958 under Kwame Nkrumah's presidency. Thanks to Hauser, George Padmore, who was organizing the gathering, sent an official invitation to Necaca for the UPNA.

The young man selected to go abroad was Holden Roberto, Necaca's nephew. Roberto was born in São Salvador on 12 January 1923, and named after the British Baptist missionary who baptized him. He was taken to the Congo by an aunt in 1925 and was later joined there by his parents. He attended the British Missionary Society school in Leopold-ville and was sent to the B.M.S. school in São Salvador in 1940–1. Returning to the Congo, he worked from 1949 to 1956 for the Belgian administration in Leopoldville, Bukavu, and Stanleyville, where he met Patrice Lumumba. His political activism began in 1951 when he was shocked by Portuguese brutality witnessed during a three-week visit to Angola.

In 1958, under pseudonyms, he travelled to the Conference via Congo-Brazzaville, the French and British Camerouns, and Nigeria, and was virtually without documents until the Ghanaian High Commission in Lagos obtained from Padmore authorization to issue the papers necessary for him to enter Ghana. In the light of criticism from recognized Pan-African leaders present for the Conference—men such as Frantz Fanon, Kenneth Kaunda, Tom Mboya, and Patrice Lumumba —Roberto abandoned for ever the dream of reviving the old Kongo Kingdom and accepted in its place the goal of an independent Angolan state. Even before the All-African Peoples' Conference opened on 5 December, Roberto had transformed the UPNA into the *União das*

Populações de Angola (UPA) and was circulating a document which declared this organization open to 'all Africans originally from Angola, without discrimination as to sex, age, ethnic origin or domicile'.[1]

In the rural south of Angola, around Nova Lisboa and Lobito, the UPA spread rapidly among the Ovimbundu and Nhaneka-Humbe peoples, despite the Portuguese belief that Sá da Bandeira, long a centre of Portuguese settlement, was so intensely Portuguese that its social and cultural life would impress itself indelibly upon the African students sent there for secondary schooling. Among these students was Jonas Savimbi, who was to become Foreign Secretary of the UPA and later lead the successful breakaway group that formed the *União Nacional para a Independência Total de Angola* (UNITA).

As recently as 1948, the Portuguese faced a serious uprising in the Humbe region, led by Chief Kassela. Two years later, a mulatto, Eduardo Vitorio Pereira, and some friends founded the *União dos Naturais de Angola* (UNATA), which held a secret meeting in Benguela in 1956, and sent an unsigned petition to Portuguese authorities in 1958. The P.I.D.E. discovered and arrested the authors and others associated with them.

Also in the south were the Cuanhama people, a subgroup of the Ovambo found in the northernmost region of South West Africa, who had a long history of armed tribal resistance to Portuguese colonialism. The emergence of nationalism in South West Africa, especially the formation of the Ovamboland People's Organization (OPO), which was later to become the South West African People's Organization (SWAPO), reinforced African nationalism on the Angolan side of the border as well. SWAPO was subsequently to establish co-operative relations with the UPA and its breakaway UNITA.[2]

The main lines along which Angola's national struggle developed are those which still divide her nationalist movements: ethnic origin and region; and the class background and education of their leaders (between relatively sophisticated *mestiço* urban elites and tribal notables with strong ties to the masses in the countryside). Political ideology and foreign sponsorship—whether from East or West, from the U.S.S.R. or China or the U.S.A., have only divided the movements further.

Movimento Popular de Libertacão de Angola (MPLA)

Inspired by the newly-formed Angolan Communist Party (PCA), which was an offshoot of the Portuguese Communist Party, the *Movimento*

---

[1] Marcum, op. cit., p. 67.   [2] Ibid., pp. 113–15.

Popular de Libertação de Angola was founded in December 1956 as a clandestine nationalist party. As explained in the previous section its immediate official predecessor was the *Partido da Luta dos Africanos de Angola* (PLUA), a grouping of small radical organizations, like the PCA in Luanda, Malange, and Catete, that had 'adopted an action programme similar to that of the PCA'.[1] Later, several other small groups which had also been controlled by the PCA, in particular the *Movimento para a Independência de Angola* (MPIA), joined the MPLA.

In the late forties, members of the Portuguese Communist Party reportedly began proselytizing among the predominantly European and *mestiço* students and intellectuals in Luanda. The organizers were mainly European civil servants, secret members of the Portuguese party, assigned to posts in Angola. Of course the party was—and remains—banned in Portugal and its overseas territories. Marxists also dominated the influential *Sociedade Cultural* and through it reached student groups.

This handful of communists would perhaps have had little influence but for the extraordinary wave of cultural nationalism then sweeping through Angolan intellectual circles. The rallying point of this 'Let us discover Angola' movement, as it was called, was the review *Mensagem*, founded in 1950 by Viriato da Cruz, a talented *mestiço* poet. Born on 25 March 1928, at Kikuvu, da Cruz was educated in Luanda. In *Mensagem*, he published poetry, fiction, and articles of protest concerning the brutalities of the colonial regime and, against Portuguese assimilationism, affirmed the values of African indigenous culture and the dignity of the black man. Not surprisingly, the Governor-General of Angola tolerated only two issues of such a subversive publication. In 1957, some of its contributors set up the equally short-lived *Cultura*.

Although inspired by Portuguese communists and joined by a few African *assimilados*, the MPLA was essentially a *mestiço* organization and its activities were confined to Luanda and other urban centres. As might be expected, the MPLA's orientation was highly intellectual. Its first president, Illidio Tomé Alves Machado (born in 1915 in Luanda), had been an influential leader of the *Liga Nacional Africana* before it was discredited. Although possessing only a junior secondary school certificate and working as a postal employee, Machado was considered to be 'a man of ideas rather than mass appeal'.[2]

The MPLA's first secretary-general was Viriato da Cruz, the former editor of *Mensagem*. A graduate of the *liceu* in Luanda, he had worked

[1] Mário de Andrade, 'Et les colonies de Salazar?' *Democratie nouvelle* (Vol. 14, No. 9, September 1960), p. 35, quoted in Marcum, op. cit., p. 28.

[2] Segal, *Political Africa*, p. 164.

for the Department of Education until, in 1952, he was fired for his political activities. He was subsequently employed as a bookkeeper by a private business until 1957, when he fled to Portugal and eventually France to escape arrest. There he became one of the key organizers of the MPLA in exile, remaining secretary-general of the organization until 1962, when grave differences developed between the MPLA leaders.

The mass arrests in Angola in 1959 were far more extensive than the MPLA had expected, although it was well aware of P.I.D.E. surveillance and feared agents had penetrated its ranks. Da Cruz commented later that the arrests, beginning in March 1959, 'made it impossible for the MPLA (in other words, the proletariat of Luanda and other Angolan cities) to effectively lead the armed peasant movement.'[1] A convinced Marxist-Leninist, da Cruz viewed the struggle in Angola as the consequence of the 'violent social contradictions provoked by the establishment and development of capitalism in that country.'[2]

Hundreds of persons were caught in the P.I.D.E. dragnet, including Illidio Machado who was arrested during a visit to Lisbon and returned to prison in Luanda. On 8 June 1960, another leading member of the MPLA, Dr. Agostinho Neto, was arrested. Born in the village of Bengo, near Catete, on 17 September 1922, Neto was the son of a Methodist pastor. After secondary education in Luanda, he received a Methodist scholarship to study medicine in Portugal, first at the University of Lisbon and then at Coimbra. While a student, he became a leader of an anti-fascist youth movement, the *Movimento de Unidade Democrática-Juvenil* (MUDJ). He also was a poet, and his political activities and poems of protest earned him arrest in 1952 and arrest followed by rustication from February 1955 to June 1957. Nevertheless, he successfully completed his medical training in 1958. Dr. Neto returned to Angola in 1959 to take up a general practice. He also became chairman of the Steering Committee of the clandestine MPLA.

Following his arrest, villagers from Bengo went to Catete to demonstrate for his release. Portuguese troops fired on them, killing thirty and wounding more than 200 others. A day later, the troops totally destroyed Bengo and its twin village of Icolo, killing or arresting everyone in the two villages.[3]

Although this genocidal violence was not then repeated elsewhere,

[1] Viriato da Cruz, 'What Kind of Independence for Angola?', *Revolution* (Vol. 1 No. 9, January 1964), p. 15.

[2] Ibid., p. 20.

[3] Marcum, op. cit., pp. 38–9.

the mass arrests in the cities were clearly decimating MPLA cadres, who had been concentrating their efforts on building a working-class movement among the black and *mestiço* proletariat, who were living in conditions of growing misery as a result of the swiftly increasing numbers of European settlers. In 1955, the European population was twelve times that in 1900. Long-urbanized Africans and peasants recently emigrated to town found themselves nearly on the same level of (in da Cruz's words) 'underemployment, unemployment and insecurity'. He adds:

The rivalries between African and European workers, abetted by the capitalist firms in Angola, also aided in developing all sorts of discrimination and racial conflict, because the fact that the great majority of Portuguese settlers belonged to the lower social strata encouraged them all the more to try to benefit from their 'racial quality'.[1]

However, contacts between the relatively sophisticated intellectuals and the generally illiterate masses were not easy. The P.I.D.E. had struck before a mass organization could become viable. Thus, in some desperation, remaining MPLA cadres decided to risk everything in one bold action in Luanda on 4 February 1961. The MPLA had also been galvanized by rumours of peasant uprisings in the north. There was no direct contact between the peasant revolutionaries and the Marxist intellectuals, who were as fearful of a tribal *jacquerie* as the colonial authorities. In Cassange, in early January, the followers of a messianic cult called Maria, after António Mariano their leader, rose in insurrection, singing hymns to Patrice Lumumba, the Bakongo Protestant leader José Eduardo Pinock, and Maria himself. Portuguese planes and troops eventually crushed this quasi-religious crusade for independence. In March, Maria was captured and mutilated. He was confined within a Portuguese prison, where he presumably died. No reports of 'Maria's War' appeared in Angolan or Portuguese newspapers, and outsiders were banned from entering the region until long after Portuguese troops had completed their mopping-up operations. However, the thousands of refugees who fled to the Congo later told of the fighting.[2]

On 22 January 1961, Portuguese opposition leader Captain Henrique Galvão and a group of followers hijacked the liner *Santa Maria*. They eventually reached Brazil eleven days later, but many had believed that Galvão might head for Angola in the hope of taking over the country. Consequently, Luanda was full of expectant foreign journalists at the beginning of February. Another factor encouraging a *coup de main* in

---

[1] Da Cruz, op. cit., p. 15.
[2] See Marcum, op. cit., pp. 124–6.

Luanda was the expected United Nations consideration of the MPLA's appeal from the previous September for an investigation of the situation in Angola.

The MPLA decided to free members held in the prisons and police posts of the colonial capital. On 4 February, before dawn, several hundred militants attacked a police station and São Paulo fortress, which was being used as a prison. Seven Portuguese police were reportedly killed, while some forty Africans died in the futile assault. On 5 February after the funeral of the seven policemen, armed settlers ran amok in Luanda, killing blacks indiscriminately. On 10 February another raid on a prison ended in failure and resulted in the deaths of seven persons and the wounding of seventeen others. This was followed by a full-scale massacre of Africans and *mestiços* by police and civilian vigilantes. The exact death toll will probably never be known, but certainly many hundreds were killed. Thus, in any case, the myth of racial harmony in the Portuguese colonies drowned in blood.

The MPLA also became purely an exile organization. Viriato da Cruz was already in France. He had been joined there by other mulattos, among them the poet Mário de Andrade and Lucio Lara, scion of a rich plantation-owning family. In 1959, da Cruz and Andrade had participated in the Second International Congress of Negro Writers and Artists, held in Rome. In October 1958, they had taken part in the Afro-Asian Writers' Conference in Tashkent, but they had not attended the First All-African Peoples' Conference in Accra in December 1958, where Holden Roberto finally abandoned tribal politics and announced the Tunis meeting, but rejected an invitation to join FRAIN.

Andrade was born on 21 August 1928, at Golungo Alto in the Dembos region of Angola. After finishing his secondary education in Luanda, he studied in Europe, first at the University of Lisbon, for six years, then at the Sorbonne, where he frequented leftist intellectual circles. In 1957, with exiles from other Portuguese colonies, Andrade helped to organize in Paris the inter-territorial *Movimento Anti-Colonialista* (MAC). In January 1960, at the Second All-African Peoples' Conference, held in Tunis, this was transformed into the *Frente Revolucionaria Africana para a Independência Nacional* (FRAIN). Holden Roberto also attended the Tunis meeting and rejected an invitation to join FRAIN.

Congolese independence in June 1960 stimulated the exiles' fantasies of a swift end to colonial rule in Angola and other Portuguese territories. In November, the U.N. General Assembly's Fourth Committee held that Portugal's 'overseas provinces' were in fact colonies, and, under the provisions of the U.N. Charter, demanded information from Lisbon concerning them. Andrade was then still speaking of MPLA hopes for a 'pacific solution to the colonial problem', while his colleague da Cruz warned frankly of coming 'direct action to win independence'. The MPLA leadership in exile was to claim later that these contradictory statements in Paris had in fact been a signal to MPLA forces in Luanda to make their attack on 4 February.[1]

But the attack, launched by only a few hundred militants, was a failure. None of the prisoners was freed and the urban cadres of the MPLA were wiped out or took flight. However, in the countryside, on 15 March, a genuine revolutionary uprising spread throughout the north of Angola, led by the UPA. Although gratified by this massive blow against colonialism, MPLA leaders were also horrified by accounts of the alleged primitive savagery of the Bakongo people in dealing with white settlers, *mestiços*, and blacks of other tribes. Manifestly exaggerated by Portuguese propaganda, these tales of atrocity have nonetheless been used repeatedly since as proof of the 'backward' tribal nature of Holden Roberto's UPA. The allegedly 'racist excesses' committed by the fighting peasants convinced the MPLA leadership that they offered the only 'decent' road to progress, guiding the ignorant peasantry to salvation.[2]

The police repression that began in 1959, the failure of the 4 February 1961 uprising in Luanda and the success of the UPA's mass revolt in the north were all bitter blows to the MPLA. The organization fought desperately to survive, launching diplomatic offensives for international support. While Roberto seemed to look to Western sources, especially American missionary groups, for assistance, the MPLA found its natural sympathizers among European communists and other leftists. It also made some gains on the Afro-Asian front, replacing the absent UPA on the Steering Committee of the Third All-African People's Conference in Cairo in March 1961, and it took part in the third session of the Council of the Afro-Asian Peoples' Solidarity Organization, held that April in Bandung.

Also in April, the MPLA and its allies in FRAIN met in Casablanca to form a new inter-territorial organization, the *Conferência das Organizações Nacionalistas das Colónias Portuguêsas* (CONCP). Although invited, the UPA did not attend the meeting, which set up a permanent secretariat in Rabat under Marcelino des Santos, the Mozambican secretary-general of the CONCP. Andrade was elected chairman of the CONCP. By now, as acting-president (since the arrest of Neto), he was running the MPLA in exile from Conakry. In October

[1] Marcum, op. cit., pp. 43–6.   [2] Da Cruz, op. cit., pp. 17–18.

1961, Andrade transferred his headquarters to Leopoldville, where the UPA had long operated unchallenged.

Among the small group of MPLA militants that survived the abortive February coup and fled Luanda into the countryside was a young man named Ferraz Bomboko. Finding himself in a UPA-controlled area of the Dembos region, he hid his real organizational affinity and accepted orders from UPA headquarters in Leopoldville. Later known as Commander Bomboko, he led a guerrilla band that seized the town of Nambuangongo, reportedly attempting to transform it into a 'People's Socialist Republic of Nambuangongo'.[1] On 9 August 1961, Portuguese troops recaptured the town and the 'guerrillas withdrew into the bush and into the mountains to create pockets of resistance.'[2]

Bomboko sent a five-man mission to Leopoldville to urge MPLA representatives there to send help. Eventually, Commander Tomas Ferreira, a former UPA militant who had switched to the MPLA, tried to lead a squad of twenty men from the Congo to Bomboko's guerrilla republic. They died while trying to cross UPA-held territory. Later, Holden Roberto confirmed that UPA forces had been ordered to wipe out any MPLA column trying to enter Angola. Clearly, the UPA did not intend to have its control inside northern Angola subverted. The possibility of such subversion was most acute, not in the Bakongo north but in border areas where two ethnic groups met and sometimes clashed, such as Nambuangongo, between Bakongo and Ovumbundu. When political rivalries were added to ethnic tensions and the everyday black suspicion of *mestiços* (who dominated the leadership of the MPLA), the results were often tragic.[3]

Nevertheless, the MPLA failed to mobilize large tribal groups, as UPA had done with the Bakongo. This and the menace of even more fratricidal attacks upon intruders in UPA-held areas, halted MPLA efforts to subvert UPA units or to build up its own guerrilla forces inside Angola. Moreover, although it was soon to begin training military cadres in Ahmed Ben Bella's newly-independent Algeria, as Holden Roberto was already doing, it could not follow his example in the Congo. Roberto enjoyed the personal friendship of too many Congolese leaders, from the then-Premier Cyrille Adoula to General Joseph Mobutu, head of the Army, who was eventually to take over the presidency. UPA also enjoyed the support of the mass of Angolan

[1] Marcum, op. cit., p. 212.

[2] Commander João Gonçalves Benedito,' Five Months of Independence in Angola', *African Revolution* (Vol. 1, No. 1, May 1963).

[3] See Robert Davezies, *Les angolais* (Paris, Editions du Minuit, 1965), for a very pro-MPLA account of the Ferreira incident.

émigrés in the Congo, mainly among whom were recruited the cadres to structure the *Exército de Libertação Nacional de Angola* (ELNA)— National Army of Liberation of Angola—under the command of a former Cuanhama corporal in the Portuguese Army, João Batista, and a Ganguela non-com, Marcos Xavier Kassanga. Roberto was commander-in-chief, while these two southerners were appointed respectively field commander inside Angola and chief of staff in Leopoldville. They strove to gain control of the anarchic mass uprising in the north, while waiting for their first batch of recruits to be trained by the Algerian National Liberation Army. When they returned as trained officers, they were installed in a camp at Kinkuzu, north of Thysville, which was to become military headquarters of the ELNA in the Congo. The MPLA never had similar facilities. Its leaders were obliged to make numerous proposals for unity with the UPA in the hope of benefiting from its obvious material advantages and gradually replacing 'reactionaries' like Roberto with MPLA leaders in order to carry out a classic 'National-Democratic Revolution' in Angola.

In July 1962, Agostinho Neto rejoined the MPLA leadership. An international campaign on his behalf had prompted the Portuguese to transfer him from prison to house arrest in Portugal. Dr. Neto wasted no time in escaping to Morocco. From Rabat he went shortly to Conakry and then to Leopoldville, where he reasserted his leadership of the MPLA. The 'Honorary President' became in fact the movement's chief executive, displacing Mário de Andrade and especially antagonizing Viriato da Cruz, the secretary-general, who was among those who suspected that Neto's escape might have been arranged by the P.I.D.E. as part of a Portuguese 'plot' to change the orientation of the MPLA.

In Leopoldville, Neto tried in vain to unite the MPLA with the UPA, but the UPA had now entered into an alliance with the smaller *Partido Democrático Angolano* (PDA), which was based on the Zombo tribe of the Bakongo, and created the *Frente Nacional de Libertação de Angola.* The FNLA had been set up in March and by April it had created the *Govêrno Revolucionário de Angola no Exílio* (GRAE)—Revolutionary Government of Angola in Exile—under Roberto as premier and with Emmanuel Kunzika of the PDA as first vice-premier.

MPLA had hoped that Neto's personal prestige would force unity on MPLA terms or at least counter the dynamism of GRAE. But the Congolese Government recognized GRAE in June 1963 and paved the way for wider African acceptance. To the UPA's FNLA, the MPLA countered with its own front, the *Frente Democrática de Libertação de Angola* (FDLA), created in July 1963. Joining with the MPLA were four heterogenous groups, the *Mouvement de Défense des Intérêts de l'Angola* (MDIA), *Ngwizani a Kongo* (*Ngwizako*), the *NtoBako* and the *União Nacional dos Trabalhadores* (UNTA). Although favouring eventual independence for Angola, three of these groups—MDIA, *Ngwizako*, and *NtoBako*—had been 'opposed to the present revolt and seem to have, on one level or another, some kind of co-operative arrangement with the Portuguese authorities', according to George Hauser of the American Committee on Africa.[1] UNTA, a communist-oriented labour union, had always been close to the MPLA so that a merger was not surprising. On the other hand, MDIA, which broke away from the UPA in 1961, was committed to non-violence and opposed UPA's strategy of revolutionary warfare. The *Ngwizako* was a non-violent Bakongo royalist faction that supported the Catholic placed on the Kongo throne by the Portuguese in 1955. The third group, *NtoBako*, was closely allied to Congolese President Joseph Kasavubu's *Abako* party and shared its dreams of a greater Kongo State extending from Angola to the Congo. *NtoBako* had also been willing to work with the Portuguese in the past.

Surprising company though these groups might have been for the MPLA, Dr. Neto (who had been elected president in December 1962) desperately needed forces to cope with a split in MPLA ranks between his own supporters and the hard-core revolutionaries who followed Viriato da Cruz. The MPLA Steering Committee met in May 1963 and removed da Cruz from the post of secretary-general, which he had held since the founding of the movement in 1956. Besides Neto's personal animosity to da Cruz, the decision to remove him and set up a three-man secretariat was prompted by the latent crisis in the international communist movement that erupted with the Sino-Soviet split. Da Cruz was viewed as too militant, too much of a hard-line Marxist-Leninist by Neto and his revisionist associates. (In January 1962, Andrade had gone to the United States to plead for support, swearing that the MPLA was not communist or even pro-communist.)[2] The inner-party struggle was virtually won by Neto when he completely bypassed da Cruz and his group at the MPLA's First National Conference in Leopoldville in December 1962, setting up a new executive committee of ten.

Da Cruz had his revenge. He informed the newly-formed Organization of African Unity's African Liberation Committee (A.L.C.), when

[1] George M. Hauser, 'Nationalist Organizations in Angola: Status of the Revolt', in John A. Davis and James K. Baker (eds.), *Southern Africa in Transition* (New York, Praeger, 1966).
[2] Marcum, op. cit., p. 220.

it visited Leopoldville in July 1963, that the MPLA's claims to have an effective fighting force inside Angola were false. He declared that only the GRAE was then actually in combat against the Portuguese. Shortly afterwards, da Cruz asked to be allowed to join the FNLA. He was subsequently admitted, but never played an active role in its leadership. Two of his close associates, Matias Migueis and José Miguel, who had followed him to the FNLA from the MPLA, were arrested at Brazzaville Airport on 12 November 1965, while *en route* to Kinshasa from Indonesia via Paris and Algiers. They were turned over to their former comrades of the MPLA, who murdered them.[1] The MPLA was also to claim that some of its members had been killed or imprisoned by the GRAE in Zaïre (formerly Congo-Kinshasa).[2]

Not only did the Goverment of Zaïre (formerly Congo-Kinshasa) recognize Holden Roberto's GRAE, it also closed down MPLA offices in Leopoldville. A haven was found across the river in Congo–Brazzaville where, especially after Alphonse Massamba–Debat came to power, the MPLA could freely denounce the GRAE over Radio Brazzaville, and train its men, under Soviet, Algerian, and Cuban instructors, for an attack on the only part of Angola to which it then had access—the Cabinda enclave.

At the time, Cabinda was the only area where the MPLA had a chance to prove itself a fighting movement of the same calibre as the UPA. Later, after the nadir of its decline, the MPLA was to claim vehemently that it was the sole 'authentic' Angolan movement and the only one fighting against the Portuguese. And yet the Cabinda operation was essentially a failure.

Following the fall of the Government of Fulbert Youlou in Congo–Brazzaville, the new regime of Massamba–Debat authorized the MPLA to liberate from Portuguese rule the tiny enclave with its 60,000 inhabitants. However, the MPLA found that the Cabindans had their own nationalist party, the *Front pour la Libération de l'Enclave de Cabinda* (FLEC), which had been set up in Brazzaville before the arrival of the MPLA. FLEC wanted total independence for Cabinda, not only from Portugal but also from Angola.

MPLA infiltration of Cabinda did not result in any spectacular battles. It was principally aimed at control over the local population and recruitment of the able-bodied for the guerrilla forces. Until the discovery of on- and off-shore oil, Cabinda's principal natural resource

---

[1] *Le Monde* (6–7 February 1966).

[2] In this section, Congo-Leopoldville becomes Congo-Kinshasa in any reference after 2 May 1966, when the main cities of the Congo were renamed.

was timber. The dense virgin forest made excellent terrain for guerrillas. In 1966, in Dar es Salaam, a senior MPLA official told the author that the forest was the guerrillas' most reliable ally.

All the Portuguese can try to do is hold the roads. The Portuguese Air Force cannot hurt us much because of the dense cover of the forest. Really, it is not a classic guerrilla war because the Portuguese do not try to hold the terrain, only the roads. And along them it is a war of ambushes. The Portuguese used to patrol in convoys of jeeps, but were hit by so many MPLA ambushes that they now use armoured trains—and they are still attacked![1]

This official repeated the MPLA claim at the time that the MPLA controlled 'one-quarter of Cabinda'. Yet then and later, reliable observers found no evidence to substantiate this claim.[2] Writing in the OSPAAAL publication, *Tricontinental*, in 1969, Agostinho Neto himself avoided making any claims, but rather commented that there was a 'dense concentration of Portuguese soldiers' in the territory. 'Cabinda was the school in which were trained the essential elements for the development of the struggle in other regions,'[3] says Neto, who refers to the Cabinda operation in the past tense throughout this article. The fact was the campaign had virtually collapsed in 1967 and 1968, due to renewed Portuguese interest in Cabinda after the oil discovery, the MPLA's failure to win the support of the local population and a change of attitude on the part of the authorities of Congo–Brazzaville, especially Massamba–Debat's fall in 1968. Congo–Brazzaville army officers had looked with great suspicion on the presence of the MPLA forces, said at one point to have been four times the size of their own, and the MPLA's Russian, Algerian, and Cuban advisers. The 200 Cubans posed a special problem as they also functioned as the praetorian guard of the president.

The MPLA failure in Cabinda was also assisted in 1966 by the defection to the Portuguese of Alexandre Taty, who had earlier been denounced by Holden Roberto as a Portuguese agent. In June 1965, Taty, then GRAE defence minister, and André Kassinda, leader of the anti-Roberto *Conselho do Povo Angolana* (CPA)—Council of the Angolan People—had seized and held the GRAE office in Leopoldville until evicted by Congolese troops. Taty subsequently joined the MPLA

[1] Interview with Daniel Julio Chipenda, MPLA Representative (Dar es Salaam, 18 March 1966).

[2] See George Martelli, 'Conflict in Portuguese Africa' in Abshire and Samuels op. cit., pp. 407–8.

[3] Agostinho Neto, 'Angola: People in Revolution', *Tricontinental* (No. 12, May–June 1969).

in Brazzaville. Following his defection to the Portuguese, he reappeared
in Cabinda as a Portuguese officer working against the MPLA, successfully encouraging many Cabindan refugees to return from the Congo–
Brazzaville. At the same time, MPLA communiqués continued to
boast of victories, thousands of soldiers under its command, and
hundreds of political cadres leading the masses throughout Angola.
Concerning these MPLA claims, a French sympathizer of the MPLA,
Gérard Chaliand, complained finally that 'the figures were not only
considerably blown up. They were frankly in the realm of fantasy.'[1]
The Cabinda operation did, however, make the MPLA more of a
competitive force, especially after a series of grave splits within the
GRAE, in particular the breakaway of Jonas Savimbi and the eventual
formation of UNITA, which at that time did not appear to menace the
MPLA. Holden Roberto's troubles were increased by Moïse Tshombé's
regime in the other Congo. The GRAE was accused by the MPLA of
working with the reactionary Tshombé, whereas Tshombé harassed the
GRAE as much as possible and only just stopped short of banning it in
Congo–Leopoldville altogether.

In any case, the tide had turned. The O.A.U. African Liberation
Committee recognized that the MPLA was now actually in combat by
giving it half the subsidy that had been allocated to the GRAE. It was
soon to receive more than GRAE.[2] The O.A.U. money was amply
complemented by Soviet aid. MPLA's communist origins had not been
forgotten in Moscow, especially as the Chinese were already showing
an interest in the GRAE.

With the men who had experienced some form of combat in Cabinda,
MPLA set up a base in Zambia in 1966 and shortly afterwards launched
a second front in eastern Angola. MPLA was able to expand its eastern
front after the Zambian Government expelled UNITA in 1966 because
of its rash attack on the Benguela Railway that carries Zambian copper
to the Atlantic. UNITA managed to survive, but virtually without
supplies from outside. If it had not had strong popular support in
south-eastern Angola, its cadres would have been gunned down by the
well-equipped MPLA force. As in the past, GRAE had left unheeded
MPLA appeals for unity, so now MPLA turned a deaf ear to similar
appeals from UNITA. In the north of Angola, GRAE still appeared to
block penetration by MPLA guerrillas. Farther south, in Bié, Moxico,

[1] Gérard Chaliand, 'Problèmes du nationalisme angolais', *Les Temps Modernes*
(August 1965).
[2] In 1967, Roberto complained that the GRAE received only $73,000 from the
O.A.U.

and Malange, the two hostile organizations were able to maintain isolated pockets of resistance, virtual guerrilla republics, except that they had little contact with the Portuguese forces or with the local population. The principal threat was from Portuguese aircraft. In the far south of Angola, the tenacious hold of UNITA on the populace prevented any serious implantation of MPLA forces. In private, the MPLA bitterly criticized SWAPO for co-operating with UNITA, and accused the South West African organization of secretly supplying UNITA, after that group had been expelled from Zambian bases.

By 1970, MPLA had clearly made a considerable comeback. It was receiving more aid from the A.L.C. than GRAE and, in 1969, had almost succeeded in having GRAE de-recognized. (A U.A.R.-sponsored effort to bring together the rival groups had foundered in 1966 and had never been refloated.) The Soviet Union and Moscow-line communist parties, as well as some 'Western' progressives, gave full support to MPLA, apparently steadily increasing the flow of money and arms, backed by instructors. MPLA had failed to drive the Portuguese out of the minuscule Cabinda enclave. If the embarrassing question was brought up, it blamed its failure on the Cabindan separatist groups, FLEC and the *Comité Révolutionnaire de Cabinda* (CRC), accusing them of being 'under the direct influence of Portuguese colonialism' and playing 'the game of Balkanizing imperialism'.[1] Admittedly, relations with the Government of Congo–Brazzaville were no longer as warm as they had once been. As the eastern front developed, MPLA headquarters were transferred from Brazzaville to Lusaka and a major base was set up on the Zambian–Angolan border. Officially, MPLA headquarters were somewhere inside Angola, allegedly near Teixeira da Sousa, but this was mainly a diplomatic fiction to prevent embarrassment to the Zambian Government.

Reliable observers have estimated the total of guerrilla forces in Angola in mid-1969 at around 15,000.[2] At times it has seemed that the efforts of MPLA's well-equipped forces were directed more against GRAE and UNITA guerrillas than against the Portuguese. In 1968, MPLA was reported to have massacred many UNITA men in an attempt to move southwards, but by the end of the year UNITA had

[1] *Le Monde* (2 February 1967).

[2] Whitaker, 'Angola, Guinea, Mozambique', p. 24, says: 'The guerrilla forces may total 15,000, but most informal estimates place the number of rebel troops between 3,500 and 5,000 each for GRAE and MPLA, and 500 to 1,500 for UNITA, with a tendency to stress the lower figures in each case.' In *The Economist* (10 May 1969), a special correspondent estimated GRAE strength at 8,000 and MPLA strength at 4,000. He gave no figures for UNITA.

beaten back the MPLA forces. Observers also reported that MPLA sought to hold well-defined areas by conventional military measures rather than by adherence to classic tenets of guerrilla warfare. Soviet doctrine seemed to have greater influence on MPLA tactics than the teachings of Chairman Mao, militarily as well as politically. Moreover, the mulatto leaders still had great difficulty in winning the support of the tribesmen in the sparsely populated scrub land of eastern Angola. Determined efforts made to break the existing social structures and to impose new relations of production of course provoked angry resentment and sometimes active opposition.[1] Nevertheless, Neto claims that Cuaodo Cubango and Moxico in 1969 constituted 'a firm base for the military and political training of the guerrillas; the people there lead a near-normal life and give great support to the combatants.'[2] This simply was not true. At the end of 1970, despite patrols roaming over large areas of Angola, and holding firmly several zones near the Zambian base, its headquarters were in Lusaka, not inside Angola.

Attempts to win support in the West were made by Mário de Andrade, who by then was running CONCP headquarters in Algiers, and by Neto, with whom he had quarrelled. These attempts met with little success except in Sweden, where the Swedish International Development Authority and the Social Democratic Party actively supported MPLA, as well as its allies FRELIMO and PAIGC. A leading British sympathizer, Basil Davidson, again pleaded the case of MPLA in October 1970. Urging Western support for MPLA, against 'a vigorous propaganda which comes partly from Maoist groups', for UNITA, and GRAE which 'has not been able, nor apparently even wished to free itself from ethnic separatism,' Davidson launched out with equal ferocity against Washington and Peking, while maintaining that the Moscow-line MPLA was a revolutionary movement 'of a type not seen before'.[3] Despite Davidson's strictures, Neto himself considered it worthwhile enough to risk Soviet displeasure by visiting Peking in July 1971. Addressing a banquet given in his honour by the Chinese–African Peoples' Friendship Association, the MPLA leader energetically assured his hosts that 'the Angolan guerrilla fighters and their leadership in their fight draw inspiration from the voice of Chairman Mao Tsetung, the great leader of the Chinese people, and the voice of the Chinese people, to which they always listen attentively.'[4] But in its tactics inside

[1] See 'UNITA et MPLA: La guerrilla et la lutte de libération nationale', *Analyses et documents* (Paris, No. 181, 18 December 1969).
[2] Neto, 'Angola: People in Revolution', p. 68.
[3] Basil Davidson, 'The Seed of Midwinter', *New Statesman* (30 October 1970).
[4] Hsinhua News Agency Daily Bulletin (27 July 1971).

Angola and in relations with other liberation movements, the MPLA was slow to reveal any indication of a profound change of heart. The hard fact remained that MPLA, although it has indeed made progress from an urban-based *mestiço* intellectual group to a functioning politico-military force, had not won the fratricidal struggle within Angola; it had neither exterminated its rivals nor modified the ethnic reality of the country that, along with ideology, still provided an objective basis for the persisting disunity of the forces fighting colonialism.

Govêrno Revolucionário de Angola no Exílio — Frente Nacional de Libertação de Angola (GRAE/FNLA)

The armed struggle in the Angolan countryside was launched on 15 March 1961 by the *União das Populações de Angola* (UPA). Transforming itself later into a front called the *Frente Nacional de Libertação de Angola* (FNLA), the UPA eventually controlled the Revolutionary Government of Angola (GRAE), which it set up in Zaïre (formerly Congo-Kinshasa) on 3 April 1962. Although recognized by the Congolese Government and admitted to the Organization of African States, the GRAE, like its parent FNLA, represented in essence two northern Angolan parties. However, they were solidly linked with the major ethnic group of northern Angola, the Bakongo peoples, and had individual members and sympathizers from virtually every region of the country.

The UPA began its existence in July 1957 as the *União das Populações do Norte de Angola* (UPNA),[1] formed by Angolan exile groups in the Congo who, since 1954, had been embroiled in the struggle for the throne of the old Kongo Kingdom. They wanted a strong king who would restore the independence of the ancient realm, separating it from the rest of Angola as well as from Portugal. This effort was thwarted by the Portuguese, who maintained tight control over the royal court in São Salvador. The royal oppositionists fled to the Congo, where some of their kinsmen had long been settled in Leopoldville and Matadi. Groups from those two cities, although they subsequently lost interest in seizing the throne, joined in forming an authentic party of Bakongo nationalism.

Shortly before the UPNA was formally constituted, those who were to become its leaders petitioned the United Nations for an on-the-spot investigation of the brutalities of Portuguese colonialism. The letter to

---

[1] Concerning this date, three years later than that usually given, see Marcum, op. cit., p. 63.

the U.N. Secretary General was sent in the name of the Kongo Kingdom, 'not introduced by the country called Angola'.[1]

In November 1957, the UPNA leaders decided to follow up this initiative by sending a representative abroad to speak on their behalf in independent Africa, in the United States, and at the United Nations. Holden Roberto, nephew of Manuel Barros Necaca, UPNA president, was selected and, in 1958, he left Leopoldville clandestinely for Accra, to attend the First All-African Peoples' Conference organized by Ghana's President Kwame Nkrumah and George Padmore. In Ghana, where he met leading Pan-Africanists from Africa and America, Roberto abandoned Bakongo nationalism for an Angolan national movement. He hastily changed the name of the UPNA to *União das Populações de Angola* (UPA). But in the Congo, and even more inside Angola, the new national party was almost exclusively Bakongo and heavily influenced by Protestants, who had long fought against Portuguese Catholic control of the Kongolese monarchy.

In September 1959, Holden Roberto visited the United States to lobby the Fourteenth Session of the U.N. General Assembly. He travelled on a Guinean passport and worked closely with the Guinean Mission to the U.N. He also furthered his American contacts, especially through the American Committee on Africa, headed by the Reverend George Hauser. Roberto received much encouragement and assistance, in particular from American Protestant groups and missionary societies, who had long been aware of the Catholic–Protestant conflict in the struggle against the Portuguese for the Kongolese throne.

When Roberto attended the Second All-African People's Conference in Tunis in January 1960, he resisted strong pressure to merge UPA with the mulatto-led MPLA. At the same time, Roberto established close relations with the Tunisian Government, headed by President Habib Bourguiba, and was later to receive considerable assistance from Tunisia. From Tunis, Roberto returned to Accra, where he now found himself pressured by the Ghanaian Government to merge with the MPLA. Roberto's stubborn refusal to do so was approved by Frantz Fanon, the French West Indian psychiatrist who had joined the Algerian FLN and was then the ambassador to Ghana of the Provisional Government of the Algerian Republic (GPRA). Fanon had already written scathingly of the divided loyalties and pretensions to quasi-divine leadership of half-castes.[2]

[1] Quoted in Abshire and Samuels, op. cit., p. 390.

[2] See Frantz Fanon, *Peau noire, masques blancs* (Paris, Maspero, 1952), *Black Skin, White Masks* (New York, Grove Press, 1967).

Throughout this time, the Angolan exiles in the Congo were under close surveillance by the Belgian colonial authorities. After political rioting in Leopoldville in January 1959, the Belgians arrested and expelled many Angolans in the belief that they had sparked the national-ist demonstrations. Manuel Barros Necaca and José Eduardo Pinock, founders of the old UPNA and both of them uncles of Holden Roberto, were interrogated and threatened with deportation to Angola, which would have meant imprisonment and possibly death at the hands of the Portuguese. However, Belgian rule was ending faster than anyone realized at the time and, in July 1960, under an independent Congo headed by Roberto's old friend Patrice Lumumba, the UPA rapidly gained strength and structured itself, with Roberto at its head. Lumumba permitted the UPA to broadcast over the Congolese radio and to recruit openly among Angolan *émigrés*.

The fall of Lumumba in September 1960 was a serious blow, especially as President Joseph Kasavubu, although he had abandoned the former hopes of his *Abako* party for a Bakongo state stretching from Angola to the Congo, retained a deep-seated hostility towards the UPA. Roberto had to go into hiding to avoid arrest by Kasavubu for allegedly planning to 'establish Communism in neighbouring Angola'.[1] He eventually fled to Ghana, where he was astonished to hear the secre-tariat of the All-African Peoples' Conference inform him there would be no help for him 'because you are in the pay of America'.[2]

Throughout his travels and despite the various troubles in the Congo and elsewhere, Roberto demanded that his colleagues make a maximum effort organizing in northern Angola. The colony was suffering an economic recession as well as the usual misdeeds of Portuguese coloni-alism. As John A. Marcum noted: 'By the beginning of 1961 Angola was a black powder keg with a ready fuse.' Until then, the UPA had professed non-violence, but, despite numerous appeals and the lobbying at the United Nations and in Washington, it was obvious that the Portuguese were not prepared to negotiate decolonization.

On 15 March precisely as the U.N. Security Council was preparing to discuss the situation in Angola, first reports of a vast uprising throughout northern Angola reached New York. Holden Roberto, who was in New York for the debate, confirmed that the uprising was the first stage of a revolutionary war of liberation. Although later deploring the

[1] Hélio Felgas, *Guerra em Angola* (Lisbon, Livraria Classica, 1961), p. 57. Quoted in Marcum, op. cit., p. 96.
[2] Holden Roberto, Speech before the Organization of African Unity, Assembly of Heads of State and Government (Cairo, 21 July 1964).

reported ferocity of the attacks on Portuguese settlers and officials, he maintained that this was the inevitable consequence of 500 years of Portuguese terrorism against Africans. The Portuguese replied immediately with terror and atrocities that proved 'Portuguese soldiers and colonists are no less atavistic than their African opponents'.[1] The exact toll in the carnage may never be known, but it is estimated that 750 Portuguese lost their lives in the first three months of fighting, while Portuguese forces killed some 20,000 Africans in a campaign to exterminate all who supported the revolution. Some 150,000 black survivors had fled to the Congo by the end of 1961.[2] African losses ran high because of the scarcity of weapons and appalling ignorance of the most elementary principles of guerrilla warfare. The young UPA organizers who carried out Roberto's orders to unleash the uprising lacked military instruction and could barely control the rampaging African bands, who, nevertheless, were no match in the open for Portuguese troops and militia.

The UPA was well aware of its military deficiencies. Two African deserters from the Portuguese Army, Corporal João Batista and another non-commissioned officer, Marcos Xavier Kasanga, took command of the *Exército de Libertação Nacional de Angola* (ELNA)—Army of National Liberation of Angola. Both were southerners, though the UPA had a northern tribal basis. Kassanga was appointed chief of staff in the Congo, while Batista took over as field commander inside Angola. At the same time, after Algeria had gained her independence in 1962, some two dozen others were sent there for training by Holden Roberto, the overall commander-in-chief.

Writing in 1961, Fanon had commented approvingly:

We may remember that on the 15th March 1961 a group of two or three thousand Angolan peasants threw themselves against the Portuguese positions. Men, women and children, armed and unarmed, afire with courage and enthusiasm, then flung themselves in successive waves of compact masses upon the districts where the settler, the soldier and the Portuguese flag held sway. Villages and aerodromes were encircled and subjected to frequent attacks, but it must be added that thousands of Angolans were mown down by colonialist machine guns. It did not take long for the leaders of the Angolan rising to realize that they must find some other methods if they really wanted to free their country. So during the last few months the Angolan leader Holden Roberto has reorganized the National Angolan Army, using the experience gained in various other wars of liberation, and employing guerrilla techniques.[3]

[1] Duffy, *Portugal in Africa*, p. 216.   [2] Marcum, op. cit., pp. 143–4.
[3] Frantz Fanon, *The Wretched of the Earth* (London, MacGibbon and Keel, 1965), p.107.

In the Congo, the position of the UPA was improved greatly after Cyrille Adoula, another old friend of Roberto, became Premier in August 1961. He gave permission for the construction of a large ELNA base north of Thysville, at Kinkuzu.

After the initial explosion, despite the massive Portuguese reaction and the hasty shipment of reinforcements from Lisbon, nearly all northern Angola remained under UPA control.[1] Subsequently, opponents of the UPA claimed that Roberto's cousin, José Kiasonga Manuel Peterson, was instructed by him to liquidate any non-Bakongo Africans found in the ranks of the guerrillas or anywhere in northern Angola. Survivors who fled to the north after the MPLA's 4 February attack in Luanda were said to have been summarily dealt with by UPA forces. Jorge Alicerces Valentim, an Angolan who, then a student in Portugal, was later to support the breakaway *União Nacional para a Independência Total de Angola* (UNITA), claimed: 'The killings perpetrated in the north by Holden Roberto's men was always the most serious handicap to the development of the national struggle until 1966, the year of the formation of the new national party, UNITA.'[2] As we have already seen, the MPLA also accused the UPA of annihilating its units that attempted to cross UPA-held territory. Roberto himself confirmed that no MPLA forces would be permitted to operate and he rejected out of hand all MPLA offers of unity.

However, pressures for some form of unity were so great that in March 1962 the UPA entered into an alliance with the smaller *Partido Democrático Angolana* (PDA), which was based on the Zombo tribe of the Bakongo peoples. Together, they formed the *Frente Nacional de Libertação de Angola* (FNLA) on 28 March 1962, and a month later set up the Revolutionary Government of Angola in Exile (GRAE), with Roberto as premier, Emmanuel Kunzika of the PDA and Msgr. Manuel Mendes das Neves, the former Vicar-General of Angola, as vice-premiers, and an Ovimbundu, Jonas Savimbi, as foreign minister. Neves, a mulatto prelate who had been jailed as a nationalist by the Portuguese in Luanda in April 1961, was then 71 years old and the post of second vice-premier was purely honorary. Both MPLA and Portuguese propaganda continued to denounce the GRAE for the alleged genocide of mulattos.

Shortly before this political victory, the UPA had barely escaped

---

[1] Perry Anderson, *Le Portugal et la fin de l'ultra-colonialisme* (Paris, Maspero, 1963), p. 108.

[2] Jorge Alicerces Valentim, *Qui libère l'Angola* (Brussels, Michèle Coppens, 1969), p. 12.

splitting when the ENLA chief of staff, Marcos Kassanga, and Andre Kassinda, secretary-general of the *Liga Geral dos Trabalhadores de Angola* (LGTA), a Congo-based trade unionist, also accused Holden Roberto of waging a 'fratricidal' war. They claimed that Roberto had ordered the murder of João Batista, the ELNA field commander in Angola, although subsequent reports indicated that Batista had been killed in action on 6 February 1962, while attacking a Portuguese fort at Bembe. There was also said to have been no dissension between Batista and Roberto at the time of Batista's death.[1] Kassanga further charged that '8,000 ′Angolans were savagely massacred by tribal elements in the UPA.'[2]

If the GRAE leadership was multi-ethnic, its followers were mainly Bakongo and its forces were concentrated in northern Angola. But hopes of resolving this contradiction were raised when the MPLA suffered a serious split in 1962 and its one-time secretary-general Viriato da Cruz publicly refuted MPLA claims to have more than a thousand men fighting inside Angola. Alleging the political 'decomposition' of the MPLA under the influence of the 'revisionist trend' of Agostinho Neto, da Cruz declared the FNLA/GRAE was the 'sole Angolan fighting front'. Applying for membership in the FNLA, da Cruz lambasted the hastily arranged, heterogeneous—and eventually short-lived—*Frente Democrática de Libertação de Angola* (FDLA) put together by Neto in opposition to the FNLA. But da Cruz still felt constrained to raise a number of questions crucial to the future of FNLA and GRAE:

> Will it [FNLA] succeed in uniting all the Angolan revolutionary forces? Will it transform itself into a vast organization, solid from a political, ideological and organizational point of view, functioning well and serving as an effective base for the armed struggle? Will it succeed in transforming the peasants, raising their level of revolutionary consciousness? Will it succeed, during the very course of the armed struggle, in resolving the vital problems of the peasantry, the principal source of fighters? Can it spread the armed struggle throughout the entire territory of Angola? Will it have the courage to bring to the benefit of the people of Angola the support of a sincere revolutionary internationalism?[3]

Although admitted to the FNLA, da Cruz and his followers who came from MPLA never got the unequivocable answers for which they were looking. They never played a leading role in the FNLA/GRAE and

---

[1] See Marcum, op. cit., pp. 236–43.
[2] The *Observer* (18 March 1962).
[3] Da Cruz, op. cit., p. 22.

da Cruz eventually, after the Tshombé regime prevented him from returning to the Congo, took up residence in China.

African leaders meeting in Addis Ababa at the first conference of the Organization of African Unity, in May 1963, decided overwhelmingly to give concrete assistance to the armed struggles against colonial and white-minority rule. An African Liberation Committee was charged with the task of co-ordinating this aid and seeing that it was used effectively. Persisting fratricidal rivalry between MPLA and GRAE was deemed an obstacle to the liberation struggle in Angola and a goodwill mission was sent to Leopoldville in July 1963. The six-nation mission was composed of representatives of Algeria, Congo-Leopoldville, Guinea, Nigeria, Senegal, and Uganda.

On 29 June, on the eve of the third anniversary of Congolese independence and, reportedly, despite the opposition of President Kasavubu and the U.S. ambassador, the Adoula Government had recognized Holden Roberto's GRAE as the 'de jure' government in exile of Angola.[1]

The subsequent O.A.U. goodwill mission was unable to reconcile the two parties and instead recommended exclusive recognition and support of the GRAE. But material assistance from the O.A.U. was slow in arriving, and inside Angola the ENLA was unable to score any decisive victories over the steadily mounting numbers of Portuguese troops, which soon reached 50,000, backed by militia and reservists.[2] Seventy-five per cent of these troops were Europeans. Portugal could no longer depend on African auxiliaries to fight her colonial wars.

The MPLA was obliged to close its Leopoldville offices and move to the Congo–Brazzaville, where it received substantial Soviet aid and prepared its attack on the Cabinda enclave which, though ultimately unsuccessful militarily, served to rehabilitate the MPLA politically. And in November 1964, the O.A.U. African Liberation Committee announced it would thenceforth grant material assistance to the MPLA.

The GRAE was experiencing serious difficulties. The first was caused by an internal struggle between Holden Roberto and his foreign minister Jonas Savimbi. Savimbi and his followers charged Roberto and Angolan *émigré* circles around him with tribalism and 'corruption', alleging that they had set up a 'commercial empire' in the Congo, in which some GRAE staff members were merely 'wage-earners and profiteers' who enriched themselves on the 'money of New York

---

[1] Pierre A. Moser, *La Révolution angolaise* (Tunis, Société l'Action d'Édition et de Presse, 1966), pp. 79–80, and Pierre Pascal Rossi, *Pour une guerre oubilée* (Paris, Julliard, 1969), p. 72.

[2] George Martelli, 'Conflict in Angola', in Abshire and Samuels, op. cit., p. 410.

financial circles and other international organizations.'[1] Savimbi also had protested against the entry into the FNLA of da Cruz and his followers, but attacks on the Marxist–Leninist poet ceased soon after da Cruz settled in Peking. And it was Roberto who eventually visited the Chinese capital before Savimbi. The latter finally announced his resignation from the GRAE in Cairo in July 1964. Savimbi was succeeded by Dr. José Liahuca, head of the nominally apolitical refugee relief *Serviço de Assistência aos Refugiados de Angola* (SARA), that worked closely with the GRAE.

In the Congo-Leopoldville, the GRAE was now also the target of the hostility of Premier Moïse Tshombé. Supported by the Portuguese in Katanga during his previous abortive effort to create a separate state, Tshombé clearly would have outlawed the GRAE and banned its activities altogether but for fear of adverse O.A.U. reaction. Not daring a direct move, Tshombé resorted to indirection, encouraging the take-over attempt of dissident GRAE defence minister Alexandre Taty and André Kassinda, the anti-Roberto trade unionist, and his so-called *Conselho do Povo Angolano* (CPA)—Council of the Angolan People. When Taty and Kassinda seized the GRAE office in Leopoldville, Congolese soldiers had to drive them out, but Tshombé then used the incident as a pretext for further restrictions on GRAE activities in the Congo. Taty went to the MPLA briefly and finally wound up as a colonel in the Portuguese forces in Cabinda. At the beginning of February 1965, the Tshombé regime even tried to prevent Roberto from visiting Zambia and Tanzania at the request of the governments of those countries.

Tshombé was finally overthrown in October 1965 by General Joseph Mobutu, who was another of Roberto's old Congolese friends, and restrictions on GRAE activities were immediately lifted. Mobutu pledged full support for the Angolan revolution. In October 1966, he formally broke off relations with Portugal. Inside Angola, the ENLA forces stepped up their operations in the Cassange district of Malange. A number of raids were mounted from ENLA bases in the Congo, across the border, deep into Angola. GRAE fighters were now also, for the first time, striking into eastern Angola from bases in Katanga. A number of liberated areas hundreds of miles inside the country were reinforced and supplied. But by now Savimbi had set up UNITA and was successfully maintaining guerrillas inside southern and eastern Angola. With the men trained in the unsuccessful Cabinda operation, the MPLA also launched its eastern front, across the Zambian border.

[1] Valentim, op. cit., p. 32.

Generally better armed and as well trained as its African rivals, MPLA initiated a particularly bloody fratricidal confrontation with both GRAE and UNITA. By the end of 1967, MPLA claimed its forces were ranging as far as Moxico and Cuando Cubango.

Now came the turn of MPLA to claim that its forces were the only ones fighting inside Angola. This statement was patently untrue, although echoed by the MPLA's friends in Moscow and elsewhere. After the U.A.R.-sponsored effort to reconcile MPLA and GRAE in 1966, there was to be no further talk of unity. MPLA even rejected UNITA proposals for tactical unity of action against the Portuguese and for a while probably killed more UNITA fighters than Portuguese.

Repeated efforts to reunite UNITA and GRAE also failed. Savimbi was clearly desperate for unity; however, he wanted to return with UNITA as a fully-fledged member-party of the FNLA. Roberto refused to accept this proposal, demanding instead that Savimbi and his associates merely resume their places in the existing constituent parties of the Front, but Savimbi in turn would not disband UNITA. Sympathizers of GRAE circulated a copy of a letter dated 30 May 1969, allegedly by Savimbi to the then-Congolese foreign minister Justin Bomboko, which declares his 'profound desire' for unity with Roberto's forces; it says he has already written to Congolese President Mobutu and hopes that Mobutu and Bomboko will use their influence with Roberto to effect a reconciliation. Representatives of UNITA did not deny the existence of some such letter, but strongly hinted that the text of the copy circulated might have been 'doctored' somewhat to place Savimbi in an unfavourable light. Whatever the truth, the long-awaited reconciliation still had not taken place by the end of 1971, despite renewed appeals from UNITA to both GRAE and MPLA.

GRAE forces were now estimated conservatively at 5,000 to 8,000 men.[1] Although accused by its critics of *attentisme*, sheltering in the safety of Congolese sanctuaries, Portuguese spokesmen conceded that GRAE, as well as the other two nationalist parties, had increased military operations since 1970. The hoary myth of major American assistance to GRAE was dying, however, as it was becoming quite evident that the ENLA had nothing similar to the abundant modern Soviet equipment in the hands of MPLA fighters. A reliable U.S. reporter, George Thayer, claimed that both Roberto's GRAE and the late Eduardo Mondlane's FRELIMO had received 'a small amount of financial aid from U.S. sources'.[2] Other students of the African libera-

---

[1] *The Economist* (10 May 1969).
[2] George Thayer, op. cit., p. 138.

tion movements believed Chinese assistance had also gone to GRAE.[1] While the Chinese communists preach the doctrine of 'self-reliance' as revolutionary policy, official U.S. policy was clearly stated by Secretary of State William Rogers who, while reaffirming U.S. support for the right of self-determination for the peoples of the Portuguese colonies, declared American encouragement for 'peaceful progress toward that goal'. He said the U.S. Government believed that 'resort to force and violence is in no one's interest'.[2]

During 1970–1, ELNA operations increased throughout the north of Angola as Holden Roberto reportedly came under pressure from younger militants to launch a campaign of urban terrorism against the Portuguese, complementing rural guerrillas. He was said to fear that the Portuguese might react by indiscriminate bombing of civilians in rebel-controlled areas of the country. Moreover, during a visit to Morocco and Tunisia in July, Roberto was reported to have expressed concern that the United States, which he believed was pressuring Portugal to negotiate with GRAE, was now resigned to continued colonial rule. No end to the war of liberation was in sight, and the GRAE still remained a formidable political and military force that would have to be dealt with in one way or another before anyone else could rule Angola.

União Nacional para a Independência Total de Angola (UNITA)

Although the youngest and smallest of the three Angolan nationalist parties, the *União Nacional para a Independência Total de Angola* has had surprising success since it was founded in March 1966, inside Angola, near Luso. Its future president, Jonas Savimbi, demanded that the inaugural congress be held in the *maquis* inside Angola. Ever since, UNITA spokesmen have repeatedly pointed out that their movement was the first in the history of African struggle for liberation born of action within the country, instead of being created in the military camps and *émigré* milieu in neighbouring countries. Within a short time of its founding, UNITA had succeeded in implanting inside Angola a solidly structured politico–military organization, capable of striking against the Portuguese colonial forces and defending itself from its brother-enemies, especially the MPLA.

[1] See Paul M. Whitaker, 'External Aid and the Portuguese African Liberation Movements', *Africa Report* (Vol. XV, No. 5, 1970).
[2] Secretary of State William Rogers, op. cit.

According to a publication in English by the Central Committee of UNITA, *Angola—Seventh Year*, the principles guiding the party were:

1. The systematic mobilization and organization of the peasants inside the country, as a main force of struggle.
2. Integration of intellectuals and military cadres inside and outside Angola in the struggle, side by side with the broad masses.
3. Refusal to rely on military camps created in neighbouring countries for the sake of external propaganda.
4. Active participation of all the people from both rural and urban areas in the general resistance against foreign domination.
5. Refusal to be led by big foreign powers. The big powers are trying today more than ever another *Yalta* and this time through peaceful competition.
6. Faith in *unity* and *co-operation* of all the Angolans in this phase of National Liberation.[1]

Despite the appeal for unity, UNITA came into existence as the consequence of a split in the GRAE, of which Savimbi was foreign minister at its founding in April 1962. Since 1961, he had been secretary-general of UPA and was one of the key, non-Bakongo collaborators of Holden Roberto—proving at least that the leadership was multi-ethnic, even if the party in Angola was still mainly based on the Bakongo peoples.

Jonas Malheiro Savimbi was the son of a prominent Ovimbundu family, whose home was at Chilesso, in the Bié district. However, Savimbi was born, on 3 August 1934, at Munhango in the Moxico district where his father, Lot Savimbi, was working for the Benguela Railway. The father had been converted to Protestantism and was active in founding Protestant churches and schools wherever he was transferred by the Railway, despite Catholic opposition. Jonas Savimbi received his primary schooling at the Protestant school in Chilesso, beginning a brilliant academic career that eventually took him to the University of Lisbon on a scholarship from the United Church of Christ. Despite the fact that he seems to have had little or no contact with Angolan *mestiço* students, who later became leaders of the MPLA and CONCP, Savimbi was harassed by the P.I.D.E. He refused to become their informer and, during the university holiday of 1960, left Portugal for Switzerland. His Protestant sponsors permitted him to study briefly at the University of Fribourg and afterwards at the University of Lausanne, where he eventually received a doctorate in political and juridical sciences.

Savimbi thus brought to the UPA not only his non-Bakongo origins,

[1] UNITA Central Committee, *Angola: Seventh Year* (Leyden, International University Exchange Fund, 1968). Italics in original.

but intellectual brilliance and academic achievements. It was under-
standable that the Kongo tribesmen who created the UPA were anything but intellectuals. But some observers also had the impression that
Holden Roberto, whose intellectual horizons were far broader than
theirs, was nevertheless anti-intellectual. His close personal friendship
with Frantz Fanon, however, would seem to belie this, though it is
more likely they shared a common suspicion of 'assimilated' intellectuals
in the colonial situation. For his part, Savimbi reportedly agreed to
join the UPA on the advice of Kenya's Tom Mboya, whom he had met
at a student conference. Savimbi's decision influenced many Angolan
students who, as one of them later commented bitterly, 'had naively
believed that the UPA was a national organization defending the
general interests of the broad masses.'[1] At the time, however, as John
Marcum has pointed out, Savimbi's decision helped to bring the PDA
into the FNLA with the UPA, and paved the way for the formation of
Roberto's government in exile.[2]

Within a relatively short time, Savimbi and his associates found
themselves in serious disagreement with the *émigré* milieu in Leopoldville. The barely organized chaos that reigned in the GRAE offices
offended their bureaucratic sensibilities. They resented even more the
aspect of an extended family in the leadership around Roberto and the
tolerance of incompetence and petty venality, which they judged more
severely as corruption. Themselves influenced by Marxism–Leninism
and aware of the high calibre propaganda of MPLA (which at that time
masked its virtual non-existence as a guerrilla fighting organization),
Savimbi and his friends wanted drastic revision of UPA's style of
political work and the elaboration of a coherent and progressive
ideological position. Finally, they wanted more emphasis on extending
throughout the country the armed struggle within Angola, and more
attention to the political indoctrination of the peasant masses: more
stress on the teachings of great revolutionaries like Mao Tsetung and
Ho Chi Minh, less Protestant Bible-reading.

Savimbi later maintained that his post as secretary-general of UPA
was purely titular and that he lacked the power to effect any of these
desired reforms. But, oddly enough, the dissension in GRAE did not
become apparent until the MPLA split and Viriato da Cruz applied
for membership of GRAE in July 1963. Although da Cruz was generally
considered a sincere Marxist–Leninist with excellent fraternal ties
to the Chinese communists, and Savimbi had already scandalized some
conservatives with his own leftist views, the latter apparently tried to

[1] Valentim, op. cit., p. 14.   [2] Marcum, op. cit., p. 245.

block da Cruz's admission. The Swiss journalist Pierre-Pascal Rossi believes that Savimbi was 'probably anti-Chinese' or sought, in any case, to reach a separate arrangement for Chinese support without da Cruz acting as intermediary. According to Rossi, Savimbi, who reportedly had formed his caucus of southerners within the GRAE, may also have feared the influence of da Cruz's strong personality on the nascent group.[1] Although there appears to have been no later *rapprochement* between Savimbi and da Cruz, neither Savimbi himself nor UNITA has shown any trace of anti-Chinese sentiment. Rather, MPLA and other Moscow-line critics have variously described UNITA as a 'tool of U.S. imperialism' somehow in the employ of Peking.[2]

Savimbi resigned from the GRAE on 16 July 1964, in Cairo, where he had gone to attend the O.A.U. summit conference. In the statement issued on his resignation, Savimbi complained of the deficiencies of the GRAE, and especially its alleged failure to mobilize the popular masses inside Angola. His departure was followed within days by the resignations of José Liahuca, Jorge Valentim, José N'Dele, and others. Accompanied by an anti-Castro black Cuban of Jamaican origin, Carlos More, Savimbi left Cairo for Lausanne.[3] He was followed there by Florentino Duarte, formerly a UPA student in Switzerland and then GRAE representative in Cairo. Rejecting an invitation to join Savimbi's group, Duarte publicly denounced his former friend and colleague. Nevertheless, Savimbi spent a year studying once more at the University of Lausanne, during which he also visited Brazzaville for contacts with the MPLA. These were followed up later, but Savimbi found the clique around Agostinho Neto even more obdurate than the group around Holden Roberto. Moreover, the revisionist Marxist ideology of the MPLA leaders was totally incompatible with the People's War that Savimbi wanted to conduct inside Angola. Their peer by intellect, educational achievement, and class origin, although not himself a mulatto, Savimbi was reportedly viewed by Neto as an unstable personality and, worse still, a budding ultra-leftist. Finally, they felt there was no need to replace the troublesome da Cruz with a blacker version of the same tendencies—Savimbi.

[1] Rossi, op. cit., pp. 84–8.

[2] For example, Basil Davidson, in the *New Statesmen* (30 October 1970), decried 'a vigourous propaganda' on behalf of UNITA 'which comes partly from Maoist groups'.

[3] More went to Paris shortly afterwards, where he long campaigned in African circles against alleged racism in revolutionary Cuba. See Carlos More, 'Le peuple noir a-t-il sa place dans la Révolution Cubaine?' *Présence Africaine* (No. 52, 4e trimestre, 1964).

In March 1966, Savimbi and his associates formally constituted UNITA. At its first conference, held inside Angola, an extremely succinct, nine-point programme was adopted that was not exceptional nor essentially different from the programmes of the already-existing movements. UNITA pledged itself, as they had done, to full independence, anti-imperialist solidarity, a planned economy, a programme of industrialization, and adherence to the U.N. Charter and the principles of the Organization of African Unity. UNITA also promised to 'struggle constantly for the formation of real *United Front* of all the Angolan nationalist forces without any discrimination whatsoever'.[1] Even in the midst of subsequent fratricidal combat with MPLA forces, UNITA leaders repeated this appeal for a united front against the Portuguese.

The party was structured, under a collective leadership, on the Leninist principle of democratic centralism from a General Assembly and Central Committee at national level to the cell, the basic unit of the party, with provincial, district and regional committees between. Warning that the national struggle 'might be long and bitter', UNITA created its military wing, the *Forças Armadas de Libertação* (FALA).

Operating on a politico-social level as well as the purely military, FALA cadres, political officers, and social and medical workers developed their action on five fronts—along the Zambian border, central, and southern Angola—in Lunda, Malange, Moxico, Bié, Cuando Cubango and, beginning in May 1969, in Huila. Unlike the MPLA, with its policy of overt hostility to existing tribal structures, UNITA has attempted to bring about important changes in the organization of Angolan rural life without destroying the existing communal society, which in some cases has only marginal contact with the Portuguese cash economy. Improving farming techniques, it attempts to create where possible an 'independent' economy. Where security permits, schools and clinics are opened and other medical and social services provided. The 'liberated' regions are sparsely populated. In principle, they are divided into twelve zones (each with twenty-five guerrillas) and twenty-five sub-zones.

Despite the lack of substantial external aid (except for an initial trickle of Chinese arms and medical supplies), UNITA had surprising success. Even its setbacks indicated how fast the organization had grown—as on 31 December 1967, when a *New York Times* correspondent in Lisbon wrote of major clashes between Portuguese forces and UNITA in the heart of Angola, near Luso, with the Portuguese

[1] UNITA Central Committee, op. cit., p. 25.

reportedly capturing a hundred members of UNITA. The struggle continued and the *Times of Zambia* (Lusaka) published in September 1969 a series of articles by their reporter Steve Valentine who had spent four weeks travelling 500 miles deep inside Angola with UNITA guerrillas. Valentine claimed that UNITA's main source of weapons was the Portuguese Army, whose N.A.T.O. weapons were seized in UNITA raids. Despite repeated denials by N.A.T.O. officials, serial numbers and other marks indicated that the Portuguese Army was indeed diverting these arms to the colonial war in Africa. Valentine concluded his series: 'Jonas Savimbi's only failure has been to convince the world that the organization exists.'

Zambian authorities knew UNITA existed and apparently no longer approved. In August 1967, following accusations by the Portuguese that UNITA guerrillas had blown up a section of the Benguela Railway, key supply line between Zambia and the Atlantic, Savimbi was forced to leave Zambia. According to the *Zambia News* of 13 August 1967, the Portuguese had threatened to cut the rail line completely if Zambia did not take action against UNITA, which then maintained an office in Lusaka. Although the party had never been officially recognized by the Zambian Government 'and, while UNITA was scoring more proven successes in Angola than the other two organizations, the Government—with an eye to Angola—remained strictly non-committal about the future of that party,' the newspaper reported. Eventually, Zambia suspended Savimbi's temporary residence permit and forced him to leave for Cairo.

Savimbi did not remain long in the U.A.R. capital. Somehow he managed to reach guerrilla-held areas inside Angola, and from there he later pleaded by letter with Zambian President Kenneth Kaunda for permission to reopen UNITA's Lusaka office. The closing of the office, Savimbi said, 'creates a lot of difficulties'; it prevented arms, medical supplies, and clothing from outside from reaching his men. He agreed that he had broken the strict conditions laid down by the Zambian Government to control freedom fighters in Zambia. These were that the Benguela Railway was not to be harmed and that Angolan *émigrés* in Zambia were not to be recruited. However, he pledged himself to abide by these rules in future. Nevertheless, Zambian authorities would not rescind the order against him and at the beginning of 1972 UNITA was still outlawed in Zambia.

The expulsion of UNITA officials from Zambia also exposed to reprisal UNITA sympathizers and members among the growing Angolan refugee community in Zambia. Their situation became critical and many, in despair, were forced to swear allegiance to MPLA or, if they were lucky, to the GRAE, whose President Holden Roberto made a personal visit to Lusaka to discuss their fate. Roberto had already visited Lusaka in September 1966 to discuss with Savimbi a possible unification of the GRAE and UNITA. Aware of the breakaway group's difficulties, Roberto's conditions for reunification were harsh:

1. Dissolution of UNITA inside and outside the country and integration of the UNITA militants and adherents into the framework of UPA (GRAE) membership.
2. Jonas Savimbi must write a letter of apology for his declaration of resignation from UPA in 1964 and he must solicit his possible readmission to his former post of Secretary-General of UPA.
3. Savimbi must issue a communiqué condemning his Cairo declaration of 1964 through which he resigned from the post of secretary-general of UPA and foreign minister of GRAE.[1]

These conditions were rejected by UNITA, but it still urged a meeting of leaders of all three Angolan liberation movements, under O.A.U. auspices, to negotiate political and military co-operation.

Inside Angola, UNITA was also encountering difficulties. There were reports of differences between the regional commissioners of peasant origin (who are also chiefs of the UNITA people's militia) and the political commissioners and military leaders of the FALA (who are generally of urban and petty bourgeois origin).[2] The level of political consciousness and ideological sophistication between the two groups varied greatly, and political education classes, discussions with the political leadership, criticism, and self-criticism could barely prevent the differences widening into a split in the organization.

The most ominous threat came from the MPLA's new drive into eastern Angola from Zambian bases. UNITA officials realized that the arrival of the MPLA was partly a consequence of Zambia's decision to ban UNITA. In a score of clashes with the aggressive MPLA units, UNITA lost many men and had to cede considerable territory, falling back to the south and centre of the country. In the south, UNITA maintained co-operative fraternal relations with the South West African People's Organization (SWAPO), whose guerrillas often transited southern Angola *en route* to Ovamboland, where they were trying to create a *foco* in South West Africa.[3] MPLA eventually

[1] UNITA Central Committee, op. cit., p. 37.

[2] *Analyses et Documents*, (Paris, No. 181, 31 December 1969).

[3] In Douglas L. Wheeler and René Pélissier, *Angola* (London, Pall Mall, 1971), p. 225; Pélissier maintains that the 'main trump-card of the UNITA is its ethnic appeal to the Ovimbundu'.

accused SWAPO of bartering much-needed supplies for UNITA assistance, and demanded—but apparently never got—SWAPO help in liquidating UNITA in that region of the country.

At the time, UNITA's military forces were modest. Moises Kayombo, an FALA military commander, claimed to have 3,000 fighters under his command in 1969, but weapons for only 1,600 of them.[1] While it was obviously impossible for them to launch a general offensive, they were more than capable of protecting the politico-social infrastructure that UNITA was extending through south central Angola.

Somewhere in this vast area, the Second Congress of UNITA met in ordinary session on 24–30 August 1969. It 'reaffirmed that its general line was to carry out a protracted people's war for national liberation and steadily develop guerrilla warfare in Angola by relying on its own efforts.'[2] The radical anti-imperialist direction being taken by UNITA was indicated by the expression of greetings to the Provisional Revolutionary Government of South Vietnam, created by the National Liberation Front of South Vietnam; the convocation of the Ninth Congress of the Communist Party of China and on the occasion of the re-election of Chairman Mao Tsetung. With these expressions, there were condemnations for the 'continuation of American aggression against the heroic people of South Vietnam fighting for their national independence,' and the 'naked invasion of the Republic of Czechoslovakia, followed by another aggression against the People's Republic of China by the Soviet Union'.[3]

Shortly after the congress, through 1970, the FALA stepped up operations against the Portuguese and also successfully repulsed the fratricidal onslaught of its MPLA rivals. Jonas Savimbi and his associates were able to document their success in the combat against the Portuguese. They chose to remain silent concerning the battle imposed upon them against their own brothers.

When, in June 1970, the Italian Communist Party organized in Rome an International Conference in Support of the Struggle of the Peoples of the Portuguese Colonies, only the Moscow-supported parties of the CONCP were invited—the Soviet wing of the Afro-Asian Peoples' Solidarity Organization and the World Council of Peace. Commenting on the sole presence of the MPLA, UNITA's foreign secretary Jorge Sangumba said that the sponsoring organizations had:

[1] Ibid.

[2] 'Triumphant Development of Angolan Armed Struggle', *The Afro-Asian Journalist* (Peking, No. 2, July 1970), p. 22.

[3] 'Final Communiqué of the Second Congress of UNITA,' *Afro-Asian Journalist* (Peking, No. 2, July 1970), p. 24.

... proved to be international mouthpieces of the U.S.S.R.'s diplomatic efforts to influence the course of events in the liberation movements of Southern Africa. However, history has demonstrated that no foreign country, big or small, has ever succeeded in imposing solutions upon other countries and peoples without their full and conscious consent. Only the Angolan people are masters of their own struggle and destiny. Therefore, to determine a priori that only MPLA represents the Angolan people is no more, no less, than wishful thinking and mere mental exercise. This does not reflect the objective conditions inside Angola.[1]

Nevertheless, the search for unity remained one of the keystones of UNITA's programme. Jonas Savimbi declared himself still ready and willing to negotiate a unity-of-action pact with other nationalist leaders. Without unity, no matter how brilliant the successes achieved locally, he insisted, victory in the liberation struggle and consequent independence for Angola would remain impossible.

[1] 'Press Statement on the Rome Conference' by Jorge Sangumba (London, 22 June 1970).

II. GUINÉ AND THE CAPE VERDE ISLANDS

Partido Africano da Independência da Guiné e Cabo Verde (PAIGC)

Frente para a Libertação e Independência da Guiné Portuguesa (FLING)

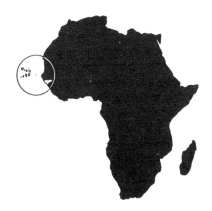

The Background

A humid, low-lying wedge of land, only 150 miles in depth, Guiné (Portuguese Guinea or Guinea-Bissau—so-called to distinguish it from the neighbouring independent Republic of Guinea, whose capital is Conakry) was discovered by the Portuguese in 1446. From forts on the coast, the Portuguese obtained black slaves, and gold and ivory for goods manufactured in Europe. The military forces of the Islamic kingdoms of Mali and Wolof effectively blocked Portuguese penetration of the interior of the Guinea coast; nevertheless, the trade in slaves flourished thanks to continuing tribal wars. The unfortunate captives were dispatched to Brazil, or the Cape Verde Islands, a crescent-shaped archipelago located in the Atlantic about 300 miles west of Senegal. These uninhabited islands, of volcanic origin, were also discovered in the middle of the fifteenth century. Today's population on the islands descends from a handful of Portuguese adventurers and the many thousands of African slaves brought from Guiné. The Portuguese were more secure on the islands, built up a plantation economy, and from them administered their various forts and trading posts along the entire Gulf of Guinea. The Province of Guiné was separated administratively from the Cape Verde Islands only in 1879, and even then the interior of the swampy, heavily-forested country was not completely under Portuguese control. In the twentieth century, *mestiços* from Cape Verde settled in Guiné and developed the cultivation of rice, the country's main crop and basic food. Before the war of liberation swept the country, 100,000 tons of rice were grown annually. Also produced for export were palm kernels and groundnuts. The farms were generally African-owned, but the trade and its profits were monopolized by the *Companhia União Fabril* (CUF) and its associated companies. So great is the stake of the CUF in Guiné that 'sceptics in Lisbon call this war "the Company's war".'[1]

Sandwiched between the Republic of Senegal and the Republic of Guinea, Guiné is relatively flat. The highest point is only 950 feet above sea level. Its coastal plain is dented by many river estuaries, bordered

[1] Basil Davidson, *The Liberation of Guiné* (Harmondsworth, Penguin, 1969), p. 26.

by mangrove mud flats, and dotted with swamps. Clusters of sandy islands lie offshore. The rivers, meandering, sluggish, yet deep enough for shallow-draught vessels to steam seventy or eighty miles upstream, are the main arteries of transport across most of the country's 13,948 square miles—about two-fifths the size of Portugal or nearly the size of Switzerland. Along the river banks are located the majority of the population of 800,000 and most of the urban centres, including the capital, the port of Bissau, with 25,000 inhabitants. Other major towns are Bolama (15,000 inhabitants), and Cacheu (10,000)[1] which are also ports.

At least five months of the year are very wet, characterized by a monsoonal climate and violent tropical storms. Relative humidity often reaches saturation point during this season. The remainder of the year is drier, but the humidity remains high. At all times the interior, which has a savannah-type climate, is drier than the coastal plain. While mangroves, fresh-water swamp forest and Casamance woodland predominate on the coast, the hills of the interior are covered by very thick grass.[2]

With forty persons per square mile, on average, Guiné is one of the most densely populated countries of Africa. This population, composed of some thirty tribes, is basically rural, despite strenuous efforts by the Portuguese to regroup it in centres under military control—a standard counter-insurgency tactic.

The major ethnic groups are:

Balante	250,000
Manjaco	140,000
Fula	100,000
Malinke	80,000
Pepel	50,000
Mancagne or Brame	35,000
Felup	15,000
Bissagos	15,000
Others (Beafada, Bairote, Cassanga, Banhun, Sarakollé, Balanta-Mané, Pajadinca, etc.)	115,000[3]

[1] Colin Legum (ed.), *Africa Handbook* (Harmondsworth, Penguin, 1969), p. 439.
[2] See R. J. Harrison Church, *West Africa* (London, Longmans, 1960), p. 275.
[3] See Gérard Chaliand, *Lutte armée en afrique*, p. 23.

Constituting 30 per cent of the total, the Moslems, mainly the Fula and Malinke, live in feudal-type societies led by customary chiefs. The animists, who make up the remaining 70 per cent of the population, live, except for the Manjaco, in societies without customary chiefs, with age-grades constituting the major form of social organization. They are governed by councils composed of heads of families. Almost all these varied peoples are farmers living on their privately- or communally-owned land. Few are Christians. Well over 90 per cent of Africans are illiterate. Their *lingua franca* is the Cape Verdian Creole, a melange of Portuguese and African languages, brought from the islands to the mainland by the mulatto functionaries who traditionally have administered the colony.

In the 1950 census, less than 2 per cent of the population were classified by the Portuguese as 'civilized'. The wet climate and the presence of malaria and yellow fever discouraged European settlement in the best of times, so that, excluding the ever-growing number of Portuguese troops, only about 3,000 whites and 3,500 *mestiços* from the Cape Verde Islands lived in Guiné in 1970. Since the outbreak of the liberation struggle in 1962, more than 30,000 Portuguese troops have been sent to crush the black revolutionaries. They have had little visible success against an intelligent, elusive enemy in the mangrove swamps and rain forests.

Although some bauxite and phosphate have reportedly been discovered, no minerals are exploited and the country's sole wealth comes from the produce of the African-owned farms. The CUF has long battened on that, but in ordinary imperialist terms the colony has clearly become a heavy burden on Portugal. It has never been an easy place to rule. Nuno Tristão, its Portuguese discoverer, was killed while trying to land on an offshore island. And, although the trading posts later established on the coast did send home slaves and gold, the great cost of the expeditions to set up and protect them made the operation a deficit one for Prince Henry the Navigator, who died in debt. In 1971, the territory was nearly worthless to Portugal and large portions of it were in the hands of the guerillas, but the Portuguese colonialists clung to the urban centres and declared their determination to resist African liberation here, as in Southern Africa.

When visiting Guiné in February 1968, Portuguese President Américo Tomas declared:

Guinea does not stand in so-called Southern Africa but that does not matter, for we attach to it the same importance as to other sacred portions of national territory. Within the healthy principles that are the guidelines of our collective

life, our decision to defend it against foreign attacks could not be any
other. It is a part of the same body, which to function perfectly must be kept
intact.[1]

In other words, abandonment of Guiné might lead to defeat in Angola
and Mozambique as well.

The relationship between the inhabitants of the fourteen Cape Verde
Islands and those of Guiné and others of Portugal's African mainland
territories is both close and ambiguous. On one hand, the islanders are
largely of African descent. They number more than 200,000 in a plantation society dominated by a small group of white landowners.[2] This
society is divided subtly according to shades of colour, as in the West
Indies, with blackness synonymous with poverty. But as Frantz Fanon
observed in the French West Indian islands, the ruling class contains
many mulattos and other persons of mixed blood, some of whom are
more than 95 per cent African but are nevertheless considered 'white'
and staunchly identify themselves with the metropolitan power,
rejecting any identification with Africa. For example, Alfredo Margarido
reports that some of the most determined resistance to African insurrection in northern Angola in 1961 was found in areas administered
by Cape Verdian functionaries.

Conversely, Cape Verdian intellectuals have played a major role in
the organization of the liberation movement in Guiné. Their radical
political initiation generally occurred when they were students in
Portuguese universities and came in contact with black and mulatto
youths from other territories as part of their re-Africanization. These
revolutionaries of petty bourgeois origin later made 'in-depth' studies
of Guinean society, carrying out a sort of revolutionary anthropological
research in order to overcome their initial ignorance of African life
and to discover means of mobilizing traditional African societies for a
People's War. Amílcar Cabral, before becoming Secretary-General of
the *Partido Africano da Independência da Guiné e Cabo Verde* (PAIGC),
the leading nationalist party, spent several years travelling about Guiné,
studying the various peoples and societies, as an agronomist in the
employ of the colonial administration. The agricultural census that

[1] The *Guardian* (28 November 1968), quoted in Abshire and Samuels, op. cit.,
p. 419.

[2] In 1920, there were 8,186 landowners, making up 2 per cent of the total population of 159,675. Of these landowners, only slightly more than 3,000 were persons of
colour. Whites owned the largest holdings. See Alfredo Margarido, 'Portugais des
"provinces d'outre-mer d'Afrique",' *Revue française d'études politiques africaines*
(No. 12, December 1966).

Cabral carried out from 1952 to 1954 was also to provide the basis of the PAIGC's revolutionary strategy.[1]

However, Cape Verdian intellectuals, even including some alleged Marxist–Leninists, were—and still are—far from agreement on the wisdom of complete identification with Guiné. They rather follow the example of Leitão da Graça, leader of the *União das Populações das Islas do Cabo Verde* (UPICV), who urged concern for the preservation of the unique personality of the people of Cape Verde. Graça criticized those leaders who, while calling for the liberation of both Guiné and Cape Verde, have limited their energies mainly to Guiné. Another Cape Verdian, based in Dakar, Mello e Castro, leader of the *Movimento de Libertação das Islas do Cabo Verde* (MLICV), even called for an autonomous armed struggle against Portuguese rule on the islands.[2] In fact, neither the MLICV nor the PAIGC has yet had much success in the difficult conditions on the islands. And, even after eventual loss of Guiné, Portuguese colonialism might still be able to retain possession of these African islands.

The Resistance

The original Portuguese interest in the territory they called *Os Rios de Cabo Verde* was one not of settlement but merely of trade for slaves and gold. From the security of the Cape Verde Islands, they established a fleeting hegemony over the entire Gulf. Forts were built at strategic mainland points, generally on the coast. Portuguese dominance was uncontested, except by the Moslem kingdoms of the interior, until the beginning of the seventeenth century, when the Dutch captured Arguim in Upper Guiné and São Jorge da Mina on the Gold Coast. The Dutch were beaten off at Cacheu in Guiné and in the islands.

In the nineteenth century, after the suppression of the slave-trade, the Portuguese lost interest in Guiné and the territory was nearly seized by the French advancing from neighbouring Senegal. However, the British also made claims on the territory. The dispute between the British and the Portuguese was arbitrated in favour of the Portuguese in 1870 by President Ulysses S. Grant of the United States. The conflict between the French and the Portuguese was settled by the Luso-French Convention of 1886. By relinquishing the port of Zinguinchor on the

---

[1] Cabral made an excellent résumé of this analysis of the social structure of Guiné in a talk at the now-defunct Centro Frantz Fanon in Milan in May 1964. See Amilcar Cabral, *Revolution in Guinea* (London, Stage 1, 1969), pp. 46–61.

[2] See Alfredo Margarido, 'L'archipel du Cap-Vert: perspectives politiques', *Revue française d'études politiques africaines* (No. 25, January 1968).

south bank of the Casamance in exchange for the previously French-held Cacine district, Portugal consolidated and obtained international recognition for its Guiné colony, which had been separated from Cape Verde since 1879. The capital was initially established at Bolama, where it remained until 1941 when the administration was transferred to Bissau.

But Portuguese nominal sovereignty in no wise implied effective control over the territory. Most of the African peoples remained hostile to Portuguese rule. Any attempt to extend that rule was met by armed resistance. Hence, a period of 'pacification' was necessary before Portugal could benefit from its title to the land.

Portuguese troops attacked one after the other the various tribes in the country. In 1878–80, they marched against the Felup and Manjaco peoples. The Fula and Beafada were struck in 1880–2. In 1883–5 came the turn of the Balante. A series of campaigns followed in the 1890s, but none was particularly successful and occasionally Portuguese losses were high. In 1901, 1903, 1904, and 1907, further expeditions were mounted against resisting African tribes. Only between 1913 and 1915 did the Portuguese finally extend some measure of control over the entire country, thanks to the military prowess of a Captain João Teixeira Pinto and a Sengalese adventurer, Abdul Injai. Teixeira Pinto was transferred to East Africa, where he died in battle against the Germans, and Abdul Injai was made chief of the Oio tribe. He quarrelled with the Portuguese and was removed and exiled to Cape Verde a few years later.

Despite the 'pacification', according to a Brazilian report, Portuguese settlers and traders in Bissau were obliged in 1915 to live 'behind the defence of their town walls, and no one could go safely into the interior. Bissau was really a camp. Its walls formed a triangle based on the sea, and its people lived inside these walls,' outside which they feared the vengeance of the 'fearsome Pepels', while 'even those who were able to go on trading missions had to pay for the Pepel Chief's permission.'[1]

More campaigns were mounted against the stubbornly-resisting Africans, beginning with the Pepels in 1915. Fighting reoccurred in 1917, 1925, and 1936. Then, as repeatedly in the past, the Portuguese claimed that Guiné was 'definitely' pacified and for ever theirs.

Even so, in the countryside, this tradition of militant resistance to European encroachment remained in the forefront of popular consciousness. As Basil Davidson has pointed out, Portuguese occupation was 'undoubtedly real when at last achieved. It might have been peacefully

[1] M. Archer, *Terras onde se Fala Portugues* (São Paulo, 1962), quoted in Davidson, *The Liberation of Guiné*, p. 23.

accepted, as colonial occupation often was elsewhere, but for the nature of Portuguese rule.'[1] The previous squalid and shabby practices of Portuguese colonialism were exacerbated by Salazar's *Estado Novo*. In the fascistic conditions imposed by the regime in the colonies (as well as at home), the oligarchy had broad licence to plunder overseas territories and reduce their populations to near-servitude. In Guiné, where the Portuguese felt no need or inclination to develop the country's infrastructure, Africans at least suffered less the exactions of forced labour than in the other Portuguese colonies.

Tensions produced by Portuguese rule were most acute among the wage-earners of the towns. As Gérard Chaliand has said, they were not a classic industrial proletariat.[2] Numbering around 25,000 to 30,000, most of these workers had only recently arrived from the countryside and still preserved a peasant mentality. The jobs they held were often artisanal or semi-skilled: they were garage mechanics, assistant machinists, as well as salesmen, and domestic servants. The most organized were the port and transport workers. Just below these workers was the fluid mass of the urban *lumpenproletariat*—or *déclassés*, as Amílcar Cabral prefers to call them—many of whom also had only recently arrived in town. Unable or unwilling to find regular employment, the members of this class eked out existences by odd jobs, petty crime, prostitution, and begging. Because of crime, they often came in contact with the police. The experience of the liberation movement was that many were willing to become police informers in return for small favours or a blind eye turned by authorities to their criminal occupations. Nevertheless, a number of youths from this class were eventually mobilized in the struggle against Portuguese rule.

In November 1950, the Portuguese established the one and only official African trade union, the *Sindicato Nacional dos Empregados do Comércio e da Indústria*. It was a totally controlled corporate body, whose members were forbidden to strike or demonstrate. This sham organization naturally could not remedy workers' grievances, and numerous local illegally constituted associations were formed in quasi-clandestinity, but nevertheless highly vulnerable to police exposure and repression. Africans were also permitted for a while to associate overtly in sporting clubs. These clubs became rallying points for protest and dissent. In 1954, when all Africans, whether 'assimilated' or not, were to be allowed to become members, the Sports and Recreation Association was banned by the colonial authorities.

---

[1] Davidson, *The Liberation of Guiné*, p. 23.
[2] Chaliand, *Lutte armée en Afrique*, p. 32.

Cape Verdian and Guinean graduates of Portuguese universities were the fuse that detonated the explosive tensions that had been developing since the Second World War. Among these graduates were Amílcar Cabral and Henri Labery, two of the founders of the first nationalist organizations in Guiné. The very first—the *Movimento para a Independência Nacional da Guiné Portuguesa* (MING)—was organized clandestinely in Bissau, in 1954, by Cape Verde and Guiné commercial workers and civil servants, but had failed to gain strength.

In the Cape Verde Islands, the more complex social structure, as well as a measure of racial integration and assimilation, with the resulting false consciousness of belonging to a Portuguese cultural and national community, delayed and kept weak the commitment to a struggle of national liberation. But the Cape Verdian students and intellectuals had also absorbed in Europe strong doses of Marxism–Leninism and African nationalism. At first grouped around the revue *Claridade*, the protests of the Cape Verdian elites were purely regional and non-political. They demanded a better utilization of Cape Verde's limited resources and, above all, recognition by Portuguese rulers of the specific character of their islands' history and culture. More practically, they demanded the removal of all barriers to the employment and advancement of island intellectuals in the hierarchy of the Portuguese State. As we have already seen, some of these Cape Verdian intellectuals also protested against the continuing association of their islands with Guiné, and it is worth noting that the first clandestine nationalist party established in Guiné, the MING, made no reference to Cape Verde in its name or programme.[1]

Partido Africano da Independência da Guiné e Cabo Verde (PAIGC)

Abandoning the moribund MING, almost the same group of African intellectuals, 'together with several craftsmen and manual workers',[2] joined again in the mid-fifties to organize clandestinely in Bissau the *Partido Africano da Independência da Guiné e Cabo Verde*, which has become the major nationalist party in Portuguese Guinea, although there were only six founding members. The PAIGC set as its main objectives:

(a) Immediate conquest of national independence in Guinea and the Cape Verde Islands.

[1] See Margarido, 'L'archipel du Cap-Vert: perspective politiques'.
[2] Cabral, op. cit., p. 30.

(b) Democratization and emancipation of the African populations of these countries, exploited for centuries by Portuguese colonialism.

(c) Achievement of rapid economic progress and true social and cultural advancement for the peoples of Guinea and the Cape Verde Islands.[1]

Despite the intimate knowledge of rural life of Amílcar Cabral, the Secretary-General (founder of the party with Rafael Barbosa, who became its Chairman), the PAIGC began its activities by creating an urban underground organization.

Cabral had studied agronomy in Lisbon and, immediately after graduation in 1950, began working for the colonial agricultural service. His most important work was carried out from 1952 to 1954, when he travelled throughout Guiné, conducting the agricultural census that gave him detailed acquaintance with traditional life and customs. Born in 1920, of parents who had emigrated from Cape Verde to Bafatá, Cabral began his real political education at Lisbon's *Casa dos Estudantes do Império*, where, among other African students, he met Agostinho Neto and Marío de Andrade of Angola. Not only did they encourage his 're-Africanization', they equally stimulated his clandestine studies of Marxist–Leninist classics. The friendship and ideological identity of views of the three men were to continue long after their student days. Cabral in fact worked for a private sugar plantation in Angola and even went back there shortly after the founding of the PAIGC. In December 1956, he, with Neto, was one of the founding members of the *Movimento Popular de Libertação de Angola*.

The PAIGC and MPLA held similar traditional views concerning the priority of political work in the urban centres. Every effort was to be made to build a working-class base for the parties in the towns. Both parties were led mainly by petty bourgeois intellectuals, and attracting real workers into their ranks was a difficult task, but the PAIGC did eventually recruit successfully among the port and transport workers of Guiné. Later, a clandestine trade union, the *União Nacional dos Trabalhadores da Guiné* (UNTG) was formed. This phase of PAIGC development led to a wave of strikes throughout 1958, culminating in a strike of dock workers at Pidgiguiti, in Bissau, on 3 August 1959. The strike was crushed by Portuguese officers and civilians who, when African troops refused to do so, opened fire on the striking workers, killing fifty of them. Many of the strikers were arrested and twenty-one were later convicted on charges of subversion and sentenced to from one to five years' imprisonment.

The Pidgiguiti massacre prompted a drastic revision of the PAIGC's

[1] Article 4 of the PAIGC Statutes, quoted in ibid., p. 30.

plan of action. Cabral, who was still in Angola at the time, returned to Guiné to take personal control of the party. He summoned his colleagues to a meeting on the outskirts of Bissau on 19 September. Reaffirming their commitment to the liberation of Guiné from Portuguese rule 'by all possible means, including war', the PAIGC faced up to the bankruptcy of their urban tactics. A confidential party record states that, after three years of political work, the party leaders, acting on the principle of 'expect the better but prepare for the worse', adopted the following new plan of action:

1. Without delay mobilize and organize the peasant masses who will be, as experience shows, the main force in the struggle for national liberation.
2. Strengthen our organization in the towns but keep it clandestine, avoiding all demonstrations.
3. Develop and reinforce unity around the Party of the Africans of all ethnic groups, origins and social strata.
4. Prepare as many cadres as possible, either inside the country or abroad, for political leadership and the successful development of our struggle.
5. Mobilizé emigrés in neighbouring territories so as to draw them into the liberation struggle and the future of our people.
6. Work to acquire the means that will be needed for success.[1]

Finally, in order to 'guarantee the security of a part of the leadership', the PAIGC decided to transfer its party headquarters to outside Guiné.

Shortly afterwards, Cabral left Guiné for the Republic of Guinea, which had gained its independence from France in 1958. The PAIGC general secretariat was established in Conakry. But inside the country, the transfer from the towns to the countryside was no easy task. For one thing, the PAIGC had only about fifty members at the time, and half of them were in Bissau. Moreover, although convinced that only a rural-based struggle could defeat the Portuguese, who were almost entirely confined to the towns, Cabral was nevertheless sharply critical of Fanon's thesis that the peasantry were the revolutionary class *par excellence* in Africa. In the analysis of Guiné's social structure that he presented to the Centro Frantz Fanon in Milan, Cabral declared:

. . . one key problem, which is of enormous importance for us, as we are a country of peasants, and that is the problem of whether or not the peasantry represents the main revolutionary force. I shall confine myself to my own country, Guiné, where it must be said at once that the peasantry is not a revolutionary force—which may seem strange, particularly as we have based the whole of our armed liberation struggle on the peasantry. A distinction

[1] Quoted in Davidson, *The Liberation of Guiné*, p. 32.

must be drawn between a physical force and revolutionary forces; physically, the peasantry is a great force in Guiné: it is almost the whole of the population it controls the nation's wealth, it is the peasantry which produces; but we know from experience what trouble we had convincing the peasantry to fight. . . . The conditions in China were very different: the peasantry had a history of revolt, but this was not the case in Guiné, and so it was not possible for our party militants and propaganda workers to find the same kind of welcome among the peasantry in Guiné for the idea of national liberation as the idea found in China. All the same, in certain parts of the country and among certain groups we found a very warm welcome, even right at the start. In other groups and in other areas all this had to be won.[1]

While this would seem to underestimate the importance of the tradition of tribal primary resistance to Portuguese rule, the Guinean and Cape Verdian *mestiço* intellectuals in the PAIGC leadership went farther and faster than their friends in Angola in recognizing and accepting the key role of the black peasantry in the liberation struggle.

In the towns, the PAIGC continued its clandestine organizing of cadres, but prudently avoided any overt acts that would provoke further Portuguese repression in the urban conditions favourable to the police and army. Heading the underground organization was Rafael Barbosa, the Chairman of the PAIGC. On the information of an informer, Barbosa was arrested only in March 1962, after eighteen months of clandestine activity, including a systematic campaign of sabotage which went on long after his arrest.

On 25 September 1960, the PAIGC made an appeal to the Portuguese to open negotiations for 'the installation of a process of parliamentary advance such as would assure the territories of their own organs of democratic self-rule.' This was reiterated in December 1960. A further appeal to the Portuguese Government was made by Cabral on 13 October 1961, urging the Salazar regime to 'follow the decolonizing example of other colonial powers in Africa'. Cabral warned that if the Portuguese persisted in refusing to negotiate independence 'nothing will stop our Party from accomplishing its historic mission: the mission of developing our struggle for national liberation, of replying by violence to the violence of the Portuguese colonialist forces.'[2]

While issuing these futile appeals to the Portuguese regime, the PAIGC was structuring its forces in the countryside, building a secure base in neighbouring, friendly Guinea, where President Ahmed Sékou Touré gave his country's full backing. In Conakry, Amílcar Cabral had set up an exile organization, the *Movimento de Libertação da Guiné e*

[1] Cabral, op. cit., p. 50.
[2] Quoted in Davidson, *The Liberation of Guiné*, p. 94.

Cabo Verde (MLGCV). In this body, affiliated to the PAIGC, he brought together exiles from Guiné in Conakry and Dakar. As Cabral told the United Nations Special Committee on Territories under Portuguese Administration, which visited Conakry in June 1962, in the previous forty years some 50,000 *émigrés* had left Guiné to settle in the neighbouring countries, and their support was vital to the PAIGC as it approached an armed confrontation with the Portuguese. Among those joining the MLGCV was Henri Labery, who had set up a *Front de Libération de la Guinée Portugaise et du Cap-Vert* (FLGC), which grouped some 30,000 Cape Verdian *émigrés* and exiles from Guiné. A rival group, called the *Movimento de Libertação da Guiné* (MLG), was organized by François Mendy Kankoila, a Manjaco who had spent most of his life in Senegal. In July 1961, Cabral drew Labery and some other exile leaders into the *Front Uni de Libération de Guinée et du Cap-Vert* (FUL). However, the MLG remained outside the newly formed Front, which consequently failed to take on life. Cabral's efforts to establish a base in Senegal also failed, and he returned to the security of the Republic of Guinea as the FUL collapsed.[1]

Inside Guiné, the sabotage campaign, which had been intended to demonstrate the power of the PAIGC to the Portuguese and induce them to sit down at a conference table, merely infuriated the colonial authorities. The P.I.D.E., the Portuguese secret police, arrived in force in Guiné, along with military reinforcements. A number of suspected PAIGC militants were arrested, among them, in March 1962, Rafael Barbosa,[2] the Chairman of the Central Committee of the PAIGC, who had been living in clandestinity. Despite these arrests, the sabotage campaign grew in intensity until, on the night of 30 June/1 July, 1962, the entire southern part of Guiné was cut off. Bridges and ferries were burned, roads and telephone and telegraph lines cut, but no military attack followed the sabotages. All the while, militants of the PAIGC were working in the countryside, seeking to win the peasantry to the cause of national liberation. We already know, from Cabral himself, that it was no easy task. Two years of careful planning, indoctrination and preparation preceded the launching of the armed struggle in the closing months of 1962.

By then, the PAIGC had secured significant international support in independent black Africa and, more important, from the Soviet Union and other Eastern European socialist countries, and China. Funds,

---

[1] See Chilcote, *Portuguese Africa*, p. 100.

[2] After seven years of detention and perhaps torture, Barbosa defected to the Portuguese, but his place had long since been effectively filled.

arms, and worldwide propaganda were made available to the PAIGC. Eager to preserve as much liberty of action in Guiné as possible and to obtain the maximum of material assistance, Cabral generally stuck to the Soviet side in the growing Sino-Soviet split.[1]

When the Soviets, or the leading Moscow-line party in Africa, the South African Communist Party—which largely controlled the African National Congress of South Africa—pressed too hard on the PAIGC, Cabral's tactic was to lavish praise on the quasi-independent line of Fidel Castro's Cuba and extol the 'Cuban example', while avoiding any involvement with the genuinely disruptive Chinese communists. Cabral's speech to the Tricontinental Conference in Havana in January 1966 pushed this line to its farthest point, as he reaffirmed an old truism:

However great the similarity between our various cases and however identical our enemies, national liberation and social revolution are not exportable commodities; they are, and increasingly so every day, the outcome of local and national elaboration, more or less influenced by external factors (be they favourable or unfavourable) but essentially determined and formed by the historical reality of each people, and carried to success by the overcoming or correct solution of the internal contradictions between the various categories characterizing this reality.[2]

Fortunately for the PAIGC, the Soviets did not push any harder and it was the Chinese who eventually showed signs of resigned disappointment at the opportunistic policy of the PAIGC.

The armed struggle began with the infiltration of small bands of men into Guiné from the Republic of Guinea. They carried out a campaign of persuasion and, if absolutely necessary, terror, to enrol tribesmen in the fight against the Portuguese. While this campaign was successful among the Balante, the Fula chiefs remained loyal to Portugal and asked for and obtained arms to create an African militia to combat the guerrillas. Nevertheless, the Portuguese were unable to seize the initiative from the revolutionaries or even to recapture the island of Como, south of Bissau, which had become the rebel strongpoint. Portuguese efforts to seal the frontiers with Guinea and Senegal were repeatedly thwarted as the guerrillas demonstrated their

[1] Davidson, *The Liberation of Guiné*, claims that, although some PAIGC military commanders were trained in China in the early sixties, the Chinese reduced their support for the revisionist-oriented Guinean movement. The Chinese Hsinhua News Agency, however, has never ceased publishing reports of military engagements of the 'Guinean (Bissau) Patriotic Armed Forces', but references to the PAIGC itself were extremely rare for several years and only reappeared in late 1970.

[2] Cabral, op. cit., pp. 74–5.

manoeuvrability and the country-wide extent of their popular support. Under Governor Arnaldo Schultz, a tactic of village fortification was systematically carried out by the Portuguese in the hope of isolating the villagers from the rebels. Initially, this seemed to work as the defences and Portuguese troops were able to keep out the guerrillas, but the increasing fire-power of the freedom fighters made the attacks more costly in Portuguese lives, especially after the PAIGC brought Soviet-made, recoilless rifles into widespread use.

The PAIGC military organization was three-tiered. Assisting the Party's regular forces, the Revolutionary Armed Forces of the People (FARP), was an emergency militia of local peasants concerned mainly with small operations and defence; a classic guerrilla force of part-time farmer-soldiers assisted either the regular armed forces or the militia.

As an additional counter to the fortified villages of the Portuguese, the PAIGC extended widely its own educational and medical facilities. This system of social services was intended to create a revolutionary ethos and a unified national consciousness to overcome the heterogenous ethnic divisions of Guinea society. By the end of 1967, the PAIGC controlled well over half of Guiné. Governor Schultz recommended abandonment of the territory, but he was replaced by a new Governor, with additional Portuguese troops. The arrival of a squadron of twelve Fiat jet fighter-bombers created some temporary problems for the guerrillas. However, their expanding base areas were soon dotted with modern Czech and Soviet anti-aircraft guns that kept the planes at high altitude and rendered their bomb-runs highly inaccurate, if still occasionally deadly. On the ground, the Portuguese were yet unable to move far from the towns, and the fortified village policy had been demonstrated a failure. More and more, the planes strafed and napalmed African civilian populations as the enemy clearly became the Guinean people as a whole. This murderous policy naturally strengthened the political hold of the PAIGC on the population and stiffened popular resolve to resist and eventually win.

The key to the strength of the PAIGC lies in its close links with the rural masses, with whom the party is dialectically involved in a process of social and economic change. For the Marxist–Leninist–oriented PAIGC, national liberation necessarily implies social revolution and cannot be limited solely to the acquisition of formal sovereignty. The party has representatives throughout the country and in every village, acting as agents of revolutionary mobilization, stimulating the activities and learning from the experiences of the *tabanca* committees. (*Tabanca* is Creole for village.) Not only does PAIGC's system of information feed-back operate to the Central Committee at the top, but high-ranking party officials able to take action are located on the spot in every major region; in some other African liberation movements, leadership is found only in exile headquarters in Dar es Salaam or Lusaka. The village committees watch over vital farm production and support the local militia and guerrilla units. As far as possible, agricultural produce is marketed through the party's outlets in neighbouring countries and not through the Portuguese monopolies. In fact, wherever possible, the PAIGC has systematically destroyed the warehouses of the CUF. The crops bring the party foreign exchange and make the liberated zones self-sufficient for food.

The formal party structure is a Leninist one, in which democratic centralism is the main principle of organization. But, as the struggle has developed, greater emphasis had been placed on local responsibility at all levels. Pragmatism and common sense reign. Regions and zones were created by the PAIGC party congress, held in the forests of southern Guiné on 13 to 17 February 1964, which also reconfirmed Amílcar Cabral as Secretary-General. The PAIGC hierarchy consists of a Political Bureau of twenty—fifteen with full membership and five candidate members. The Political Bureau elects from its ranks an Executive Committee of seven members. All belong to the sixty-five member Central Committee—twenty of the sixty-five are candidate members.[1]

In 1964, the Central Committee was divided into seven departments, but in 1967 these were reduced to five, which are:

1. a control commission;
2. a security commission;
3. a commission for foreign relations;
4. a commission for national reconstruction;
5. a commission for the organization and orientation of inner-Party relations.[2]

Because of similar ideological orientation and the past close personal relations between Cabral and the *mestiço* intellectuals who head some of the liberation movements of other Portuguese colonies, the PAIGC has long taken a leading role in the *Conferencia de Organizações das Colónias Portugesas* (CONCP), which was founded in 1961, replacing the *Frente Revolucionária Africana para a Independência das Colónias Portuguesas* (FRAIN), which Cabral had helped to set up a year earlier

---

[1] Chaliand, *Lutte armée en afrique*, p. 37.
[2] See Davidson, *The Liberation of Guiné*, p. 80.

at a meeting in Tunis. With the exception, at times, of FRELIMO, the CONCP group have generally steered a cautious pro-Moscow course internationally. In return, Moscow-line communist parties in Western countries, as well as the Eastern European and Cuban parties, support only the CONCP. The CONCP leaders have also visited the United States, addressed the United Nations, and sought whatever aid might be available in the West. The successes of the PAIGC have served as a precious alibi and cover for the setbacks of other CONCP parties, which have not always fared well in their separate struggles, despite massive propaganda on their behalf by such tireless partisans as Basil Davidson in Britain and Robert Davezies in France, who repeatedly assured their readers that all rival bodies were figments of the imagination of the C.I.A. or 'Peking's propagandist aid'.[1] At the beginning of 1971, PAIGC and UNITA of Angola were the only movements in the Portuguese colonies on the offensive, although neither GRAE nor COREMO was doing as poorly as the CONCP propagandists claimed.

In June 1970, Cabral represented the PAIGC at the Rome conference in support of the peoples of the Portuguese colonies, organized by the Italian Communist Party for the World Council of Peace and the Afro-Asian Peoples' Solidarity Organization. Cabral, Marcelino dos Santos, and Agostinho Neto were jointly received on 1 July by Pope Paul VI. Although to those who take their ideologies seriously the thought of the three communist revolutionaries on their knees before the Supreme Pontiff was outrageous, Cabral quite correctly declared: 'This was a great victory for us.'[2] The PAIGC leader added: 'By receiving us, the Pope made a concrete political gesture and created a situation in which the Portuguese Catholics who are against the colonial war will have arguments to counter the Government propaganda that the fighting in Africa is to safeguard the Christian faith.'

The total numbers of PAIGC forces, now divided into three fronts—north, south, and east—are probably no more than 10,000 men in arms. Composed of around 5,000 men, the FARP is supported by 2,000 to 3,000 guerrillas and around 2,000 local militia.[3] Given its mass base, the PAIGC could probably increase these figures in a relatively short time.

[1] Basil Davidson, 'Portugal's Colonies: The Seed of Midwinter'.

[2] As reported by the Cuban Prensa Latina News Agency when Cabral visited Havana for the celebrations of 26 July 1970. In this interview, Cabral again praised the Soviet Union and complained that African aid given through the O.A.U.'s Liberation Committee was 'insufficient'. The principal support of the PAIGC came from the socialist countries, mainly the U.S.S.R., he said, 'which gives us almost all the war material, the arms and ammunition, we use in our struggle.'

[3] See Paul M. Whitaker, 'The Revolutions of "Portuguese" Africa', *Journal of Modern African Studies* (Vol. 8, No. 1, April 1970).

Despite enormous difficulties, the PAIGC was solidly in control of at least 50 per cent of the country and militarily dominant in another 10 to 20 per cent. The Portuguese General António Spinola, a veteran anti-guerrilla fighter in Angola, despairingly declared of Guiné that 'a Portuguese military victory would be a miracle.'[1] On the other hand, although the guerrillas have driven the Portuguese from much of the land, a clear-cut military victory that would expel the colonial forces from Guiné would also be a miracle. And so the war was expected to drag on, until some political change in Portugal itself brought to power a regime that would face up to African realities.

Frente para a Libertação e Independência da Guiné Portuguesa (FLING)

Though the earliest and certainly the most successful, the PAIGC has not been the sole African nationalist party in Guiné. A number of smaller groups have been nurtured in Senegal and maintained a presence there, if only an office in Dakar. Most of these groups joined together in 1963 to create the *Frente para a Libertação e Independência da Guiné Portuguesa*. The fears of the Government of President Leopold Senghor concerning the revolutionary militancy of Sékou Touré's regime in the neighbouring Republic of Guinea naturally extended quickly to the leftist PAIGC, which was backed by Conakry. Hence, the Senegalese Government was more than willing to support, if not actively foster, rivals to the PAIGC. In addition, there are more than 65,000 Guinean *émigrés* living in Senegal, representing many ethnic groups. The PAIGC has never devoted much attention to this exile community. The most needy refugees are maintained on the borderline of poverty by international relief organizations. Among this human mass, FLING found its main popular base—in Senegal, not inside Guiné.

Long the main group in FLING, François Mendy Kankoila's *Movimento de Libertação da Guiné* (MLG) was the first to launch an armed struggle inside Guiné. In July 1961, while Amílcar Cabral was trying to vitalize the *Front Uni de Libération de Guinée et du Cap-Vert* (FUL), the MLG launched an attack across the border from Senegal against the Portuguese post of Suzana and a resort hotel in Varela. Approximately seventy-five men, in three units, took part in this hit-and-run raid. Swift Portuguese retaliation against Senegal made that country the first in Africa to break off diplomatic relations with

[1] René Lefort, 'Avec les nationalistes de Guinée portugaise', *Le Monde*, 6–7 November 1970.

Portugal. But the Senegalese Government had no intention of going to war against Portugal over Guiné, nor could the MLG follow up its initial raid with the creation of liberated zones within Guiné. Still, the MLG remained the most militant group within the loose alliance that made up FLING.[1]

Other parties in FLING included Henri Labery's *União das Populações da Guiné* (UPG)—after Labery's break with Cabral; the Malinke-based *Rassemblement Démocratique Africaine de la Guinée* (RDAG); the *União dos Naturais da Guiné Portuguesa* (UNGP); and the *União Popular para a Libertação da Guiné* (UPLG). Except for the MLG, most of these groups expressed the most moderate views about constitutional progress towards autonomy and possibly independence in Guiné. The UNGP, which did not join FLING until late in 1963, continued even afterwards to press for non-violent means to obtain independence. And it was the UNGP Chairman Benjamin Pinto-Bull, formerly a high school teacher in Dakar, who became President of FLING in 1966.

Another characteristic of all the groups that joined together in FLING was their omission of any reference to the Cape Verde Islands. Their objectives were limited solely to Guiné and many of their leaders and followers were, in fact, violently hostile to Cape Verdians as a people. They resented the islanders' mixed blood, their relatively superior education and higher ranking in the hierarchy of the Portuguese colonial system. Many could never forgive or forget that the Cape Verdians had been the direct administrators of Portuguese rule in Guiné.

Although its military activities seem to have halted in 1963, FLING continued to press for recognition as a liberation movement on a footing of equality with the PAIGC. Beginning in 1963, and until 1967, the O.A.U. tried repeatedly to encourage a merger of the two rival groups. President Senghor of Senegal personally encouraged such a fusion, but by 1967 the clear superiority on the terrain of the PAIGC and the obvious incompatibility of the political views of the two groups made further efforts out of the question. According to Basil Davidson, by the end of 1967 the Sengalese Government had reluctantly accepted the PAIGC's supremacy; he adds: 'It seems that agreements had in fact been signed early in 1967 which fully regularized the position of the PAIGC on Senegalese soil, giving the PAIGC something of the same formal as well as practical position as they already enjoyed in relation to Guinea.'[2] Nevertheless, three years later, in 1970, PAIGC spokesmen

---

[1] See Chilcote, *Portuguese Africa*, pp. 100–2.
[2] Davidson, *The Liberation of Guiné*, p. 87.

were complaining to a French journalist of the hostility encountered by their party in Senegal. Senegalese authorities were reported even to have ordered the closing of the PAIGC's hospital in Ziguinchor, forcing the evacuation from Guiné of seriously wounded persons—who often had to be carried on the backs of porters—to another hospital at Boké, in the Republic of Guinea.[1] Yet another specialist claimed that, in addition to a base camp in Kindia, near Conakry, the PAIGC was permitted to establish a camp at Kolda in Senegal. Kolda was said to have become the 'principal training and supply center of PAIGC, although Cabral's own headquarters remained at Conakry.'[2]

As for FLING, Paul M. Whitaker has reported its claims that it had a hundred soldiers trained by the Senegalese Army, but no outside observer has ever seen this force or heard of its activity.[3] Sympathizers feel there may be truth in persisting rumours of Portuguese P.I.D.E. and American C.I.A. support for FLING, as a moderating force that could be brought into any eventual negotiations with the PAIGC. In 1963, Benjamin Pinto-Bull flew to Lisbon to plead directly with Salazar for reforms. One of his brothers, Jaime Pinto-Bull, was briefly Portuguese Secretary General of Guiné and the province's representative in the Portuguese National Assembly. Another brother, a doctor, was also said to live in Lisbon, which was frequently visited by Benjamin Pinto-Bull's wife while he remained in Dakar.[4] In 1970, Pinto-Bull himself was rarely seen in Dakar and it was believed he was living mainly outside Africa.

Four members of the FLING Central Committee were reported to have fallen into the hands of the PAIGC during 1970. According to reliable African sources, these four leaders had contacted Cabral and claimed they were interested in merging FLING with PAIGC. Cabral seemingly encouraged the initiative but, when the four reportedly asked to tour PAIGC bases and liberated zones inside Guiné in order to see at first hand what the PAIGC was bringing to the proposed merger, Cabral arranged for the arrest of all four as soon as they crossed into Guiné. These sources, which were clearly favourable to the PAIGC, insisted that FLING had ceased to exist as an effective, functioning organization. And as 1971 ended, it was impossible to prove that declaration false, but in African politics amazing resurrections are not unheard of.

[1] *Le Monde* (5 September 1970).
[2] George Martelli, 'Conflict in Portuguese Africa', in Abshire and Samuels, op. cit., p. 418.
[3] Whitaker, 'The Revolutions of "Portuguese" Africa'.
[4] Ibid.

III. MOZAMBIQUE

Frente de Libertação de Moçambique (FRELIMO)

Comité Revolucionário de Moçambique (COREMO)

The Background

The Portuguese explorer Vasco da Gama landed in Mozambique in March 1498. One aspect of his voyage of discovery was the search for the legendary Christian kingdom of Prester John, with which the Portuguese realm hoped to make an alliance against the Moslems, but da Gama found the East African coast completely in the hands of Arabs and Islamized African peoples, who used Swahili, a blend of Arabic and Bantu languages, as a lingua franca. More important to the Europeans than the promotion of Christianity was control of the great trading complex of East Africa. In addition to the gold and ivory from the African interior, its ports and entrepôts were vital to the commerce with India, South-east Asia, Indonesia and China. Spices, gold, ivory, and silks were transported in Arab dhows from the Orient, up the Red Sea and Persian Gulf and then overland to Eastern Mediterranean ports, whence they were carried in Venetian and Genoese ships to Europe. Da Gama's visit to East Africa was short. He pressed on to India in about eight weeks. In 1499, he called at Malindi on his home-ward voyage, before sailing down the coast and on to Europe, carrying with him first-hand knowledge of the vital role of the East African coastal cities in the trade across the Indian Ocean.

In 1500, a Portuguese adventurer, Pedro Alvares Cabral, made an unsuccessful attempt to capture the port of Sofala. The real beginning of Portuguese rule dates, however, from 1502 when Vasco da Gama sailed back into the Indian Ocean with nineteen ships. He seized Kilwa, which he considered the most important town for the gold trade with the interior, imprisoned the sultan, Ibrahim, and only freed him after he acknowledged Portuguese sovereignty and agreed to pay the Portuguese an annual tribute. By 1509, the entire East African coast lay under Portuguese rule. It is important to note that 'at this period the Portuguese sought only to establish a *commercial* empire, not a *colonial* one,' as G. S. Were and D. A. Wilson have pointed out. 'This is, they did not want to take over and rule large areas of foreign territory; they simply wanted to have enough control of ports and seaways to have the largest share in eastern trade.'[1] Thus, the Portuguese

---

[1] G. S. Were and D. A. Wilson, *East Africa Through a Thousand Years* (London, Evans, 1968). Italics in orginal.

were to remain in constantly imperilled predominance over the East African coast for the next 200 years, but during this period the trade stagnated and the effects of Portuguese rule upon the peoples were almost entirely negative.

Portuguese control was firmest on that portion of the coast between Quelimane and Sofala. From here, the Portuguese struck inland, seeking the source of the gold that trickled down to them from Zimbabwe.[1] A colonization scheme on the Zambezi failed because of disease and African resistance. Throughout this period, the centre of Portuguese authority was located in distant Goa, whence orders and occasional reinforcements were sent to the white adventurers on the East African coast. Historians generally attribute the ruination of the Zambezi area to the Portuguese *prazo* system, which continued in Mozambique 'right up to the 1880s and influenced directly and indirectly the formation of the three great land companies in Mozambique.'[2] A *prazo da coroa* was a Crown grant to Portuguese who had distinguished themselves in the colonial service. According to the regulations, which were rarely followed, a *prazero* was not to receive more than three square leagues of African land, had to reside on that land or at least within the province, marry a European wife, and cultivate and colonize the land. The *prazeros* did more or less what they liked, extending their domains over vast areas, reducing the African inhabitants to serfdom or full slavery if they were unable to pay the taxes they imposed on their tribes.

While marriage with Europeans was stipulated, there were, in fact, few white women in the colony and in a few generations the *prazeros* were almost completely *mestiços*, with Goan Indian added to African and European stock. As for slavery, the trade had existed in East Africa before the arrival of the Portuguese. The difficulty of transporting blacks around the Cape to America and the high domestic use of African slaves on the *prazos* kept the trade to a minimum, until it soared in the nineteenth century when Portuguese Guiné and Angola were no longer able to satisfy the demand for slaves. But slaving in Mozambique never reached the devastating proportions that it did in Angola or Guiné.

During the first 200 years of their presence, the Portuguese were mainly interested in monopolizing the commerce for the gold that flowed from the kingdom of the Monomotapa, the area that today is Zambia and Rhodesia. Eventually, the kingdom and direct control of the gold mines fell into the hands of the Portuguese. But in time the refusal of the Portuguese to co-operate with the Arabs brought economic

[1] See Duffy, *Portugal in Africa*, pp. 83–9.   [2] Ibid., pp. 92–5.

stagnation. By the end of the seventeenth century, the Omani Arabs drove the Portuguese from many of the cities and forts on the northern part of the East African coast. After a long siege, the key Fort Jesus at Mombasa fell to the Omanis in 1698. By the beginning of the eighteenth century, the Portuguese had withdrawn south to Cabo Delgado, which today is one of the northern districts of Mozambique bordering Tanzania.

With a total area of 297,846 square miles, Mozambique is Portugal's second largest colony in Africa, about eight and a half times the size of Portugal itself. The largest city is Lourenço Marques, the capital, with a population of 180,000. It is a busy port, handling cargoes for the Transvaal in the neighbouring Republic of South Africa and landlocked Rhodesia. Beira, the second city, with a population of 85,000, is also a major port, handling cargoes for Rhodesia and Malawi. Other major urban centres are Quelimane (20,000 inhabitants), Nampula (15,000), and Tete (12,000).

The country is generally low-lying along the coast, but in its west-central and north-western portions the interior African plateau rises from 3,500 to 5,000 feet, with a number of higher points. The coastline is 1,750 miles long. A number of wide bays make excellent harbours. Elsewhere, the coast tends to be low and sandy, with shallow offshore waters and shoals.

Most of the country lies in the tropical belt, with two seasons annually: a hot rainy season from November to March; and a cooler dry season the rest of the year. The hottest months are January and February, when temperatures average between 80° and 85°F. On the interior plateau, temperatures are more than 10 degrees cooler on average. Relative humidity is about 80 per cent everywhere. Because of the warm winter temperatures, many white South Africans flock to the beaches around Lourenço Marques in June and July.

According to the census of 1960, Mozambique had a total of 6,578,600 persons, of whom only 97,300 were Europeans and 31,500 were *mestiços* and 19,300 Asians. At the beginning of 1970, population was estimated at more than 7 million, of which more than 6 million were African. The European population was about 130,000. The highest densities of population are found along the coast, especially in the districts of Zambézia and Moçambique. In the northern interior, forming part of the border with Tanzania, Niassa is the least populated district. As elsewhere in Africa, Portugal's 'civilizing' effect in Mozambique can only be described as monumental in its failure; the 1960 census listed slightly more than 2 per cent of the total population as 'civilized' by

Portuguese standards—that is, excluding the Europeans and Asians only about 5,000 Africans.

Mozambique's African population belongs to various Bantu-speaking tribal groups. In the north is the largest group, the Makua–Lomwe, who made up 40 per cent of the total African population. In the 1950 census, this farming people, divided into small tribal units without a strong central political structure, numbered 2,293,000. The second largest group, the Thonga, is found south of the Zambezi and numbered 1,460,000. Many of its men work as migratory labourers in South African mines. The Shona, who live to the north of Thonga, numbered 1,155,000, while an even larger number of Shona live in Rhodesia. Other major tribes are:

Chopi (Tonga)	240,400
Nyanja and Chewa	166,000
Makonde	136,200
Yao (Ajua)	119,900
Barore	44,400
Ngoni (Nguru)	14,300

The Yao, who also live in the north, are Islamized, whereas their neighbours, the Makonde, resisted conversion to Islam. In the past, the Makonde were also noted for their successful resistance to the slave-traders who preyed on other tribes. They are the second largest northern tribe and 300,000 of their kin live across the border in Tanzania. Since the beginning of the guerrilla war in Mozambique, some 10,000 Makonde refugees have fled across the border into Tanzania, where many of them have joined the ranks of the *Frente de Libertação de Moçambique* (FRELIMO). No single ethnic group is dominant throughout the country and most preserve their traditional animist religions, as neither Islam or Christianity has spread to more than 40 per cent of the African population.

Mozambique is essentially an agricultural country, with cotton the major export crop, followed by sugar, cashew nuts, tea, and tobacco. However, farming is not the only natural resource. Petroleum and iron ore deposits have been discovered and are beginning to be developed. Mozambique Gulf Oil has discovered two natural gas fields. In addition to this American company, other U.S. and a consortium of South African, French, and West German firms are prospecting for oil and gas. The iron ore deposits are being mined by Japanese and South African, as well as Portuguese, companies. And near the frontier with Swaziland, a South African company has been granted a concession to exploit the deposits of diamonds, manganese, and asbestos. However, the greatest expansion has taken place in industry, especially textiles.

The future expansion of the colonial economy and its further integration with that of South Africa/Rhodesia, will depend upon the construction of the vast Cabora Bassa Dam on the Zambezi, in Tete District. If finished, it would be the largest in Africa, generating at the completion of the first phase of construction—scheduled for 1974—1,200 megawatts, and eventually up to 4,000 megawatts. An area of 1,100 square miles would be flooded, forcing the transfer of 24,000 Africans to 'protected billages' on less desirable lands, while the rich, newly irrigated land would be settled by a million European immigrants.

The Portuguese Government gave the highest priority to the project and has sought to associate all major Western interests in its construction, but South Africa was obliged to take the biggest stake in the £145 million deal as African pressures mounted on potential overseas investors. Sweden barred any Swedish firm from taking part, and Italy did likewise after a direct appeal from Zambia's President Kaunda, who labelled the scheme a 'crime against humanity'.[1] On the other hand, the Johannesburg *Star* declared that the dam 'heralds the establishment of a South African economic community' composed of the white-minority regimes of Southern Africa, directed from Pretoria.

Naturally, both FRELIMO and the *Comité Revolucionário de Moçambique* (COREMO) vowed to thwart the project. They launched attacks in the Tete region, but without significant success as the Portuguese Army reinforced its defences in the area and received full assurances from South Africa that South African forces would be ready to come to its aid if need be.

Portuguese settlers in Mozambique are much more under the influence of white South Africa than their kin in Angola. English has become the second language of the colony, especially with the growth of tourism and South African investment. Should the crumbling heritage of Salazar in Lisbon eventually collapse, with, possibly, a radical shift in Portugal's determination to cling to its colonial possessions, the settlers would be greatly tempted to carry out a Rhodesian-type secession, seeking the eventual formation of a white federation with South Africa. Despite increasing immigration from Portugal, the small number of whites in Mozambique could not hope to maintain dominance over the restive blacks without an alliance with Pretoria and Salisbury.[2]

---

[1] See *Le Monde* (10 September 1970) and the *Daily Telegraph* (29 December 1970).

[2] See Alfredo Margarido, 'Portugais des "provinces d'outre-mer" d'Afrique'.

The Resistance

Despite the sharp differences and complete divergence of interests between them, the Arabs and Islamized Africans on the East African coast did not receive the fifteenth century Portuguese adventurers with unyielding hostility. So great were the rivalries between the rulers of the Arab ports that at times some were shortsighted enough to make common cause with the Portuguese interlopers in the Indian Ocean. The most serious and determined resistance to Portuguese aggrandizement came instead from the African tribes in the interior, in particular from the kingdom of the Monomotapa. This was overcome, but in general, as elsewhere in the Portuguese African colonies, administration was marked by its absence over vast areas and by corruption and inefficiency where it was present.

Individual tribes, such as the Makonde, fought with some success against the slavers, who took on average 10,000 slaves annually between 1780 and 1800. But, because of virtual depopulation elsewhere, there was a rising demand for blacks. Increased activity by slavers was also favoured by persisting tribal wars, whose losers were sold into slavery by their conquerors. The conquerors in one war sometimes became the losers in conflict with other neighbours and so followed their own victims into slavery. James Duffy reports that the number of slaves exported from Mozambique rose sharply to 15,000 a year and reached 25,000 annually for a decade, then declined after 1850; this was long after the decree of 1836 which in principle abolished slaving in the Portuguese colonies.[1] However, the vicious trade did not end completely until around 1865. Even then, it persisted in another form: the transportation of so-called 'volunteer workers' to the Comoros and Réunion Island, in principle for a period of five years. The Africans shipped to the French-held islands were taken by the very same slavers as operated in the past, and marched to the coast where they were put aboard French ships as 'émigrés'. The only difference was that the Africans were subjected to an additional farcical ceremony in which they were 'asked' if they were willing to 'volunteer' for work in the islands. Woe unto the black 'émigré' who failed to answer the question affirmatively! This modified slave system was not abolished until 1864 and even then clandestine slaving continued in Mozambique for at least another fifteen years.

Africans not shipped abroad faced the cruelties of the *prazo* system. The *prazeros* made little or no distinction between a slave and a *colono*,

[1] Duffy, *Portugal in Africa*, p. 97.

the black inhabitant on their land concessions who, although allegedly a free man, was obliged to work without pay for the *prazero*. Despite their nominal freedom, many Africans were still sold into full slavery by the *prazo*-holders. Such an iniquitous system of exploitation naturally provoked resistance—or 'rebellion', as the self-righteous Portuguese and *mestiço prazeros* considered any move to check their exploitation of their fellow human beings. The *prazo*-holders maintained small private armies, often closer to Ku-Klux-Klan gangs in the South of the United States than regular military units, designed to terrorize their unwilling African subjects and crush any attempted African resistance.

Prazero arrogance knew no bounds and was often directed against Portugal itself. In the middle of the nineteenth century, a *mestiço*, Joaquim José de la Cruz (or Nyaude), on his own authority decided to levy tolls on all traffic on the Zambezi, from his headquarters at Massangano. The Portuguese governor not only failed to crush the feudal ambitions of Cruz, but was unable to prevent Cruz's son, António Vicente (Bonga) from destroying the city of Tete. Bonga defeated a Portuguese expedition in 1869 and held a vast territory until his death in 1885. The Portuguese were not able to regain control of the area from Bonga's brother for another three years.

More important was the Gaza empire created in the southern region of the same name by Ngoni tribes. Between the second decade of the nineteenth century and 1859, these Ngonis—or Gazas, as they came to be called—massacred the garrison of Lourenço Marques, attacked Inhambane and Sofala, seized the *prazos* south of the Zambezi and raided far to the north. The founder of this empire, Soshangane, died in 1859, leaving two sons who fought for control of the kingdom. The legitimate successor, Mahueva, was defeated by Umzila, or Muzila, his brother, who made a deal with the Portuguese in exchange for their support. Nevertheless, Umzila continued to treat the Portuguese with scant respect and demanded tribute from them. He died in August 1884. His son, Gungunhana, sought British protection against his Portuguese enemies. Apparently, the British at least encouraged Gungunhana to continue his struggle, which did not end until December 1895, when he and his capital were captured by the Portuguese. But the Gaza empire was not firmly in Portuguese hands until August 1897, when Gungunhana's military leader, General Maguiguana, died. Only then could the Portuguese at last declare the area 'pacified'.[1]

The corrupt, anarchical *prazo* system was finally curbed about this

---

[1] See Chilcote, *Portuguese Africa*, pp. 115–16.

time by Lisbon. Instead of more *prazeros* and their immense plantations, three land-holding companies were set up: the Mozambique, Niassa, and Zambézia. The Mozambique and Niassa virtually governed the vast territories under their control, with a monopoly on trade and the exploitation of natural resources. They even collected taxes from the inhabitants. The Mozambique ruled over 62,000 square miles in the district of Manica and Sofala. The Niassa company had a similar huge tract north of the Lrúio River. Only the Zambézia company was deprived of administrative rights in its area between Quelimane and Tete. In all three cases, the companies failed to materialize the large profits that had been awaited from this massive expropriation of African land. In 1901, all land not already privately owned by Europeans was declared government land. In effect, this meant that all African tribal claims were nullified and the land held by Africans was subjected to government disposal. In theory, African land tenure was to be protected, but in practice the system meant even speedier eviction of blacks from land coveted by European individuals or companies.[1]

The *prazo*-holders violently resisted Lisbon's efforts to bring them under the control of the colonial administrations. Troops were sent against these European, *mestiço*, and even a few African *prazeros* in various regions. But it was not until 1904 that the power of the *prazo*-holders was broken. Military expeditions had to be mounted around the same time against various restive African tribes in many regions. The Mozambique district was not subdued until 1918, while others succumbed somewhat earlier, such as the Makua and Makonde in 1909 and 1910 and the Ajáuas in 1912.

As elsewhere in Africa, military 'pacification' was followed by a temporary halt in African armed resistance, then an upsurge of non-violent and de-tribalized resistance to colonial abuses. The formation of the *Liga Africana* in Lisbon in 1920, although it gathered together only some twenty African and mulatto intellectuals, had significant repercussions in the colonies. In Mozambique, African demands for justice were first voiced by the *Grémio Africano*, also founded in the 1920s. In time, this became the *Associação Africana*, which came partially under government control. The more determined nationalist elements in the *Associação* then formed the *Instituto Negrófilo*, which was later forced by the Government to change its name to *Centro Associativo dos Negros de Moçambique*. Europeans born in Mozambique set up an organization to protect their particular interests, the *Associação dos*

[1] See Eduardo Mondlane, *The Struggle for Mozambique* (Harmondsworth, Penguin 1969), pp. 30–1.

Naturais de Moçambique. In the 1950s, this group finally opened its ranks to non-whites and fought for a non-racial society.

As in Angola, *mestiço* intellectuals and poets, such as José Craveirinha, Noémia de Sousa, and Marcelino dos Santos, explored the African past and re-evaluated African culture. In time, their work took on a more explicitly critical tone, condemning the misery and brutality of colonialism. Dos Santos, discovering communism in his European student days and later in exile, was eventually to become one of the founders of FRELIMO. Until muzzled by the fascist press laws of the Salazar regime, the weekly *O Brado Africano*, established in the twenties as one of the first African publications, provided a platform for the restive black and brown intellectuals. However, the most vigorous protests against colonial rule and exploitation came from African workers and peasants. In the thirties, the dockworkers struck in Lourenço Marques on various occasions. The dockers and plantation workers struck again in 1947. An abortive uprising followed in 1947: the Portuguese crushed it and jailed or deported its leaders and many of those who participated. In 1956, when the dockworkers again struck, forty-nine of them paid for their boldness with their lives. Finally, in 1963, another strike of Lourenço Marques dockworkers, which spread to Beira and Nacala, also ended in failure.

The countryside was far from tranquil. According to Chilcote, in April 1960, when Kibirti Diwani and other members of the Makonde tribe sought to form an association, they were arrested and deported, but only after more than 600 of their fellow Africans had been shot down by Portuguese forces.[1] The Portuguese were quick to make use of their arms against defenceless Africans on many occasions and made a practice of massive arrests wherever there was unrest.

This agitation reached secondary school students, led by some who had been sent to South Africa to study and had later formed the *Núcleo dos Estudantes Africanos Secundários de Moçambique* (NESAM), an offshoot of the *Centro Associativo dos Negros de Moçambique*. Among the youths active in NESAM was Eduardo Mondlane, who was to become the first President of FRELIMO. However, NESAM had, as Mondalne himself admitted, a 'tiny membership'.[2] Its influence was restricted to those few privileged African youths who had access to education, but at least among them it successfully countered notions of Portuguese cultural supremacy over all things African and exposed the hollow fraud of 'assimilation'. Eventually, like Mondlane, a

---

[1] Chilcote, *Portuguese Africa*, p. 118–19.
[2] Mondlane, op. cit., p. 113.

number of NESAM members were to play leading roles in the liberation movement in Mozambique.

The first genuinely nationalist organization was the *União Democrática Nacional de Moçambique* (UDENAMO), formed on 2 October 1960 among Mozambican exiles in Rhodesia and Nyasaland (now Malawi), under the leadership of Adelino Gwambe. In April 1961, it moved its headquarters to Dar es Salaam. A second group, the Mozambique African Nationalist Union (MANU) was founded in Mombasa, Kenya, during February 1961. Its members were Mozambican exiles in Kenya, Tanganyika, and Uganda who had been inspired by the successes of the Kenya African National Union (KANU) and the Tanganyika African National Union (TANU). MANU's founders, the President, Matthew Mmole, and Secretary-General, M. M. Mallianga, had worked with and been strongly influenced by these East African nationalist parties. In time, MANU also transferred its headquarters to Dar es Salaam. Mozambican exiles from the Tete district formed a third organization, the *União Africana de Moçambique Independente* (UNAMI), which in 1961 also moved to Dar es Salaam.

Strong pressures for a merger were exerted there by Tanganyikan (now Tanzanian) President Julius Nyerere. In addition, the newly-formed CONCP—whose April 1961 conference in Rabat was attended by Gwambe in the name of all three Mozambican groups—was eager to see a unified Mozambican liberation movement. In June 1962, UDENAMO, MANU, and UNAMI merged to form the *Frente de Libertação de Moçambique*. But the new-found unity was to be very short-lived.

Frente de Libertação de Moçambique (FRELIMO)

Created by the merger in June 1962 of the three existing African nationalist movements under pressure of pan-African demands for unity in the struggle against Portuguese colonialism in Mozambique, FRELIMO has nevertheless been constantly beset by fierce faction-fighting, ideological, ethnic, and personal rivalries, assassinations, defections, and splits. Such unity as remained was due largely to the active concern of President Julius Nyerere of Tanzania—who had granted FRELIMO major bases in his country from which to launch its struggle—and the necessity to justify the exclusive material support FRELIMO received from the African Liberation Committee of the Organization of African States.

The Secretary-General of the newly-formed FRELIMO was David J. M. Mabunda, from UDENAMO. The Deputy Secretary-General, Paulo José Gumane, was also from UDENAMO, while Matthew Mmole, the Treasurer, came from MANU. The Vice President was the Reverend Uria Simango, a Protestant pastor from the Beira region, who had been leader of UDENAMO. The well-known leftist poet Marcelino dos Santos, a mulatto long associated with the communist-oriented *mestiço* intellectuals who founded the CONCP, was given the post of Secretary for External Relations because of his previous contacts and lengthy experience in exile in Portugal and France.

Almost hand-picked by President Nyerere to head this heterogenous group as FRELIMO's President was Dr. Eduardo Chivambo Mondlane, a former university professor who had once worked for the United Nations as an international civil servant. At the time of the formation of FRELIMO, Mondlane was teaching anthropology at Syracuse University in the United States. He had been born in 1920 in the Gaza District of southern Mozambique, son of a minor tribal chieftain. Assisted by Protestant missionaries, he was able to attend secondary school in Lourenço Marques and obtain a primary school certificate in 1936, which was 'the highest educational achievement allowed an African in Mozambique'. In 1944, he entered secondary school in South Africa and eventually went on to Witwatersrand University. However, the new Afrikaner Nationalist government expelled him from South Africa, and returning to Mozambique, he was arrested by Portuguese authorities on suspicion of 'subversion'. Soon freeing him, the authorities recommended that he attend a Portuguese university. Supported by an American rather than a Portuguese scholarship, he entered the University of Lisbon in 1950. There, Mondlane met Marcelino dos Santos, Agostinho Neto, Amílcar Cabral, Mário de Andrade, and other future leaders of nationalist movements in the Portuguese colonies. Mondlane nevertheless was unhappy because of the close surveillance of the P.I.D.E. in Lisbon, and the next year transferred to Oberlin College in the United States. He graduated with a B.A. in 1953, then took an M.A. and Ph.D. in sociology from North-western University. In May 1957, after a year doing advanced research at Harvard University, Mondlane was employed by the United Nations as a research officer on trust territories. It was in this capacity that he met Julius Nyerere. Later, he accepted a teaching post at Syracuse University. Because Mondlane had not been involved in the disputes of the three existing Mozambican nationalist organizations, Nyerere thought that he might more easily be able to foster their unification.

FRELIMO was formed in June and Mondlane was elected its President at the first party congress in Dar es Salaam in late September 1962.[1]

In the programme adopted by the congress, no mention was made of guerrilla warfare against the Portuguese in Mozambique. But this was a deliberate omission. A reference to procuring all 'means of self-defence' and preparing the people 'for any eventuality' indicated clearly enough the direction the founders of FRELIMO were considering.

Mondlane returned to the United States after the party congress, to fulfil his teaching commitments at Syracuse. At FRELIMO headquarters in Tanganyika, he left as his personal representative Leo Milas, FRELIMO's Publicity Secretary. Within months, Milas had driven Gumane and Mabunda out of FRELIMO. They left Dar es Salaam for Cairo, where eventually they set up a rival group. In August 1964, Milas himself was expelled from FRELIMO, accused by the Central Committee of being an Afro-American impostor, actually Leo Clinton Aldridge, Jr., born in Pittsburgh, Texas, U.S.A., not in Mozambique. Milas, who by this time had been appointed FRELIMO's Secretary for Defence and Security, countered with allegations that Mondlane was working closely with the U.S. Central Intelligence Agency and accepting '£200 monthly from the Israeli Embassy in Dar es Salaam'.[2] Also expelled in 1963 was Matthew Mmole, the first Treasurer of FRELIMO. Whether the blame for these expulsions should be entirely placed on the mysterious Milas is not clear, but it was quite obvious that Mozambican nationalists were more divided than ever when Mondlane finally returned to Dar es Salaam in 1963 to take up his duties as President of FRELIMO.

Accompanying him were his white American wife, Janet Mondlane, née Johnson, and their three small children. Mrs. Mondlane, who had an M.A. in African Studies from Boston University, immediately took an active interest in FRELIMO and ran the Mozambique Institute, a mainly American-funded school for Mozambican refugees in Dar es Salaam. The Institute sought to prepare qualified youths for scholarships at universities abroad and in this scored many successes, despite great internal friction between students and staff. Perhaps largely because she was an American white woman who participated fully in FRELIMO affairs, Mrs. Mondlane was 'repeatedly accused by factions

[1] See Paul M. Whitaker, 'In Memoriam: Dr. Eduardo Chivambo Mondlane, 1920–1969', *Pan African Journal* (Vol. II, No. 1, Winter 1969).

[2] See FRELIMO Circular 'Expulsion of Leo Clinton Aldridge, Jr., otherwise known by the aliases of Leo Milas and Leo Aldridge-Milas', 25 August 1964; and S. Leo Milas, 'My Expulsion from FRELIMO and the Reason for It' (Cairo [?], September 1964).

inside and outside FRELIMO of alleged ties with the Central Intelligence Agency.'[1] The presence of other whites, including Portuguese oppositionists, in FRELIMO was welcomed by the more cosmopolitan of its leaders, such as dos Santos, as well as Mondlane, but the whites were bitterly resented by staunch African nationalist and tribal elements. Later, after Marcelino dos Santos's marriage in 1968 to a white South African woman, Pamela Beira, the same elements raised a vigorous protest. Nevertheless, by the time of Mondlane's assassination, Mrs. dos Santos was employed by him as a confidential secretary. While an act of great personal courage, dos Santos's marriage was politically inopportune and certainly contributed no more towards FRELIMO's unity than had Mondlane's.

In principle, after 1968, FRELIMO's structure greatly resembled the organization of other groups within the CONCP. The highest instance of the party is the Congress, representing all members, which meets every four years. The Congress selects the Central Committee, which handles current business and meets every six months, while an Executive Committee, appointed by the Central Committee, meets every two months or within two weeks of a call for its convocation. Daily decision-making is handled by a Politico-Military Committee appointed by the Executive Committee. In addition to their selection by the Congress, members of the Central Committee are partially nominated by the provincial bodies. These are Provincial Councils, which meet every three years, selecting a Provincial Committee for the handling of current affairs; a District Council, which meets every two years, selecting a District Committee for current affairs; and, finally, a Local Council which meets every year, creating a Local Committee to take care of day-to-day business. The Presidency can appoint members to the Local Councils, and although members are also elected, the final authority for this level rests with the Presidency. In the isolation imposed by conditions of guerrilla warfare, this structure merely represented an ideal, while virtual guerrilla autarkies grew up in the areas inside Mozambique under FRELIMO control. This also was a factor for future dissension.

Mondlane had aspired to making FRELIMO a truly national party, cutting across all tribal barriers in Mozambique. He deliberately sought a leadership that included a broad representation of all major ethnic groups. Nonetheless, as the party grew in numbers in Tanganyika, the largest percentage of its new recruits were Makonde who crossed the

---

[1] Whitaker, 'In Memoriam: Dr. Eduardo Chivambo Mondlane'.

Rovuma River into Tanzania. The Makonde and Nyanja, another tribe living on the northern border, soon provided the bulk of FRELIMO forces. But this too was to be a factor of disunity as other tribes, such as the Makua, traditional enemies of the Makonde, refused to join with them.

FRELIMO did not launch an armed struggle inside Mozambique until 25 September 1964, two years after its formation, when guerrillas trained in Algeria and the United Arab Republic went into action for the first time. This attack may have been carried out somewhat earlier than planned, after a small rival group headed by a former MANU leader made a raid into Mozambique, killing a Dutch priest and some Africans out hunting with him. Many of the band, including the leader, were killed by the Portuguese troops who pursued them.[1]

Initially, FRELIMO's military strategy called for attacks on the Portuguese in Cabo Delgado and Niassa districts in the north, bordering Tanzania, and a second front in Tete District, in the north-west, bordering Malawi, Zambia and Rhodesia, but lack of a popular base and shortage of supplies in this area forced FRELIMO to withdraw its forces and concentrate solely on Cabo Delgado. Here, the guerrillas made hit-and-run attacks from the protection of the remote Makonde plateau, but Makua hostility to the Makonde prevented extension of operations more than 100 miles south of Cabo Delgado. By 1965, fighting had spread to the Niassa District, where FRELIMO forces were mainly Nyanja tribesmen, and extended around the shore of Lake Niassa. In both cases, the Portuguese sought to regroup the population in strategic hamlets or fortified villages. As the Nyanjas are found both in Mozambique and Malawi, despite the reluctance of the Government of President Hastings K. Banda, FRELIMO forces were operating for a while from Malawian bases as well as from camps inside Mozambique. Finally, by 1968, FRELIMO was able to reopen its front in Tete District hoping, as its new President and military commander Samora Moisés Machel admitted, to prevent construction of the big Cabora Bassa dam. 'If they achieve their objective', he said, 'they will have a political triumph of international magnitude, because it will mean that the Portuguese still control Mozambique, that armed struggle does not exist, that the guerrillas are still not consolidated, and that what we say is nothing but propaganda.'[2]

[1] See George Martelli, 'Conflict in Portuguese Africa', in Abshire and Samuels, op. cit., p. 421.

[2] Samora Moisés Machel, 'Why We Fight', in *Tricontinental* (No. 18, May–June 1970), p. 10.

Unfortunately, FRELIMO has had a bad record of exaggerated war claims. Not that the Portuguese military have been any more honest—though they are somewhat more cautious than FRELIMO spokesmen, who systematically padded the toll of enemy dead and wounded, and estimates of the size of areas considered liberated, or 'semi-liberated' zones. As long ago as October 1967, *O Combatente*,[1] organ of the rival *Comité Revolucionário de Moçambique*, was able to ridicule FRELIMO claims to have liquidated 'more than 5,000 Portuguese soldiers, destroyed about 300 military vehicles, shot down 22 aircraft, destroyed various military posts and camps and sabotaged a number of bridges and roads' in three years of fighting. The pompous 'War Communiqués' issued by FRELIMO headquarters in Dar es Salaam came in time to be generally greeted with scepticism and often bitter amusement. Among those who reportedly were embarrassed by such stupidities were the Cuban, Chinese, and Eastern European instructors training FRELIMO forces in camps in Tanzania, particularly the Cubans and Chinese. Yet in a speech delivered in London on 7 March 1968 before members of the Royal Institute of International Affairs and the Institute of Race Relations, Dr. Mondlane himself was to claim FRELIMO virtually controlled 'one-fifth of the total area of Mozambique, with a population of almost 1 million out of a 7 million population'. This would have been an area as large as Portugal itself, with a population as great as Lesotho's. At the same time, FRELIMO was unable to open this area for inspection by the African Liberation Committee, or take home from Tanzania the 35,000 Mozambican refugees being cared for by the U.N. High Commission for Refugees.

While Mondlane was also extolling to his British and American listeners the growing unity in the struggle against the Portuguese, events in Dar es Salaam were proving him far from the truth. He was obliged to cut short his stay to return to Tanzania, where an African priest, Mateus Pinho Gwenjere, had led irate students of the Mozambique Institute in a riot against Mrs. Mondlane's control over the school. In May 1968, the FRELIMO office was raided by these dissidents and a resisting staff member was killed in the mêlée. The Mozambique Institute was closed and, with the aid of Tanzanian police, the dissidents were quelled. But the police could not restore unity to FRELIMO ranks.

A second congress of the party was organized inside Mozambique not far from the Tanzanian border in Niassa District, from 20 to 25

---

[1] *O Combatente* (Lusaka, Vol. I, No. 3, 31 October 1967).

July 1968. According to FRELIMO sources, altogether 170 delegates and observers attended the gathering, as well as representatives from such fraternal bodies as the ANC of South Africa, ZAPU of Rhodesia and the pro-Moscow faction of the Afro-Asian Peoples' Solidarity Organization. Also invited to cross the border into 'liberated' Mozambique was the writer Basil Davidson. He was only the second journalist to enter the country with the guerrillas. Although FRELIMO spokesmen had often boasted of the vast areas of the country under their control, they seemed unable to open them for inspection by the O.A.U. and journalists. Until early in 1968, even Mondlane himself had not seen the territory claimed to be under FRELIMO control. Accompanying the President's delegation was a sympathetic Swedish reporter, Anders Johansson, correspondent for *Dagens Nyheter* in Stockholm. Lack of confidence in FRELIMO communiqués was by then so great that it is doubtful whether many would have believed anything if a reputable newsman had not been present.[1]

The mounting tensions in FRELIMO erupted at the congress, although somehow these were not mentioned in the account given by the British observer. Structural changes were made in the party's organization, in the name of democratic centralism. The Central Committee was now to be composed of members elected from provincial bodies, representatives of mass organizations, provincial secretaries, and members elected by the Congress, the party's supreme organ. From twenty-odd members, the Central Committee grew to forty members. But its function now was to be strictly legislative. The Executive Committee, created around Mondlane and Vice-President Uria Simango, was composed mainly of the secretaries of FRELIMO departments and operated like the cabinet of a government. And, as we have already noted, a Political and Military Committee was also created to handle current business.

Whether these efforts at wider representation of FRELIMO low-level leadership and the rank and file would have had much success in bringing unity to FRELIMO ranks is impossible to say. Before the reforms had been long in operation, Dr. Mondlane was assassinated in Dar es Salaam, on 3 February 1969. Mondlane died instantly when, at about 11.20 a.m., a bomb concealed within a book exploded as he opened the package containing it. Mondlane was blown up while seated at a desk in the seaside bungalow of Betty King, a wealthy American who ran a gem company in Tanzania. Previously, she had worked as an unpaid

[1] See Anders Johansson, 'In Mozambique with FRELIMO', in *Mozambique Revolution* (Dar es Salaam, No. 35, June–September 1968).

assistant to Mondlane. At the time of her husband's death, Mrs. Mondlane was away on a fund-raising tour in Sweden. Mondlane preferred to work at Miss King's bungalow rather than at the poky FRELIMO offices on Nkrumah Street in Dar es Salaam; there, also, he was able to avoid the quarrelling factions within official organization headquarters and concentrate his efforts on finding a solution to the persisting problems that beset it. With Mondlane removed from the scene, there seemed even less chance of a successful solution.

Tanzanian police were never able to pinpoint the assassin. The book containing the bomb arrived in a package bearing the postmark of a West European country. With FRELIMO as Portugal's 'Enemy Number One', it was naturally believed that the P.I.D.E. was responsible, although the Portuguese denied the charge. Portuguese spokesmen claimed that Mondlane had been killed by 'Maoist' dissidents within FRELIMO, as it was no secret that the generally pro-Western Mondlane and his pro-Soviet Secretary for Political Affairs at that time, Marcelino dos Santos, were drawing together, seriously disturbed by the growing Chinese revolutionary influence on the rank and file. Nevertheless, FRELIMO under Mondlane had achieved the unprecedented in obtaining financial and material assistance from both the Soviets and the Chinese, as well as from Western sources. In 1965, Mondlane had boasted that he could get 'money from the West and arms from the East'.[1] And this claim at least seemed quite true.

Mondlane's death opened a period of intense crisis in FRELIMO. Although encouraged by leaders of other African liberation movements and many of the FRELIMO rank and file, FRELIMO's Vice-President Uria Simango was reluctant to declare himself the automatic successor to Mondlane. Dos Santos, encouraged by the Soviets, other Eastern Europeans, and Cubans, made a bid for the presidency, but the *mestiço* poet and world traveller lacked a firm power-base within the party. He was forced to come to terms with FRELIMO's Algerian-trained military commander, Samora Moisés Machel, who had already given his personal protection to Mrs. Mondlane, assuring her that she would continue to play a major role in the leadership of her late husband's party. Thus, when the FRELIMO Central Committee met on 21 April 1969, to fill the vacuum left by Mondlane, Simango found dos Santos, Machel, and Mrs. Mondlane allied against him. The meeting was a stormy one as the opposing factions fought over, or, in the words of the communiqué released later, held a 'profound debate' over, 'the divergent lines which have developed within the leadership concerning the concept

[1] Quoted in Martelli, 'Conflict in Portuguese Africa', p. 423.

of the process of the people's armed struggle.'[1] Unable to select one person for the presidency, the Central Committee decided to replace the office with a 'collective organ composed of three members, elected by the Central Committee and called the Council of the Presidency.' Named to this triumvirate were, of course, Uria Simango, Marcelino dos Santos, and Samora Machel. Simango still seemed the strongest of the three, as he was also named co-ordinator of the Council of the Presidency, to act as 'the link between the Council of the Presidency and the Departments of the Executive Committee.'

On 3 April 1969, shortly before this crucial Central Committee meeting, the Portuguese authorities in Mozambique had announced that Lavaro Kavandame, a tribal strong-man and onetime Provincial Secretary of FRELIMO in Cabo Delgado, had defected and was now collaborating with the Portuguese forces against the national liberation movement. Although FRELIMO spokesmen claimed the 65-year-old Makonde leader was 'completely valueless' to the Portuguese, they privately expressed deep concern about the security of FRELIMO's tribal base in Cabo Delgado. Kavandame was accused of corruption and murder and he was alleged to have fled to escape trial for the killing of one of FRELIMO's military commanders, Paulo Kankhomba, on 22 December 1968. Kankhomba was not the first FRELIMO military leader to die in mysterious circumstances. In 1966, Filipe Magaia, who had preceded Samora Machel as FRELIMO military commander-in-chief, was killed while visiting one of his own bases. Machel's first task as commander had been to re-establish a modicum of discipline among his feuding, restive troops and their leaders.

The triumvirate that replaced Mondlane was hailed with relief by anxious partisans of FRELIMO. Even before the murder of Mondlane, Basil Davidson had written hopefully, 'Mondlane, Simango, Marcelino dos Santos, Samora Machel . . . and others today form a solid and united team among whom, as far as I can see, there remains no basic disagreement.'[2] In fact, so numerous were the disagreements that FRELIMO was again in full crisis in November 1969. Uria Simango, co-ordinator of the three-man supreme body, published a thirteen-page document, accusing his two associates of plotting to murder him. He charged that FRELIMO was infected with 'strong feeling of sectarianism, regionalism and tribalism'. He complained of a series of assassinations in the past: Filipe Magaia, Mateus Muthemba, Paulo Kankhomba,

[1] *Mozambique Revolution* (No. 38, March–April 1969).
[2] *Le Monde Diplomatique* (November 1968). Author's translation from the French text.

and Silverio Rafael Nungu. 'That there was frequent, cold-blooded and deliberate killing in our army is a matter that was of heated discussions inside and outside FRELIMO,' Simango wrote. And he gave a hair-raising account of Nungu's murder at the Central Military Base in Cabo Delgado. It had been claimed that Nungu 'had died of hunger strike, had refused to eat for eight days, after he was interrogated on organizing a group against the organization and on wanting to run away to hand himself to the Portuguese authorities . . . a great absurdity!' According to Simango, Nungu had been tricked into going from Tanzania to Cabo Delgado, where he was brutally murdered on 18 July 1969, as 'fulfilment of the plan drawn and the decision taken at Janet's house at Oyster Bay by the clique of criminals on obedience of an imperialist plan' to assassinate their rivals in the leadership.

Simango demanded the expulsion of Mrs. Mondlane and her return to the United States 'because she is the source of massive corruption in FRELIMO.' He also demanded the resignation and trial for their alleged crimes of Machel and dos Santos. 'Massacres of fighters should be terminated. Unity must be restored' through the development of internal democracy within the organization, he declared. Finally, he threatened to resign if his demands were not complied with immediately. Naturally, they were not and, although he discussed the crisis with a very anxious President Nyerere, Simango was unwilling to remedy matters by force, despite his many followers in FRELIMO ranks. Seven of the nine members of the Executive Committee met urgently and announced in November that Simango was relieved of his post, for allegedly violating FRELIMO rules and regulations and committing a serious breach of discipline in publishing his thirteen-page denunciation of his colleagues. President Nyerere did not intervene beyond giving Simango a police guard. Eventually, his situation in Dar es Salaam became untenable and he left for Cairo.

At the end of 1970, Portuguese authorities in Mozambique announced another coup: the defection of Dr. Miguel Murupa, the former Secretary for External Relations who had been handpicked by the late Dr. Mondlane after Murupa received his degree in economics from Howard University in Washington. Born in 1938, Murupa had spent little more than a year working for FRELIMO before he abandoned the faction-ridden party in May 1969. However, he remained in Tanzania, where he was later arrested and turned over to FRELIMO again. In an interview with a journalist in Nampula, Mozambique, in December 1970, Murupa disclosed he was then working for the Psychological Warfare Department of the Portuguese Army. He said he had been taken by

FRELIMO to Mozambique as a prisoner and made to work as a menial for the guerrilla leaders in the north. Finally, in November 1969, he was able to make his escape and surrendered to the Portuguese forces.[1] Obviously, he had little choice.

A new splinter group, calling itself the Mozambique Liberation Front (MOLIMO), was reported in mid-1970. Headed by Henriques Nyankale, as Secretary-General, MOLIMO accused FRELIMO of having become a 'puppet organization' since the assassination of Dr. Mondlane. Claiming inspiration from Chairman Mao and Fidel Castro, MOLIMO denounced Mondlane's successors in the FRELIMO leadership as 'counterrevolutionaries' who spent their time in Dar es Salaam 'fighting with beer bottles and toasting in the name of those who have been killed.' Nyankale promised that, if given material support, MOLIMO would 'do more fighting than talking'.[2] But whether or not it received any backing, there has been no further sign of life from this breakaway organization since its founding.

In June 1971, another split occurred in FRELIMO ranks when a new group of dissidents gathered in Nairobi to form the Mozambique United Front (FUMO). Reliable sources claimed FUMO had won considerable support among Mozambican students in the United States and Europe, as well as in the rank and file in Africa. Nevertheless, the organization, headed by its Acting President Marcelino Mbule, showed no further signs of activity after its original denunciation of FRELIMO as 'powerless' to lead the liberation struggle as a result of infiltration by the P.I.D.E. and the C.I.A.[3]

Encouraged by this unprecedented chain of turmoil and disaffection within the guerrilla ranks, the Portuguese Army launched a major offensive in several areas of Mozambique at the end of 1970. The Portuguese offensive had in fact been mounting steadily since June. By Christmas, General Kaulza de Arriaga, commander of the Portuguese forces, and his wife were able to boast that they had spent the holiday at Tartibo, a captured guerrilla base near the Tanzanian border. The confident General claimed that his 60,000 troops—who faced about 8,000 guerrillas—were moving 'towards a definitive victory' over FRELIMO.[4] As the Portuguese have proved to be hardly more truthful in their claims than their FRELIMO adversaries, the validity of that claim was most doubtful. But it was quite evident that FRELIMO had

[1] See *The Times* (21 December 1970).
[2] See *Africa Research Bulletin* (1–31 August 1970).
[3] See *Le Monde* (26 June 1971).
[4] See the *Daily Telegraph* (28 December 1970).

suffered a series of stinging setbacks since the death of Mondlane, due more to internal contradictions and an incredible tendency to settle inner-party squabbles in blood than any new-found military prowess on the part of the Portuguese Army.

Comité Revolucionário de Moçambique (COREMO)

Almost two years after launching an armed struggle against the Portuguese in Mozambique, the *Comité Revolucionário de Moçambique* won *de facto* recognition at the Tenth Session of the O.A.U.'s African Liberation Committee in Kinshasa at the end of January 1967. COREMO representatives had given the A.L.C. overwhelming documentary proof of the reality of their organization and its fight against the Portuguese. But, unlike FRELIMO, the smaller group was not granted any financial or material assistance from the O.A.U., nor was it even permitted to open an office in Dar es Salaam, headquarters of the A.L.C.

The founders of COREMO were the same veteran African nationalists who, in 1962, had sought to create FRELIMO as a unified Mozambican liberation movement. Although they had worked hard for the new body, Paulo José Gumane (its Deputy Secretary-General) and David Mabunda (its Secretary-General)—both of whom had previously been leaders of UDENAMO—were driven from their FRELIMO posts within months by Leo Milas. They left Dar es Salaam for Cairo, where they reconstituted UDENAMO in May 1963.

Another group was also in existence at that time in Uganda, headed by Adelino Hlomulo Chitofo Gwambe, who had been one of the original leaders of UDENAMO before the creation of FRELIMO. However, because he had been accused of being a Portuguese agent, Gwambe was not invited to join the new organization. He then formed the *Comité Secreto da Restauração da UDENAMO* in Kampala and eventually set up another version of UDENAMO under the name of *União Democrática Nacional de Monomotapa* (called UDENAMO-Monomotapa, whereas Gumane and Mabunda's group was known as UDENAMO-Mozambique).

After his expulsion from FRELIMO, its former Treasurer, Matthew Mmole, reconstituted his previous organization, MANU. He joined with Gwambe and Sebastene Sikauke, provisional representative of the Mozambican African National Congress (MANCO), to organize, on 20 May 1963, the *Frente Unida Anti-Imperialista Popular Africana de Moçambique* (FUNIPAMO). With the expulsion of even more members of the FRELIMO Central Committee, FUNIPAMO grew and changed its name to Mozambique Revolutionary Council (MORECO). UDENAMO and MORECO merged at the beginning of 1965.

This proliferation of contending Mozambican nationalist groups was deplored throughout Africa. The Tanzanian Government, committed to FRELIMO and Dr. Mondlane, refused to admit the existence of the other groups, but in mid-1965 the Zambian Government took the initiative to convene a conference of all rival organizations in Lusaka. The Zambians hoped to effect the reunification of the Mozambican nationalist movement, but Mondlane walked out of the talks after the others had refused to disband their groups and join FRELIMO as individuals. The remaining delegates then united their five organizations in the new *Comité Revolucionário de Moçambique.* Forming COREMO were UDENAMO–Monomotapa, UDENAMO–Mozambique, MANU, MANCO, and UNAMI.[1] Lusaka was picked as COREMO headquarters. Gwambe was elected the first president, but long-standing accusations against him were revived and he was expelled after a year. Paulo José Gumane replaced him at the head of COREMO while the Secretary-General elected was Joseph Chiteji. He was replaced later in that post by Absolom T. Bahule.

Since its founding, COREMO has remained, at least on the surface, a small organization. Its strong-point inside Mozambique was said to be the Tete District, where COREMO guerrillas were reported to be in combat against the Portuguese forces. Gumane has claimed that he has some 5,000 followers inside Mozambique, armed mainly with primitive and home-made weapons. Gumane himself was also said to visit frequently his forces inside Mozambique and it was obvious that he received some support from the Zambian Government. When PAC guerrillas made an attempt to reach South Africa through Mozambique, they were assisted by COREMO guerrillas, whose bases provided them with convenient resting points on their trek southward. The PAC unit was eventually wiped out hundreds of miles inside Mozambique, near Vila Perry.

On 29 February 1968, COREMO's 25-year-old former Secretary for External Affairs, Mazunzo Million Bobo, was killed in a fire-fight with Portuguese forces at Chale Ngone Camp, in the Vila Gamito area, near the Malawi border. Two other COREMO men and five Portuguese soldiers were killed in the clash. In general, COREMO units sought to avoid contact with the enemy, concentrating rather on building up a clandestine network of cadres inside Mozambique and secretly training

[1] See Chilcote, *Portuguese Africa*, pp. 120–1.

freedom fighters in the bush for massive action at some future date.

COREMO's offices in Lusaka were bare and the organization never seemed able, or perhaps willing, to indulge in lavish propaganda. Its claims of battle victory were refreshingly modest. Gumane explained to some British journalists in 1968, 'We are in no position yet to kill thousands of Portuguese. Anyway, if all the claims made by other movements were true, there would be none left for us to kill.'[1]

In general, COREMO lined up internationally with the PAC, ZANU, GRAE, UNITA, and SWANU. Its enemies smeared it, like them, as either pro-Chinese or a creation of the C.I.A. However, there was little indication of any major outside influence, although COREMO's public statements were always the most anti-imperialist conceivable.

Nevertheless, Gumane's three-month trip to the United States and Western Europe in 1968 created much adverse comment within COREMO and a split was narrowly avoided.[2] While COREMO clearly continued to exist, outsiders had little idea of its activit:es inside Mozambique. Even the few COREMO representatives abroad complained bitterly of lack of communications from their headquarters. No one could say whether this shadowy organization, preferring clandestinity to propaganda, would eventually bring together the underground infrastructure it sought to prepare for a massive and generalized People's War throughout Mozambique. Reports of Portuguese operations in Tete indicated they were anxious never to give COREMO leisure to do so and considered the group a threat—if not an immediate one—to continuing Portuguese rule. In January 1971, COREMO scored a spectacular success by attacking Mukangadzi settlement near the site of the projected Cabora Bassa Dam, reportedly killing fifty Portuguese and capturing six others. One of the six prisoners was said by the guerrillas to have later committed suicide, but Portuguese authorities claimed the man was shot because he could not walk fast enough when the guerrilla unit returned to its base. Later the Portuguese claimed all the prisoners were dead, although COREMO said they were being released through the Red Cross. Holding the Zambian Government responsible for the activities of COREMO, the Portuguese staged an 'unofficial' boycott of cargoes bound for Zambia through Mozambican ports.[3]

[1] *The Times* News Team, *The Black Man in Search of Power* (London, Nelson. 1968).
[2] See Paul M. Whitaker, 'The Revolutions of "Portuguese" Africa'.
[3] See the *Guardian* (16 March 1971).

However, as 1971 passed, COREMO was unable to repeat this success, and with the continuing debility of FRELIMO, it was nevertheless obvious there unfortunately existed no more constant or immediate threats to the Portuguese, than those created by their own contradictions.

IV. SÃO TOMÉ E PRÍNCIPE

Comité de Libertação de São Tomé e Príncipe (CLSTP)

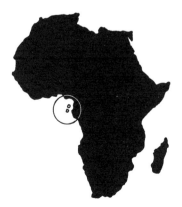

The smallest of Portugal's African provinces, São Tomé e Príncipe, is a mountainous group of islands, part of a chain that extends from the Cameroun Mountains into the Gulf of Biafra in the equatorial Atlantic. The two principal islands, São Tomé and Príncipe, are separated from each other by a distance of 82 miles and lie about 275 and 125 miles, respectively, off the northern coast of Gabon. In addition, the archipelago includes a group of islets: Cabras to the north; Santana, Quiziba, and the Seven Stones—which, in fact, are fourteen—to the east; Rolas to the south, and Gabado and Coco to the west. The total area of all islands is only 372 square miles. The provincial capital is the city of São Tomé, on the north-east coast of the island of the same name, with some 12,000 inhabitants.

Sugar and slaves dominate the early history of these islands; today, the crops are cocoa (80 per cent of exports) and coffee, and the 'slaves' are contract and convict labourers. The warm, moist climate of the islands was ideally suited to the cultivation of sugar cane, as it is to that of cocoa and coffee. Temperatures range between 66°F and 89·6°F, with March the hottest month. There is heavy rain, with annual totals as high as 150 to 200 inches on the south-western slopes of the mountains on São Tomé and 160 to 175 inches for Príncipe.

When the Portuguese João de Santarem and Përo Escobar discovered these islands between 1471 and 1472, they were uninhabited. In 1485, King João II gave the archipelago to one of his courtiers, João de Pavia, as an hereditary fief. The first white settlers arrived on the island in 1486; as well as the adults sent to the island, there were some 2,000 children of Jews expelled from Spain. Taken from their parents and baptized Christians, the children arrived in 1494, ostensibly to populate the empty islands. By 1499, malaria and other tropical diseases had reduced their numbers to 600. Only fifty or sixty survived in 1532.[1]

Unhealthy as the islands were for Europeans, they were valuable assets in the Portuguese Empire. Besides producing sugar, they were most conveniently placed on the long route to the Orient and were an ideal centre for trade with the West African coast. Of course, as elsewhere, the basis of that trade was slavery. Many of the slaves were

[1] René Pélissier, 'São Tomé ou le poids des siècles', *Revue française d'études politiques africaines* (No. 25, January 1969).

shipped on to the Americas, but tens of thousands remained on the islands to work on the plantations until freed by death. Slaves were absolutely essential to the islands' economy because of the small permanent European settlement. Although Portuguese, Spanish, and French immigrants were settled on the islands, the bulk of the population was composed of Africans. It still is today, and although slavery has been abolished for more than a century many of these Africans are contract labourers or convicts from other Portuguese colonies, especially Mozambique.

According to the 1960 census, the population of the islands was 64,263. By 1969, it was estimated that there were more than 62,000 Africans, of whom 54,500 were on São Tomé and 7,500 on Príncipe. Some 17,000 of these blacks were contracted and/or deported labourers from the mainland. In addition, there were 5,000 Creoles and 1,200 Europeans.

The sugar-cane plantations of the sixteenth to eighteenth centuries were cultivated by black slaves. Despite repeated slave revolts, the economy flourished until the second half of the eighteenth century. The first slave revolt, led by Yoan Gato, occurred in 1530, when São Tomé was the most important slave port in West Africa. The most famous revolt took place in 1585; it was led by Amador, who besieged the capital with a force of escaped slaves and *Angolares* (descendants of slaves from Angola who were shipwrecked in 1544 and clandestinely created an independent African society in the forests on the northern slopes of the massif of São Tomé). Amador's guerrilla army at one time liberated two-thirds of the island and he was proclaimed king. However, the Portuguese regained the initiative and Amador was hanged in 1596. Despite the defeat, the fugitive slaves again found refuge in the dense forests, from which they mounted repeated attacks on the whites over the next century. Additional slaves had constantly to be brought from the mainland to work the plantations.

The end of slavery in the Portuguese colonies nearly brought the islands' economy to ruin. As neither Europeans nor Creoles would consent to work in the fields, clandestine cargoes of blacks were brought in from West Africa and Mozambique, to work the cocoa and coffee that had replaced sugar-cane as the islands' main crops. The Portuguese labour code of 1899 gave legal sanction to this neo-slave trade, declaring the victims 'free' contract labourers. In principle, the contract was for five years, but at the end of that relatively short period no one was ever returned to the mainland. Disease and overseers' brutality took a frightening toll.

This sordid business was denounced in 1906 by Henry W. Nevinson, an English correspondent whose book, *A Modern Slavery*, set off a great controversy in both Britain and Portugal. The English chocolate manufacturers, Cadbury Brothers, when informed investigated the charges personally and through agents. A missionary named Charles Swan was sent by William Cadbury to conduct an inquiry and his findings, published in London in 1909 under the title of *The Slavery of Today*, prompted a boycott of São Tomé cocoa by Cadburys and other English and German manufacturers. In 1913, another Englishman, John Harris, published *Portuguese Slavery: Britain's Dilemma*, in which he revealed that 70,000 to 100,000 Angolan labourers had been sent to the islands before 1908 and that not a single one had been repatriated. The international scandal—which apologists for Portuguese colonialism still think of as a British-inspired campaign to discredit Portugal in Africa and seize her territories—forced at least a temporary halt in this new slave-trade, some reforms and the repatriation of the surviving Angolan workers.[1]

Today, the great plantations possess 93 per cent of the cultivable land. The islanders' small-holdings are minuscule, occupying 'scarcely 7% of the cultivable land and 52% of the autochthonous population lives on them.'[2] The economy is dominated by the *Banco Nacional Ultramarino* (National Overseas Bank) and the ubiquitous *Companhia União Fabril* (CUF).

As the official statistics reveal, contract labourers are still vital to the islands' economy. Many now come from Cape Verde, encouraged to volunteer for emigration by the famines that have ravaged those islands and the general persisting misery. From Mozambique are sent the convict labourers who, while serving their sentences, are as close to slaves in the traditional sense as can be imagined. In the past, they remained outside island society except as suppliers of labour-power. The 'natives' were the *mestiço* Creoles and the *Angolares* and they were rarely united on any issue. One group speaks Creole Portuguese, the other a mixture of African languages. Only after the Second World War did a new consciousness slowly develop among the islanders, beginning with the educated youth. As Paul Fordham noted: 'São Tomé is one of the most likely places where charges of "colonial exploitation" can be made to stick. . . . Whatever the liabilities of colonial ownership, São Tomé is for Portugal a very profitable piece of real estate.'[3]

---

[1] See Duffy, *Portugal in Africa*, pp. 134–7.

[2] 'St. Thomas and Prince: The People's Resistance to the Portuguese Presence', *Tricontinental* (No. 40, July 1969).

[3] Fordham, op. cit., p. 158.

In February 1953, the then Governor, Carlos Gorgulho, gave his approval to efforts by the great plantations to solve the problem of scarcity of manpower by virtually reintroducing slavery. Rather than submit to forced labour, the islanders struck and even resisted with arms. Portuguese troops and armed white settlers retaliated by killing 1,032 islanders in less than a week. The worst massacre took place at the village of Batepa, whose name has now become a symbol of Portuguese barbarity to the people of the islands.

Comité de Libertação de São Tomé e Príncipe (CLSTP)

As in other African colonies, the most advanced national consciousness and desire for liberation was developed among island students in Portuguese universities. They shared in the cultural and political awakening of the overseas students and joined in the 'reAfricanization' and Marxist–Leninist studies that went on clandestinely there among young *mestiços* and privileged blacks. In September 1960, a *Comité de Libertação de São Tomé e Príncipe* was formed. It eventually established its headquarters in Libreville, Gabon. In April 1961, the CLSTP took part in the founding conference of the *Conferência das Organizações Nacionalistas das Colónias Portuguêsas*, in Rabat.

Although able to build a clandestine organization on the islands and to play a role in the archipelago-wide strike of August 1963, the CLSTP remained weak. Many of its cadres were arrested by the P.I.D.E. Others despaired of success and abandoned the struggle. The Secretary-General of the CLSTP, Tomas Medeiros, and one other delegate represented the party at the CONCP's second congress in October 1965 in Dar es Salaam. Medeiros made one of the briefest of addresses to that gathering, praising the struggles of the MPLA, PAIGC, and FRELIMO, while pointing out that 'a geographical factor renders difficult, but not impossible, the passage to armed action' in the archipelago.[1] São Tomé and Príncipe remain vital and profitable to Portuguese colonialism in the twentieth century. In the face of the now massive Portuguese reinforcements, the likelihood of another uprising on the islands probably depends on the successful development of the struggle on the African mainland and a weakening of the Portuguese political resolve to cling to this mountainous, yet fertile, chain of islands.

[1] CONCP, *La lutte de libération nationale dans les colonies portugaises: la conférence de Dar es Salaam*, (Algiers, CONCP, 1967).

PART SIX:
THE HORN OF AFRICA AND SOME ISLANDS

I. THE FRENCH TERRITORY OF THE AFARS AND ISSAS

Front de Libération de la Côte des Somalis (FLCS)

Mouvement de Libération de Djibouti (MLD)

When the former Italian Somaliland won its independence in 1960, a considerable number of Somalis remained outside the borders of the new Somali Republic. Somalis in Ethiopia's Haud and Ogaden regions, the Northern Frontier District of Kenya, and French Somaliland hoped that the territories in which they lived would soon also become parts of the Republic. In fact, Article VI, section 4, of the Somali Constitution promised them: 'The Somali Republic shall promote, by legal and peaceful means, the union of Somali territories and encourage solidarity among the peoples of the world, and in particular among African and Islamic peoples.' The peoples who lived in the border areas of all the countries surrounding the Republic were almost all of Somali origin.[1] The new Prime Minister, Dr. 'Abd ar-Rashi explained:

Our neighbours are our Somali kinsmen whose citizenship has been falsified by indiscriminate boundary 'arrangements'. They have to move across artificial frontiers to their pastureland. They occupy the same terrain and pursue the same pastoral economy as ourselves. We speak the same language. We share the same creed, the same culture, and the same traditions. How can we regard our brothers as foreigners? Of course we all have a strong and very natural desire to be united.[2]

The British Somaliland Protectorate was united to the Somali Republic shortly after independence—achieved as a United Nations trust territory administered by Italy and not as an Italian colony. However, the further reunification of the Somali peoples proved exceedingly difficult and has yet to be accomplished.

Both Kenya and Ethiopia maintained that the contested territories in their countries were inalienable. As for the populations of Somali origin, they were mainly nomadic pastoralists, the two governments argued, who had recently migrated into the areas. In any case, Somalis in Ethiopia and Kenya expressed a desire to secede and unite with the Somali Republic. Eventually, frustrated in efforts at negotiation,

[1] Ted Gurr, in Feliks Gross, *World Politics and Areas* (New York, New York University Press, 1966), estimated that 1 million persons in Ethiopia's Haud and Ogaden regions, 240,000 in Kenya, and 37,000 in French Somaliland were Somali-speaking.

[2] I. M. Lewis, *The Modern History of Somaliland* (London, Weidenfeld and Nicolson, 1965), pp. 178–9.

Somali rebels took to arms. A declaration of emergency was made in the Northern Frontier District in December 1963 and British arms and material were supplied to the Kenya forces that went into battle against the Somalis. At the same time, Kenya and Ethiopia concluded a Defence Pact against Somalia. In February 1964, war appeared imminent when there was a new series of serious clashes between Ethiopian forces and the Somali Army, as well as Somali rebel forces.

The Organization of African Unity repeatedly appealed for negotiations between the warring parties. Although at times granting 'an embarrassed hearing'[1] to Somali irredentists at all-African conferences, the majority of African States clearly had little sympathy for the Somali cause. The O.A.U. member-states tended to take the view that there were numerous similar ethnic groups divided by artificial colonial borders throughout Africa and that, if the principle of re-examination, not to say modification by armed struggle of these borders were accepted in the case of the Somalis, African unity and stability would be seriously threatened. Somali leaders were urged to resign themselves to the *status quo*, in the name of African unity.

In fact, despite the strength of popular demands for the re-unification of the Somali people, their leaders—in the second half of 1967, after the formation of a government by the new Prime Minister, Muhammad Haji Ibrahim Egal—demonstrated willingness to normalize relations with Ethiopia and Kenya and set aside the question of re-unification of the Somali territories. So peace was restored, but the status of the Somali tribesmen remained unresolved. Popular discontent eventually found an outlet in the assassination of leaders and a military coup in October 1969.

Shortly after independence, however, before Somalis learned how difficult the task of re-unification was to be, it was assumed that, as with British Somaliland, French Somaliland would swiftly be added to the new Republic. The French had already granted the territory some autonomy in July 1957, with the creation of a Territorial Assembly elected by universal suffrage and a *Conseil de gouvernement*, presided over by the French Governor. (Later, the Council was to have an indigenous President at its head.) But France was then fighting to maintain her rule over Algeria and her other African territories. In the referendum of November 1958, these territories, with the exception of Algeria, were offered a choice of continuing association with France or independence. According to the French authorities, 75 per cent of the

---

[1] See Immanuel Wallerstein, *Africa: The Politics of Unity* (London, Pall Mall 1968), pp. 76–7.

electors in French Somaliland voted to remain under French rule. The ballot was carried out under the guns of French troops and by French civil servants who obstructed the electioneering of the pro-independence party. As soon as the result was announced, the Somali nationalists maintained that the election had been rigged. Considering as well the unscrupulous behaviour of French authorities in other African territories, such as Niger, it is not surprising that Guinea was the sole country to achieve independence through this referendum, and that the results in French Somaliland favoured continuing association with France.

France had moved into the Horn of Africa in 1885, seeking a coaling station for her steamships plying to and from the Far East through the Suez Canal. The British had long had a facility in Aden. On the other side of the Gulf, Britain also had treaties of protection with the Somali Issa clan, whose traditional home was at Zeila, some forty miles south-east of Djibouti in what is now the Somali Republic. At that time, Djibouti was merely a coral island connected to the mainland at low tide. The French had already signed treaties with the Danakils (or Afars, as they are now called) to the north. A deal for Djibouti was made with the Issa chieftains. Britain reluctantly recognized the French presence and boundaries were fixed between the protectorates in 1888.

In 1896, the armies of Emperor Menelik of Ethiopia defeated an Italian colonial army at the battle of Adowa in Eritrea. The Italians were forced to put aside their colonial pretensions—until Mussolini came to power—and negotiate with the Ethiopians for the right to colonize Eritrea and Somalia. Britain and France also negotiated with the Emperor for recognition of their claims in the Horn of Africa and in so doing fixed the boundaries of Djibouti and Northern Somalia with Ethiopia, abandoning to Ethiopian sovereignty Somali and Danakil people who had been covered by previously concluded treaties of protection. The sole justification for this abandonment was *Realpolitik*. Ancient maps and travellers' accounts 'testify to the independent status of the Somali and Danakil littoral and hinterland at that period in history; nor is there subsequent historical evidence that the Danakil and Somali coasts have ever formed "part and parcel" of Ethiopia.'[1]

In addition to the needed coaling station, French imperial strategists considered building a railway from Djibouti to French Equatorial Africa. Work on the rail link began in 1897. For numerous reasons,

[1] See John Drysdale, 'The Problem of French Somaliland', *African Report* (November 1966).

including British hostility to the project, the railway eventually ran
not to Oubangi-Chari, but 486 miles to Addis Ababa. Completed in
1917, the Franco-Ethiopian Railway has proved vital to the economy
of Ethiopia and still handles the bulk of cargo by ship and rail to and
from, Addis Ababa. The closure of the Suez Canal since 1967 and a
weakening of French resolve to cling to the possession since the departure of the late General Charles de Gaulle from the Elysée Palace, have
had little influence on Ethiopian determination to prevent the vital port
of Djibouti from falling into Somali hands. Emperor Haile Selassie
declared in September 1966 that Djibouti was an integral part of
Ethiopia. 'Djibouti indisputably is ours,' he said, 'and its people know
they belong to Ethiopia.'[1]

Actually, the peoples of French Somaliland are deeply divided
concerning the future of their territory. In 1966, the population was
said by the French authorities to be 125,000. Of these, 24,000 were
Issas and 30,500 Afars (Danakils). Europeans and citizens of other
French Community nations numbered 3,000; Arabs numbered 7,000
and 'temporary residents of nationalities' 10,200.[2] Altogether, 62,000
lived in Djibouti itself. Agriculture, fishing, and the breeding and
grazing of goats, sheep, cows, and camels lag far behind the port and
railway operations in the territory's economy. The territory, covering
8,880 square miles, is 89 per cent desert. Between May and October, the
average temperature is 92°F on the coast, and rain is rare at any time.

The French census figures have been challenged by Somali nationalists, who maintain that since 1963 the French have done everything
possible to divide Somalis and Danakils and build up the Danakils as a
barrier against Somali irredentism. Ali Aref Bourhan's Danakil
followers in the *Rassemblement Démocratique Afar* (RDA) have
consistently voted for maintaining the *status quo*. Nevertheless, another
group of Danakils, led by Mohammed Issa 'Cheiko', in the *Union
Démocratique Afar* (UDF), allied themselves with the Somali *Parti du
Mouvement Populaire* (PMP), headed by Musa Ahmed Idris.

Demands for independence and some form of association with the
Somali Republic came to a head again in August 1966 when General
de Gaulle stopped off in Djibouti while on a world tour. At least five
(and perhaps up to twenty-one) persons lost their lives in the ensuing
rioting. De Gaulle swiftly organized another referendum, after arresting
many nationalist leaders, including Mohammed Ahmed Issa 'Cheiko',
and deporting many thousands of Somalis. Again, in the presence of

[1] Quoted ibid.
[2] Colin Legum, *Africa Handbook*, p. 130.

French troops and conducted by French functionaries, the referendum of 19 March 1967, resulted in a majority in favour of continuing association with France, by 22,555 votes to 14,666. After the referendum, Ali Aref Bourhan became President of the Council of Government and, to underscore the French- and Ethiopian-backed divisions among its peoples, the name of French Somaliland was changed to the French Territory of the Afars and Issas.

In the face of mounting repression and the limitations of pro-Somali sentiments, part of the nationalist movement was obliged to go underground. Although armed struggle was not immediately launched, preparations were being made to launch it in due course. Eventually, in Somalia, there was formed the *Front de Libération de la Côte des Somalis*, headed by Robleh Awalleh. To avoid diplomatic embarrassment to the Somali Government, the FCLS transferred its headquarters to Aden, now capital of the independent People's Democratic Republic of South Yemen.

On 22 July 1968, at a meeting in Algiers, the O.A.U.'s eleven-nation African Liberation Committee officially recognized the FLCS as a liberation movement. But also recognized at the same time, as though in an act of blind impartiality, was the *Mouvement de Libération de Djibouti*, an Afar-based organization that sought autonomy for the territory and closer association with, or attachment to, Ethiopia. Since both the territorial government of Ali Aref Bourhan and France had assured Ethiopia that its vital economic interests in the port and railway would be protected, the MLD had no need to take action of any sort. The main function of the MLD would appear to be to act as a reserve force to invite and spearhead direct Ethiopian intervention if France ever chose to meet Somali demands. On the other hand, the successful struggle of the Eritrean Liberation Front and increasing revolutionary tensions within Ethiopia itself could eventually ease the task of the frustrated Somali nationalists in Djibouti, forcing a new regime in Addis Ababa to come to terms with them.

II. THE COMOROS

Mouvement de Libération Nationale des Comores
(MOLINACO)

Sadly neglected by France so far as education, health, and other social services are concerned, yet clung to because of their strategic dominating position at the northern end of the Mozambique Channel between Madagascar and the East African coast, the Comoro Islands contain one half of the total population of France's Overseas Territories. Although neo-colonialism is now more in vogue than indirect colonial rule, this anachronism persisted in the Comoros because of the alliance of historic Comoro feudalism and a handful of large French firms who dominate the economy of the archipelago.[1] The world's second largest producer of vanilla, this group of fertile volcanic islands also exports coconut fibre, essence of perfume (70 per cent of French production), sisal, cocoa, cloves, coffee, pepper, wood, and earth (lava for construction). The four islands of the archipelago—Grand Comoro, the largest (formerly known as Angazidja), Anjouan, Mohéli, and Mayotte (formerly called Mahore)—have a combined land area of 838 square miles and, at the beginning of 1971, an estimated population of 260,000. According to the 1966 census, 126,205 persons lived on Grand Comoro. There were 80,032 on Anjouan, 31,930 on Mayotte, and 10,300 on Mohéli at that time. The islands are obviously overpopulated, especially in view of the utter lack of industry, and Comorians have been obliged to emigrate to Madagascar, Zanzibar and the mainland of Tanzania, or metropolitan France. The capital, Moroni, is located on Grand Comoro and numbered 11,515 inhabitants in 1966.

Almost the entire population of the islands is Moslem, Islam having been introduced around A.D. 940 under the Omayyads. For centuries, Arabs established on the Comoros dominated the trade route to India. Archeological researches indicate that the first inhabitants arrived around the fourth century A.D. and were probably a Malayo-Polynesian people—Proto-Malagasies—who passed through the Comoros *en route* to Madagascar.[2] Whatever their remote origins, the early population adopted a social structure of a Bantu-type matrilineal chieftainship.

[1] See Michel Legris, 'Les Comores: un archipel plus une ile', *Le Monde* (31 December 1970, 14 January 1971).

[2] See Jean Martin, 'L'Archipel des Comores', *Revue française d'études politiques africaines* (No. 44, August 1969).

In addition to Arabs, who gave the islands their name, there arrived Sharazis from Persia, fleeing religious persecution at home, and they became masters of the islands in the sixteenth century. The Portuguese attempted to take over the Moslem islands at about the same time, but found them uninviting and difficult to rule. Malagasies also settled on the four islands, but the East African slave trade brought many more thousands of blacks from the mainland. Today, as a result, the Comorian resembles in no way the inhabitant of Madagascar, while 'nothing distinguishes him from the African of the eastern coast'.[1] Arabic and Swahili were the principal languages before the arrival of the French and even today the vast majority of the population still does not speak French.

From the sixteenth to the early nineteenth century, the islands were nominally governed by a Sultan of Anjouan and, under him, numerous local sultans. Feudal society depended on trade with passing ships, occasional piracy, and acting as an entrepôt for slaves from East Africa. European pirates, driven from the West Indies, also frequented the Mozambique Channel during the eighteenth century. But the most serious menace to the islanders was constituted by invaders from Madagascar. In 1816, Sultan Alaoui of Anjounan wrote to King Louis XVIII of France congratulating him on his return to the throne and requesting a French expeditionary force to defend the islands against the invaders. The French refused the troops. On Grand Comoro, Sultan Ahmed (the Tibe Mougne MKou) had no greater success with a similar appeal to the Portuguese. Only in 1841 did the desire of the French Indian Ocean naval squadron for a secure and convenient base prompt France to occupy the island of Mayotte.[2]

Later, the French attempted to consolidate their influence over Mohéli, but maladroit efforts to convert the inhabitants to Christianity antagonized the islanders and their Queen Djombe Fatima. Meanwhile, British influence was strong on Anjouan Island, where the British Consul a certain William Sunley, was also, more gainfully, employed in managing 600 slaves on a vast plantation. Dr. Livingstone was scandalized, especially since the British Government of the time was allegedly engaged in wiping out the African slave trade, and Sunley was given the choice of his diplomatic post or the life of a slave-owner. He chose to remain a slave-owner and was removed from the Foreign Service, although kept on discreetly for several more years as unofficial British

[1] Abdou Sakari Boina, 'The Comoros: Encounter with their Reality', *Tricontinental* (No. 49, April 1970).

[2] Martin, 'L'Archipel des Comoros'.

representative in the Comoros. Only the Grand Comoro remained untouched by Britain and France because of its inhospitable ports and the reputed ferocity of its inhabitants but, when a certain Dr. Schmidt of the *Deutsche Ostrafrikagesellschaft* visited that island, the French were galvanized into action. After Sunley's time, the British had lost interest in Anjouan so that the French, proclaiming a protectorate over Mohéli, Anjouan and Grand Comoro in 1886, did so without opposition. They were already well established in Mayotte.

At first, the archipelago was ruled indirectly—as today—through the local sultans, under the French Governor-General of Réunion. In 1895, the islands were used as stepping stones in the French conquest of Madagascar. This eventually proved against the interests of the Comoros, especially after 1912, when they were joined to Madagascar and governed from Tananarive.

From 1946, with the establishment of the Fourth Republic in France, the Comoros were given one seat in the French National Assembly. This was filled by Said Mohamed Sheikh, a great feudal lord and friend of France, who dominated the political life of the archipelago until his death in March 1970. He remained Deputy of the Comoros until 1962, when the archipelago was granted 'internal autonomy', then he left the Palais Bourbon to become President of the Council of Government in Moroni.

As a veteran Comorian nationalist has pointed out:

A High Commissioner of the French Republic retains almost all powers:
(a)   defence and security, foreign relations;
(b)   civil law and common right;
(c)   in charge of the protection of the people's rights and liberties, individual or collective, recognized by the French constitution: money, treasury, credit, foreign exchange and commerce, press, radio transmission, television, citizenship, the police and high education (this does not exist). He is qualified to annul or modify the decisions of the local chamber or dissolve it because of French interests; he also controls the legality of the actions of local authorities and undertakes nullification procedures; for these reasons, Comoro administrative acts and deliberations are submitted to him before being exercised, published or put into action by the Council of the Comoro Government.[1]

To back up the High Commissioner, more than four French regiments, mostly from the Foreign Legion, were stationed on the islands.

Under the guidance of the feudal chiefs and French officials, the populace voted overwhelmingly for association with France in November 1958. To make independence even more unattractive, a law of 1961

[1] Abdou Sakari Boina, 'The Comoros: Encounter with their Reality'.

guaranteed what was called the 'personality' of each island. Should Comorians at some time demand independence, it would not be granted to the archipelago as a whole under this law, but individually to each island. Nevertheless, in April 1970, even Said Ibrahim, who replaced the late Said Mohamed Sheikh as the pro-French strongman, conceded that independence might be inevitable, but 'it must be meticulously prepared.'[1]

The struggle for independence was led from abroad by Abdou Sakari Boina's *Mouvement de Libération Nationale des Comores*, formed in 1963 in Dar es Salaam. From its base in Tanzania, supported by the O.A.U.'s African Liberation Committee, MOLINACO has vigorously given the lie to French claims of complete decolonization in Africa by means of printed propaganda and broadcasts over Radio Tanzania. On the islands, the party began organizing clandestine cells and was particularly strong among youth in the secondary schools. In February 1968, these youths demonstrated for three days against French rule and the strike of lycée students continued for more than a month. Some 200 students, as well as some adults, were arrested. Many of those arrested were subsequently tried and given prison sentences of two to five years.

The programme of MOLINACO has only three main points:

(a)   The recognition of political parties in order to prepare and organize our people to accede to its total independence;
(b)   the reform of the present electoral system by a law recognizing to the Comorian citizen the right of an elector and eligibility with individual candidature and the consequent creation of electoral circonscription;
(c)   the determining of a date for the independence of the country after an election or general referendum under international arbitration (U.N.O., O.A.U.)[2]

This programme is also that of the *Parti Socialiste Comorien* (PASOCO), which maintains close relations with MOLINACO, although, unlike MOLINACO—which was banned by virtue of a French law of 1901 and Article 80 of the French Penal Code—PASOCO enjoys legal existence on the archipelago.

The pro-French government party is the *Union Démocratique des Comores* (UDC), headed by Said Ibrahim. In August 1968, in the wake of the upsurge of sentiment for independence, an official opposition

[1] *Le Monde* (1 January 1971).
[2] Memorandum presented by the National Liberation Movement of Comoro (MOLINACO), at the Preparatory Conference of the Non-Aligned Countries in Dar es Salaam, no date.

party was formed, the *Rassemblement Démocratique du Peuple Comorien* (RDPC). Condemning the 'independentist phraseology' of PASOCO, the RDPC offers what it calls a political alternative within the framework of 'internal autonomy'. Led by Mohamed Djaffar, its President, and Mouzzaoir Abdallah, Secretary-General, the RDPC, while calling for maintaining the French presence, has fought for greater political liberties. The reluctant granting of some of these liberties permitted the formation of PASOCO, although its members must endure every sort of official and unofficial threat and intimidation, loss of employment as well as arbitrary arrest and constant surveillance by the police.

Difficulties mounted too for the UDC, as Said Ibrahim was manifestly unable to cope with dissension within the ranks of his own party, faced with the overwhelming demands for independence. At the end of December 1970, five members of Said Ibrahim's Government resigned, expressing the hope that he would work out a new programme that would 'respond to the aspiration of all the peoples of the archipelago'.[1] New elections were held on 6 June 1971, but provided no immediate solution to the crisis over independence. When the crisis began, Abdou Sakari Boina visited the United Nations to speak on behalf of MOLINACO. Returning to Dar es Salaam, the nationalist leader said that a 'quiet revolution' was being prepared in the Comoros. If independence was not granted soon, MOLINACO would not hesitate to take 'appropriate measures', he warned. Thus, France was given another chance—to make her boasts of decolonization a reality or face a new armed struggle off the African coast. And the example of the Comoros appeared not to have been lost on the people of La Réunion, on the other side of Madagascar, although their struggle had not been recognized by the Organization of African Unity. This 'Overseas Department' of France—a colony since 1642—was weary of fraudulent elections, a ruinous plantation economy and persisting underdevelopment. Headed by Paul Vergès, the Communist Party of Réunion, which led an undeclared national struggle, was indicating that it might no longer allow that struggle to be sidetracked, either by an indifferent or fearful French Communist Party—which had long controlled the internal affairs of its smaller 'sister' party—or crushed by the bureaucrats and policemen of the French Fifth Republic.[2]

[1] *The Times* (29 December 1970).
[2] See 'Réunion Against Colonialism', *Tricontinental* (Bimonthly), (No. II, March–April 1969).

III. THE CANARIES

Mouvement pour l'Autodétermination et l'Indépendance
de l'Archipel Canarien (MPAIAC)

At its meeting in Algiers in July 1968, the African Liberation Committee not only recognized the two rival liberation movements of the French Territory of Afars and Issas, it also surprised some people—not in Madrid alone—by granting provisional recognition to the *Mouvement pour l'Autodétermination et l'Indépendance de l'Archipel Canarien* (MPAIAC), a clandestine political party, with headquarters in Algeria, that demanded self-determination and eventual independence for the Canary Islands. From the glossy tourist brochures lavishly distributed throughout Northern Europe by the Spanish Ministry of Information and Tourism, especially during the dreary winter months, one would not in any way connect the Canaries with Africa or political struggle. And yet, in Algiers, the Organization of African Unity, albeit with some reluctance, decided that the Canaries were not an integral part of Spain but rather an African archipelago whose liberation struggle merited the assistance of the independent African States.

The Canary Archipelago is composed of seven large islands: Lanzarote, Fuerteventura, Gran Canaria, Tenerife, Gomera, Palma, and Hierro, and six small islands. With a total area of 2,807 square miles and a population of about 860,000, the Canaries lie just off Spanish Sahara and Ifni, one a small enclave that has been returned to Morocco and the other a vast, nearly uninhabited 'sandbox'—to use René Pelissier's description.[1]

After having been claimed by the Portuguese, the Canaries were systematically conquered by Normans, under Count Jean de Bethencourt, at the beginning of the fifteenth century. The Spaniards took undisputed possession only between the seventeenth and eighteenth centuries. The cultivation of sugar-cane was introduced and Spanish fleets bound for the Americas made a stop at the islands before crossing the Atlantic. At the same time, the islands maintained close trading ties, both legal and illegal, with Morocco. In the seventeenth century, the wine of the Canaries (which was mentioned by Shakespeare) enjoyed a boom in Europe, until the port of Garachico was destroyed by a volcanic eruption and the production of wine was reduced to insignificant qualities by the grape blight of 1853. Today, the principal products of the islands are bananas, tomatoes, potatoes, and tobacco.

[1] René Pelissier, 'Spain's African Sandboxes', *Africa Report* (February 1966).

The natives of the islands, known to the Romans through accounts given them by King Juba of Mauritania, were called Guanches. The historian Pliny mentions an expedition to the archipelago some time around 40 B.C. The name of Canaries, i.e. Land of the Dogs, was given the archipelago because its inhabitants were reputed to own numerous sheep dogs to guard their flocks. The Arabs also visited the islands during the early Middle Ages, but never settled there. Portuguese men of war sailing down the African coast towards India landed at the islands, but Pope Clement VI nevertheless gave the archipelago to the Infante Don Luiz of Spain in 1344 to create a Christian Kingdom of the Canaries. Spain proclaimed its dominion in 1496, but the claim was contested by the Portuguese, as well as the French, Moroccans, Algerians, and British.[1]

The origins of the Guanches, the native population of the islands, are not known. Early European travellers provide little information concerning the social organization on the islands, but describe the population as divided into two types: one a 'Cro-Magnon people', with white skins and blue eyes, and a second also with white skins, who seemed to be the mixture of the first with a Khoisan racial type.[2] The Guanches were farmers and shepherds, basing their economy mainly on the raising of goats. Their society was apparently divided by classes, with aristocrats distinguished by their fine dress.

The Guanches heroically resisted the occupation of their islands, but were subdued by superior force. At the beginning of the nineteenth century, economic stagnation and widespread poverty again encouraged the expression of aspirations for independence. Although some Spaniards had settled on the islands, the people of Canaries remained well aware of their own distinct ethnic origins. After the loss of much of the Spanish Empire elsewhere in the world, such as Cuba and the Philippines, the separatist sentiments grew and Spanish troops had to be sent to quell the movement, which in 1909 was able to seize and hold the city of Laguna on Tenerife for three days.

Politically, Madrid made concessions by granting greater autonomy to the local councils. This calmed the situation and there were no major changes until Franco seized power in Spain in 1939. The Falangists abolished the traditional privileges of the islands and carried out a ruthless policy of assimilation and integration. Although Spanish

[1] For this account of the Canaries and the MPAIAC the author is indebted to Alfredo Margarido, 'Les Iles Canaries entre l'Europe et l'Afrique', *Revue française d'études politiques africaines* (No. 33, September 1968). Margarido has done pioneering work in writing about the archipelago.

[2] See Margarido, 'Les Isles Canaries'.

culture was accepted by the islanders, they were less happy with the limited horizons implied by economic integration with Spain and the drastic rise in the cost of living during the Second World War. During this period, many islanders emigrated to Central and South America, especially Venezuela.

After the war, with renewed prosperity for the middle classes of Western Europe, the 'ideal climate' of the islands attracted a growing number of tourists, especially in the winter months. Although the Canaries occasionally suffer from droughts, which are catastrophic to crops and livestock and have produced mini-deserts on some of the islands, average temperatures are comfortable all year round, varying only from an average of 59°F to 68°F, under prevailing clear skies.

For the Guanches, the droughts and competition from North African farm producers in European markets created constant economic crisis. Despite Franco's strict labour laws, dock workers and seamen threatened a strike in the port of Tenerife and forced an increase in their wages. In January 1961, some 500 taxi drivers broke away from the official government-controlled union to form a co-operative. In February, the dock workers and seamen renewed their struggle, and this time the authorities retaliated with the arrests of a dozen suspected militants and their lawyer, Antonio Cubillo. In May, 1,500 bakery workers who had lost their jobs launched violent demonstrations in Tenerife, during which leaflets demanding self-determination and independence made their appearance. Thus, the economic struggle of the working class on the islands became linked with aspirations of independence.

This movement was to increase in scope. In January 1962, the workers at the port of Santa Cruz de Tenerife struck. In March, the police observed a clandestine campaign in favour of independence. On 24 March Cubillo was arrested again, but released shortly afterwards. On the following day, a football match at Las Palmas in Grand Canary was halted and a vast demonstration spread out through the city as an estimated 15,000 persons shouted slogans such as 'Long live independence!' and 'Out with the Spanish!' The authorities retaliated with arrests of the separatist leaders. One of them, Fernando Sagazeta, a lawyer, was sentenced to eight years in prison, but Cubillo was released provisionally. He finally went into exile to escape a prison sentence and to organize.

The young lawyer eventually set up an office in Algiers. He had a most difficult task before him: on one hand, he had to persuade sceptical African leaders to take an interest in the Canaries and, on the other,

he had to build up from afar a clandestine organization on the archipelago. After a conference of *émigrés* from the Canaries, including some
from South America, the MPAIAC was formed in Algiers in 1964. The
organization declared its objectives were:

. . . to fight by all means and forces to obtain the sacred, legitimate and
natural right to self-determination and independence, to establish in time a
Socialist Republic on the African archipelago of the Canary Islands, a
Republic capable of representing and manifesting before other free peoples
of the world the true, just and revolutionary socialist aspirations of the
Canary peoples.[1]

Not only did this clear-cut stand on independence provoke indigna-
tion in Madrid, it brought condemnation from exiled Spanish Republican leaders, who also could not conceive of the Canaries as anything
but Spanish. Many African States, with economic and political ties to
Spain, tried to avoid the issue. At the beginning of July 1968, the
MPAIAC complained of hostility to its cause, even among the eleven
member-states of the O.A.U.'s African Liberation Committee. But
thanks to energetic support by the Algerian Government, the A.L.C.
finally accepted the legitimacy of the Canaries' struggle for liberation
on 22 July 1968. Except for *Le Monde* and some specialist publications,
the event passed unreported in the world's press. Even allegedly 'progressive' Spaniards bitterly protested that the Guanches were 'not black'
and hence not part of Africa. But the same criticism could be—and has
been—made of all African peoples north of the Sahara. As to those
who maintained that Canaries separatism was merely the figment of the
febrile imagination of one man—viz. Antonio Cubillo, almost all subsequent working class militancy and illegal strikes reported on the
archipelago have been associated with demands for self-determination
and independence.

On the mainland of Africa, Spain's remaining outposts of empire
are awaiting disposition. Equatorial Guinea became independent in
1968. The Franco regime was willing to permit eventual Moroccan
annexation of Ilni, but was still inflexibly opposed to the return of the
enclaves of Ceuta and Melilla to Morocco. Independence for Sakia-
el-Hamra and Rio do Oro (the Spanish Sahara) has been blocked
largely by the contending claims of Morocco and Mauritania to that
vast and sparsely populated territory. The phosphate-rich country of
266,000 square kilometres was inhabited in 1967 by 50,000 Africans,
9,000 Spanish civilians, and more than 10,000 Spanish troops. Reports
from Algeria, in 1970, told of the formation of a liberation movement

[1] Quoted in Margarido, 'Les Isles Canaries'.

in the Spanish Sahara, called the *Nidam* (which is simply Arabic for 'organization') demanding self-determination and an end to Spanish rule. It was obviously far too early to predict the course of this struggle and that on the Canaries which—like the struggles on Africa's many islands still in the hands of European powers—could only be bitter and difficult in the confined conditions in which they must be fought. But it was Kwame Nkrumah who insisted, long before he was swept into exile, that for numerous reasons Africa could not afford to be indifferent to the fate of her offshore islands. African liberation meant also freedom for every part of Africa, no matter how seemingly remote.

PART SEVEN:

A CONCLUSION AND A BEGINNING

The History of the world is none other
than the progress of the consciousness
of Freedom.
  – G. W. F. HEGEL, *Lectures on the*
  Philosophy of History

Superficially viewed, this survey of African liberation movements at the approach of the last quarter of the twentieth century makes gloomy reading. It could perhaps be interpreted as indicating the hopelessness of the African cause in the face of entrenched white minorities, stridently supported by kith and kin in Western Europe and North America, although clearly the African masses have been deprived of what are generally considered essential human rights and are increasingly fettered by exploitative political and economic systems.

Apologists for the white-minority regimes must either rely on intellectually feeble racist arguments that the black man is unfit to govern himself, or appeal for 'understanding' and patience on the part of censorious outsiders, because of an alleged Gordian knot of historical, social, and economic complexities that can only be unravelled in time— a very long time. We are urged to show 'realism' and resign ourselves to the fact that this, after all, is not the best of all possible worlds. Such a position was put forcefully in the face of world opinion by Britain's Conservative Government at the beginning of 1971, as Prime Minister Edward Heath sought to justify his decision to sell arms to South Africa's apartheid regime. Sir Alec Douglas-Home, the Foreign Secretary, did not attempt to defend apartheid, but rather assured critics of the Government that the white rulers of South Africa would be changed by 'the civilizing influences of the outside world'[1] that came through trade, and which apparently included even the arms deal. In a speech at Putney on 30 October 1970, the Foreign Secretary began this siren song by asserting: 'Normal relations with the world outside, coupled with inevitable economic change within, will work great changes in apartheid over time.'[2] Indeed, changes in Southern Africa are inevitable, but there is no inexorable logic of history or economic development that demands such changes should favour the oppressed

[1] *The Times* (23 July 1970).   [2] *The Times* (31 October 1970

African masses. In fact, the history of South Africa proves the contrary. Since the coming to power of the Afrikaner Nationalist Party in 1948, there have been virtually uninterrupted retrogressive measures to strip the African majority of all constitutional rights. Africans have been systematically deprived of the right to express political opinions, organize to defend their interests, move freely inside and outside the country, learn what they want, marry whom they please, accept employment with equality of pay and conditions of work, or democratically elect representatives. The same process can be seen at work in settler-ruled Rhodesia since U.D.I., and, despite the myth of multiracial harmony, in the Portuguese colonies as well, especially as South Africa's hegemony over all parts of the White Bastion grows stronger and traditional Boer prejudices are imposed far beyond the borders of the Republic.

This work has made little effort to examine the white regimes. Rather, attention has necessarily been concentrated on the organization of African resistance to them. I have been well aware that I was only describing one element of a dialectical process, as though a prize fight could be reported by describing the actions of only one of the fighters. The sole justification offered is the vast available body of work on the history and structures of the white regimes and the comparative paucity of material on the struggles of African peoples against those regimes. And, unfortunately, much of the literature that is devoted to the liberation movements has been propaganda, largely eulogistic, and outrageously biased. In passing, I have mentioned some offending authors. Their worst crime has been to try to reduce a complex struggle to the simplicities of *images d'Epinal*. Their readers have been given the wholly untrue notion that African nationalists can be divided neatly by whites or any other outsiders into the 'authentic' and 'inauthentic'. Certificates of recognition were distributed, generally in keeping with the distant political objectives in Africa of the Soviet Union, to certain parties which seemed best to fit in with those objectives, although no African liberation movement anywhere can honestly be described as merely a fabrication of Moscow. In the case of South Africa, there have been repeated attempts by white 'progressives' to deny the African nationalist character of the struggle and to suggest that black nationalists were 'reactionaries', while racist white skilled workers were merely misguided class-brothers of the blacks.

On the other hand, Pan-Africanism is in full crisis. The Organization of African Unity has not lived up to the hopes of its founders in assisting the struggle to remove the last vestiges of colonial and white-minority rule from the African continent. Probably, the fault lies in the very conditions of compromise that permitted the creation of the O.A.U., so that, instead of becoming a revolutionary body, it became merely another, if respected, regional assembly of States. The dream of Kwame Nkrumah and George Padmore has almost vanished. A few years ago a French left-wing critic naively commented: 'Today . . . the fact of being African has no more political significance than that of being born in the 15th arrondissement.'[1] But the situation of the African in the territories under white rule is objectively far different from that of the resident of rue de Vaugirard, as we have seen. Suffering indignities and deprivation, the African lives in intense contradiction with the political and economic structures in which he discovers himself as a result of history. His consciousness is of his unfreedom.

In the preceding pages, I have sketched the background and chronicled the developing struggles for liberation within their national context. But, in the course of this brief and summary survey, I could only touch on those of their specific complexities essential to an understanding of the dynamics of each situation. Throughout, I have found African pitted against African for numerous reasons—tribal, ideological, and personal. In only a few instances did I discover a territory in which a single party could honestly be said to represent the national aspirations of a united African people in opposition to the white regime. But the principal contradiction was not between African and African, rather between Africans and the whites who have sought to dispossess them of land and liberty.

After a half-century of efforts at reform and hopes for the gradual emancipation of these African majorities, there seems little rational basis for further illusions about peaceful change. If Africans have learned any lesson from their history, it is that revolutionary violence alone can break off their shackles. To become free demands more than the will to be free. The debate among African fighters has only begun as they seek the theoretical and material weapons and forms of organization necessary. Despite powerful lobbies in London, Paris, Washington, and elsewhere on behalf of preservation of the *status quo*, increasingly broader segments of world public opinion recognize the iniquity of the present situation and reluctantly concede that '*unconstitutional action is the only course left open*' to the oppressed blacks. To continue in the words of the Working Party appointed by the Department of International Affairs, the British Council of Churches, and the Conference of British Missionary Societies, presided over by Philip Mason: '*But*

[1] *Analyses et Documents* (No. 100, 14 October 1965).

there can be a just rebellion as well as a just war and we cannot sincerely withhold support from those who have decided to face the certain suffering involved in such rebellion.'[1] Nevertheless, as became evident during the sixties, there are many sincere persons in Moscow, as well as in the West, who fear revolutionary upheaval in Africa and elsewhere in the under-developed continents of the world. As the Zanzibari revolutionary and Tanzanian Government Minister Abdulrahman Mohamed Babu declared:

The national interest of the Soviet Union was henceforth to be paramount. This may be a good policy for a nationalist state, but is it compatible with the principles on which a socialist state is based? No longer was the national liberation revolution to be regarded, as in Lenin's and Stalin's days, as part of the struggle and a link in the international struggle against imperialism and capitalism.[2]

Africans were not without friends, however, though one need not be a Maoist to believe the wisest counsel was probably that which urged self-reliance. As Lin Piao explained:

Only when the people in a country are awakened, mobilized, organized and armed can they overthrow the reactionary rule of imperialism and its lackeys through struggle; their role cannot be replaced or taken over by any people from outside. In this sense, revolution cannot be imported.[3]

Rather than a conclusion, this survey of African liberation movements leads only back to the beginning of what promises to be a bitter, protracted struggle for national independence and liberty.

[1] Philip Mason et al., *Violence in Southern Africa: A Christian Assessment* (London, S.C.M. Press, 1970), p. 77. Italics in orginal.

[2] A. R. M. Babu, 'What is Leninism Today?', *Azania News* (September 1970).

[3] Lin Piao, *Long Live the Victory of the People's War* (Peking, Foreign Languages Press, 1965), p. 64.

Table 1

MAJOR LIBERATION MOVEMENTS

(Organizations recognized by the O.A.U. are printed in bold type)

South Africa:	**African National Congress (ANC)** Unity Movement (UMSA) **Pan Africanist Congress (PAC)**
South West Africa:	South West Africa National Union (SWANU) **South West African People's Organization (SWAPO)**
Zimbabwe:	**Zimbabwe African People's Union (ZAPU)** **Zimbabwe African National Union (ZANU)** Front for the Liberation of Zimbabwe (FROLIZI)
Angola:	**Movimento Popular de Libertação de Angola (MPLA)** **Govêrno Revolucionário de Angola no Exílio/Frente Nacional de Libertação de Angola (GRAE/FNLA)** União Nacional para a Independência Total de Angola (UNITA)
Guiné and the Cape Verde Islands:	**Partido Africano da Independência da Guiné e Cabo Verde (PAIGC)** Frente para a Libertação e Independência da Guiné Portuguesa (FLING)
Mozambique:	**Frente de Libertação de Moçambique (FRELIMO)** Comité Revolucionário de Moçambique (COREMO)*
São Tomé e Príncipe:	**Comité de Libertação de São Tomé e Príncipe (CLSTP)**
The French Territory of Afars and Issas:	**Front de Libération de la Côte des Somalis (FLCS)** **Mouvement de Libération de Djibouti (MLD)**
The Comoros:	**Mouvement de Libération Nationale des Comores (MOLINACO)**
The Canaries:	Mouvement pour l'Autodétermination et l'Indépendance de l'Archipel Canarien (MPAIAC)*

*Although provisional or *de facto* recognition was granted these movements, they have not subsequently been given full formal recognition by the O.A.U.

Table 2

SOME MAJOR AFRICAN CONFERENCES
WHICH DISCUSSED LIBERATION QUESTIONS

First Conference of Independent African States, Accra, 15–22 April 1958.
First Conference of the Pan-African Freedom Movement of East and Central
   Africa (PAFMECA), Mwanza, Tanganyika, 16–18 September 1958.
First All-African Peoples' Conference, Accra, 5–13 December 1958.
Conference of Foreign Ministers of Independent African States, Monrovia,
   4–8 August 1959.
Second PAFMECA Conference, Moshi, Tanganyika, September 1959.
Second All-African Peoples' Conference, Tunis, 25–30 January 1960.
Second Conference of Independent African States, Addis Ababa, 15–24
   June 1960.
Third All-African Peoples' Conference, Cairo, 23–31 March 1961.
Third PAFMECA Conference (which enlarged the organization and changed
   its name to the Pan-African Freedom Movement of East, Central and
   South Africa—PAFMECSA), Addis Ababa, February 1962.

THE ORGANIZATION OF AFRICAN UNITY (OAU)

Assembly of Heads of State and Government:
   Summit Conference of Addis Ababa, 22–25 May 1963.
   First Ordinary Session, Cairo, 17–21 July 1964.
   Second Ordinary Session, Accra, 21–25 October 1965.
   Third Ordinary Session, Addis Ababa, 5–9 November 1966.
   Fourth Ordinary Session, Kinshasa, 11–14 September 1967.
   Fifth Ordinary Session, Algiers, 13–16 September 1968.
   Sixth Ordinary Session, Addis Ababa, 6–9 September 1969.
   Seventh Ordinary Session, Addis Ababa, 1–4 September 1970.
   Eighth Ordinary Session, Addis Ababa, 21–3 June 1971.

Council of Ministers:
   Pre-Summit Conference, Addis Ababa, 15–21 May 1963.
   First Ordinary Session, Dakar, 2–11 August 1963.
   First Extraordinary Session, Addis Ababa, 15–18 November 1963.
   Second Extraordinary Session, Dar es Salaam, 12–15 February 1964.
   Second Ordinary Session, Lagos, 24–9 February 1964.
   Third Ordinary Session, Cairo, 13–17 July 1964.
   Third Extraordinary Session, Addis Ababa, 5–10 September 1964.
   Fourth Extraordinary Session, New York, 16–21 December 1964.
   Fourth Ordinary Session, Nairobi, 26 February–19 March 1965.
   Fifth Extraordinary Session, Lagos, 10–13 June 1965.
   Sixth Extraordinary Session, Addis Ababa, 3–5 December 1965.
   Sixth Ordinary Session, Addis Ababa, 28 February–6 March 1966.
   Seventh Ordinary Session, Addis Ababa, 31 October–4 November 1966.

Eighth Ordinary Session, Addis Ababa, 27 February–4 March 1967.
Ninth Ordinary Session, Kinshasa, 4–10 September 1967.
Tenth Ordinary Session, Addis Ababa, 20–4 February 1968.
Eleventh Ordinary Session, Algiers, 4–12 September 1968.
Twelfth Ordinary Session, Addis Ababa, 17–22 February 1969.
Thirteenth Ordinary Session, Addis Ababa, 27 August–6 September 1969.
Fourteenth Ordinary Session, Addis Ababa, 27 February–6 March 1970.
Fifteenth Ordinary Session, Addis Ababa, 15–19 June 1971.

SELECTED BIBLIOGRAPHY

David M. Abshire and Michael A. Samuels (eds.) *Portuguese Africa: a handbook*. New York, Praeger, 1969.

Perry Anderson. *Le Portugal, et la fin de l'ultra-colonialisme*. Paris, Maspero, 1963.

Mario de Andrade and Marc Olliver. *La guerre en Angola*. Paris, Maspero, 1971.

Giovanni Arrighi. *Sviluppo economico e sovrastrutture in Africa*. Turin, Einaudi, 1969.

Mary Benson. *The struggle for a birthright*. Harmondsworth, Penguin, 1966.

C. R. Boxer. *The Portuguese seaborne empire 1415–1825*. London, Hutchinson, 1969.

Brian Bunting. *The rise of the South African reich*. (Harmondsworth, Penguin, 1969.

Amílcar Cabral. *Revolution in Guinea*. London, Stage 1, 1969.

Gérard Chaliand. *Lutte armée en Afrique*. Paris, Maspero, 1967.

Ronald H. Chilcote. *Portuguese Africa*. Englewood Cliffs, N.J., Prentice Hall, 1967.

R. J. Harrison Church. *West Africa*. London, Longmans, 1960.

Robert Davezies. *Les angolais*. Paris, Editions du Minuit, 1965.

Basil Davidson. *Black mother*. London, Gollancz, 1961.

—— *The Liberation of Guiné*. Harmondsworth, Penguin, 1969.

John A. Davis and James K. Baker (eds.) *Southern Africa in transition*. New York, Praeger, 1966.

John Day. *International nationalism: the extra-territorial relations of Southern Rhodesian African nationalists*. London, Routledge and Kegan Paul, 1967.

Régis Debray. *Revolution in the revolution*. New York, Monthly Review Press, 1967.

Claude Delmas. *La guerre révolutionnaire*. Paris, Presses Universitaires de France, 1965.

Cosmas Desmond. *The discarded people: an account of African resettlement in South Africa*. Harmondsworth, Penguin, 1971.

James Duffy. *Portugal in Africa*. Harmondsworth, Penguin, 1962.

—— *Portuguese Africa*. Cambridge, Mass., Harvard University Press, 1959.

Michael Elliott-Bateman (ed.) *The fourth dimension of war*. Manchester, Manchester University Press, 1970.

B. Fagan. *Southern Africa*. London, Thames and Hudson, 1966.

Frantz Fanon. *Black Skin, White Masks*. New York, Grove Press, 1967.

—— *The Wretched of the Earth*. London, MacGibbon and Kee, 1965.

Edward Feit. *South Africa: the dynamics of the African National Congress*. London, Oxford University Press for the Institute of Race Relations, 1962.

François Fejtö. *Dictionnaire des partis communistes et des mouvements révolutionnaires*. Brussels, Casterman, 1971.

Hélio Felgas. *Guerra em Angola*. Lisbon, Livraria Classica Editõra, 1961.

Ruth First. *South West Africa*. Harmondsworth, Penguin, 1963.

Abram Fischer, Q.C. *Statement from the dock, Supreme Court, Pretoria.* London, Mayibuye Publications, 1966.

Walter Fitzgerald. *Africa.* London and New York, Methuen and Dutton, 1957.

Paul Fordham. *The geography of African affairs.* Harmondsworth, Penguin 1965.

T. M. Franck. *Race and nationalism: the struggle for power in Rhodesia–Nyasaland.* New York, Fordham University Press, 1960.

Vo Nguyên Giap. *People's war, people's army.* New York, Bantam Books, 1962.

André Glucksmann. *Le discours de la guerre.* Paris, L'Herne, 1967.

David C. Gordon. *The passing of French Algeria.* London, Oxford University Press, 1966.

Richard Gott. *Guerrilla movements in Latin America.* London, Nelson, 1970,

Felix Greene. *The enemy: notes on imperialism and revolution.* London. Jonathan Cape, 1970.

Feliks Gross. *World politics and tension areas.* New York, New York University Press, 1966.

Ernesto Che Guevara. *Venceremos ! The speeches and writings of Che Guevera* (John Gerassi, ed.) London, Panther, 1968.

William A. Hance. *The geography of modern Africa.* New York, Columbia University Press, 1964.

Thomas Hodgkin. *African political parties.* Harmondsworth, Penguin, 1961.

James R. Hooker. *Black revolutionary: George Padmore's path from communism to pan-Africanism.* London, Pall Mall, 1967.

Arslan Humbaraci. *Algeria: a revolution that failed.* London, Pall Mall, 1966.

George Kay. *Rhodesia: a human geography.* London, University of London Press, 1970.

Leo Kuper. *An African bourgeoisie.* New Haven and London, Yale University Press, 1965.

Vittorio Lanternari. *The religions of the oppressed.* New York, The New American Library, 1965.

Colin Legum (ed.) *Africa handbook.* Harmondsworth, Penguin, 1969.

—— *Pan-Africanism.* London, Pall Mall, 1962.

Roger Ashley Leonard (ed.) *A short guide to Clausewitz on war.* London, Weidenfeld and Nicolson, 1967.

I. M. Lewis. *The modern history of Somaliland.* London, Weidenfeld and Nicolson, 1965.

B. H. Liddell-Hart. *Strategy: the indirect approach.* London, Faber and and Faber, 1967.

Lin Piao. *Long live the victory of the people's war.* Peking, Foreign Languages Press, 1965.

Emilio Lussu. *Teoria dell'insurrezione.* Milan, Jaca Book, 1969.

Mao Tsetung. *Selected Military Writings.* Peking, Foreign Languages Press, 1963.

—— *Selected Works.* Peking, Foreign Languages Press, 1965.

John A. Marcum. *The Angolan revolution.* Cambridge, Mass., M.I.T. Press, 1969.

Philip Mason et al. *Violence in Southern Africa.* London, S.C.M. Press, 1970.

John J. McCuen. *The art of counter-revolutionary war*. London, Faber and Faber, 1966.

Eduardo Mondlane. *The struggle for Mozambique*. Harmondsworth, Penguin, 1969.

Jules Monnerot. *Sociologie de la révolution*. Paris, Fayard, 1969.

Pierre A. Moser. *La révolution angolaise*. Tunis, Société l'Action et de Presse, 1966.

George P. Murdock. *Africa: its peoples and their culture history*. New York, McGraw-Hill, 1959.

Abdul Haris Nasution. *Fundamentals of guerrilla warfare*. London, Pall Mall, 1965.

'A. Neuberg' (allegedly Ho Chi Minh, Hans Kippenberger, O. Piatnitsky, Mikhail Tukhachevsky, and Erich Wollenberg). *Armed insurrection*. London, New Left Books, 1970.

Mathew Nkoana. *Crisis in the Revolution*. London, Mafube Publications, 1969.

Kwame Nkrumah. *Handbook of revolutionary warfare*. London, Panaf Press, 1968.

Roland Oliver and J. D. Fage. *A Short History of Africa*. Harmondsworth Penguin, 1962.

George Padmore. *Pan-Africanism or communism?* London, Dobson, 1956.

P. Paret and J. W. Shy (eds.) *Guerrillas in the 1960s*. New York, Praeger, 1965.

The polemic on the general line of the international communist movement. Peking, Foreign Languages Press, 1965.

William J. Pomeroy (ed.) *Guerrilla warfare and Marxism*. London, Lawrence and Wishart, 1969.

—— *The forest*. Berlin, Seven Seas Publishers, 1965.

I. I. Potekhin. *African problems*. Moscow, Nauka Publishing House, 1968.

T. O. Ranger. *The African voice in Southern Rhodesia*. London, Heinemann, 1970.

Janet Robertson. *Liberalism in South Africa 1948–63*. Oxford, Clarendon Press, 1971.

Pierre Pascal Rossi. *Pour une guerre oubliée*. Paris, Julliard, 1969.

Edward Roux. *Time longer than rope*. Madison, University of Wisconsin Press, 1966.

Pietro Secchia (ed.) *La guerriglia in Italia*. Milan, Feltrinelli, 1969.

Leopold Sedar Senghor. *African socialism*. New York, American Society of African Culture, 1959.

Ronald Segal. *African profiles*. Harmondsworth, Penguin, 1962.

—— *Political Africa*. London, Stevens, 1961.

—— *The race war*. London, Cape, 1966.

N. M. Shamuyarira. *Crisis in Rhodesia*. London, Deutsch, 1965.

H. J. and R. E. Simons. *Class and colour in South Africa, 1850–1950*. Harmondsworth, Penguin, 1969.

J. E. Spence. *Republic under pressure*. London, Oxford University Press for the Royal Institute of International Affairs, 1965.

Sun Tzu (Samuel B. Griffith, ed.) *The art of war*. Oxford, The Clarendon Press, 1963.

Robert Taber. *The war of the flea*. London, Paladin, 1970.

George Thayer. *The war business*. London, Paladin, 1970.

The Times News Team. *The black man in search of power*. London, Nelson, 1968.

Hans Toch. *The social psychology of social movements*. London, Methuen, 1966.

Roger Trinquier. *Modern warfare: A French view of counterinsurgency*. London, Pall Mall, 1964.

UNITA Central Committee. *Angola: seventh year*. Leyden, International University Exchange Fund, 1968.

Jorge Aliceres Valentim. *Qui libère l'Angola?* Brussels, Michèle Coppens, 1969.

Luis Mercier Vega. *Guerrillas in Latin America: the technique of the counter-state*. London, Pall Mall, 1969.

Benoit Verhaegen. *Rébellions au Congo*. Brussels, C.R.I.S.P., 1966.

Immanuel Wallerstein. *Africa: the politics of unity*. London, Pall Mall, 1968.

Emile Wanty. *L'Art de la guerre*. Verviers, Marabout Université, 1967.

G. S. Were and D. A. Wilson. *East Africa through a thousand years*. London, Evans, 1968.

M. Wilson and L. Thompson. *Oxford history of South Africa*. Oxford, The Clarendon Press. Vol. 1, 1970; Vol. 2, 1971.

Jon Woronoff. *Organizing African Unity*. Metchen, N. J., The Scarecrow Press, 1970.

Jean Ziégler. *Le pouvoir africain*. Paris, Editions du Seuil, 1971.

INDEX

AAC, *see* All-African Convention

AAPSO, *see* Afro-Asian Peoples' Solidarity Organization

ADP, *see* African Democratic Party

A.L.C., *see* African Liberation Committee

ANANGOLA, *see* Associação Regional dos Naturais de Angola

ANC, *see* African National Congress

APDUSA, *see* African People's Democratic Union of South Africa

ARM, *see* African Resistance Movement

Abako party, Congo, 219, 227

Abdallah, Mouzzaoir, 313

Addis Ababa, 8, 161, 231, 304

Adoula, Cyrille, 217, 229, 231

Afana, Osendé, 7

Afars and Issas, 4, 305

African, Asian, and Latin American Peoples' Solidarity Organization (OSPAAAL), 126, 128, 221

African Communist, 69, 72, 73–4, 138

African Democratic Party (ADP), 46–7, 83

African Liberation Committee (A.L.C.), 5, 7–9, 66, 74, 123, 135, 138, 161, 164–5, 219–20, 222, 231, 276, 287

African National Congress (ANC), 9, 26, 38–76, 83, 90, 91, 98, 125, 282; decline and revival, 43–50; failure and schism, 50–55; and Freedom Charter, 52–5; in exile, 55–76; Youth League, 38, 44–5, 46, 48, 60, 82–3; and SWAPO, 138–9; and ZAPU, 67–8, 165

African National Congress of Southern Rhodesia, 154, 158

African National Council, 184

African People's Democratic Union of South Africa (APDUSA), 79–80

African Resistance Movement (ARM), 58, 63

African Voice Association, 154

African Voters League, 152

Afro-Asian People's Solidarity Council, 156

Afro-Asian Peoples' Solidarity Organization (AAPSO), 9, 75, 123, 125, 126, 128–9, 177, 216, 241, 260, 282

Afro-Asian Writers' Conference, 215

Alexander, Dr. Neville, 80

Algeria, 3, 8, 65, 135, 161, 163, 228, 231, 320; *see also* National Liberation Front

Algerian National Liberation Army, 57, 218

All-African Convention (AAC), 38, 43, 44, 46, 76–7

All-African Convention (Rhodesia), 154, 158

All-African Peoples' Conference, 156, 158, 210, 215, 216, 226, 227

All-African People's Convention, 83

All-In African Conference of 1961, 57

Amador, 294

American Committee on Africa, 210, 219, 226

Andrade, Mario de, 192, 208, 215, 216–17, 218, 219, 224, 253, 277

Angola, 4, 67, 137, 191; background, 199–202; the Resistance, 202–11; *see also* GRAE, MPLA, UNITA

Angolan Communist Party (PCA), 208, 211

Angolan United Front, *Frente de Unidade Angolana* (FUA), 206–7

Anjouan, 309, 310

Anti-Apartheid Movement, 69, 72

Apartheid, 4–5, 21–2, 24, 113, 326;
    U.N. Seminar, 100
Associação Africana, 274
Associação dos Naturais de Moçam-
    bique, 274–5
Associação Regional dos Naturais de
    Angola (ANANGOLA), 205–6
Awalleh, Robleh, 305
Azania, 88; *see also* South Africa

BPP, *see* Botswana Peoples Party
Babu, Abdulrahman Mohamed, 328
Bahule, Absolom T., 288
Bakongo people, 201, 209, 216, 217,
    218, 225, 227
Balante people, 246, 250, 257
Bambata Rebellion, 29, 32, 83
Bamjee, Omar, 70, 71
Banda, Hastings Kamuza, 84, 162–3
Bantu Authorities Act, 50
Bantu Congress (Rhodesia), 154
Bantustan policy, 20–1, 22, 24;
    South West Africa, 131
Barbosa, Rafael, 253, 255, 256
Bashee River, 62, 92
Basner, Senator Hyman, 47
Basutoland, 40, 59, 94; *see also*
    Lesotho
Basutoland Congress Party, 6, 94, 95
Batepa massacre, 296
Batista, João, 218, 228, 230
Beafada people, 250
Bechuanaland, 40, 59; *see also* Bot-
    swana
Beira, Pamela, 279
Beira, 149, 269, 275
Belgium, 4, 227
Bengo massacre, 213
Benguela, 200, 203, 204, 205; rail-
    way, 222, 239
Benson, Mary, 50, 53
Berlin Conference, 109, 190, 205
Beukes, Hans, 118–19, 120
Bié, 222, 238
Bissagos people, 246
Bloemfontein, 34; Conference, 43
Bobo, Mazunzo Million, 288
Boer Rebellion of 1914, 40–1
Boer War, 26, 28–9

Boina, Abdou Sakari, 312, 313
Bomboko, Commander Ferraz, 217
Bondels people, 115
Bondelswarts, rebellion, 117
Bonga (António Vicente), 273
Botha, General Louis, 41, 111
Botswana, 40, 67, 68; *see also*
    Bechuanaland
Botswana (Bechuanaland) People's
    Party (BPP), 128
Bottomley, Arthur, 176
Bourguiba, Habib, 226
Bourhan, Ali Aref, 304, 305
Brazil, 188, 245
Britain, 3, 4, 26–7, 29, 150, 191, 249;
    and Rhodesia, 146–7, 148–9, 151,
    156, 175–6, 178, 180, 184
British Somaliland Protectorate, 301
British South Africa Company, 146–
    147, 151
Bungas, village councils, 46, 79
Bunting, Sidney, 35, 37, 42, 63
Bushmen, 22–3, 27, 111
Butler, R. A., 160, 175–6

C.I.A., *see* Central Intelligence
    Agency
CLSTP, *see* Comité de Libertação
    de São Tomé e Príncipe
COD, *see* Congress of Democrats
CONCP, *see* Conference of National-
    ist Organizations of the Portuguese
    Colonies
COREMO, *see* Comité Revolu-
    cionário de Moçambique
CPA, *see* Conselho do Povo Angolano
CPSU, *see* Communist Party of the
    Soviet Union
CRC, *see* Comité Révolutionnaire de
    Cabinda
CUF, *see* Companhia União Fabril
Cabinda, 4, 200, 220–2, 231
Cabora Bassa Dam, 271, 280–1, 289
Cabral, Amilcar, 10, 74, 192, 248,
    252, 253, 254–5, 257, 259, 260,
    277
Caetano, Marcelo, 187, 195
Cadbury, William, 294
Cairo, 122, 124, 125–6, 216

Cajee, Amin, 70, 71
Calheiros e Menezes, S., 204
Cameroun, 6–7
Camões, Luis Vaz de, 188
Canaries, 4, 317–21
Cape Native Voters' Association, 43
Cape Verde Islands, 4, 188, 190, 199, 245–61
Castro, Fidel, 126
Catete massacre, 213
Central African Federation, 3, 145, 154, 176
Central Intelligence Agency, 75, 88, 194, 263, 278
Centro Associativo dos Negros de Moçambique, 274
Ceuta, 187, 188, 320
Chaka, King, 28
Chaliand, André, 222
Champion, George, 35
Charter of Algiers, 10–11
'Cheiko', Mohammed Issa, 304
Chikerema, James, 67, 154, 155, 160, 161, 163, 164, 165, 169, 172, 173, 178, 184
Chilembwe, John, 31
China, 8, 65, 67, 74, 85, 123, 128, 161, 194, 237, 256; attitude to liberation movements, 9–10; and ANC, 75–6; and GRAE, 234; and MPLA, 224; and PAC, 84; and SWAPO, 141; at Tricontinental Conference, 125; and ZANU, 181
Chinese-African Peoples' Friendship Association, 224
Chirimuhuta, 152
Chisiza, Dundura, 154–5
Chitebo, Herbert, 174, 180–1, 182, 183, 184
Chiteji, Joseph, 288
Chitziga, Nicholas, 177
Chokwe-Lunda people, 201, 202
Christian Catholic Apostolic Church in Zion, 31
Church of Christ Uprising, 31
Coast of Afars and Issas, 4, 305
Cold Comfort Farm, 163, 171
Collins, Canon John, 70
Coloured People's Congress (for-merly Organization), 51, 60–1, 96–7
Coloureds: South Africa, 22, 23, 39, 78, 97; South West Africa, 111, 113, 119; see also Mestiços
Comité de Libertação de São Tomé e Príncipe (CLSTP), 296
Comité Révolutionnaire de Cabinda (CRC), 223
Comité Revolucionário de Moçam-bique (COREMO), 104, 260, 271, 287–90
Comité Secreto da Restauração da UDENAMO, 287
Communist parties, 36–7, 42, 45–6, 125; Angola, 208; Lesotho, 94; Portugal, 212; Reunion, 313; Soviet Union (CPSU), 65; see also South African Communist Party
Como, Island of, 257
Comoro Islands, 4, 272, 309–12
Companhia União Fabril (CUF), 245, 247, 259, 295
Conakry, 255–6, 263
Conference of Nationalist Organiza-tions of the Portuguese Colonies (CONCP), 9, 195, 216, 241, 259, 260, 276, 296
Congo-Kinshasa (Zaïre), 6, 8, 199, 217–18, 220, 227, 229
Congo-Brazzaville, 220, 223; MPLA activity, 221, 222
Congo-Leopoldville, 231, 232
Congress Alliance (South Africa), 39, 51, 53, 55, 57, 58, 59, 69, 73, 74, 83, 105, 140
Congress of Democrats (COD), 51, 53, 60, 88
Congress of the People, 53
Conselho do Povo Angolana, Council of the Angolan People (CPA), 221, 232
Convention People's Party, Ghana, 82
Cruz (or Nyaude), Joaquim José de la, 273
Cruz, Viriato da, 192, 206, 208, 212–213, 215, 216, 218, 219, 220, 230–231, 232, 236–7

Cuanhama people, 202, 204, 211
Cuba, 8, 65, 74, 123, 124, 221
Cubillo, Antonio, 319, 320
Cultura, review, 206, 208, 212

Dadoo, Dr. Yusuf, 45, 73
Damara people, 111, 116, 119
Danakil people, 303, 304
Dar es Salaam, 8, 66, 72, 95, 122, 124, 136, 278, 282, 296; liberation army headquarters, 159, 276, 312
Davezies, Robert, 260
Davidson, Basil, 224, 250, 262, 282, 284; support for CONCP, 260
Day, John, 155, 157, 175
De Keyser, Ethel, 69
Desai, Barney, 61, 97
Dias, Bartolomeu, 19, 187
Dingaan, Chief, 28
Diwani, Kibirti, 275
Djaffar, Mohamed, 313
Djibo, Bakary, 5–6
Djibouti, 4, 303, 304
Djombe Fatima, Queen, 310
Dos Santos, Marcelino, 192, 279, 283, 284, 285
Douglas-Home, Sir Alec, 150, 151, 325
DuBois, Dr. W. E. B., 41, 82, 207
Duarte, Florentino, 237
Dube, John Langalibalele, 40
Dumbutshena, Enoch, 157
Duncan, Patrick, 54, 88; joins PAC, 94
Dutch settlers, 19, 22–3, 28

ELNA, *see Exército de Libertação Nacional de Angola*
Ebrahim, Ahmed Gora, 86
Eritrean Liberation Front, 305
Estatuto dos Indigenas, 195
Ethiopia, 4, 6, 8, 112, 301–5
Ethiopian Church, 31, 32, 92
Exército de Libertação Nacional de Angola (ELNA), 218, 228, 232, 234

FALA, *see Forças Armadas de Libertação*

FARP, *see* Revolutionary Armed Forces of the People
FDLA, *see Frente Democrática de Libertação de Angola*
FLCS, *see Front de Libération de la Côte des Somalis*
FLEC, *see Front pour la Libération de l'Enclave de Cabinda*
FLGC, *see Front de Libération de la Guinée Portugaise et du Cap-Vert*
FLING, *see Frente para a Libertação e Independência da Guiné Portuguesa*
FLN, *see* National Liberation Front
FNLA, *see Frente Nacional de Libertação de Angola*
FRAIN, *see Frente Revolucionaria Africana para a Independência Nacional*
FRELIMO, *see Frente de Libertação de Moçambique*
FROLIZI, *see* Front for the Liberation of Zimbabwe
FUA, *see* Angolan United Front
FUL, *see Front Uni de Libération Guinée et du Cap-Vert*
FUMO, *see* Mozambique United Front
FUNIPAMO, *see Frente Unida Anti-Imperialista Popular Africana de Moçambique*
Fanon, Frantz, 210, 226, 228, 248
Fearless, H.M.S., 150, 164, 179
Felup people, 246, 250
Ferreira, Commander Tomas, 217
Field, Winston, 161
First, Ruth, 118
First World War, 41, 204
Fischer, Abram, 25–6, 30, 49, 61–2
Forças Armadas de Libertação (FALA), 238, 241
Foley, Maurice, 164, 179
France, 3, 4, 193, 249, 303, 310, 311
Freedom Charter (South Africa), 25, 26, 52, 53–4, 83
French Somaliland, 4, 301, 302–3, 304–5
Frente de Libertação de Moçambique (FRELIMO), 74, 103, 104, 224,

233, 260, 270, 271, 275, 276–87
Frente Democrática de Libertação de Angola (FDLA), 218, 230
Frente Nacional de Libertação de Angola (FNLA), 218, 225–34; *see also* GRAE
Frente para a Libertação e Independência da Guiné Portuguesa (FLING), 261–3
Frente Revolucionária Africana para a Independência Nacional (FRAIN), 215, 259–60; *see also* CONCP
Frente Unida Anti-Imperialista Popular Africana de Moçambique (FUNIPAMO), 287
Front de Libération de la Côte des Somalis (FLCS), 305
Front de Libération de la Guinée Portugaise et du Cap-Vert (FLGC), 256
Front for the Liberation of Zimbabwe (FROLIZI), 183–4
Front pour la Libération de l'Enclave de Cabinda (FLEC), 220, 223
Front Uni de Libération de Guinée et du Cap-Vert (FUL), 256
Fula people, 246, 247, 250

GPRA, *see* Provisional Government of the Algerian Republic
GRAE, *see Governo Revolucionário de Angola no Exílio*
Galvao, Captain Henrique, 214
Gama, Vasco da, 19, 187, 267
Gandhi, Mahatma, 30, 39
Geingob, Gottfried Hage, 132
Germany, in South West Africa, 109–117
Ghana, 3, 8, 82, 91, 128, 161, 164, 210, 226
Gold Coast, 82; *see also* Ghana
Goldreich, Arthur, 62, 73
Gorgulho, Carlos, 296
Göring, Dr., 115
Governo Revolucionário de Angola no Exílio (GRAE), 137, 194, 218, 220, 222, 225–34, 260; *see also* FNLA
Graça, Leitão da, 249

Gremio Africano, 205, 274
Group Areas Act, 24, 50
Guanche people, 318
Guiné (Guinea-Bissau), 4, 189, 190, 245–61
Guinea, 8, 128, 231, 255–6, 257
Guinea-Bissau, *see* Guiné
Gumane, Paulo Jose, 277, 278, 287, 288, 289
Gumede, James, 42
Gwambe, Adelino Hlomulo Chitofo, 276, 287, 288

Hadebe, James, 71
Haroun, Imam Abdullah, 97–8
Harris, John, 62–3
Hauser, George, 210, 219, 226
Heath, Edward, 150–1, 325
Herero Chiefs' Council, 122, 132
Herero people, 109, 110–11, 115, 116, 119, 120
Herero War, 110, 115
Hertzog, General, 29, 43, 77
Holtby, Winifred, 36
Houphout-Boigny, Felix, 7
Humbe rising, 211

ICU, *see* Industrial and Commercial Workers' Union
IWW, *see* Industrial Workers of the World
Ibrahim, Said, 312, 313
Idris, Musa Ahmed, 304
Ifni, 320
Imbumba Yama Afrika (Union of Africans), 30, 39
India, 74, 125, 188
Indian Congress, 51, 60
Indians in South Africa, 24–5, 48, 51, 86
Industrial and Commercial Workers' Union (ICU), 33–7, 42, 81, 92; in Rhodesia, 153, 154
Industrial Workers of the World (IWW), 34
Injai, Abdul, 250
Instituto Negrofilo, 274
International Congress of Negro Writers and Artists, 215

International Court of Justice, 112–113, 176
International Defence and Aid Fund, 70
International in Support of the Struggle of the Peoples of the Portuguese Colonies, 241–2
Israel, 181, 278
Issa clan, 303, 304
Italian Somaliland, 301
Italy, 271, 303

Jabavu, Dr. D. D. T., 43, 76
Jacobs, Hoosain, 70, 71
Japan, 25, 82, 128
Jehovah's Witnesses, 152
Jessup, Judge Philip C., 112
'Jinga', Queen, 203
Jonathan, Chief Leabua, 6, 95

KANU, see Kenya African National Union
Kadalie, Clements, 33, 35, 36, 42, 81, 153
Kahn, Sam, 49
Kambona, Oscar, 66, 104–5
Kangueehi, Gerson, 131
Kankhomba, Paulo, 284
Kankoila, François, 256, 261
Kapuuo, Clements, 120, 121, 131, 135
Kasavubu, Joseph, 219, 227, 231
Kassanga, Marcos, 218, 228, 230
Kassela, Chief, 211
Kassinola, André, 221, 230, 232
Katimo Mulilo air base, 140
Katjiuongua, M., 127, 129, 137
Katutura affair, 122, 131, 133
Kaukuetu, Uatja, 121
Kaunda, Kenneth, 84, 102, 151, 160, 161, 162, 163, 173, 183, 210, 239, 271
Kauraisa, Charles, 124, 129, 130
Kavandame, Lavaro, 284
Kawawa, Rashidi, 98, 159
Kenya, 3, 11, 128, 301, 302
Kenya African National Union (KANU), 3, 276
Kenyatta, Jomo, 11, 82

Kerina, Mburumba, 114, 118, 119, 120, 121, 122, 132–4, 135
Kgosana, Philip, 90–1
Khartoum Conference, 9, 66, 74, 104, 138
Khoisan peoples, 22–3, 27, 28
Kimbundu people, 201
King, Betty, 282, 283
Kinzkuzu Camp, 218, 229
Kitawala cult, 151–2
Kliptown Congress, 53
Kongo Kingdom, 189, 201, 202, 203, 208–9, 225
Kongwa Camp, 71–2
Kooper, Reverend Marcus, 119
Kotane, Moses, 49n, 73
Kozonguizi, Jariretundu, 118, 119, 121, 122, 123, 124, 126–7, 129–30, 132, 133, 135
Kuhangua, Jacob, 121, 132, 137
Kunzika, Emmanuel, 218, 229
Kutako, Hosea, 120, 121

LGTA, see Liga Geral dos Trabalhadores de Angola
LNA, see Liga Nacional Africana
Labery, Henri, 252, 256, 262
Land law, Mozambique, 274; São Tomé e Príncipe, 295; South African Republic, 20, 43, 48, 77; Southern Rhodesia, 148, 154
Langa massacre, 29, 56, 90
League Against Imperialism, 42
League of African Rights, 35, 36, 42
League of Nations, 112, 117–18
Leballo, Potlako Kitchener, 23, 55, 83, 92–3, 94, 95, 98–100, 101, 103, 104–5
Lee, Frantz, 80
Lembede, Anton Muziwakhe, 38, 44, 47, 60, 82–3
Lesotho, 6, 21, 40, 95, 205; see also Basutoland
Lesotho Communist Party, 94
Letlaka, T. T., 103
Letsie II, Chief, 40
Lewis, Ethelreda, 36
Liahuca, Dr. José, 232, 237
Liberal Party of South Africa, 61, 88

Liberation movements, authenticity, 326; foreign aid, 8–10; ideological programmes, 10–11
Liga Africana, 274
Liga Angolana, 207
Liga . Geral dos Trabalhadores de Angola (LGTA), 230
Liga Nacional Africana (LNA), 207, 212
Livingstone, Dr. David, 28, 151, 190–1, 310
Lobito, 199, 200, 211
London Missionary Society, 109, 151
Lourenço Marques, 269, 273, 275
Luanda, 199, 200, 201, 202, 203, 214–215, 229
Lumumba, Patrice, 210, 227
Lusaka, 98, 163, 172, 173, 181, 223, 288, 289
Lutuli, Chief Albert J., 50–1, 53, 55, 56, 58–9, 72, 90, 129

MAC, *see Movimento Anti-Colonialista*
MANU, *see* Mozambique African Nationalist Union
MANCO, *see* Mozambican African National Congress
MDIA, *see Mouvement de Défense des Intérêts de l'Angola*
MINA, *see Movimento de Independência Nacional de Angola*
MING, *see Movimento para a Independência Nacional da Guiné Portuguesa*
MLD, *see Mouvement de Libération de Djibouti*
MLG, *see Movimento de Libertação da Guiné*
MLGCV, *see Movimento de Libertação da Guiné e Cabo Verde*
MLICU, *see Movimento de Libertação das Islas Cabo Verde*
MOLIMO, *see* Mozambique Liberation Front
MOLINACO, *see Mouvement de Libération Nationale des Comores*
MORECO, *see* Mozambique Revolutionary Council

MPAIAC, *see Mouvement pour l'Autodetermination et l'Indépendance de l'Archipel Canarien*
MPIA, *see Movimento Para a Independência de Angola*
MPLA, *see Movimento Popular de Libertação de Angola*
MUDJ, *see Movimento de Unidade Democratica-Juvenil*
Mabunda, David J. M., 277, 278, 287
Machado, Illidio, 212, 213
Machel, Samora, 280, 283, 284, 285
Magaia, Filipe, 284
Magombe, George, 8, 73, 103, 105
Makarero, Chief Samuel, 115
Make, Vusumzi, 59
Makhubu, Lawrence, 70
Malan, Dr. D. F., 29, 47–8
Malawi, 3, 145, 205, 280
Malianga, Moton, 157, 162
Malianga, Washington, 159, 182
Mallianga, M. M., 276
Mandela, Nelson, 45, 55, 57, 58, 62
Mandume, King, 117
Manjaco people, 246, 247, 250
Mao Tsetung, 9, 12, 64, 89
Marcum, John A., 209, 227, 236
Marenga, Chief Jacob, 115
Maria cult, 214
Marks, J. B., 73, 75
Marney, Cardiff, 61, 97
Masabala, Samuel, 34
'Mashona Rebellion', 147
'Matabele Rebellion', 147
Matos, Norton de, 205
Matthews, Joe, 65, 73, 94
Matthews, Professor Z. K., 44, 49, 52
Mayotte, 309, 310
Mbaeva, Nathanael, 122, 135
Mbanderu people, 119
Mbeki, Govan, 62
Mbeya Bagamoyo, 66
Mboya, Tom, 210, 236
Mbule, Marcelino, 285
Mbundu people, 202
Medeiros, Tomas, 296
Mello e Castro, 249
Mensagem, 206, 208, 212
Meroro, David, 131

Mestiços, 200–12, 248, 268; *see also* Coloureds
Milas, Leo, 278
Military training, 76, 161, 168–9, 217, 218, 220, 228, 281
Mmole, Matthew, 276, 277, 278, 287
Mobutu, Joseph, 217, 232, 233
Moheli, 309, 310
Mokhehle, Nstu, 94
Mokone, Mangena M., 31
Mondlane, Dr. Eduardo Chivambo, 14, 103, 194, 275, 277, 281, 282–3, 288
Mondlane, Janet, 278, 279, 281, 282, 285
Monomotapa kingdom, 268, 272
Morogoro, 66–7; Conference, 72, 73–74
Moroka, Dr. James S., 48, 49, 50
Mosaka, Paul, 46–7, 83
Moshi Conference, 75, 98
Mouvement pour l'Autodetermination et l'Indépendance de l'Archipel Canarien (MPAIAC), 317, 320
Mouvement de Défense des Intérêts de l'Angola (MDIA), 219
Mouvement de Libération de Djibouti (MLD), 305
Mouvement de Libération Nationale des Comores (MOLINACO), 312, 313
Movimento Anti-Colonialista (MAC), 215
Movimento para a Independência de Angola (MPIA), 212
Movimento de Independência Nacional de Angola (MINA), 208
Movimento para a Independência Nacional da Guiné Portuguesa (MING), 252
Movimento de Libertação da Guiné (MLG), 256, 261
Movimento de Libertação das Islas Cabo Verde (MLICV), 249
Movimento de Libertação da Guiné e Cabo Verde (MLGCV), 256
Movimento Popular de Libertação de Angola (MPLA), 74, 202, 208, 211–25, 230, 233, 253; guerrilla

activities, 220–2, 231, 232–3; Luanda rising, 214–15, 216; and UNITA, 138, 223–4, 240; and UPA, 216, 217, 218
Movimento de Unidade Democratica-Juvenil (MUDJ), 213
Moyo, J. Z., 162, 163, 169–71, 172, 184
Mozambican African National Congress (MANCO), 287, 288
Mozambique, 4, 19, 67, 102, 146, 190, 205, 267–76
Mozambique African Nationalist Union (MANU), 276, 287, 288
Mozambique Institute, 278, 281
Mozambique Liberation Front (MOLIMO), 286
Mozambique Revolutionary Council (MORECO), 288
Mozambique United Front (FUMO), 286
Mtambanengwe, Simpson, 176, 177
Mthombeni, Maurice, 70, 71
Mugabe, Robert, 162, 175, 176, 179, 180, 184
Multiracialism, 52–3, 54, 57, 64, 72, 86, 105, 206–7, 279
Murupa, Dr. Miguel, 285–6
Muundjua, John, 131

N.A.T.O., *see* North Atlantic Treaty Organization
NDP, *see* National Democratic Party
NESAM, *see* Nucleo dos Estudantes Africanos Secundários de Moçambique
NUDO, *see* National Unity Democratic Organization
Nama people, 109, 111, 115–16, 119
Nambuangongo, 217
Namibia, 113, 133; *see also* South West Africa
Namibia Liberation Army, 139
Natal Indian Congress, 30, 39
National Committee of Resistance, 58
National Consultative (*formerly* Action) Committee, 53

National Democratic Party (NDP), 155–6, 157, 159
National Liberation Front (FLN), 10–11, 57
National Party, Lesotho, 95
National Unity Democratic Organization (NUDO), 120, 131, 135
Nationalist Party (South Africa), 26, 29, 47–8, 94, 326
Native Land Husbandry Act (Southern Rhodesia), 155
Native Representative Council, 43, 46, 49, 77, 79
Native Trust and Land Bill, 40, 43, 77
Natotsibeni, Queen Regent of Swaziland, 40
Ndebele people, 23, 146, 173
Ndongmo, Monsignor Albert, 7
Ndongo kingdom, 202–3, 208
Necaca, Manuel Barros, 210, 226 227
Nelengani, Luis, 132, 135, 137
Neto, Dr. Agostinho, 213, 218, 219, 221, 224, 237, 253, 260, 277
Neves, Manuel Mendas das, 229
Nevinson, Henry W., 294
Ngavirue, Zedekia, 124
Ngcobo, A. B., 98, 100
Ngoni tribes, 270, 273
Ngubane, Jordan, 53
Ngwane, see Swaziland
Ngwizani a Kongo (Ngwizako), 219
Nhaneka-Humbe people, 211
Niassa, 269, 280; company, 274
Nicosia meeting, 128, 177
Nidam, 320–1
Nigeria, 8, 231
Nkoana, Matthew, 97, 103–4
Nkoloso, E. F. Mukuka, 179
Nkomo, Joshua, 67, 154, 155, 156–7, 158–62, 164, 171, 174–5, 176, 184
Nkomo Camp, 66
Nkrumah, Dr. Kwame, 13, 82, 84, 105, 226
Nokwe, Duma, 89–90
Non-violence, 30, 57, 64, 90
North Atlantic Treaty Organization, and Portugal, 191, 193–4, 239
Ntantala, T. M., 103

Nto Bako, 219
Nucleo dos Estudantes Africanos Secundários de Moçambique (NESAM), 275
Nujoma, Sam, 121, 122, 132, 133, 134, 135, 139, 140
Nungu, Silverio Rafael, 285
Nyandoro, George, 154, 155, 158, 163, 172, 173, 176, 184
Nyanja and Chewa people, 270, 280
Nyankale, Henriques, 286
Nyasaland, 31, 276; see also Malawi
Nyasaland African National Congress, 154
Nyerere, President Julius, 8, 66, 105, 160, 276, 277, 285
Nyirenda, Romo, 151, 152
Nzo, Alfred, 73

O.A.U., see Organization of African Unity
OPO, see Ovamboland People's Organization
OSPAAAL, see African, Asian, and Latin American Peoples' Solidarity Organization
Organization of African Unity, 5–8, 13, 102, 123–4, 161, 177, 231, 262, 302, 326–7; see also A.L.C.
Orlando Branch of ANC, 89
Ovambo tribe, 110, 116, 117, 133–4, 136–7
Ovamboland People's Congress, 119
Ovamboland People's Organization (OPO), 119, 121, 132, 211
Ovimbundu people, 201, 204, 211, 217

PAFMECA, see Pan-African Freedom Movement for East and Central Africa
PAIGC, see Partido Africano da Independência da Guiné e Cabo Verde
PASOCO, see Parti Socialiste Comorien
PCA, see Angolan Communist Party
PCC, see People's Caretaker Council

PDA, *see Partido Democrático Angolano*

P.I.D.E., *see Polícia Internacional e de Defesa do Estado*

PLUA, *see Partido da Luta dos Africanos de Angola*

PMP, *see Parti du Mouvement Populaire*

PNA, *see Partido Nacional Africano*

Paarl police station, 61, 92

Padmore, George, 35, 36, 37, 84–5, 226

Pan African Congress, First, 41, 82; Third, 207; Fifth, 82

Pan African Freedom Movement Conference, 57

Pan-African Freedom Movement for East and Central Africa (PAFMECA), 8

Pan Africanist Congress, 38, 46, 54, 55–6, 59–60, 61, 62, 70, 82–105, 124–5, 129, 166–7, 288

Pan Africanist Manifesto, 52–3

Parti du Mouvement Populaire (PMP), 304

Parti Socialiste Comorien (PASOCO), 312, 313

Partido Africano da Independência da Guiné e Cabo Verde (PAIGC), 10, 74, 224, 248, 252–61, 262–3

Partido Democratico Angolano (PDA), 218, 229

Partido da Luta dos Africanos de Angola (PLUA), 208, 212

Partido Nacional Africano (PNA), 207

Pass laws, 44, 55–6, 90–1

Paton, Alan, 61

Paul VI, Pope, 260

People's Caretaker Council (PCC), 162, 163

Pereira, Eduardo Vitorio, 211

Pidgiguiti massacre, 253

Pinock, José Eduardo, 214, 227

Pinto-Bull, Benjamin, 262, 263

Plaatje, Solomon, 40, 41, 82

Polícia Internacional e de Defesa do Estado (P.I.D.E.), 137, 206, 208, 211, 213, 256, 263, 296

Poqo, 61; and PAC, 93–4

Portugal, 4, 19, 109, 116, 117, 137–8; involvement with Africa, 187–96, 245

Portuguese Guinea, *see* Guiné

Positive Action Campaign, 82, 90, 134

Potekhin, I. I., 88–9

Prazo system, 268, 272–3

Príncipe, *see* São Tomé

Prohibition of Political Interference Act, 61

Provisional Government of the Algerian Republic (GPRA), 226

RDA, *see Rassemblement Démocratique Afar; Rassemblement Démocratique Africain*

RDAG, *see Rassemblement Démocratique Africain de la Guinée*

RDPC, *see Rassemblement Démocratique du Peuple Comorien*

Rand, 34, 41–2

Rashi, Dr. Abd ar-, 301

Rassemblement Démocratique Afar (RDA), 304

Rassemblement Démocratique Africain (RDA), 6

Rassemblement Démocratique Africain de la Guinée (RDAG), 262

Rassemblement Démocratique du Peuple Comorien (RDPC), 313

'Rehoboth Basters', 111, 120

Resha, Robert, 75, 129

Réunion Island, 4, 272, 313

Revolution, journal, 64–5

Revolutionary Armed Forces of the People (FARP), Guiné, 258, 260

Rhodes, Cecil, 26–8, 145, 191

Rhodesia, 137–8, 147, 165–6, 205, 276, 326; agreement with Britain, 151; guerrilla warfare, 166–8; sanctions, 149–50; U.D.I., 146, 149, 163–4, 176, 178; *see also* Southern Rhodesia; Zambia; Zimbabwe

Rhodesia Railways African Employees' Association, 158

Rhodesian Front, 149, 157

Rivonia trial, 62
Roboroko, Peter, 45, 98, 100
Roberto, Holden, 137, 194, 210–11, 215, 217, 221, 222, 226, 227, 228, 231, 232, 233, 234, 236, 240
Rome, 215, 260
Roux, Edward, 32, 34, 36, 49, 82
'Rudd concession', 147

SACP, *see* South African Communist Party
SANROC, *see* South African Non-Racial Olympic Committee
SARA, *see Serviço de Asistência dos Refugiados de Angola*
SPP, *see* Swaziland Progressive Party
SWACO, *see* South West Africa Coloureds' Organization
SWADU, *see* South West Africa Democratic Union
SWANIO, *see* South West Africa United National Independence Organization
SWANLIF, *see* South West Africa National Liberation Front
SWANU, *see* South West Africa National Union
SWANUF, *see* South West Africa National United Front
SWAPA, *see* South West Africa Progressive Association
SWAPO, *see* South West African People's Organization
Sagazeta, Fernando, 319
Sakia-el-Hamra, 320
Salazar, Antonio de Oliveira, 4, 187, 195, 251
Sangumba, Jorge, 241
Santos, Marcelino dos, 216, 260, 275, 277
São Jorge da Mina, 190, 249
São Paulo, 202, 215
São Salvador, 209, 225
São Tomé e Príncipe, 188, 189, 190, 199, 293–6
Sauer, Paul, 91
Savanhu, Godfrey, 184
Savimbi, Jonas, 138, 211, 222, 229, 231, 232, 233, 234, 235–8, 239

Sawaba Party, 5
Schultz, Governor Arnaldo, 258
Scott, Michael, 118, 121
Sechaba, periodical, 69, 72
Second World War, 44, 45, 154
Sékou Touré, President Ahmed, 255, 261
Seme, Dr. Pixley Ka Izak, 39–40, 42, 43, 47
Senegal, 8, 231, 257, 261, 262–3
Senghor, Leopold, 11, 261
Separate Representation of Voters Act, 50
September, Reg, 73, 98
Serviço de Assistência dos Refugiados de Angola (SARA), 232
Shamuyarira, N., 160, 176, 184
Shangaan people, 23
Sharpeville massacre, 29, 56, 90
Sheikh, Said Mohamed, 311
Shihepo, Hiuanua, 141
Shona people, 146, 173, 174, 270
Shopala, Leo, 137
Sikauke, Sebastene, 287
Silundika, T. George, 149–50, 163, 168, 172
Simango, Uria, 277, 283, 284–5
Sindicato Nacional dos Empregados do Comércio e da Indústria, 251
Sinoia clash, 164, 178
Sisulu, Walter, 45, 48, 50, 51, 60, 62
Sithole, Ndabaningi, 159, 160, 162, 164, 174, 176, 179, 180, 184
Siwela, Shelton, 184
Slave-trade, 5, 187, 188–90, 204, 245, 268, 272, 293–4, 310
Slovo, Joe, 73, 74
Smith, Ian, 67, 146, 150, 151, 162, 163, 164
Smuts, General J. C., 41, 42, 44, 111, 117
Sobantu, Jerry, 152
Sobukwe, Mangaliso Robert, 45, 56, 83–4, 89, 90, 93
Socialist Youth Movement, 70
Sociedade Cultural de Angola, 207–8, 212
Sofala, 267, 268, 273
Somali Republic, 301, 302

Somalis, 301–302
Sousa, Noémia de, 275
South Africa, 4–5, 205, 325, 326;
background, 19–23; detribalization, 23–4, 30–1; education policy,
61; international measures against,
91–2; labour laws, 21–2; and
Portugal and Rhodesia, 137–8,
165, 201, 271; refugees from, 59,
65; repression, 47–8, 59; resistance,
29, 37–8; and South West Africa,
112–18
South African Coloured People's
Organization (later Congress), 39;
see also Coloured People's Con-
gress
South African Communist Party
(SACP), 25, 26, 35, 36, 41–2, 45,
48–9, 61, 62, 63–4, 65, 75
South African Congress of Trade
Unions, 51
South African Institute of Race
Relations, 24, 62, 78
South African Native National Con-
gress, 39–40, 42, 154
South African Non-Racial Olympic
Committee (SANROC), 62–3
South African Trade Union Con-
gress, 34–5
South West Africa, 4, 48, 139; back-
ground, 109–12; incorporated into
South Africa, 118; League of
Nations mandate, 112, 116–17;
the resistance, 114–20, 139–40; and
United Nations, 113, 114
South West African Coloureds'
Organization (SWACO), 119, 120
South West Africa Company, 110
South West Africa Democratic Union
(SWADU), 120
South West Africa National Libera-
tion Front (SWANLIF), 135
South West Africa National Union
(SWANU), 23–4, 119, 120–31,
134–5
South West Africa National United
Front (SWANUF), 120, 135
South West African People's Or-
ganization (SWAPO), 9, 74, 119,
122, 123, 132–41, 211, 223, 240
South West Africa Progressive Asso-
ciation (SWAPA), 119, 121
South West Africa Student Body,
119, 121
South West Africa United National
Independence Organization
(SWANIO), 119
Southern Rhodesia, 3, 4, 147–53;
independence negotiations, 148–9;
1961 Constitution, 157; see also
Rhodesia, Zimbabwe
Southern Rhodesia ANC, 155–6
Southern Rhodesia Congress Com-
mittee Abroad, 156
Southern Rhodesia Native Associa-
tion, 152
Soviet Union, 8–9, 65, 66, 67, 135,
177, 194, 222, 223, 242, 256
Spain, 4, 317
Spanish Guinea, 320
Spanish Sahara, 320–1
Sports and Recreation Association,
Guinea-Bissau, 251
Strijdom, J. G., 54
Strikes, 34, 41–2, 55, 57, 253, 275, 319
Sunley, William, 310–11
Suppression of Communism Act, 49,
50
Swazi people, 23
Swaziland, 40, 59
Swaziland Progressive Party (SPP),
128
Sweden, 70, 124, 224, 271

TANU, see Tanganyika African
National Union
Tabata, Dr. I. B., 46, 77, 80
Takawira, Leopold, 162, 176, 179,
180
Tambo, Oliver, 45, 56, 59, 60, 67, 68,
71, 72, 73, 74–5, 165
Tanganyika, see Tanzania
Tanganyika African National Union
(TANU), 66, 159, 276
Tanzania, 8, 65–6, 91, 104–5, 128,
276, 288
Taty, Alexandre, 221–2, 232
Terrorism Act, 81

Tete District, 269, 271, 273, 280
Thelope, Seme, 41
Thomson, George, 164, 179, 180
Tiger, H.M.S., 150
Todd, Garfield, 159, 184
Toivo, Toivo Herman ja, 119, 121, 132
Tomas, Américo, 247–8
Transvaal Congress, 83
Treason Trial, 54–5
Tricontinental, 221
Tricontinental Conference, 124–7, 257
Tricontinental Organization, 123
Tripoli Programme, 10
Tshombe, Moïse, 222, 231, 232
Tunis, 215, 260
Tunisia, 226

UDC, *see Union Démocratique des Comores*
UDENAMO, *see União Democrática Nacional de Mozambique*
UDENAMO — Monomotapa, *see União Democrática Nacional de Monomotapa*
UDENAMO — Mozambique, *see União Democrática Nacional de Moçambique*
UDF, *see Union Démocratique Afar*
UMSA, *see* Unity Movement of South Africa
UNAMI, *see União Africana de Moçambique Independente*
UNATA, *see União dos Naturais de Angola*
UNGP, *see União dos Naturais da Guiné Portuguesa*
UNIP, *see* United National Independence Party
UNITA, *see União Nacional para a Independência Total de Angola*
UNTA, *see União Nacional dos Trabalhadores*
UNIG, *see União Nacional dos Trabalhadores da Guiné*
UPA, *see União das Populações de Angola*
UPC, *see Union des Populations du*

Cameroun
UPG, *see União das Populações da Guiné*
UPICV, *see União das Populações das Islas do Cabo Verde*
UPLG, *see União Popular para a Libertação da Guiné*
UPNA, *see União das Populações do Norte de Angola*
Uganda, 8, 231
Uirab, Bamba, 127
Umkhonto we Sizwe, 58–9, 62
Umzila (Muzila), 273
União Africana de Moçambique Independente (UNAMI), 276, 288
União Democrática Nacional de Moçambique (UDENAMO), 276, 277, 287, 288
União Democrática Nacional de Monomotapa (UDENAMO-Monomotapa), 287, 288
União Nacional para a Independência Total de Angola (UNITA), 104, 138, 211, 222, 223, 229, 232, 234–242, 260
União Nacional dos Trabalhadores (UNTA), 219
União Nacional dos Trabalhadores da Guiné (UNTG), 253
União dos Naturais de Angola (UNATA), 211
União das Populações de Angola (UPA), 200, 210–11, 215, 216, 225, 226, 227–8, 229, 230, 236; *see also* FNLA, GRAE, UPNA
União dos Naturais da Guiné Portuguesa (UNGP), 262
União das Populações da Guiné (UPG), 262
União das Populações das Islas do Cabo Verde (UPICV), 249
União das Populações do Norte de Angola (UPNA), 209, 210, 225, 226
União Popular para a Libertação da Guiné (UPLG), 262
Union Démocratique Afar (UDF), 304
Union Démocratique des Comores (UDC), 312, 313

Union des Populations des Cameroun (UPC), 6–7

United Arab Republic, 8, 65, 67, 91, 125, 135

United National Independence Party (UNIP), 160

United Nations, 46, 59, 100–1, 149, 159, 176, 215–16, 225–6, 227; Committee on Colonialism, 168; and South West Africa, 4n, 112, 114, 118–19, 122–3, 132–3; on Portuguese territories, 256; on apartheid and racial discrimination, 24; on Rhodesia, 159; on Angola, 206

United Party, 26

United States, 61, 112, 113, 194, 233, 234

Unity Movement of South Africa (UMSA), 64, 76–81, 124–5

Valentim, Jorge, 229, 237

Valentine, Steve, 239

Veii, Gerson, 127, 130

Venda people, 23

Vergès, Paul, 313

Versailles Peace Conference, 41

Verwoerd, Hendrik, 24, 56, 61

Victoria Falls Conference, 161

Vorster, John, 113, 136, 140

Wankie battle, 68, 69, 71, 165–6, 167

Whitehead, Edgar, 155–6

Wilson, Harold, 150, 164, 176

Windhoek Review, 129, 131, 137

Windhoek, 113, 122, 131

Winneba conference, 75

Witbooi, Hendrik, 115

Witbooi, S. H., 120

World Council of Peace, 9, 241, 260

Worral, John, 68, 166

Wu Hsueh-tsuen, 125

Xuma, Dr. A. B., 46, 48, 76

Xuma-Dadoo Pact, 51

Youth League (Southern Rhodesia), 154, 158; *see also* ANC

ZANU, *see* Zimbabwe African National Union

ZAPU, *see* Zimbabwe African People's Union

Zaïre, 6; *see* Congo-Kinshasa

Zambia, 3, 8, 65, 137, 139, 140, 145, 164, 184, 199, 223, 239, 288, 289; liberation army camps, 66, 165, 168–9, 222; and liberation movements, 98, 102–3, 105

Zimbabwe, 67–8, 158; *see also* Rhodesia, Southern Rhodesia

Zimbabwe African National Liberation Army, 178, 182

Zimbabwe African National Union (ZANU), 89, 104, 129, 161, 162, 163, 164, 174–84; *see also* FROLIZI

Zimbabwe African People's Union (ZAPU), 9, 67, 149, 151, 157, 158–174, 177, 282; Students' Union, 177; *see also* FROLIZI

Zimbabwe Students' Union, 181n

Zinguinchor, 249, 263

Zionist church, 92

Ziyambi, Frank, 179

Zulu people, 23